German Modernism

CALIFORNIA STUDIES IN 20TH-CENTURY MUSIC

Richard Taruskin, General Editor

1. *Revealing Masks: Exotic Influences and Ritualized Performance in Modernist Music Theater,* by W. Anthony Sheppard
2. *Russian Opera and the Symbolist Movement,* by Simon Morrison
3. *German Modernism: Music and the Arts,* by Walter Frisch

German Modernism

MUSIC AND THE ARTS

Walter Frisch

UNIVERSITY OF CALIFORNIA PRESS
BERKELEY LOS ANGELES LONDON

The publisher gratefully acknowledges the generous contribution to this book provided by the Ahmanson Foundation Humanities Endowment Fund of the University of California Press Associates.

University of California Press
Berkeley and Los Angeles, California

University of California Press, Ltd.
London, England

First paperback printing 2006

Library of Congress Cataloging-in-Publication Data

Frisch, Walter, 1951–.
German modernism : music and the arts / Walter Frisch.
p. cm. — (California studies in 20th-century music ; 3)
Includes bibliographical references and index.

ISBN-13: 978-0-520-25148-9 (pbk : alk. paper)
ISBN-10: 0-520-25148-2 (pbk : alk. paper)

1. Music—Germany—19th century—History and criticism. 2. Music—Germany—20th century—History and criticism. 3. Modernism (Art)—Germany. 4. Art and music. I. Title. II. Series.

ML275.F75 2005
780'.943'09034—dc22 2004012678

Manufactured in the United States of America

14 13 12 11 10 09 08 07 06
10 9 8 7 6 5 4 3 2 1

The paper used in this publication meets the minimum requirements of ANSI/NISO Z39.48–1992 (R 1997) (*Permanence of Paper*).

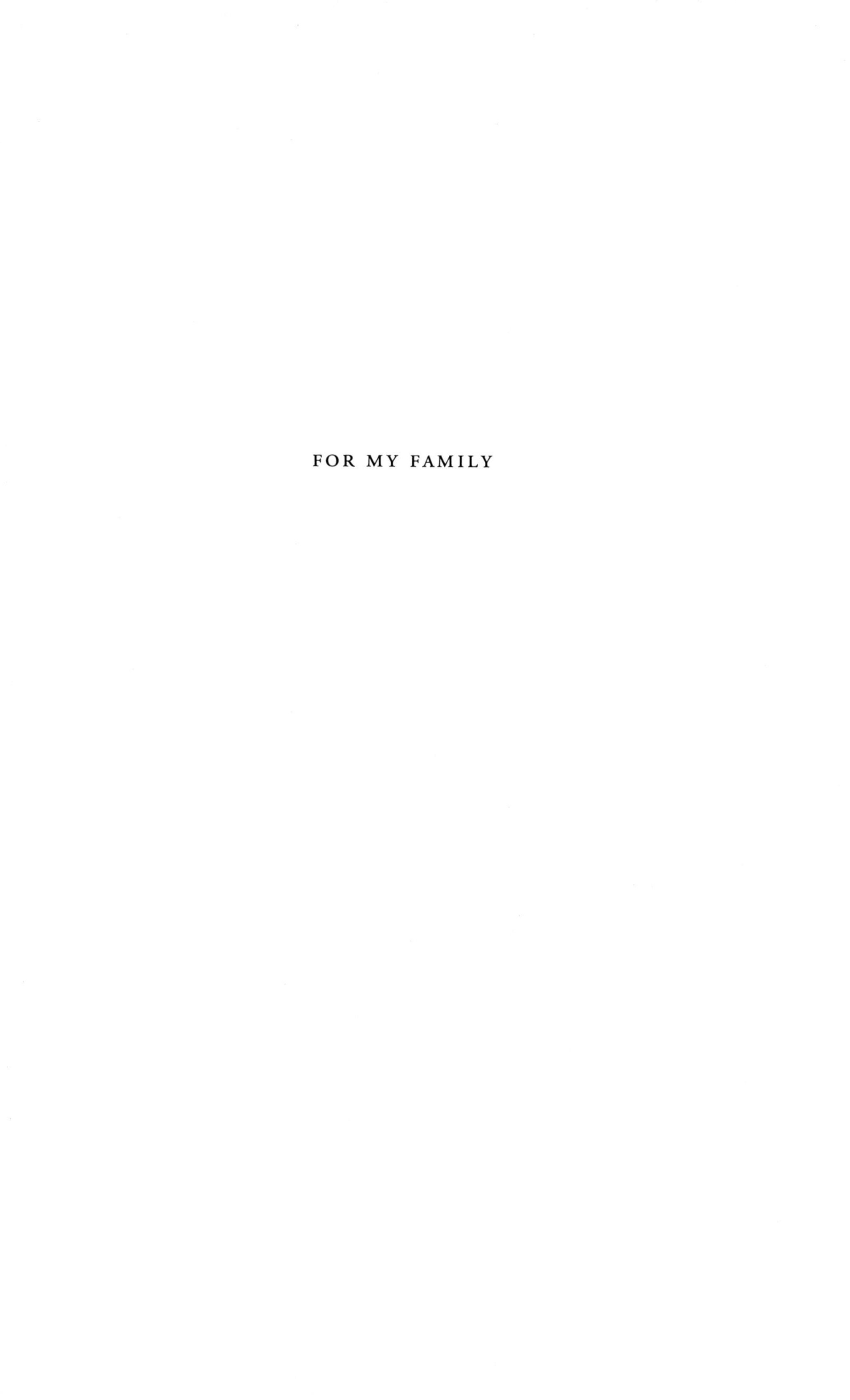

FOR MY FAMILY

CONTENTS

ACKNOWLEDGMENTS

Work on this project began as long ago as the late 1980s, in various graduate seminars and an undergraduate course (called Music in Fin-de-Siècle Europe) taught at Columbia University. It continued during a sabbatical year in Germany in 1990–91 under the auspices of the Alexander von Humboldt-Stiftung, and reached near-fulfillment during a rewarding year spent as a Fellow at the Center for Scholars and Writers at the New York Public Library in 2000–2001. The director of the Center at that time, Peter Gay, is far more than an éminence grise in German cultural-historical studies; he might justly be called the *éminence platinée,* so authoritative have been his achievements and his insights. Peter proved a wonderful interlocutor and counselor for me during my year at the Center. I also profited greatly from discussions with the other fourteen fellows, several of whom were both enthusiastic and knowledgeable about the musical repertory treated here. The staff at NYPL, at both the Humanities and Social Sciences Library and the Performing Arts Library, was always responsive and helpful; and these collections are without equal in the United States for their richness in the area of Austro-German modernism.

I am grateful to Columbia University for the release time over many years and perhaps even more for the "engaged" time spent in stimulating discussions with students and colleagues, both within and outside the classroom. As sometime chair and long-standing board member of Columbia's

Society of Fellows in the Humanities, I have found it a great privilege to be part of a truly interdisciplinary enterprise. The Society is an ideal laboratory for exploring ideas that transcend conventional boundaries. I have tried out some portions of this book at the Society's lunchtime lecture series (and at a public lecture at NYPL's Center for Scholars and Writers) and in less formal discussions with the fellows and other faculty. I am especially thankful to members of graduate seminars taught at Columbia University and University of Pennsylvania in the fall of 2003; together we explored issues and ideas in ways that helped me to get this book into its final shape. Elizabeth Davis, Nick Patterson, and the staff of the Music and Arts Library at Columbia provided gracious assistance. Joseph Auner read the entire manuscript and offered valuable advice. Peter Gay, Harro Müller, Bernhard Schlink, and Ernest Sanders helped me translate or decipher some difficult passages from German. Maja Cerar provided expert help in preparing the bibliography.

I am grateful to Prof. Rose-Carol Washton Long for helping me to identify the Kandinsky sketch reproduced as figure 8, and Mme. Annick Jean and M. Robert Groborne of the Centre Georges Pompidou in Paris for arranging access to the Kandinsky materials. Karin Maas of the Hotel Kempinski Vier Jahreszeiten found and provided me with the historical photograph of the Jahreszeitensaal. Christoph Wolff kindly located and sent me from Leipzig some of the Bach-related sources used in chapter 4.

The staff at the University of California Press has, as always, been wonderful to work with. In particular I want to thank Lynne Withey and Mary Francis, the editors who solicited and waited patiently for the book; David Anderson, the copy editor; and Rose Vekony, the project manager. Don Giller, another long-time collaborator, did a fine job with the musical examples.

I am grateful to the University of Chicago Press for permission to adapt in chapter 3 material that appeared in *Critical Inquiry* 17 (1990), © 1990 by the University of Chicago, all rights reserved; and to the University of California Press and University of Nebraska Press, respectively, for permission to adapt in chapter 4 material that appeared in *19th-Century Music* 25 (2002), © 2002 by the Regents of the University of California, and in *Bach Perspectives 3: Creative Responses to Bach from Mozart to Hindemith,* ed. Michael Marissen, © 1998 by the University of Nebraska Press.

Introduction

THIS BOOK IS A STUDY of relationships between concert or "Classical" music and early cultures of modernism in German-speaking centers. My focus is on the years between 1880 and 1920, a period extending roughly between the later years and death of Richard Wagner (1883), the most influential figure in any of the arts at the time, and the end of World War I (1918), which marked a major turning point in European culture.

Although the later phase of German modernism, during the Weimar Republic and the years leading up to World War II, has received considerable attention as a coherent or at least delimitable phenomenon, the preceding decades have remained underexplored.[1] This is in part because of a seemingly magical hold exerted by the year 1900, which serves as a dividing line in most histories of music and of the other arts. Romanticism is seen to be more or less coextensive with the nineteenth century, modernism with the twentieth. Creative artists who came to maturity in the 1880s and 1890s—in music these would include Busoni, Mahler, Pfitzner, Reger, Wolf, Zemlinsky, and the early Strauss and Schoenberg—are often included within rubrics (or chapters) like "Twilight of Romanticism" or the "Dawn of Modernism." It is the goal of the present book to isolate heuristically the four decades straddling 1900—to give them their due, so to speak, without seeing them as "transitional," as being on the way from Romanticism or to modernism.

Carl Dahlhaus, the most distinguished historiographer of music writing in the second half of the twentieth century, was probably the first to argue against what might be called the tyranny of the year 1900. In his book *Nineteenth-Century Music* he follows to some extent in the tradition of historians who see a "long" nineteenth century extending from the French Revolution to World War I. Dahlhaus actually posits what might be called a "displaced" nineteenth century: he moves its starting point in music history to 1815. Dahlhaus interprets the last decade of the nineteenth century and the first of the twentieth as a coherent period of early modernism in German music. The era is framed on one end by the emergence of a distinctive "breakaway mood," an élan vital, characterized in music by the opening of Strauss's tone poem *Don Juan* (composed in 1889), and on the other by the emancipation of the dissonance and the transition to atonality beginning in 1908. Dahlhaus thus argues that "without imposing a fictitious unity of style on the age, we could do worse than . . . speak of a stylistically open-ended 'modernist music' extending (with some latitude) from 1890 to the beginnings of our own twentieth-century modern music in 1910."[2]

In such a periodization Dahlhaus sees the possibility of demonstrating "the interaction of the Schönberg school with Mahler and composers such as Zemlinsky and Schreker, who did not take full part in the march to atonality but nonetheless continued even later to represent modernism." He also considers extending this earlier modernist phase to about 1920, since it could be said that "a revolution in musical technique around 1910 was succeeded by a profound transformation of aesthetic outlook around 1920."[3] Here Dahlhaus is referring to the neoclassicism of Stravinsky, Hindemith, and the early twelve-tone Schoenberg.

Dahlhaus ends his own history of nineteenth-century music with a chapter entitled "1889–1914" (which is then followed by a reflective coda, "End of an Era"). His approach is what might be called contextualist formalism. Dahlhaus organizes his chapter around short musical analyses that assess the technical and expressive qualities of individual works, ranging from Pfitzner's *Der arme Heinrich* (1893) to Ives's *Concord* Sonata (1916–19, according to the most recent thought). He always embeds these discussions in a framework that treats genre, intellectual or social history, and aesthetics. Dahlhaus's account of early modernism is a tour de force that no music historian has equaled. But like other less distinguished accounts of this slice of music history, it is nonetheless appended to a book that is defined by the calendar. (The scope of *Nineteenth-Century Music* was predetermined by the German series in which Dahlhaus's volume initially appeared.)

Beyond Dahlhaus, there is a large and often impressive specialized literature on individual composers in the Austro-German realm in the decades around 1900, especially Mahler, Strauss, and Schoenberg, but also increasingly on less well-known figures like Busoni, Pfitzner, Reger, Schreker, and Zemlinsky. Recent years have also seen the appearance of many recordings of once-obscure works by composers of that generation. Yet to date no musicologist has sought to place the composers and their activities into a broader artistic and cultural context of early German modernism. Although German modernism was strongly affected by broader European currents during this time, especially by French realism, symbolism, and impressionism, it has many special characteristics that justify a more closely defined study. As I will argue in chapter 1, German modernism is also broader than its manifestations in regional cultural centers like Vienna, Berlin, and Munich.

The present book is not an intellectual or conceptual history (what the Germans call *Begriffsgeschichte*) of the terms "modern" and "modernism." But some clarification of terminology is appropriate here. "Modern" as an adjective dates back at least to the Middle Ages, and since then it or its variants have been employed to characterize many different ideologies and practices seen to represent contemporary values.[4] "Modern" has frequently been part of a binary opposition that sets the present against the past, as in the "Querelle des Anciens et des Modernes" in seventeenth- and eighteenth-century France. In the more restricted sense of the present study, modern*ism,* or *die Moderne* as it was often called in German, refers to a set of beliefs and principles that in the broadest sense were shared by many creative artists in Europe from about the 1850s on. Some commentators point to Baudelaire's conception of "modern," articulated in 1859, as foundational for this phase of modernism. For Baudelaire, modernity (not yet an -ism) connoted not merely the presentness of an era, but rather a special quality of "le transitoire, le fugitif, le contingent" that could be found in any period.[5] The modern was thus set against not the "old," but the "eternal."

The adjective "modern" and the substantive "die Moderne" appear frequently in German writings both from within and about the period 1880 to 1920. The nominal form can have the connotation of either or both of the English words "modernity" and "modernism." In English, however, these words can have different meanings. I tend to understand "modernity" more as the condition or state of being modern; in this sense modernity comprises a situation that is almost passive, inevitable. Modernism is a more ideologically charged and "voluntary" phenomenon; it is in most cases an actual *movement,* propelled by a group of like-minded thinkers, artists, or critics.

In the present study I do not view musical modernism—or at least do not view it primarily—in the way that many other historians of music, art, and literature have done: as defined by the use of a technically advanced language and a clear sense of moving away from the past. In Western art music, the "story" of modernism is often told as that of an increase in chromaticism (Chopin, Liszt, and Wagner) leading eventually to atonality. There is a concomitant breakdown of phrases of four and eight measures into asymmetrical, more atomized structures. The later Wagner, Wolf, and the early Schoenberg are seen as the composers who forged this path to modernism. Debussy and Stravinsky also participate, from outside the German realm. (Even Dahlhaus subscribes to this basic narrative, although he complicates it.) In the visual arts, the analogous development is proposed in the abandonment of representation as a principal goal and in the liberation of color and line from their former roles in serving that goal. Here Manet, Cézanne, Picasso, and Kandinsky are the major figures. In literature, modernism is seen in the weakening of narrative structures and the loosening of meaning. Words become unmoored from their usual grammatical, syntactical function, like colors and lines in painting, and chords in music. Mallarmé and Hofmannsthal are among the pioneers in these areas.

These aspects of the arts around 1900 are real and significant, but they tell only part of the story of modernism. One of the main goals of the present study is to explore connections among the different arts (and artists) that are a defining feature of modernist culture in the years around 1900. The Nietzsche-Wagner relationship, which is treated in the first chapter, is paradigmatic—and proleptic—in this regard. For Nietzsche, Wagner at first represented a potential regeneration for German culture. The philosopher later soured on Wagner's art, which he saw as calculated, manipulative, and decadent. Nietzsche's ambivalence toward Wagner is symptomatic of much of modernist thought in the later nineteenth century. Wagner's last opera, *Parsifal,* is, as I argue, an embodiment of ambivalent modernism.

Naturalism was the first widespread movement in German modernism that energized creative figures in the arts. Although Wagner was implicated, naturalism sought in many respects to move beyond Wagner into a genuinely contemporary world, as is discussed in chapter 2. The most fruitful and rewarding exchanges between artists, however, took place outside the confines of naturalism. Significant artists of the early modern era who had not only personal contact with each other but also some degree of reciprocal influence include Max Klinger and Johannes Brahms, and more famously, Arnold Schoenberg and Wassily Kandinsky. In both cases, as will be discussed in chapter 3, there was pleasurable mutual recognition of technical and expressive goals. The collaboration between Richard Strauss and Hugo von Hofmannsthal, two of the greatest creative figures of their era, represents a still greater degree of artistic symbiosis. Two of their operas, *Der Rosenkavalier* and *Ariadne auf Naxos,* will be examined in chapter 6.

Another key aspect of musical modernism overlooked (or at least overshadowed) in most writing is its relationship to the past, both recent and remote. Far from turning their backs on the past, many artists around 1900 appropriated it in significant ways, and their engagement with the past is an integral part of their modernism. For Reger and Busoni (chapter 4), the music of Bach served as both a stimulus to new sounds and forms and a bridge to the past. Thomas Mann created a modern ironic style to a large extent out of his relationship to and assimilation of Wagner (chapter 5). Strauss and Hofmannsthal (chapter 6) responded to the operas of Mozart and Wagner in ways that are at once sophisticated, humorous, and moving. Pfitzner (also examined in chapter 6) used the musical past more as a stick to beat the present.

The plethora of "isms" that have been used since the early modernist period—naturalism, realism, impressionism, primitivism, expressionism, symbolism, to name just some—are indication enough of its polyvalence. My goal is not to create more categories or -isms, but rather to take a contextual and cross-disciplinary approach in exploring those especially characteristic of Austria and Germany in the decades surrounding 1900. If readers come away with some puzzlement about just what "modernism" is or was (or continues to be), but with a greater understanding of the artists and their work, this book will have attained its goals.

EDITORIAL NOTE

In this book I cite extensively from German-language sources. English titles are used if the works (such as Nietzsche's writings or Mozart's operas) are widely known by them. Where possible I have also used published English translations of texts, sometimes amending them in light of the original sources. For all other German materials, the translations are my own unless otherwise noted. Because it is my hope that this book will be of interest and use to readers who do not know German well, I have translated citations, excerpts, and certain key terms, expressions, and titles. To make the book as user-friendly and uncluttered as possible, I have normally given English titles in the text and have put the German in the notes.

ONE

Ambivalent Modernism

Perspectives from the 1870s and 1880s

UNTIL 1871 THERE WAS NO coherent political entity called Germany, but rather a loose "German Confederation" of thirty-eight states that had been created in 1815, at the Congress of Vienna. The two largest and strongest parts of the Confederation were Austria and Prussia, who dominated the political and cultural stage for most of the century and were frequently in conflict. When he was appointed prime minister of Prussia in 1862, Bismarck hoped to exclude Austria from the Confederation and ensure Prussian dominance; this was the so-called *kleindeutsch* vision of German unity. War ensued between Austria and Prussia, and Prussia's victory in 1866 led to a North German Confederation that excluded Austria and the southern German states. The Prussian victory over France in 1870–71 consolidated Prussian power still further; a larger German empire or Reich was declared that now encompassed all the German-speaking lands except Austria.[1]

Despite the political tensions between Austria and the Prussian-dominated Reich, both may be said to be encompassed within a broader German culture that was effectively *großdeutsch.* As Peter Gay has reminded us, in the later nineteenth century "the boundaries of German culture were wider than the boundaries of the German Reich."[2] One thinks of a figure like Johannes Brahms, who was north German by birth and temperament, and a fervent supporter of Bismarck, and yet who chose from the early 1870s to live full time in Vienna, where he was warmly welcomed by, and became an integral part of, Viennese bourgeois liberal society. The modernist aesthetic of Arnold Schoenberg a generation later has often been associated with—and its origins traced to—his native Vienna. Yet for a substantial part of his early career he resided in Berlin, where not only were the professional opportunities and contacts better, but where his "Viennese" modernism was in many respects better appreciated than in his native city.

There were, to be sure, considerable differences between Vienna and Berlin, or Berlin and Munich. The particular quality of culture in these individual cities has been explored in a number of distinguished writings over the past two decades.[3] Yet Gay is right to assert that "what tied all these regions to one another was more important than what divided them. Language was the great unifier, language and the free migration of writers, artists, composers, and performers from court to court, city to city."[4] Since at least the early nineteenth century, well before the founding of the Reich, the German language had fulfilled this function of creating what Hinrich Seeba has called the "immaterial presence" of a German spirit.[5]

Notions of Germanness and modernity were closely linked for many writers and artists in the period from about 1870 until 1915, roughly from the formation of the German Reich up until the outbreak of World War I. The emergence in this period of what came to be perceived or presented as "modern" in German art and culture intersected—and often came into conflict—with national consciousness. As the art historian Françoise Forster-Hahn has put it, "the languages of modernism are intricately intertwined with discourses of nationalism in Germany."[6] As a result, German modernism took on a particular profile, a *Sonderweg* or special path, which can be characterized by the notion of "ambivalent modernism," a term I borrow from the historian Marion Deshmukh. Deshmukh understands ambivalent modernism as a "a type of turn-of-the century modernism echoed by many cultural and intellectual figures. . . . It can be described as a generally positive outlook toward the rapidly changing social, economic, and scientific German landscape, but tempered by an occasional nostalgia for features of a preindustrial community in which quality workmanship and value were recognized."[7] German modernism is ambivalent in admiring and fostering the new, at the same time as clinging fervently to the past out of a sense that the past (especially the German past) was an essential part of the German character that could not be abandoned. Other European nations certainly had their share of modernist ambivalence at this time, but nowhere was it as extreme or as fundamental as in Austro-German culture.

WAGNER AND GERMAN MODERNISM

Richard Wagner is the most important figure of ambivalent modernism in German music. His music was recognized (including by himself) as advanced in technique and expression; it was the acknowledged inspiration for countless works conceived and perceived as "modern" in the last quarter of the nineteenth century. Yet for Wagner himself, *die Moderne* was not a meaningful aesthetic category. After about 1850 he almost never wrote about the music of his contemporaries, with the exception of his essay on Liszt's symphonic poems of 1857. For Wagner, modernism was essentially a social-cultural evil, and a concept diametrically opposed to Germanness or *Deutschtum,* which resided deep within the German soul and had ultimately little to do with politics or even nationhood.

Early in 1878 the *Bayreuther Blätter* published two essays by Wagner that would seem neatly to encompass the concerns of the present study. One was entitled "What Is German?" and the other simply "Modern." The essay on Germanness had been drafted in 1865 as a diary entry intended for King Ludwig II, then shelved when some of its points were taken up at much greater length in the first segments of "German Art and Politics" from 1867.[8] When Wagner chose to publish "What Is German?" in 1878, the political landscape of Germany had changed dramatically because of the founding of the German Reich in 1871. As Wagner makes clear from the comments he added in 1878 after the end of the original essay, he was already disillusioned with many aspects of the new political order. He felt that the true German "spirit" *(Geist)* was now being submerged by rampant capitalism, by what he calls the overemphasis on "business" (*Geschäft,* a word he places in quotation marks several times).

In the body of "What Is German?" (the portion written in 1865), Wagner tries to clarify "das eigentlich deutsche Wesen," the real essence of Germanness. Relying on what he describes as recent research—he cites the brothers Grimm—Wagner notes that the term "deutsch" originated not as the name of an actual people but as a character attribute. "Deutsch," he says, is related to the verb "deuten"; thus "deutsch is what is plain *[deutlich]* to us, the familiar, the wonted, inherited from our fathers, the offspring of our soil" (PW 4:152). The *Deutsches Wörterbuch* of the brothers Grimm does in fact, as Wagner implies, draw a connection between *deutsch* and *deutlich,* though no priority is given to *deutsch* as a character attribute. The Grimms observe how in his translation of the Bible Luther uses "undeutsch" to mean "unverständlich" or unclear. More recently, philologists have established that *deutsch* comes from *diutsic,* an adjective derived from the Old High German *diot,* which means "people." *Deutsch* thus indicates the vernacular language, in distinction to the official administrative language of the Middle Ages, Latin.[9]

Wagner points out that the word "Deutschland" arose after the period of Charlemagne, as a geographic designation for the area occupied by those people who remained east of the Rhine and north of the Alps, while others, including the Goths, Franks, Vandals, and Lombards wandered away: "Consequently it ["Deutschland"] denotes those peoples who, remaining in their ancestral seat, continued to speak their ur-mother-tongue, whereas the races ruling in Romanic lands gave up that mother tongue." Wagner manages thus in a single stroke to establish the authenticity of Germans, who "could reap the advantage of fidelity to their homeland and their speech, for from the bosom of that home there sprang for centuries the ceaseless renovation and freshening of the soon decaying outland races." Although many people associate "the so-called German glory *[Herrlichkeit]*" with the rise of the Holy Roman Empire after Charlemagne, in fact, says Wagner, the German essence or *Wesen* began to emerge only later, with the collapse of the empire after 1600. Wagner sees in music, especially that of J. S. Bach, the resurrection of the German spirit after the disasters of the Thirty Years' War. He calls Bach a *Wundermann* who is the "history of the innermost life of the German spirit" (PW 4:162). (As we will see in chapter 4, this image of Bach was to retain considerable force well into the twentieth century.)

In "German Art and Politics," Wagner adds to this "history" in suggesting that the German spirit was further "resurrected" in the last half of the eighteenth century by Winckelmann, Lessing, Goethe, Schiller, Mozart, and Beethoven. But the German spirit has never manifested itself at the political level—among the rulers—and is threatened, he says, by its diametric opposite, "French civilization," Wagner's catchphrase in this essay for things non-German. (Frederick the Great comes in for special criticism for having favored aspects of French culture over German.) French civilization is, Wagner says, superficial and imposed from above, while the German spirit arises from the *Volk.* As Wagner summarizes in a "brief antithesis": "French Civilization arose without the people, German Art without the princes; the first could arrive at no depth of spirit because it merely laid a garment on the nation, but never thrust into its heart; the second has fallen short of power and patrician finish because it could not reach as yet the court of princes, not yet open the hearts of rulers to the German Spirit" (PW 4:41).

In "What Is German?" Wagner likewise suggests that the German people have allowed the German spirit to become "penetrated" by an "utterly alien element." Here that element is less French civilization than it is the Jews. With an unabashed profit motive, the Jews have sought to capitalize on Germany's resources. The result is "an odious travesty of the German spirit." Unless German rulers take care, the German spirit will disappear under foreign influences. "How are we to conceive a state of things in which the German Folk remained, but the German Spirit had taken flight?" he asks. "The hardly-thinkable is closer to us than we fancy" (PW 4:158–59, 164). As Hannu Salmi has pointed out in an excellent study, Wagner saw Germanness very much in terms of binary oppositions: things were either *deutsch* or *undeutsch.* These sentiments—and, indeed, many of those expressed in Wagner's essays of the mid-1860s—closely resemble the philosophizing on art and Germanness in *Die Meistersinger,* whose libretto Wagner had completed in 1862 and which was premiered in 1868; they could almost come out of Pogner's speech to the Masters in act 1, or from Hans Sachs's final monologue.[10]

Wagner's conception of Germanness touches on several themes that would continue to remain important for early German modernists. One is that there is something definably "German" that must be preserved and encouraged through artistic institutions and creations. This position implies a direct connection between Germanness and culture. Another theme is that there is an inevitable relationship between art and politics, because the latter must have as part of its goal to support the former. Salmi has argued that for Wagner, as for many Germans around midcentury, the demand for political unification was justified because of Germany's status as an "imagined community." Salmi draws here on Benedict Anderson's evocative and by now well-known concept, by which a nation is "imagined" because its members "will never know most of their fellow-members, meet them, or even hear of them, yet in the minds of each lives the image of their communion."[11] The notion of an "imagined community" is analogous to Hobsbawm's idea of an "invented tradition," whereby a group will observe a ritual or practice that may be quite recent but derives its authenticity from an appeal to a fictitious past. Wagner's Nuremberg in *Die Meistersinger* is filled with such inventions and imaginings.

Here is how Salmi paraphrases what he calls Wagner's "national vision," based on the writings of this period:

> The new rising Germany would develop into a cultural power comparable to Classical Antiquity, provided it fulfilled certain conditions. Germany

> would be modeled on a united monarchy, in which the highest executive power would be given to the King; art would be given a central position in society, and the German genius would rise to be the spiritual leader of the nation: This genius would be Wagner, whose *Gesamtkunstwerk* would take its position as the channel to an understanding of the world, and *Deutschtum* would be comprehended in its original significance as genuine, creative, and universal. . . . Germany would attain her true political and spiritual greatness.[12]

A reader today coming to Wagner's essay "Modern," written and published in 1878, might be surprised that it is concerned not at all with modernism or modernity in art—not with style or technique—but with a political and cultural modernism that is linked directly with Judaism and liberalism. Wagner is responding to a recent publication (unidentified by him) in which "an important Jewish voice" (apparently so called in the publication itself, since Wagner puts the phrase in quotation marks) praises the modern world over the "old world of orthodoxy" and applauds the leading role played by Jews in German culture and science. After citing the passage, Wagner rips into it. He asks just what the "old orthodoxy" really is, and what is new. His answer: the Jews themselves, who can never really enter German culture, are the only novelty. What the Jews really are, says Wagner, is "a consciously unproductive set of Epigones" who seek "to cast adrift the irksome earnestness of their forerunners and proclaim themselves 'Modern.'" Wagner asserts that to explain what "modern" really means "is not so easy as the Moderns imagine; unless they will admit that it stands for a very shady thing, most perilous to us Germans in particular" (PW 6:45–46). What that "shady thing" comes down to for Wagner is essentially liberal Judaism, a phrase he uses repeatedly. He implies that liberal Judaism is basically an urban, middle-class phenomenon that is of little real help to the German *Volk.*

CROSSCURRENTS IN WILHELMINE GERMANY

For Wagner, "modern" is an ideological category that is incompatible with true *Deutschtum* or Germanness, which resides in the language and especially in the *Volk.* His attitudes, as reflected in the essays discussed above, are characteristic of one important trend in cultural and political thought in the wake of German unification, during the years called the *Gründerzeit,* or foundation period. This was the dark underside of modernism. Like Wagner, some commentators took anything but a rosy view of the economic boom and the rapid urbanization and industrialization of the main cities of Germany, especially Berlin. As the historian David Blackbourn puts it, these were "critics of modernity who preferred their society, like their carrots, 'organic' rather than 'mechanical.'"[13] In the epilogue of "What Is German?" Wagner mentions two of the most prominent such cultural critics. Admitting (with his characteristically false modesty) that "I must hold myself unqualified for further answering the question" posed by the title of the essay, he defers to Constantin Frantz and Paul de Lagarde (PW 4:169). These two cultural conservatives were among the most prominent spokesmen for what Fritz Stern has called the "idealism of antimodernity" in the latter part of the nineteenth century.[14] Frantz had been cited prominently by Wagner at the opening of "German Art and German Politics," which uses as a springboard Frantz's notion (set forth in 1859) that Germany must assert its "forces of mind and spirit" over those of "French civilization" (PW 4:37). Frantz was also the dedicatee of the second edition of Wagner's *Opera and Drama,* published in 1868.

Frantz in fact took up the invitation extended by Wagner in "What Is German?" He responded with a lengthy "open letter" to Wagner that appeared in the *Bayreuther Blätter* in June 1878, five months after the composer's article. Frantz argued that German art and politics are—or should be—intimately related because both go well beyond "questions of mere power or material interests" and encompass "the broader issues of mankind's development."[15] Frantz repeats the themes of his other writings, arguing that Germany's political thought, like its art, has been operating for too long under narrow concepts of "nation" and "state." These are really of secondary importance for a German, who should turn back to the model of the Holy Roman Empire, which made clear that Germany's essence was supranational. German politics must thus become metapolitics, standing in the same relationship to conventional politics as metaphysics to physics.[16]

In the 1850s Lagarde had begun to address the question "What Is German?" in the writings that were collected as *Deutsche Schriften.* These appeared in 1878, the same year as Wagner's essays "What Is German?" and "Modern," and were much admired at Bayreuth. Lagarde attacks many of the same institutions as Wagner, including political liberalism, commerce, banking, and the press, all of which he likewise associates with the Jews. According to Stern, this mixture of anticapitalism and anti-Semitism was a common thread among cultural conservatives in the later 1870s. Stern stresses that "the identification of Jew and modernity," which Wagner and Lagarde both make explicitly, became "an immensely powerful component of anti-

Semitism."[17] Wagner's essays, then, are almost certainly reflections of Lagarde's thought and more generally of what Stern called "the politics of cultural despair." When the *Deutsche Schriften* arrived in Bayreuth, Cosima Wagner wrote Lagarde that she and Wagner would "do everything in our power" to ensure a wide circulation. The personal ties between Lagarde and Wagner were never close because Lagarde apparently had little interest in or sympathy for the actual music of Wagner or the circle of *Zukunftsmusiker.*[18] This fact points up the paradox referred to above: Wagner's conservative thought did not match up with the modern style of his music.

A highly influential tract that linked issues of modernity and nationalism was Ferdinand Tönnies's *Gemeinschaft und Gesellschaft* (Community and Society) of 1887. Tönnies argued that there was a fundamental difference between a rural, agrarian "community" and the modern, urban, commerce-based "society." The former, more truly representative of Germany, is founded on family relationships, mutual possession, and direct contact with nature; it is "organic." Society is "a multitude of natural and artificial individuals, the wills and spheres of whom are in many relations with and to one another, and remain nevertheless independent of one another and devoid of mutual family relationships."[19] Society is based on the production of commodities by a labor class, and on their consumption by a bourgeois class. Tönnies's book became the basis for many arguments about the values of the German *Volk,* which were seen to be threatened by modern urbanization. The notion of *Heimat* (literally, "home" or "homeland") became a kind of German ideal for antimodern critics. A whole genre of *Heimat* literature and art grew up in the years around 1900, much of which presented idealized, often nostalgic, views of rural life.

The 1870s and 1880s were not without significant counterpoint to the writings of Wagner, Frantz, Lagarde, Tönnies, and other cultural conservatives. In a recent study, Kevin Repp has shown that their variety of radical antimodernism was only one strand of a complex social-cultural-political fabric in Wilhelmine Germany. There was in fact a "thick web of crisscrossing paths" and a search for "alternative modernities," especially apparent in what Repp calls the "generation of 1890," reformers and critics who came to maturity in the last decade of the century. These figures included Adolf Damaschke, a prominent member of the National Socialists Association (founded in 1896) and populist land reformer, who could seem at once anti- and philo-Semitic, at once a cultural despairist and a promoter of scientific and technological advances through what he called "organic progress."[20] Damaschke and others in this "Wilhelmine reform milieu" present no unified picture. Above all, Repp shows (as do other scholars cited by him), we should avoid trying to identify a clearly defined "special path" or *Sonderweg* leading to Germany's demise under Hitler. For Repp and others, this is a historiographic model that for too long has hampered a richer contextual view of the period from about 1880 to World War I.

NIETZSCHE AND WAGNER

The most important and sophisticated response to the Wagnerian-Lagardian-Frantzian brand of antimodernism came from Friedrich Nietzsche. Although he launched himself from a Wagnerian platform with *The Birth of Tragedy* in 1872, by the end of the 1870s Nietzsche had broken with the aesthetic-cultural program embodied by Wagner. Nietzsche was far from an unabashed modernist; indeed, he called one major collection of essays *Unzeitgemäße Betrachtungen* (literally Uncontemporary Observations).[21] He comments only seldom upon contemporary writers, artists, or musicians. Rather, it is his ruthless, penetrating critique of cultural attitudes and practices in the 1870s and 1880s—and his own ambivalence about them—that makes him such a key figure in early German modernism. Nietzsche's intellectual trajectory across two decades in many ways prefigures the course of German modernism. It is for that reason that he merits the bulk of the commentary in this chapter.[22]

Most of *The Birth of Tragedy* is a closely argued account of the nature of Attic tragedy according to the two aesthetic poles of the Apollonian and Dionysian. But Nietzsche begins by acknowledging a "seriously German problem," which is taken up at length in the final sections of the book.[23] Echoing Wagner and Frantz, Nietzsche criticizes French culture as superficial and suggests that, by contrast, Germany must reach deeper into its soul to awaken a "glorious, intrinsically healthy, primordial power" (p. 136). German art and culture can be reborn through a better knowledge of Greek art and culture; especially to be hoped for is a "renovation and purification of the German spirit through the magic fire of music" (adapted from p. 123). The reference to Wagnerian *Feuerzauber* (magic fire) is, of course, unmistakable, and the book concludes with a paean to Wagner's works as embodying the modern rebirth of Attic tragedy in Dionysian music (pp. 139–44).

Nietzsche turned his attention more specifically to questions of Germanness and modernity in the first of his *Unfashionable Observations,* "David Strauss as Confessor and Writer," written and published in 1873. This essay was written in the aftermath of the Prussian victory over France and the declaration of a German Reich. Ostensibly an attack on David Strauss's popular book *The Old and the New Faith: A Confession,* the essay is more fundamentally a polemic against the book's enthusiastic readership, whom Nietzsche famously dubbed the *Bildungsphilister* ("cultivated philistines," in a recent translation). The Strauss essay seems to have been written in part as an effort to please Wagner, who was a long-standing critic of Strauss's work and had vilified the Strauss book in conversations with Nietzsche at Bayreuth during Easter of 1873. Nietzsche began his essay soon thereafter and wanted to complete it in time to present to Wagner for his birthday on May 22.

Like Wagner in the essays discussed above, and as at the end of *Birth of Tragedy,* Nietzsche is concerned in the Strauss essay with the fate of the German *Geist.* He warns that the triumph over the French could in fact lead to "the defeat—indeed, the extirpation—of the German spirit for the sake of the 'German Reich.'"[24] Nietzsche is more overtly worried than Wagner about German "culture": he attacks the prevalent notion that the German military victory is also one for German culture. In fact, he says, German culture is in a miserable state. The achievements in war, science, technology, and scholarship—hallmarks of the *Gründerzeit* and of which Germans are so proud—are not signs of culture, says Nietzsche. Culture is rather "a unity of artistic style that manifests itself throughout all the vital self-expressions of a people." Modern Germany is characterized by the "absence of style" or a "chaotic hodgepodge of all styles" (p. 9). The cultivated philistines that dominate Germany are complacent, unadventurous. They have created "an age of epigones" (p. 15), characterized by "either imitation of reality to the point of apishly reproducing it in idylls or gently humoristic satires, or free imitations of the most recognized and famous works of the classical authors" (p. 16).[25] Nietzsche, who names no names beside Strauss, undoubtedly shared Wagner's disdain for much "modern" art. But his focus on style—and much of the essay is concerned with the stylistic failings of Strauss's prose—presented a stumbling block to the composer, who, as he told Nietzsche, had little interest in style as such.[26]

In the third of the *Observations,* "On the Utility and Liability of History for Life," Nietzsche follows up many of these points. The cultivated philistines again make an appearance. Here Nietzsche's target is their "historical sickness," an obsession with history manifested in a supposedly scientific objectivity that fails to really understand and learn from the past. "The historical sensibility," says Nietzsche, "when it rules *uncontrolled* and is allowed to realize all its consequences, uproots the future because it destroys illusions and robs existing things of that atmosphere in which they alone are able to live." The best way out of this mind-set, this "excess of history," is to take what Nietzsche calls the antidote, the "suprahistorical" viewpoint. This comprises "those powers that divert one's gaze from what is in the process of becoming to what lends existence the character of something eternal and stable in meaning, to *art* and *religion.*"[27] Nietzsche may be said to reaffirm here the power of art that he articulated in *Birth of Tragedy* and to argue against science, or *Wissenschaft.*

On the face of it, Nietzsche's fourth essay in the *Unfashionable Observations,* "Richard Wagner in Bayreuth," written in 1875–76, would seem to update *Birth of Tragedy* by presenting Wagner as the greatest modern German artist and Bayreuth as the site of artistic regeneration through a festival presentation of the music dramas. Wagner's poetry, music, dramatic theory, and stage management all come in for adulation. And yet, as several commentators have noted, the seeds of Nietzsche's break with Wagner are already present in this essay. Gary Brown has described "Richard Wagner in Bayreuth" as "an equilibrist's act," balancing an acknowledgment of Wagner's consummate mastery with a growing distrust of the whole Wagnerian enterprise. Ronald Hayman notes that Nietzsche sneaks "his stowaway criticism on board the vessel of praise."[28] There are, for example, (at least) two ways of reading a passage like the following:

> All previous music, when measured against Wagner's, seems stiff or timid, as if one should not look at it from all sides and as if it were ashamed. Wagner seizes every degree and every coloration of feeling with the greatest firmness and determination; he takes the most tender, most remote, and most tempestuous emotion into his hand without fear of losing it, and he holds on to it like something that has become hard and firm, even though everyone else may regard it as an elusive butterfly. His music is never indefinite, mood-like; everything that speaks through it, human being or nature, has a strictly individualized passion; in his music, storm and fire take on the compelling force of a personal will.[29]

On the one hand, Nietzsche is praising Wagner's ability to exert total control of structure and detail, to shape all dimensions of the listener's musical experience. On the other hand, we can sense here a mistrust of Wagner's "coercive power," of his carefully calibrated manipulation of the listener. It seems a short step to Nietzsche's blistering attack in *The Case of Wagner* from 1888, where he writes of Wagner's music: "The whole no longer lives at all: it is composite, calculated, artificial, and artifact." Lurking behind the professed admiration in the earlier essay for Wagner's ability to capture "every grade and every color of feeling" is the later criticism of Wagner as "miniaturist," whose "wealth of colors, of half shadows, of the secrecies of dying light spoils one to such an extent that afterward almost all other musicians seem too robust."[30]

NIETZSCHE'S NEOCLASSICAL TURN

Only a month after the appearance of "Richard Wagner in Bayreuth" in July 1876, Nietzsche fled the Bayreuth festival in disillusionment. The intellectual consequences of this experience are clear in a fragment from his *Nachlass* (unpublished writings and notes) prepared sometime between the end of 1876 and the summer of 1877: "To readers of my earlier writings I want expressly to clarify that I have given up the metaphysical-artistic viewpoints that in essence held sway there; these viewpoints are pleasant but unsustainable. He who is permitted early on to speak publicly is customarily soon also forced publicly to contradict himself."[31] This passage may have been drafted for the preface to *Human, All Too Human,* which appeared in 1878 and was the first work that clearly reflected Nietzsche's distancing from Wagner's music and aesthetics. *Human, All Too Human* is often regarded as Nietzsche's first truly philosophical work. In it, he renounces the essay form of his earlier *Birth of Tragedy* and *Unfashionable Observations* in favor of aphorisms or paragraphs arranged thematically. A year after the publication of *Human, All Too Human,* Nietzsche published as an "appendix" a further set of aphorisms called *Assorted Opinions and Maxims* (1879). Still a year later came another collection, *The Wanderer and His Shadow* (1880). In 1886 Nietzsche republished all three collections, with new prefaces, under the title *Human, All Too Human.* The original book of that name became volume 1; the *Assorted Opinions and Maxims* and *The Wanderer and His Shadow* together became volume 2.

In the fourth section of *Human, All Too Human,* entitled "From the Soul of Artists and Writers," Nietzsche explicitly signals a break with the Romantic metaphysics of art and music, in particular Schopenhauer's (and by extension, Wagner's). One of his first tasks is to demystify the category of the "artist-genius." In a series of aphorisms that are widely recognized as referring at least in part to Wagner, Nietzsche argues against "worshipping the genius." Certain artistic figures or their works give the impression of having been created as a kind of miracle or act of grace, as the result of pure "inspiration." Nietzsche argues strongly for the importance of craft and hard work in artistic creation. "Do not talk about giftedness, inborn talents!" he writes. "One can name great men of all kinds who were very little gifted. They *acquired* greatness, became 'geniuses' (as we put it) through qualities the lack of which no one who knew what they were would boast of: they all possessed that seriousness of the efficient workman which first learns to construct the parts properly before it ventures to fashion a great whole."[32] Nietzsche draws attention to the Beethoven sketchbooks, of which he must have been made aware by Gustav Nottebohm's publications of the 1860s and early 1870s.[33] "We can now see from Beethoven's notebooks how the most glorious melodies were put together and as it were culled out of many beginnings. . . . All the great artists have been great workers, inexhaustible not only in invention but also in rejecting, sifting, transforming, ordering" (p. 83).

After dismantling artistic genius, Nietzsche sets about demystifying music itself. "Music is, of and in itself, not so significant for our inner world," he argues, "nor so profoundly exciting, that it can be said to count as the *immediate* language of feeling" (p. 99). Since differently disposed or trained people can experience music in different ways, meaning cannot reside in the music itself, but is projected onto the music by the listener. Referring directly to—and apparently rejecting—the categories of Schopenhauer and Kant, Nietzsche says that music does not speak of the "will" or the "thing in itself." Only in an age that had conquered the entire sphere of inner life for musical symbolism could the intellect entertain this idea. The intellect has projected this meaning into the sound.

In this context, "symbolism" *(Symbolik)* and "symbolic" seem to be Nietzsche's terms for the apparent power of music (or any art) to be understood without being explicit. For Nietzsche, music has evolved from an earlier state in which sounds without physical gesture (such as dance) are unintelligible, to a state, in the present day, where "the ear reaches a level of rapid understanding such that it no longer requires visible movement, and understands the composer without it." According to Nietzsche, "One then speaks of absolute music, that is to say of music in which everything is at once understood symbolically without further assistance" (p. 100).

Nietzsche finds much to dislike in what he calls "modern" music. In a section called "The desensualization of higher art," Nietzsche suggests that music has become extremely complicated, making great demands on the listener: it has forced our ears to grow "more and more intellectual." He explains that "the ugly side of the world, the side originally hostile to the senses, has now been conquered for music; its sphere of power especially in the domain of the sublime, dreadful and mysterious, has therewith increased astonishingly: our music now brings to utterance things which formerly had no tongue. . . . What will be the consequence of all this? The more capable of thought eye and ear become, the closer they approach the point at which they become unsensual: pleasure is transferred to the brain, the sense-organs themselves grow blunt and feeble" (p. 100).

It is not clear to which composers, works, or techniques Nietzsche is referring here. One can imagine the symphonic poems of Liszt and music dramas of Wagner being indicted for extending music's power to "speak." But the emphasis on the brain might seem also to criticize Brahms, whose First Symphony of 1876—one of his densest and most "intellectual" works, in Nietzsche's sense—was widely performed (and criticized for those very qualities) in Austria and Germany at the time *Human, All Too Human* was being written.[34]

Nietzsche seems to be criticizing not only composers, but also listeners. He points to what he calls a "twofold" trend among audiences in modern Germany: "on the one hand a host of ten thousand with ever higher, more refined demands, listening ever more intently for the 'meaning,' and on the other the enormous majority growing every year more and more incapable of comprehending the meaningful even in the form of the sensually ugly and therefore learning to seize with greater and greater contentment the ugly and disgusting in itself, that is to say the basely sensual in music" (pp. 100–101). Whatever his specific targets, Nietzsche's stand against modern music and its listeners is in line with the more generally classical and antimetaphysical tone of *Human, All Too Human.* In its 1878 version, the book was dedicated to the memory of Voltaire. Nietzsche holds up a Hellenic ideal of balance and moderation, very different from the spirit in which he had idealized the Greeks in *The Birth of Tragedy* six years earlier. Now he presents Voltaire as the last artist or writer who was able "to subdue through Greek moderation a soul many-formed." Voltaire was "one of the last men able to unite in himself the highest freedom of spirit and an altogether unrevolutionary disposition without being inconsistent and cowardly" (p. 103).

Nietzsche goes on to condemn the "modern spirit" that "has come to rule in all areas, with its unrest, its hatred of moderation and limitation." And yet, Nietzsche's is not a destructive or hostile viewpoint. At the end of the section "From the Soul of Artists and Writers" Nietzsche seems to predict, or at least accept, the end of art as an aesthetic, sensuous phenomenon. He asks: when we have given up a metaphysics of art, of art as transcendent, as well as the cult of genius, "what place still remains for art"? He says that for thousands of years art has taught us "to look upon life in any of its forms with interest and pleasure." If we gave up art, we would still not forfeit what it has taught us to do, just as in giving up religion we have not abandoned "the enhancement of feeling and exaltations one has acquired from it." Nietzsche concludes: "As the plastic arts and music are the measure of the wealth of feelings we have actually gained and obtained through religion, so if art disappeared the intensity and multifariousness of the joy in life it has implanted would still continue to demand satisfaction. The scientific man is a further evolution of the artistic man" (p. 105).

The last sentence, "Der wissenschaftliche Mensch ist der Weiterentwicklung des künstlerischen," is perhaps the single most striking sentence in the "Artists and Writers" section of *Human, All Too Human.* The word "scientific" is an imperfect translation of *wissenschaftlich,* which in this context can be taken to mean "knowledge-oriented" or perhaps even "experience-oriented," as opposed to the aesthetic connotation of *künstlerisch.* The idea that the knowledge-oriented man is an extension of the artistic one is in many ways a revolutionary one. Certainly, nothing speaks more directly to Nietzsche's break with Wagnerian-Schopenhauerian metaphysics. We note too how far Nietzsche has traveled from his position in *The Birth of Tragedy* and *Unfashionable Observations,* where he vilified *Wissenschaft* and associated it with the cultivated philistines.

What does *Wissenschaft* really mean for Nietzsche? As Giorgio Colli explains: "Certainly not science in the old sense, that is, a system of hypotheses which are founded on universal principles, which are closely linked with one another, and of which one, with the help of another, can be derived and proven. But also not science in the modern sense—knowledge gained from collecting, induction, and experiment and then also carried over into the deductive mechanism." Colli observes that even the aphoristic form of *Human, All Too Human* points to Nietzsche's mistrust of logical, deductive thought, of the productiveness of chains of proof. Nietzsche is clearly not a modern positivist of the later nineteenth century. For Nietzsche, Colli argues, "scientific" ability "means above all the capacity for judgment, a judgment whose elements are united not through a necessity inherent in the reason of all men, but through a bond which not all are given to understand."[35]

In a recent study Christopher Cox employs the concept of "naturalism" to explain Nietzsche's turn to *Wissenschaft* in the wake of abandoning metaphysics. Cox is using the term "naturalism" in the more purely philosophical sense it has assumed in modern Anglo-American philosophy (especially since Quine). Naturalism in this context, according to Cox, "denies the existence of supernatural entities and explanatory principles and endorses a broadly scientific conception of the world."[36] Cox argues that Nietzsche occupies such a position in his emphasis on the completeness of "the world of life, nature, and history" (Nietzsche's phrase, from *The Gay Science*). Cox makes no reference at all to naturalism in the historically and culturally specific sense it took on in Europe in the 1880s as an artistic-cultural program. Yet the terminological identity suggests that Nietzsche's post-Wagnerian turn might be fruitfully considered in the light of the naturalist movement of the mid-1880s, to be examined in the next chapter.

For Nietzsche, "science" and the "scientific man" are not the endpoints of his antimetaphysical, antireligious quest. Art and aesthetics continue to play an important, perhaps *the* most important, role. In *The Birth of Tragedy,* Nietzsche had famously suggested that "it is only as an *aesthetic phenomenon* that existence and the world are eternally *justified*" (p. 52). He also says of the spectator who experiences the Dionysian aspect of Greek tragedy: "Art saves him, and through art—life" (p. 59). Although his outlook changes radically over the next decade, Nietzsche's faith in art and the artistic experience does not diminish. He continues to believe, as he argued in the "Attempt at a Self-criticism" appended to *The Birth of Tragedy* in 1886, that "all of life rests upon semblance, art, deception, points of view, and the necessity of perspectives and error" (p. 23). Art is ultimately more effective than science in helping us interpret the world and life—art, which affirms appearance, and "in which precisely the *lie* is sanctified and the *will to deception* has a good conscience." Cox suggests persuasively that for Nietzsche, art affirmed his highest values: it "prizes experimentation and innovation and thus affirms change and becoming."[37]

It is thus important to emphasize that Nietzsche is *not* suggesting that science replace art, or that artists become scientists. Rather, he advocates what he calls a "double-brain" that can accommodate both art and science: "[A] higher culture must give to man a double-brain, as it were two brain-ventricles, one for the perceptions of science, the other for those of non-science: lying beside one another, not confused together, separable, capable of being shut off; this is a demand of health. In one domain lies the power-source, in the other the regulator: it must be heated with illusions, onesidednesses, passions[;] the evil and perilous consequences of overheating must be obviated with the aid of the knowledge furnished by science" (p. 119). The double-brain notion is an updating of the Apollonian-Dionysian dichotomy from *The Birth of Tragedy,* which likewise posited an intellectual, knowledge-based side to humankind, and a more passion- and feeling-driven one. Unlike Wagner and the cultural despairists such as Lagarde, Nietzsche is not especially pessimistic, despite the fact that he seems to predict the death of art as it has been known and practiced. Although the whole section on "Artists and Writers" points toward the final aphorism on "the sunset of art" and the sentiments summarized above, the tone is neither resigned nor bitter. There seems to be no real regret about the abandoning of metaphysics, the transcendence of art, or the "worshipping of genius." *Human, All Too Human,* manifesting a certain detachedness absent in his earlier works, represents what Rüdiger Safranski has called the philosopher's "cooling-down experiment."[38]

It is in *Assorted Opinions and Maxims* and *The Wanderer and His Shadow,* the two successors to the original *Human, All Too Human,* that Nietzsche presents somewhat more explicitly his vision of what kind of art and artist should succeed the Wagnerian/metaphysical model. The art that Nietzsche advocates to replace the monstrous Wagnerian apparatus and the flight into the metaphysical is an art that reflects "reality." The poet of the future, he says, "will depict *only reality* and completely ignore all those fantastic, superstitious, half-mendacious, faded subjects upon which earlier poets demonstrated their powers. Only reality, but by no means every reality!—he will depict a select reality" (p. 240). Here we find an example of the "naturalism" noted by Cox and a striking anticipation of the agenda of the German naturalists.

Nietzsche also may be said to anticipate in significant respects the trends that begin to emerge clearly in music only thirty-five years later, in about 1915, and that have been called neoclassical. Nietzsche begins this discussion in an earlier segment of *Human, All Too Human,* where he admires the formal and expressive constraints of what he calls the "Franco-Hellenic art" of Racine, Corneille, and Voltaire, and derides later "revolutionary" tendencies. In *Assorted Opinions and Maxims* and *The Wanderer and His Shadow,* Nietzsche elaborates on these ideas, espousing a neo-Hellenic program of art that will beautify life—an art of purity, politeness, of "speaking and being silent at the proper time" (p. 255). This does not mean that good art is to lack spirit or feeling. For the new art is to be, in Nietzsche's memorable phrase, "dancing in chains" *(in Ketten tanzen).* This means that good art arises from the imposing of constraints, limits, or conventions upon one's imagination. Nietzsche's example is the Greek artist: "What is the *new constraint* he has imposed upon himself and through which he charms his contemporaries (so that he finds imitators)? For that which we call 'invention' (in metrics, for example) is always such a self-imposed fetter. 'Dancing in chains,' making things difficult for oneself and then spreading over it the illusion of ease and facility—that is artifice they want to demonstrate to us" (p. 343). For Nietzsche, the Greeks observed convention in order to communicate with their audiences. The Greek artist "wants to conquer *immediately* with each of his works . . . which is possible, however, only through convention. . . . Obstinately to avoid convention means wanting not to be understood" (p. 339).

In these writings from 1878–80, then, Nietzsche boldly sets forth aesthetic programs that will be fulfilled by the first generations of modernists over the next fifty years. In his 1886 preface to part II of *Human, All Too Human,* Nietzsche confirms retrospectively the "anti-Romantic attitude": the opposition to Romantic pessimism and its presentation of a "spiritual cure." He says too that it was time "to make a farewell" to Wagner. And yet it is important not to see the Nietzschean attitudes of *Human, All Too Human* as generated solely or even primarily by his break with Wagner. As Colli observes, "*Human, All Too Human* is not to be understood as a reaction, aided by the break-up of the friendship, to a world view that was strongly influenced by Wagner, but rather as the expression of a new spiritual maturity, which was at first helped by the relationship to Wagner, but in the end became hindered by it."[39]

As any reader of Nietzsche will know, Wagner remained central to Nietzsche's thought to the very end. Rather than ignoring Wagner, as might be expected of someone having said "farewell," Nietzsche continues to discuss the composer and his work, like a dog worrying a bone. In the later writings, the assaults become stronger and at times bitingly ironic, attitudes that might be taken as a clear indication of Nietzsche's continuing fascination and even love for the music. As Frederick Love has observed, "The student of psychology must surely question the vehemence, the defensiveness, even the desperation of these attacks on Wagner and Wagner's art. . . . The music of Wagner—possibly inseparable in Nietzsche's memory from the remembrance of his total Wagnerian experience—persisted to the end in its hold over him."[40] There is no greater example of ambivalent modernism, or modernist ambivalence, than Nietzsche's complex attitudes toward Wagner.

NIETZSCHE'S "GERMAN DEPTH," "MUSIC OF THE SOUTH," AND THE "GRAND STYLE"

By the mid-to-late 1880s Nietzsche repeatedly confirmed the anti-Romanticism of *Human, All Too Human* and continued to interrogate Germanness. In a segment of the "People and Fatherlands" chapter of *Beyond Good and Evil* from 1885–86, he turned his gaze on the attribute of *deutsche Tiefe* (German depth). "The German soul contains within it a maze of passageways," Nietzsche remarked. "There are caverns in it, hiding places, castle keeps; its disorder has much of the charm of the mysterious; a German knows about the secret paths to chaos." These qualities contribute to German depth, which for all his skepticism Nietzsche sees as basic to the German soul and which, as we have been recently reminded by Bernd Sponheuer, is an "ideal type" of long standing in German music.[41] Nietzsche urges his contemporaries not to "sell our old reputation as a deep people too cheaply in exchange for Prussian 'dash' and Berlin wit and sand."[42]

Yet Nietzsche felt German depth had pretty much run its course in music. He implied as much in the next section of *Beyond Good and Evil* (§245), where Romantic music from Schumann on is seen as too narrowly German and "threatened by its greatest danger: to cease being *the voice of Europe's soul* and to deteriorate into mere fatherland-ism."[43] At around the same time as he was writing *Beyond Good and Evil,* Nietzsche remarked in a letter to Erwin Rohde of 1886 that in place of Wagner "we need the south, sunshine 'at any price,' bright, harmless, innocent Mozartian happiness and delicacy of tones."[44] Love has shown that Nietzsche's appeal to the south—*Musik des Südens* (music of the South), *südliche Musik* (southern music), and *mein Süden in der Musik* (my South in music) are phrases that appear in the writings—is a common thread in his writings from the early 1880s on. These are references not to music that is necessarily composed in Italy, Spain, or Provence, but to the ideal qualities of music. Music of the South is "effectively a private tag for music that has agreed" with Nietzsche physically and emotionally. When Nietzsche is more specific about what such music is, he uses terms similar to those he uses to describe his own literary style: in Love's account, "deceptive naiveté combined with great subtlety *(heiter und tief);* refined awareness of its own modernity and a conscious delight in the deliberate exploitation of tradition." Nietzsche's Music of the South is also a kind of antidote or alternative to decadence, a term he also begins to use in the mid-1880s and that he derived from Paul Bourget. Music of the South is healthier, more listenable than decadent music (of which Wagner is, of course, Nietzsche's prime example); it has, as Love notes, "an unmistakable therapeutic component."[45] This notion of healthy, restorative music will resurface later in the rhetoric of the fin de siècle, especially in connection with Bach reception, as will be argued in chapter 4.

Nietzsche found these abstract ideals manifest in a number of composers and works. At first he seems to have projected them onto, or through, his friend Peter Gast (an alias for Heinrich Köselitz), whom he called the "new Mozart." Gast became a kind of puppet or vehicle for some of Nietzsche's ideas on music and a hoped-for embodiment of a post-Wagnerian musical idiom in opera based largely on Gluck and Piccini.[46] In fact, Gast proved a musical disappointment to Nietzsche, as did August Bungert, the composer in whom Nietzsche took a brief interest in 1883. Bungert was seeking to outdo the Bayreuth master with an operatic tetralogy about Odysseus called *Die homerische Welt* (The Homeric World). Nietzsche also took an interest in Rossini, of whom by 1888 he knew eight operas.[47] Yet it was ultimately Bizet whom Nietzsche claimed to embody his newer musical and aesthetic values. As Nietzsche famously observed of *Carmen* in *The Case of Wagner,* written in 1888: "This music seems perfect to me. It approaches lightly, supplely, politely. It is pleasant, it does not *sweat.* 'What is good is light; whatever is divine moves on tender feet': the first principle of my aesthetics" (p. 157).

And yet, for all his admiration of Bizet, it seems clear that in Nietzsche's scheme of the mid-1880s Bizet is not truly *modern.* If anything, he may be postmodern; like Gast, he represents a neoclassical style that Nietzsche might hope to see replace the excesses of Wagner. It is Wagner who for Nietzsche is "the *modern artist par excellence.*" Wagner is modern in his decadence, in his seeking after "effect, nothing but effect," and in the fact that despite the large scale of his music, "the whole is no longer a whole. . . . It is composite, calculated, artificial, and artifact" (p. 170).

Despite his accusing Brahms of "melancholy of impotence," Nietzsche thought more highly of the composer than he made out in *The Case of Wagner.* According to Gast, Nietzsche "respected Brahms" and "particularly admired his North German seriousness, his austere masculine manner, his rejection of directionless, confused music, his sense of logic and construction."[48] In *The Case of Wagner* Brahms is also "modern" for Nietzsche in important respects: "Brahms is touching as long as he is secretly enraptured or mourns for himself—in this he is 'modern'; he becomes cold and of no further concern to us as soon as he becomes *the heir* of the classical composers" (p. 188). This statement implies that Nietzsche admires Brahms's subjectivity and finds it "modern," but that the more historicist aspects of Brahms's work are not—or rather, the sense of historical continuity with the past is not. Nietzsche's antihistoricism, so well documented in his "On the Utility and Liability of History," is clearly in evidence here.

There is much in *The Case of Wagner* that is contradictory or ambivalent. The ironic tone of the essay certainly complicates any attempt to read it as a "straight" account of Nietzsche's ideas on modern music. But it is clear that much as he disparages both Wagner and Brahms, Nietzsche sees them as emblematic, in different ways, of modern German music. Wagner is modern in his manipulativeness, shallowness, and decadence, Brahms in his "melancholy of impotence." Neither composer, it seems, can avoid the modern condition.

One of the key elements of modernity for Nietzsche—and here again he is in many respects prophetic—is the impossibility of large-scale coherence, of structural unity in works of art. In literature (in particular the literature he refers to as decadent), "the word becomes sovereign and leaps out of the sentence, the sentence reaches out and obscures the meaning of the page, the page gains life at the expense of the whole—and the whole is no longer a whole" (p. 170). These thoughts seem to anticipate the *Sprachkrise* articulated almost fifteen years later by Hofmannsthal in his *Lord Chandos Letter* of 1902, where Chandos writes, "I have utterly lost my ability to think or speak coherently about anything at all. . . . Everything fell into fragments for me, the fragments into further fragments, until it seemed impossible to contain anything at all within a single concept."[49] This work is considered one of the prime documents of turn-of-the-century subjectivity.

With his comments in *The Case of Wagner* Nietzsche renounces an important principle of his earlier aesthetics, that of the Grand Style or *großer Stil.* For him, the Grand Style implied ambitious art on a large scale, constructed with logic, structural coherence, and balance. Music in the Grand Style need not be complex, elaborate, or fussily detailed; rather, it shows "disdain for the beauty that is small and brief; it is a feeling for the minimal and the maximal *[Weniges und Langes].*" Elsewhere Nietzsche noted that "the Grand Style originates when the beautiful triumphs over the immense."[50] As Love suggests, the concept of the Grand Style "became the single cypher for virtually all the unattained and even unattainable goals that Nietzsche had ever conceived for music, a term implicitly antithetical to the 'decadent' condition of contemporary musical art."[51]

For Nietzsche, not even the great German composers seem to have attained the Grand Style—not Bach, nor Beethoven in the Ninth Symphony, which is perhaps the work that would come most readily to a nineteenth-century mind as an example, and that Nietzsche specifically mentions as *not* being in the Grand Style.[52] Nietzsche's favorite example of the Grand Style—and the only concrete one he adduced, on several occasions, though without any elaborating explanation—was the Pitti Palace in Florence. In the spring of 1888, at about the same time he was writing *The Case of Wagner,* Nietzsche notes in a fragment called "Music—and the Grand Style" that "all the arts have ambitions toward the Grand Style," except music: "Why is it lacking in music? Why up to now has no musician constructed in the manner of the architect of the Pitti Palace? . . . Does music perhaps belong in that culture where the realm of all sorts of powerful men is coming to an end? In the end does the concept of the Grand Style contradict the soul of music—the 'woman' in our music?"[53] Nietzsche goes on to wonder whether all modern music is not decadent—for him the category in opposition to the Grand Style. The problem, then, seems to lie not with specific composers or works, but with the art of music itself.

The fragment can perhaps help shed some light on the contemporaneous *Case of Wagner,* where Wagner is depicted as the most modern and decadent of musicians, in part because he works with "small units." Wagner is, Nietzsche remarks with what would appear to be a counterintuitive stance, "our greatest miniaturist." But Wagner may also just be the only modern musician to understand that such a small-scale perspective is necessary, inevitable. As Nietzsche notes: "Everything in music today that lays claim to a 'great style' *either* deceives us *or* deceives itself." He continues,

> What can be done well today, what can be masterly, is only what is small. Here alone integrity is still possible.—
>
> Nothing, however, can cure music *in* what counts, *from* what counts, from the fatality of being an expression of the physiological contradiction—of being *modern.* (p. 188)

Just what constitutes that "physiological contradiction" becomes clear from the end of the Epilogue of *The Case of Wagner.* Nietzsche views the modern condition as fraught with contradictions and oppositions: "Biologically, modern man represents a *contradiction of values;* he sits between two chairs, he says Yes and No in the same breath. . . . [A]ll of us have unconsciously, involuntarily in our bodies values, words, formulas, moralities of opposite descent—we are, physiologically considered, *false.*" For Nietzsche, Wagner is the "most instructive" case of such a contradiction among modern men.

WAGNER'S *PARSIFAL* AND AMBIVALENT MODERNISM

Wagner's last opera, *Parsifal,* composed between 1877 and 1882, can serve as a fulcrum for the issues raised in this chapter. As a work created on the cusp of the early modern era, it is a striking example of ambivalent modernism. The ambivalence might be said to reach right into the compositional techniques of the opera; chorale-like melodies and the "Dresden Amen," evocative of the old, the antique, coexist with anxious chromatic harmonies that sound ultra-new. *Parsifal* also reveals the tension between modernism and German national identity. As Wagner's most socially and culturally regressive work, it promulgates an even more restricted notion of "community" than *Die Meistersinger,* in which the strong community-based values of Nuremberg are challenged, and ultimately enriched, by the incursions of a more complex urban "society" (envy, riots, elopement). Admission to the community of the Grail in *Parsifal* is restricted to chaste Christian men. They are also by implication Aryan men.

Paul Lawrence Rose, in what is often a heavy-handed treatment of Wagner's anti-Semitism and attitudes on race, provides what is nonetheless a persuasive explanation of the connection between the later writings and *Parsifal.* In these essays from 1877–81, into which fits "What Is German?" discussed above, Wagner promoted the idea of an Aryan Jesus and an Aryan Christianity, purified of any Judaic association. "That the God of our Saviour should have been identified with the tribal God of Israel," he wrote, "is one of the most terrible confusions in all world-history."[54] For Rose and for the contemporary critics of *Parsifal* that he cites, the opera was recognized as a kind of manifesto of racial and not simply religious regeneration. In this interpretation Klingsor "embodies the corruption of Judaized Christianity"; he in turn uses Kundry (described by Wagner himself as "a kind of Wandering Jew") to corrupt and destroy the Grail knights. Rose claims that "Wagner intended *Parsifal* to be a profound religious parable about how the whole essence of European humanity had been poisoned by alien, Jewish values. It is an allegory of the Judaization of Christianity and of Germany—and of purifying redemption. In place of theological purity, the secularized religion of Parsifal [the character] preached the new doctrine of racial purity."[55] Rose's position is extreme but plausible. Whether we understand *Parsifal* as racial or religious ideology, as a piece of "nostalgic medievalism" (Lucy Beckett's term), or simply as a ceremonial work (Wagner called it a *Bühnenweihfestspiel,* a stage-consecrating festival play), it has an unmistakably strong antimodernist cast that is so characteristic of Wagner and his like-minded contemporaries.[56]

Parsifal was, significantly, the work of Wagner's that brought out Nietzsche's ambivalence most strongly. In a letter to Peter Gast of January 1887, he wrote: "I recently heard for the first time the introduction to *Parsifal.* . . .

[D]id Wagner ever compose anything better? The finest psychological intelligence and definition of what must be said here, expressed, *communicated,* the briefest and most direct form for it, every nuance of feeling pared down to an epigram; a clarity in the music as descriptive art, bringing to mind a shield with a design in relief on it."[57] In *The Case of Wagner,* written a year and a half later in May 1888, he now called *Parsifal* a decadent work that, Circe-like, lures its listeners in: "In the art of seduction, *Parsifal* will always retain its rank—as *the stroke of genius* in seduction.—I admire this work; I wish I had written it myself; failing that, *I understand it*" (p. 184). Wagner's powers make him the "Klingsor of all Klingsors," the greatest of all magicians. In *Nietzsche contra Wagner,* written in December 1888 just before his final collapse, Nietzsche attacked *Parsifal* still more strongly. He responded not to any anti-Semitic dimensions of the opera, but to its cloying religiosity. Wagner was "a decaying and despairing decadent," who in *Parsifal* "suddenly sank down, helpless and broken, before the Christian cross." The opera is "a work of perfidy, of vindictiveness, of a secret attempt to poison the presuppositions of life—a bad work. The preaching of chastity remains an incitement to anti-nature: I despise everyone who does not experience *Parsifal* as an attempted assassination of basic ethics."[58]

Nietzsche's first assessment, in the letter to Gast, puts in positive terms what he would condemn in *The Case of Wagner,* where the composer is depicted as a decadent "miniaturist" capable (or desirous) only of working with "small units." In this nexus of concepts and attitudes lies an important key to the musical style of *Parsifal,* which can be called ambivalent, or at least conflicted, because Wagner seems at once to aim for and to renounce the Grand Style. A closer look at the act 1 Prelude singled out by Nietzsche can help illuminate these issues.

The slow tempo of the Prelude *(Sehr langsam),* and indeed of much of the music connected with the Grail Temple in acts 1 and 3 of the opera, is characteristic of what in 1885 Ludwig Nohl identified as a German predilection for Adagio movements. Nohl was writing specifically about chamber music, but one could extrapolate from the immediate context to operatic music. (Nohl would certainly have known *Parsifal* by this point.) In her article that begins with the citation of Nohl, Margaret Notley points out that for most of the nineteenth century, at least from late Beethoven on, Adagio movements held a special status for both composers and critics in German lands. Many sought to emphasize the ideal of a form in which the standard structural archetypes were governed or shaped by melodic processes. By late in the century, Notley suggests, Wagner's notion of *unendliche Melodie* or unending melody was seen as a guiding principle for Adagios.[59]

The Wagnerian Adagio might be the most self-conscious example of what Nietzsche identified (disparagingly) as German depth. Lasting close to fifteen minutes in most performances, the Prelude to act 1 of *Parsifal* is the longest of any of Wagner's preludes—that is, of the post-*Tannhäuser* orchestral pieces that precede the operas and are designated as preludes *(Vorspiele),* not overtures. Its time scale is even more extensive than the *Tristan* Prelude, which normally clocks in at about eleven minutes. Nietzsche's terms "brief," "direct," and "epigrammatic" might not be the first to come to mind when contemplating the expansive *Parsifal* Prelude. Yet he is definitely onto something about this work, as was Theodor Adorno, who in his essay "On the Score of 'Parsifal'" of 1956–57 describes "a tendency towards simplification" *(Vereinfachungstendenz),* which I take to mean both the epigrammatic quality identified by Nietzsche as well as the scarcity of leitmotives in comparison with Wagner's other mature operas (a point made by Adorno). For Adorno, the motives of *Parsifal* are "somewhat fractured and inessential *[Gebrochenes und Uneigentliches].*"[60]

With the notion of simplification, Adorno also alludes to a clarity that is the sonic analogue to the chastity and purity *(Reinheit)* that are the opera's main values. Indeed, Wagner may have thought along those precise lines. In the spring of 1881, he was visited at Bayreuth by the racial theorist Arthur Gobineau, whose work he greatly admired. On this occasion, Wagner took pleasure in reading aloud some favorite pages from Gobineau's treatise *Essay on the Inequality of the Human Races* (1853–55).[61] These came from book 3, chapter 4, where Gobineau argues that before the seventh century, B.C., the "Aryan Greeks" had attained a "great period of literary and artistic glory" in epic poetry, architecture, sculpture, and philosophy—all of which then declined through Semitic influence.[62] After reading to Gobineau, Cosima reports, Wagner sat down and played him the Prelude to *Parsifal.* The direct juxtaposition of racial theory and music seems more than coincidental.

Wagner may be said to begin his Prelude with pure Melody: arching over six long measures, the *Liebesmahl* theme is played unaccompanied, in unison, by strings and woodwinds (example 1). The initial gesture is an A♭-major triad that climbs upward and is completed by a scalar ascent to the high A♭ an octave above the point of departure. However "direct" or "simple," this theme is no mere unfolding of a scale. The *Liebesmahl* is as ambiguous in rhythm and meter as it is clear in its initial harmonic implications. Although Wagner notates the theme in $\frac{4}{4}$, it does not at first fit comfortably into a clear metrical grid. It begins on a weak notated beat (the second), although listeners will not likely know where the beat is unless they have their eyes on the conductor or score. Rhythmically, the theme is highly syncopated.

Just as the theme completes its octave ascent, harmonic stability is undermined. Rather than serving as a point of resolution for the rising scale, the high A♭ is unstable. It falls on a weak beat, lasts only an eighth note, then sinks down to G. This G is, in fact, the first note of the theme to fall on a strong beat—the downbeat—and its *forte* dynamic represents the culmination of a crescendo. This is an extraordinary moment because as the leading tone, G represents the least stable note in an A♭-major scale. And yet this G is made to serve as the endpoint of the opening gesture and proceeds to derail or redefine the harmonic trajectory of the theme. It shifts its identity from that of leading tone in A♭ to the dominant in C minor. Moving resolutely down to C, by fifth, it generates the first real cadential gesture, toward C minor, or iii of the initial A♭. The D♮ on the second beat is the first nondiatonic note to be heard. It lies outside the scale of A♭ and confirms the motion of the theme toward the realm of C minor.

Measure 3 is the most metrically and rhythmically regular of all six measures of the theme; all its notes fall on the beat, and there are no syncopations within the measure. But the final E♭ begins to lead us back to the sound world of the opening. It serves at once as an implied iii, but also as V of A♭. Rhythmically it resumes the ambiguity of the opening, by being tied over the bar line to m. 4. Yet the overall thrust is now toward resolution. The strong D♭ on beat three of m. 4 firmly corrects the D♮ of the preceding measure and facilitates a resolution of the line to C, the third degree of A♭. Once the C is reached, the rest of the orchestra joins in, confirming the A♭-major harmony through arpeggios and repeated chords. These are the first chords sounded in the Prelude. Harmony has now joined Melody to make a complete whole.

Within these six measures Wagner manages to convey much of the essence of *Parsifal,* especially the opposition of its two worlds—the realm of the Grail and that of Klingsor. The juxtaposition is in part harmonic: the more stable A♭-major "frame" encloses a turbulent C-minor middle segment, much as the Grail acts of the opera, acts 1 and 3, surround Klingsor's act 2. Yet the rhythmic design of the theme presents almost the opposite image. The A♭-major segments are syncopated and irregular, and thus from this point of view unstable; the C-minor central segment is aligned with the

Example 1. Wagner, *Parsifal* Prelude

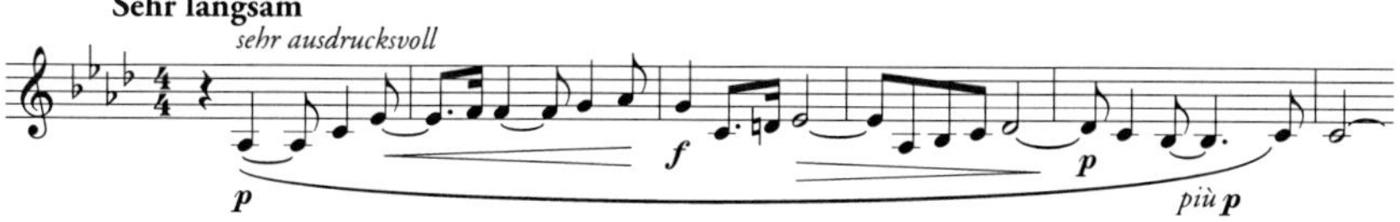

bar line, and its rhythmic profile is much more direct. Thus we sense that for all its apparent serenity, the realm of the Grail is far from secure. Klingsor's realm can seem more confident and assertive. As the opera unfolds, we see how much these two spheres intersect: Amfortas's anguish dominates the Grail scenes, and Parsifal as "pure fool" infiltrates and eventually conquers Klingsor's realm. Harmony and rhythm are thus in tension in the Prelude.

The sense in which the irregularity on the local level obscures a larger design brings Wagner's Prelude into line with the fragmentation and miniaturization observed by Nietzsche and later identified by Hofmannsthal as key aspects of modernism. When we listen to something as spread out as the Prelude, we might experience something of a musical analogue to the language crisis of Hofmannsthal's Lord Chandos, for whom sentences fell into bits and no coherent whole could be perceived. But there is an important difference. In Wagner's Prelude we get no sense of musical crisis, no sense of a *Tonkrise* similar to Hofmannsthal's *Sprachkrise.* Rather, subject and object, or listener and work, are kept in balance.

Another aspect of *Parsifal* conveyed by the Prelude is the relationship between time, space, and motion. Within the six measures we seem to have traveled far and yet in a sense have gone nowhere, since we end up at the harmony where we began. The effect of motion within stasis, or stasis within motion, is an explicit aspect of *Parsifal.* It is what Parsifal observes as he walks to the Grail Temple with Gurnemanz in the transformation scene between scenes 1 and 2 of act 1: "Ich schreite kaum, doch wähn ich mich schon weit" (I scarcely tread, yet seem to have come far). To this, Gurnemanz famously replies, "Du siehst, mein Sohn, zum Raum wird hier die Zeit" (You see, my son, time becomes space here).

It was in this light that Adorno observed how in *Parsifal* "the master of the art of transition ends up composing a *static* score" (p. 384). What contributes to the static quality is that the first large formal unit of the Prelude is generated by varied repetition of the entire nine-measure theme. Then on a still broader scale, the initial theme in unison and its accompanied repetition (mm. 1–19) form a larger unit in A♭ major that is treated as the model for a large-scale sequence down a third in C minor (mm. 20–38). These first thirty-nine measures represent the first large formal unit (A) in a prelude whose overall form might be analyzed as A–B–C–Coda. The structure of A is:

a (mm. 1–8), A♭ major

a′ (mm. 9–19), A♭ major

a (mm. 20–27), C minor

a′ (mm. 28–39), C minor

Wagner thus magnifies on a vaster harmonic plane the implied harmonic move to C minor in m. 3 of the Prelude. This A segment of the Prelude, all based on the *Liebesmahl* motive, takes almost five minutes to unfold. It is followed by a section (B) based on the "Dresden Amen" and "Grail" motives, which are treated mainly in bold sequences. This segment wanders harmonically, but returns to A♭ in m. 78. Then begins a quasi development (C) based on the *Liebesmahl* motive. This is the most unstable, modulatory section of the Prelude, the one in which thematic fragmentation dominates. But no "recapitulation" follows. Instead, the music subsides onto the dominant, E♭, which is sustained and leads, without resolution onto the tonic A♭, directly into act 1.

Adorno claims that an aspect of the originality of *Parsifal* is its demand for a distinctive kind of listening: *Nachhören,* or after-hearing. The *Liebesmahl* theme "reverberates" *(verhallt)* through the four bars after its last note has sounded (mm. 6–9), while the A♭-major chord is being unfolded. Adorno explains: "It is as though the style of *Parsifal* sought not merely to represent musical ideas, but to compose their aura as well, as this constructs itself not at the moment of execution, but rather during the music's subsequent decay. This intention can be understood only by whoever surrenders more to the echo of the music than to the music itself" (p. 384). Although Adorno is writing almost a century after *Parsifal,* his insights are not anachronistic; they point directly to the modernity of the opera and its techniques. The idea of after-hearing, of listening for the echoes rather than the "thing itself," would seem to be something new around 1880.

After-hearing can be associated with Nietzsche's double-brain metaphor for the scientific-artistic man. For Nietzsche, we recall, in the postmetaphysical, post-Romantic world, the scientific man would be the "further development" of the artistic one. His double-brain would contain both the artistic "power-source" and the scientific "regulator." It may be that such a dual apparatus is necessary, or desirable, to take in the *Parsifal* Prelude, in which an idea (or sound) is followed by its equally important aura (or echo). It is this succession of idea and aura that makes for the temporal and sonic spaciousness of this music. In his last score Wagner mastered fully the science of sound—the ability to compose out the after-echoes—and thus became the first truly "scientific" composer in Nietzsche's sense of the word. That Wagner accomplished this feat of modernism in the service of a social-cultural message that is so regressive and antimodern points up the ambivalence that lies at the heart of his achievement.

TWO

German Naturalism

EVEN AS THE SOUNDS OF *PARSIFAL,* at once modern and regressive, echoed through the Bayreuth Festspielhaus in 1882, newer trends were on the rise in Germany. Naturalism was the first self-conscious, programmatic movement of German modernism. It had its beginnings around 1880, primarily in two urban centers, Berlin and Munich, and began to decline by the mid-1890s. German naturalism drew much of its inspiration from France, specifically from the realism of Courbet, Flaubert, and Zola. Ibsen also became an influential figure. Although music was not central to the program of the German naturalists, their concerns overlapped with those of musicians and commentators on music. At least in Austria and Germany, these concerns were more aesthetic than political and social. Most naturalists were concerned less with how their art could or could not rescue the working class or emancipate women than with how social conditions could and should be represented or captured in art. As such, in the decades around 1900, arguments about music's ability or obligation to be naturalistic took on a new urgency in considerations of opera, Lieder, and instrumental works.

In this chapter, after examining some of the foundational notions of German naturalism in the 1880s, I will discuss the ways in which Wagner was accommodated to the naturalist agenda, aspects of declamatory naturalism in German text-setting, and German responses to and adaptations of Italian verismo as a way of getting beyond Wagner. Finally I will consider how what was considered the "overcoming" of naturalism in the 1890s led to a kind of hyper-naturalism in the works we normally consider expressionist, including Strauss's *Salome* and *Elektra.*

NATURALISM: DEFINITIONS AND PERSPECTIVES

Naturalism arose in the wake of the founding of the German Reich, the advance of technology and of the natural and social sciences, and the rise of the city and its attendant sociopolitical problems. Naturalists manifested some of the same ambivalence as other early modernists. They were at once attracted by technical and scientific progress and repelled by its antihumanism. They were supportive of German national identity and appalled at imperial ambitions. Many of the naturalists' agendas were played out in two leading periodicals: in Munich, *Die Gesellschaft* (Society), published from 1885 to 1902; and in Berlin, *Freie Bühne für modernes Leben* (Free Stage for Modern Life), which began publication in 1890 and through several name changes still appears today. Fritz Schlawe has succinctly summarized the goals of the naturalists, as reflected especially in these and similar periodicals, as "the contemporary struggle of the young against the old, against the flattening and corruption of intellectual life, against the devaluation of literature through the scourge of family magazines and the industrialization of journalism, against the mendacious idealism of the philistines—all in the service of a resolutely realistic worldview."[1]

In the new Germany—imperialistic, capitalistic, militaristic, and increasingly industrial and urban—the early naturalists called for greater social equality, greater individual spiritual freedom, and an enhanced status of the artist.[2] "We have swallowed more iron and blood than our nature can bear," Michael Georg Conrad wrote in 1893 about the militarism of Wilhelmine Germany. "The dumbest soldier is worth more than the best poet."[3] Yet the early naturalists were also strongly nationalistic. Like Wagner they felt that the true German spirit was being eclipsed or buried in imperial Germany.

Despite their dissatisfaction with many aspects of life in the new Reich, most of the naturalists valued the advances in science and technology and sought to associate artistic creation with them. Although few of these writers mention Nietzsche, their attack on metaphysics and their advocacy of a link between the natural sciences and art clearly reflect the positions of Nietzsche examined in the last chapter. In an article called "Realism and Natural Science" of 1888, Karl Bleibtreu, one of the most prominent theorists of naturalism, baldly asserts, "The fundamentals of the scientific outlook emphasized here must reshape all aesthetics and artistic creation from the ground up, since ideas of beauty and ugliness, justice and injustice are changed according to nature, and a healthy new morality is constructed. . . . The realistic poetry of the future no longer knows any metaphysics other than as a symbol for those apparently transcendental, immanent ideas that we can today analyze inductively from natural life." Elsewhere Bleibtreu claims: "The spirit of scientific [or scholarly, *wissenschaftlicher*] research must link itself up with the spirit of poetry."[4] Many of Bleibtreu's remarks sound Nietzschean, but they have a more pragmatic aim of someone in the trenches, of someone (unlike Nietzsche) actively engaged in the literary-cultural scene of Germany.

Bleibtreu uses the term "realism," which during this period in Austria and Germany is virtually interchangeable with naturalism, even though the two words can have different nuances. Many later historians and critics have also used both terms, realism and naturalism, to describe essentially the same phenomena in the nineteenth century. In the strictest sense, one should perhaps reserve "realism" for the movement in French painting in the mid-nineteenth century of which the acknowledged master was Courbet. In his most famous canvases, such as *The Stonebreakers* of 1849, Courbet tends to strip peasants or workers of an idealized veneer of pastoralism. Naturalism can be more directly associated with the writer and novelist Émile Zola, who preferred that term to realism. In 1868 he described the goal of his novel *Thérèse Raquin* as "first and foremost a scientific one" and likened the approach to his characters as "the analytical method . . . that surgeons apply to corpses." Zola sought to distance himself from "realists" like Dickens by avoiding any moral judgment on what he was presenting.[5] In the present chapter, I will, to be consistent, stick with the term "naturalism," because that was the one used most often to represent the set of beliefs and practices being treated here.

Zola was a beacon for the German naturalists. Remarks by him appeared in 1885 in the third issue of *Die Gesellschaft,* where he argued that an artist should be true to himself and to his subject: "What I demand from the artist is something very different from asking him to please me or conjure up fearsome visions. I want him to give of himself completely; I want him to reveal to me a strong, unique spirit, to put before my eyes with a bold hand a piece of nature, as he sees and takes hold of it." This comment reflects Zola's more-often cited credo, "Une oeuvre d'art est un coin de la nature, vu à travers un tempérament" (A work of art is a corner of nature seen through a temperament).[6]

Within German-speaking lands between 1850 and the mid-1890s, an important group of novelists, including Theodor Fontane, Gottfried Keller, and Conrad Ferdinand Meyer, wrote detailed depictions of middle-class German life that were influenced by Balzac, Flaubert, Zola, and Dickens. The styles and methods of these "bourgeois realists," as they came to be known, seemed inadequate to the first generation of German naturalists, who turned their attention to the nitty-gritty of urban life and/or to the plight of laborers in general, as in Gerhart Hauptmann's famous play *Die Weber* (The Weavers) of 1892. Visual artists followed a similar path. One of the most renowned realist paintings from the earlier phase is Adolf Menzel's *Eisenwalzwerk* (Iron-Rolling Mill) of 1872–75, which has been called "the first artistically valid representation of an industrial scene in European art."[7] Later, factories and railways in Berlin were depicted starkly by Hans Baluschek (1870–1935), himself the son of a railway engineer. Käthe Kollwitz (1867–1945), who lived in Berlin from 1891, created powerful prints of laborers, including a set, *Das Weberaufstand* (Weavers' Revolt, 1895–98), directly inspired by Hauptmann's play. The painter Max Liebermann (1847–1935) began as a hard-core naturalist and turned to a more impressionist style in the 1890s. He was especially attracted to the Netherlands, where he painted such works as *Netzflickerinnen* (Net Menders, 1887–89), showing Dutch women working on a flat windswept landscape.

Among the most important examples of naturalism are the poems of Arno Holz about life in modern Berlin. Berlin had grown exponentially over the latter half of the nineteenth century from a population of 400,000 in 1850 to over 2,000,000 by 1910.[8] Much of this growth was spurred by the *Gründerzeit,* or foundation period, of the German empire after 1871. Many residents of metropolitan Berlin, the imperial capital, were the new working class. Between 1895 and 1907 alone, the number of workers living in Berlin grew by 300,000.[9] In the "Großstadt" (Large City) segment of Holz's *Das Buch der Zeit: Lieder eines Modernen* (The Book of the Age: Poems of a Modern Man, 1886), a major collection of naturalist verse, a slice of Berlin life is captured with photographic precision by a poem called "Ein Andres" (Another Thing):

> Five worm-eaten steps lead up
> to the top floor of a workers' tenement;
> the north wind likes to linger here,
> and the stars of heaven shine through the roofing.
> What they catch sight of, oh, it is plenty enough

to make us weep sympathetically at the misery:
A small crust of black bread and a pitcher of water,
a worktable and a stool with three legs.
The window is nailed shut with a board,
and yet the wind whistles through now and again,
and on that bed stuffed with straw
a young woman is lying, sick with fever.
Three small children are standing around her . . .

[Fünf wurmzernagte Stiegen gehts hinauf / ins letzte Stockwerk einer Mietskaserne; / hier hält der Nordwind sich am liebsten auf, / und durch das Dachwerk schaun des Himmels Sterne. / Was sie erspähn, oh, es ist grad genug, / um mit dem Elend brüderlich zu weinen: / Ein Stückchen Schwarzbrot und ein Wasserkrug, / ein Werktisch und ein Schemel mit drei Beinen. / Das Fenster ist vernagelt durch ein Brett, / und doch durchpfeift der Wind es hin und wieder, / und dort auf jenem stroh-gestopften Bett / liegt fieberkrank ein junges Weib danieder. / Drei kleine Kinder stehn um sie herum . . .][10]

One could scarcely assemble a list of images more brutally realistic than Holz's. The numbing, proselike multiplication of detail makes for the deliberately grim depiction of the underbelly of capitalist prosperity in the booming metropolis Berlin.

Not all naturalist poetry was this severe. It could also describe in similar detail more pleasant settings outside the city, or the festive clink of glasses and smoke of cigarettes in an urban cafe. For Holz and many of his contemporaries, the subject matter was less significant than the quality of the description. Holz's formula for the naturalist objective was: *Kunst = Natur–x,* or Art = Nature minus *x,* where *x* is the "material" of art, or its "conditions of reproduction purely as such" *(Reproduktionsbedingungen rein als solchen).* Holz explained: "Art has the tendency to revert to nature. She will do this according to the standards of her specific conditions of reproduction and their manipulation."[11]

One key element of Holz's program was what came to be called *konsequenter Naturalismus,* or sequential naturalism, which was intended to give a moment-to-moment description of situations, events, impressions, and verbal exchanges. There would be no governing, overarching perspective, no omniscient narrator or perceiver.[12] This approach was also dubbed *Sekundenstil,* or second-by-second style.[13] Sequential naturalism was first put systematically into practice in an 1889 collection of short stories, coauthored by Holz and Johannes Schlaf and called *Papa Hamlet* after one of the main stories. The stories are filled with minute details, frequent shifts of perspective, and a kind of indirect speech that deliberately confuses the narrative voice with that of an individual character.

Papa Hamlet itself, like much realist or naturalist literature, is the story of a family's struggle and decline. Niels Thienwiebel, an unemployed actor who once played Hamlet, lives in a squalid attic room (similar to the one described in "Ein Andres") with his wife, who is ill with tuberculosis, and his small son Fortinbras, who is subject to seizures. The family is threatened with eviction for nonpayment of rent. Niels drinks heavily and is abusive. At the end of the story he is found frozen in the snow by a small boy at play. The story is presented almost exclusively in dialogue, with much use of North German dialect and many contractions; there is minimal intervention from a narrator.

The second-by-second style is clear in a portion of the story when Niels cruelly forces a pacifier on the whining Fortinbras. Holz and Schlaf capture every nuance of the verbal exchanges. There is virtually no narration and no specific identification of the speakers (in this case, Niels and his wife). Punctuation, including *Gedankenstriche* (the dash used by Germans to separate segments of a paragraph) and ellipses, is applied with almost scientific precision:

> He had found the pacifier now and wiped it on his underwear.
> "It's really cold! Well? Will it be soon? Well? Take it, camel! Take it! Well?!"
> The little Fortinbras gasped!
> His little head spasmed at the nape of the neck, and in despair he rotated it in all directions.
> "Well? Do you want it, or not?! — — Brute!!"
> "But — Niels! For God's sake! He's having it again — the seizure!"
> "So what! Seizure! — — There! Eat!!"
> "Dear God, Niels . . ."
> "Eat!!!"
> "Niels!"
> "Well? Are you — quiet now? Well? — Are you — quiet now? Well?! Well?!"
> "Oh God! Oh God, Niels, what, what — do you think you're doing?! He, he — is not screaming anymore! He . . . Niels!!"
>
> [Er hatte den Lutschpfropfen jetzt gefunden und wischte ihn sich nun an den Unterhosen ab. "So'ne Kälte! Na? Wird's nu bald? Na? Nimm's

> doch, Kameel! Nimm's doch! Na?!" Der kleine Fortinbras jappte! Sein Köpfchen hatte sich ihm hinten in's Genick gekrampft, er bohrte es jetzt verzweifelt nach allen Seiten. "Na? Willst Du nu, oder nich?! — Bestie!!" "Aber — Niels! Um Gotteswillen! Er hat ja wieder den — Anfall!" "Ach was! Anfall! — — Da! Friss!!" "Herrgott, Niels . . ." "Friss!!!" "Niels!" "Na? Bist Du — nu still? Na? — Bist Du — nu still? Na?! Na?!" "Ach Gott! Ach Gott, Niels, was, was — machst Du denn bloß?! Er, er — schreit ja gar nich mehr! Er . . . Niels!!"][14]

Moments later in the story, Holz and Schlaf indicate the dripping of melting snow on the roof onomatopoetically and visually, with a series of carefully calibrated ellipses that capture the passage of time:

> Tipp . . . .
> . . . . Tipp . . . . . .
> . . . . . . Tipp . . . .
> . . . . Tipp . .
> . . . .[15]

Holz advocated for poetry something analogous to sequential naturalism. By the later 1890s, in a campaign he called a "Poetry Revolution," Holz demanded the elimination of rhyme, meter, and strophic form, goals he would realize in his large collection of poems *Phantasus* (1898). In a *Selbstanzeige* (Self-advertisement) for *Phantasus,* Holz referred to these structural conventions (rhyme, meter, strophic form) as "fetters" that tended to aestheticize the word. In the older style of poetry that uses these devices, says Holz, there is "a striving toward a certain music by using words for their own sake." More precisely, such poetry employs "a certain rhythm that not only comes to life because of that which struggles through it toward expression, but which moreover owes its existence to that." Holz's own "Ein Andres" might be an example of this phenomenon; its brutal naturalist imagery is still couched in regular rhyme and meter (as is apparent in the original German, given above). To this Holz contrasts a newer poetry that "renounces any music produced by words for their own sake and which is carried, purely formally, simply through a rhythm that lives only by that which struggles toward expression." In other words, the pure nature or essence of the poetic words should not be mediated—or compromised, in Holz's view—by the artificial structural aspects of rhyme, meter, or strophic form. In this connection Holz developed his theory of *notwendiger Rhythmus,* or obligatory rhythm, for poetry. Obligatory rhythm is not preconceived, but "grows anew from the content each time, as if nothing else before it had ever been written."[16]

Holz laid out each of the *Phantasus* poems typographically in a symmetrical form along an imaginary middle axis. He felt that this style could best reveal or release the obligatory rhythm of the poetry. In addition, Holz noted, when lines of widely varying length were oriented on a middle axis, the eye would not need to travel as far from the end of a long line to the beginning of a short one, as it would in poetry oriented to the left margin.[17]

This so-called *Mittelachse* design, the elaborate title page, and the typeface of *Phantasus* seem more in the spirit of Jugendstil, the German decorative style around 1900 (to which I return in chapter 3), than naturalism per se. But many of the poems in *Phantasus* clearly reflect the second-by-second style and the "natural" flow of thoughts that we observed in *Papa Hamlet.* In the first poem (originally published in 1891), of which I give the first part here, we find some of the same punctuation devices as in the earlier short story:

Night.

The maple tree in front of my window rustles,
the dew from its leaves sparkles in the grass,
and my heart
beats.

Night.
A dog . . . barks, . . . a branch . . . cracks,—still!
Still!
You? . . . You?

Ah, your hand! How cold, how cold!
And . . . your eyes . . . broken!
Broken!!

[Nacht. / Der Ahorn vor meinem Fenster rauscht, / von seinen Blättern funkelt der Thau ins Gras, / und mein Herz / schlägt. / Nacht. / Ein Hund . . . bellt, . . . ein Zweig . . . knickt,—still! / Still!! / Du? . . . Du? / Ah, deine Hand! Wie kalt, wie kalt! / Und . . . deine Augen . . . gebrochen! / Gebrochen!!][18]

Holz's views on poetic rhythm and structure represent another formulation of his principle that Art = Nature–*x*. The "means of reproduction"—

in this case the form, meter, and rhythm—should be minimal and should not stand in between nature and art. Holz evokes music as a kind of model for the view of poetry he is rejecting. He associates rhyme, meter, and strophic form with "music," with the "fetters" that bind the word or the poetic thought. Such music must never be the goal in itself, only a means to the thought that is seeking expression. Roy Pascal has suggested that Holz's theoretical views are "of the crudest, mechanical, positivistic type" and that they represented "the most determined effort to assimilate art into science, even so far as to reject the saving grace of the artist's temperament with which Zola had tempered his fierce scientism."[19] Yet it must be said that Holz was the most systematic in carrying through the naturalist project to its logical consequences.

It was in drama rather than in prose or poetry that naturalism found perhaps its most comfortable berth, especially in the works of Hauptmann, whose first play, *Vor Sonnenaufgang* (Before Sunrise) of 1889, catapulted him to national and then international fame. This play and Hauptmann's slightly later and equally famous *Die Weber* of 1892 were widely considered the epitome of naturalist drama—drama that dealt with real people in real-life situations. Both plays center around Silesian life, that of farmers and coal miners in *Vor Sonnenaufgang,* and of weavers in *Die Weber.* In the former we witness a middle-class family rent asunder by alcoholism and suicide. In the latter, poor and hungry Silesian weavers rise up in revolt. Both plays make use of Silesian dialect; indeed, *Die Weber* was first drafted in it (and later was published in that form as well as in *Hochdeutsch*). Both plays are innovative in the way in which the audience is made to sympathize with no single figure. In *Die Weber,* Hauptmann creates what Peter Bauland has called a "collective protagonist" and a "hero-less play in which the community of people whose story is being told becomes the main 'character.'"[20]

In this overview of German literary naturalism we can detect two main strands, which might be called roughly the social and the aesthetic. Several of the naturalists were committed socialists, at least at the beginning of the movement. Like Holz's "Ein Andres" or *Papa Hamlet,* many naturalist works tend to focus on the miserable situation of the poor and working class in large cities or rural communities, and on the negative effects of industrial capitalism. But as Pascal has observed, this kind of "socialism" was different from politically active engagement. For the naturalists, socialism often "simply meant sympathy with the suffering of the destitute and helpless and indignation over social injustice." Pascal suggests that as early as 1885, even before the publication of *Das Buch der Zeit* (which contained "Ein

Andres"), Holz sought "an aesthetic that excluded ethical (national or social) constituents."[21] In other words, Holz and others gravitated ultimately toward to the second, more purely aesthetic strand of naturalism. The goal of the artist would be to develop techniques like sequential naturalism and obligatory rhythm that reduced as much as possible our awareness of the "means of reproduction," the problematic *x* variable, in the naturalist formulation of art.

As many writers pointed out at the time, aesthetic naturalism was in a sense nothing new; such impulses had been evident in art for a long time. Exasperated with the aggressive or self-promoting rhetoric of many advocates of naturalism, the philosopher and psychologist Christian von Ehrenfels observed in 1891, in one of the most thoughtful and dispassionate contemporary discussions of the phenomenon: "Naturalism does not mean identification of art with nature, only—after a period of distancing and stereotyping *[Schablonisierung]*—the approaching of the former to the latter, the seeking out again of a connection that has gotten lost, the taking up of new elements of reality that have hitherto been unnoticed or at least unused by artists, the broadening of the artistic horizon, and along with this the predominance of the beauty of thought over the beauty of sensuous impression." Ehrenfels notes some of the numerous precedents for modern naturalism in Greek sculpture and Shakespearean drama:

> We can recognize naturalistic movements in numerous epochs of the history of art. Greek sculpture is naturalistic in comparison to Egyptian, its model; the same relationship holds between Byzantine and Italian painting; Shakespeare is a naturalist in relation to the drama that preceded him. It seems that the life of the imitative arts plays itself out in two phases of development. In one, the artist tries chiefly to collect elements of reality—to "grasp" *[auffassen]* them, as the apt expression says; in the other, he seeks to work up "what he has grasped" *[das Aufgefaßte]* into ever clearer and purer forms of beauty.[22]

For Ehrenfels, then, naturalism is a cyclic impulse or phenomenon in the arts, which was having a resurgence in the 1880s and 1890s, but was hardly revolutionary.

Even as Ehrenfels wrote, in 1891, the Viennese critic Hermann Bahr was proclaiming the "overcoming" of naturalism. Bahr found German naturalism, especially as manifested on the stage, to be a pale imitation of French naturalism. "German naturalism wants truth," he wrote, "the unfalsified and genuine truth, the full and bare truth." But this goal suffocates the individual artist, forces him to subsume his artistic personality in the material.[23] What can and should rescue naturalism, Bahr says, is psychology: "The modern need is for psychology, which can work against the one-sidedness of naturalism. But we require a psychology that takes into account the long-standing practices of naturalism—a psychology that is penetrated by and goes beyond naturalism" (p. 50).

Bahr specifies that he seeks no return to older psychological models. The "old" psychology was concerned with the "results" of feelings, as they were expressed in consciousness. The "new" psychology delineates the preparations for those feelings, before they have entered into consciousness. The older psychology captured feelings after they already had become idealized, as they appear in memory; the new psychology seeks out those feelings at an earlier stage, in the realm of the senses, *before* they are stamped in consciousness and memory: "The new psychology will be displaced from the intellect to the nerves" (p. 58).

Bahr's shift toward psychological naturalism marks an important moment in the evolution—if not the overcoming—of German naturalism. As many commentators have pointed out, Bahr's emphasis on nerves and on raw, unmediated feelings anticipates, and forms an intellectual-cultural network with, the writings of Freud, Mach, and other fin-de-siècle Viennese men of science and medicine.[24] In one of the best-known passages of his essay, Bahr writes: "Sensations alone are truth, reliable, incontrovertible truth; the I is already a construction, arbitrary ordering, reinterpretation, and refitting of truth. . . . There is no comparison between the I and truth; the latter cancels out the former, and vice versa; one or the other has to be renounced. . . . Sensations, nothing but sensations, independent, momentary images of fleeting events upon the nerves—that is what characterizes the most recent phase into which truth has now forced literature" (p. 84).

For Bahr there are clear links between older and newer art. Both are essentially antinaturalistic in being concerned with the expression of human beings *(Ausdruck des Menschen):* "But when Classicism says *Mensch,* it means reason and feeling; and when Romanticism says *Mensch,* it means passion and intellect; and when modernism says *Mensch,* it means nerves. . . . Thus I believe that naturalism will be overcome by a nervous Romanticism; or rather I would like to say, through a mysticism of nerves" (p. 86).

Bahr concludes his essay with large segments on Zola and Maeterlinck. Zola is vilified for his bone-dry naturalism, including the endless description of milieu which (according to Bahr) is so divorced from the individual characters. Maeterlinck, on the other hand, is a kind of hero to Bahr because he shows "the reaction of the inner person against the external objectivity of naturalism" (p. 99). The great discovery made by Maeterlinck, says Bahr, is of "a new language that seeks to express and communicate the condition of the nerves, to which are attached characteristic colors and sounds that are inseparable from them" (p. 100). Maeterlinck's characters are "only signs of their sensations, like shadows cast upon the world by their moods; and the events that accumulate are only symbols of many stories told by the nerves" (p. 100).

Bahr finds in symbolism an answer to his quest to transcend naturalism. We may not immediately think of something like Maeterlinck's drama *Pelléas et Mélisande* as an art of nerves and sensations. The characters move about in a haze of allusion and indirect gestures. But in Bahr's splendid image, these gestures are like "shadows cast upon the world." Symbolism is thus in a sense naturalism once removed. I will return to symbolism in the next chapter, for it too links up with musical thought and practice around 1900.

NATURALISM AND WAGNER

Music plays a significant role in the two major naturalist literary-cultural periodicals, *Die Gesellschaft* and *Freie Bühne.* These two journals, based in the two main centers of naturalism (Munich and Berlin, respectively), carried a wide range of genres—fiction, poetry, essays, criticism—written by some of the most important authors of the day.[25] There are a number of ways in which music was either fitted or at times opposed to a naturalist agenda and aesthetic. It may initially surprise a reader of the above summary of naturalist ideology that the composer who is at the center of early naturalist accounts of music is Richard Wagner.

As we saw in the last chapter, Wagner was himself antimodern and antiscience in ways that would seem very out of phase with the naturalists. Yet in the very first issue of *Die Gesellschaft,* Hans Frank contributed a brief article entitled "The Master of Bayreuth and the German Position in the World." Frank sets aside personal, biographical, and technical aspects of Wagner's work to assert the "indubitably German-national stamp" of Wagner and his work.[26] "Among the heroes of our national German political life," says Frank, "Wagner deserves for all times the first place as the hero of the artistic renewal of the people." Frank, who wrote mainly on the Munich art scene for *Die Gesellschaft,* is not a significant music critic, and his little paean to Wagner is hardly a major contribution to the naturalist agenda. But it reminds us how important Wagner was, in the years after his death, especially in Bavaria, the site of Bayreuth. It also indicates how Wagner became a major cultural icon who transcended his individual art to become a symbol of German nationalism that was not only palatable, but also instrumental, to the naturalists.

In the first year of its existence, *Die Gesellschaft* brought Wagner closer to the core of naturalist aesthetics in a small article by Oskar Bie, reprinted from the *Allgemeine-Musik Zeitung*, with the title "Naturalism in Music." Bie (1864–1938), who was trained mainly in art history, wrote widely on music; his musical essays were collected into several books. This must be one of his earliest published efforts (he would have been only twenty-one), and it was certainly one of the first in Germany to broach directly the association between music (especially Wagner's) and naturalism. Bie suggests that the history of music has essentially been a struggle in which the representational aspect of music has gained "gradual dominance" over the architectonic aspect. Bie equates this conflict with "the struggle of naturalism against idealism." For him, Berlioz represents an important moment in this process, as "the artist in whom the music appears as a naturalistic, truly representative art, in which the architectonic element is only a means to an end." Berlioz's ideas were imported to Germany by Liszt and manifested in his program music and that of the New German School. Naturalism is especially evident in Wagner's music, says Bie, through the emphasis on the "poetic" element, the stress on the dramatic, the plastic corporeality of the accompanying music, as shaped by Wagner's leitmotives, and Wagner's strong individualization of instrumental voices, which results in chromaticism. "This naturalism," concludes Bie, "is thus the soil from which the future of our music is to develop; its conservative opposition should no longer be called idealism, but schematism."[27]

Bie's fighting words make clear that the old program-versus-absolute music battle of midcentury—also cast by him as a conflict between representation and idealism—is very much alive in a new guise in the early modernist era, now as a naturalistic-versus-schematic one. The list of those features that Bie considers "naturalistic" in music, and especially in Wagner, is perhaps too broad to give us any firm foothold or answer to the question "What is naturalism in music?" The "representational" impulse alone is surely an insufficient condition for naturalism.

The idea of art as imitation of nature—*imitatio naturae*—is, of course, one of the fundamental components of European aesthetics from the Renaissance through the early nineteenth century. Carl Dahlhaus lists succinctly six different ways in which music has been associated with imitation or mimesis: imitation of nonmusical sounds *(Tonmalerei);* imitation of spatial movement, such as rising and falling; representation of speech intonations; the depiction of emotion, or "internal" nature; musical structure as a representation of a concept (as when the word "rule" is conveyed musically as a canon); and music as a reflection of the world as a whole.[28] This list could undoubtedly be refined or expanded. But it is not my purpose here to revisit the broader aesthetic question of music's ability to imitate nature. Rather, I am interested in this issue as it relates to the debates about naturalism in the early period of German modernism, from about 1880 on.

Bie and Frank were by no means the first to associate Wagner with naturalistic tendencies. Already in 1866, the writer Eduard Krüger had described as "realist" (and indicated his disapproval of) Wagner's mature vocal style, which tended toward the speechlike. Dahlhaus, who brings Krüger into his discussion of "musical realism," suggests that from the perspective of the mid-nineteenth century, Wagner's style might be considered as realistic on three counts: it tends to abandon traditional four-square phrase structure for the purposes of expression, it seeks to evoke everyday speech, and Wagner claimed it to be the representative style of the era, rather than a passing phenomenon.[29]

For many critics writing about music in the 1880s and 1890s, even those of the naturalist bent, Wagner was still the most significant and "modern" musician. As such, he was fitted to the naturalist agenda even when the fit was not an especially good one. This was largely because of his status, which certainly grew after his death, as a German national figure. Wagner continued to feature in the pages of *Die Gesellschaft* into the later 1880s. Erich Stahl began a series called "Wagneriana," which commented on various publications of Wagner's writings and letters, as well as other Wagnerian matters. The series was taken up by other contributors, including the editor, Michael Georg Conrad. The editors confessed in 1886 that "the ardently Wagnerian standpoint of *Die Gesellschaft* is . . . widely known."[30] The journal's Wagnerian stance is also readily apparent in Stahl's attacks on contemporary operettas.[31]

In 1891 Ehrenfels published in *Freie Bühne* a remarkable article entitled "Richard Wagner and Naturalism," which took a more sophisticated approach to assimilating Wagner with naturalism. Ehrenfels, we recall, was the philosopher-critic who also tried to inject some coolness into the general debate about naturalism. Here he applies similar logic specifically to the case of opera. Ehrenfels sees Wagnerism and naturalism as representing two essentially different artistic directions. Naturalism is promulgated by a "closed phalanx" of artists, writers, and playwrights, all of whom share similar principles, but none of whom is at the level of Wagner. On the other side are a number of modern artists in the realm of poetry, the novel, drama, and painting—including Gottfried Keller, Gustav Freytag, Hans Makart, and Arnold Böcklin—who retreat from naturalism and show "an affinity with the Wagnerian artistic direction."[32]

In a kind of thought experiment Ehrenfels paints Wagner as both naturalist and nonnaturalist. With the depiction of the Forest Bird and the strokes of the forging hammer in *Siegfried,* Wagner is a naturalist in a literal but also superficial sense. These effects constitute mere tone-painting (though Ehrenfels does not use this term), only "clothing and scaffolding for the real artistic essence." In a more profound and important way, Wagner turns his back on the real world, Ehrenfels observes: in all his operas except *Die Meistersinger* he relies on *Wunder,* on magic or the supernatural, which is the opposite of naturalism (p. 13). Wagner also goes distinctly against the grain of naturalism, says Ehrenfels, in that he is a believer in the "ideal man," not in an evolutionist theory that suggests that man improves and develops. Naturalism, as Ehrenfels points outs, pays homage to evolutionary, Darwinian theory, which suggests progress and forward motion. Wagner has "a blazing hatred of the natural sciences and all empirical-experimental methods of thought and research" (p. 15).

Having constructed Wagner first as naturalist, then as opponent of naturalism, Ehrenfels stages a final reversal. He suggests that the psychological and emotional aspects that are captured by Wagner's music in the end make him a naturalist—at least in the sense preferred by Ehrenfels. The key here is the psychological element, in particular Wagner's probing of the unconscious:

> Music is the art which is able to awaken that life of impulse and drives that slumbers half in the unconscious and to capture it in firm shapes. And the first musician who has dared to descend into the heart of that twilight realm, in order to make concrete the indistinct shapes that fly in all directions and to raise them to the light of day in a form that is artistically articulated—is Richard Wagner. The real subject matter of Wagner's art are those things for which almost no account is taken by language and which fall under the amorphous concepts of moods, feelings, and drives of collective psychical stimuli. (p. 18)

For Ehrenfels, Wagner's principal tool in plumbing this inner world is the leitmotive. Today it is a truism that Wagner's leitmotivic method is a powerful psychological mechanism and not simply a system of "calling cards" (as Debussy suggested).[33] But in 1891 Ehrenfels may have been among the earliest critics to understand this aspect of Wagner's art, and certainly one of the first to consider it "naturalistic": "The nature of the leitmotive is often misunderstood. Many see in it only a musical tag that pops up in Wagner's orchestra as soon as a certain person or thing comes on to the stage or is mentioned. . . . In truth each leitmotive represents in the first place a feeling or mood that is distinctly psychic (unconscious)" (pp. 18–19). Ehrenfels thus sees in Wagner's leitmotivic technique a real contribution to the "ever more path-breaking scientific viewpoint of our time." Specifically, the leitmotivic technique or principle is reflective of "a naturalistic tendency in art."

In another essay published in *Freie Bühne* later in 1891, "Das musikalische Drama der Zukunft" (The Musical Drama of the Future), Ehrenfels reflects further on the relationship between Wagnerian practice and naturalist drama. Once again he begins by separating the two, pointing out a fundamental incompatibility. Music drama, he says, works with moods and feelings; Wagner probes the realm of inner drives, the "twilight underground of the human psyche" (p. 38). The naturalist writers are more concerned with thought, with the level of the intellect, although darker elements of the soul are not excluded: "The true power of the naturalistic mode of presentation consists in allowing us to glimpse a magnitude of individual feelings which can be characterized psychologically either directly as thoughts, or which nonetheless, like definite wishes, viewpoints, hopes, cares, etc., do not prevent their being designated in the world of concepts" (p. 38).

Ehrenfels adduces a scene from a recent play by Hauptmann, *Einsame Menschen* (Lonely People) of 1891, which he calls "certainly the most perfect that naturalism has up to now created" (p. 38). The scene involves an encounter between Anna Mahr, a Swiss student who is visiting Berlin, and a painter named Braun.[34] Ehrenfels discusses the complex psychological and emotional aspects of their dialogue: the two characters are meeting each other again after a long hiatus, and it is not initially clear to the spectator just what their prior relationship was (it was, in fact, a romantic one). Ehrenfels explores the question of whether the dramatic material of this scene would invite or permit the addition of music. After describing in detail the "crisscrossing of observations and reflections" in the encounter between Anna and Braun, Ehrenfels wonders how "thematic intertwinings in the orchestra" could "do justice to" them, since "the complications to which the musician would have to have recourse" would be "monstrous" (pp. 39–40).

Such a scene cannot be "set to music" easily, says Ehrenfels. "For music extends the duration of the words and sentences that are to be set and thus demands a conciseness of phrase construction in a fashion that is not appropriate to everyday speech. Prose can certainly be set to music, but thereby takes on a rhythmic shape that imparts to it a verselike character; composed prose is no longer freely unfolding speech." What music must do, he says, is go against the naturalistic elements of a text; it must ignore "individual coincidences, depart from reality, and intensify and concentrate linguistic expression as well as psychical impulses, exclude elements of thought that are without mood, and simplify the characters as well as the dramatic structure" (p. 40).

Ultimately, Ehrenfels asserts, music drama and naturalistic drama are incompatible: "The musical element works against one of the basic tendencies of naturalism, which approaches the reality of actual life, and directs the dramatist from the inner world of thoughts to the inner world of the life of mood and drives, where on the other hand music retains a definite advantage. The respective advantages of naturalistic and musical drama can be no more be united than can those of absolute and dramatic music" (p. 40). Ehrenfels hits here upon a fundamental issue of musical naturalism, at least as it would apply to opera. If one interprets the naturalist agenda in a literal way—as manifested in the Hauptmann play—then music would seem incompatible with it.

Returning to his hero Wagner, Ehrenfels suggests that Wagner "took a powerful step toward naturalism" in *Die Meistersinger* and in parts of his other operas. Ehrenfels even asserts—anticipating Bernard Shaw by some seven years—that the *Ring* is a critique of capitalist tendencies in modern society. Moreover, he says, the *Ring* reflects another important aspect of the modern condition, the "breaking apart of a worldview," specifically the loss of a "religious myth" that has prevailed for two thousand years (p. 42). Though he does not name Nietzsche, Ehrenfels is clearly referring here to a post-Nietzschean world in which God is dead. He interprets the downfall of the Gods in Wagner's *Götterdämmerung* as a confirmation of the end of traditional religious faith. Like Wagner's characters, says Ehrenfels, "we live in a time of the twilight of the gods. But the disappearing god is not the bearded Wanderer with one eye—but the God whom our mother taught us to worship" (p. 43).

In his endeavors to cast Wagner as a naturalist, Ehrenfels pays no attention to one dimension of both Wagner's art and vocal music more generally that concerned other writers on musical naturalism: the delivery of the text by the singer. Here declamation was seen as a key element, which was taken up by the critic Ernst Otto Nodnagel in an essay of 1902, "The Naturalistic Melodrama." Nodnagel wanted to return to the basic issues of post-Wagnerian vocal music and to the same problems that occupied Ehrenfels a decade earlier: "I want to investigate from the standpoint of modern aesthetics whether music drama, as Wagner bequeathed it to us, is really an empty shell, whether it is really exceptional in a process of continual organic development."[35] Nodnagel sees the dramas of Ibsen and Hauptmann as having created "a new dramatic technique, a new style," and, like Ehrenfels, he wonders to what extent their brand of naturalism can or should be carried over into musical genres.

Nodnagel notes that Wagner was deemed a naturalist by some because in his subject matter he "paid no attention to prudish people."[36] Nodnagel may be referring here to the position of the earlier naturalists like Conrad and Ehrenfels, who saw a naturalistic bent in Wagner's understanding of sexual relations. Yet, Nodnagel observes, Wagner's libretti are far from naturalistic in a stricter sense. In Wagner nature is "stylized" or "idealized" because the texts are sung. In spoken drama, declaimed verse is already stylized and removed from nature; Wagner's music drama is still more stylized because in it the "elevated" *(gehobene)* speech of declamation is further "elevated." Wagner tends to pay strict attention to the prosody and cadence of the text; the result is, says Nodnagel, what is called *Sprechgesang* or speech-song.

Indeed, as Edward Kravitt has shown in illuminating detail, Wagner was largely responsible for the more naturalistic style of singing that emerged in the mid-to-late nineteenth century and that, as we saw above, Eduard Krüger already criticized in 1866. Wagner was the most prominent and forceful of those who reacted against the Italian style that had dominated vocal training up through the first third of the nineteenth century.[37] He deplored the way in which German singers enunciated texts, and he called for a specifically German method of singing.[38] The summons was answered first by Friedrich Schmitt, with a *Grosse Gesangschule für Deutschland* (Large Singing Method for Germany), published in 1854, and later by Schmitt's disciple Julius Hey, who helped train singers under Wagner's supervision and who wrote *Deutsche Gesangs-Unterricht* (German Singing Instruction, 1884–86). The efforts to standardize or at least rationalize enunciation in singing paralleled efforts to create a more uniform *Bühnen-Deutsch,* or stage German, among actors and directors.

The newer standards of German enunciation were applied to both Lieder and opera. The main principle was that of *Sprechgesang,* which is described by Kravitt as "crisp and chiseled enunciation, as precise in singing as in contemporary recitation." Consonants like *k, t, d,* and *g* were enunciated explosively, Kravitt explains, suggesting that speech-song is also characterized by the avoidance of elision and by "elevated speech," in which singers would "hover between singing and speaking dramatic passages."[39] Kravitt's conclusions confirm what Nodnagel observed in 1902.

After reviewing these aspects of naturalistic declamation, Nodnagel formulates his central concern for the future of naturalistic singing: "How is it possible to have a combination of Wagner's principles and his stylistic achievements with those of Hauptmann? This combination would surely be the most immediate goal of any further development." In beginning to answer this question, Nodnagel turns first to Ehrenfels's article of 1891, which, he argues, started from the wrong premises. Ehrenfels selected "at random" a scene from a Hauptmann drama and then argued that such everyday language was impossible to set to music. But it is completely wrong to choose as an example a work never intended for musical setting, says Nodnagel. Ehrenfels did not understand that the whole notion of "naturalistic stage singing" is a contradiction in terms. For Nodnagel, the future lies in melodrama, and he sees his ideas manifested in several contemporary works, including Paul Geisler's one-act *Musikspiel* (play with music) *Der Herr Baron,* which he labels a "*satire* of Wagner and Hauptmann."[40]

A still closer approximation of what Nodnagel envisions is Humperdinck's *Königskinder* (Royal Children), a melodrama of 1896 that in 1907 became the source for the composer's popular *Märchenoper* (fairy-tale opera) of the same name. Yet, says Nodnagel, Humperdinck is also on a false path in that he seeks to fix the melody of the spoken words in *Sprechnoten* (spoken notes). Humperdinck's score puts ×'s in the place of note heads, but otherwise specifies pitch and rhythm (example 2). With this procedure, according to Nodnagel, Humperdinck overlooks the fundamental difference between the prosody of speech and song in German: "Language measures rhythm through rise and fall, thus qualitatively; song prosody on the other hand measures quantitatively, according to long and short."[41] Humperdinck's spoken notes do not resolve the problem, Nodnagel says; *Königskinder* is thus

Example 2. Humperdinck, *Königskinder*

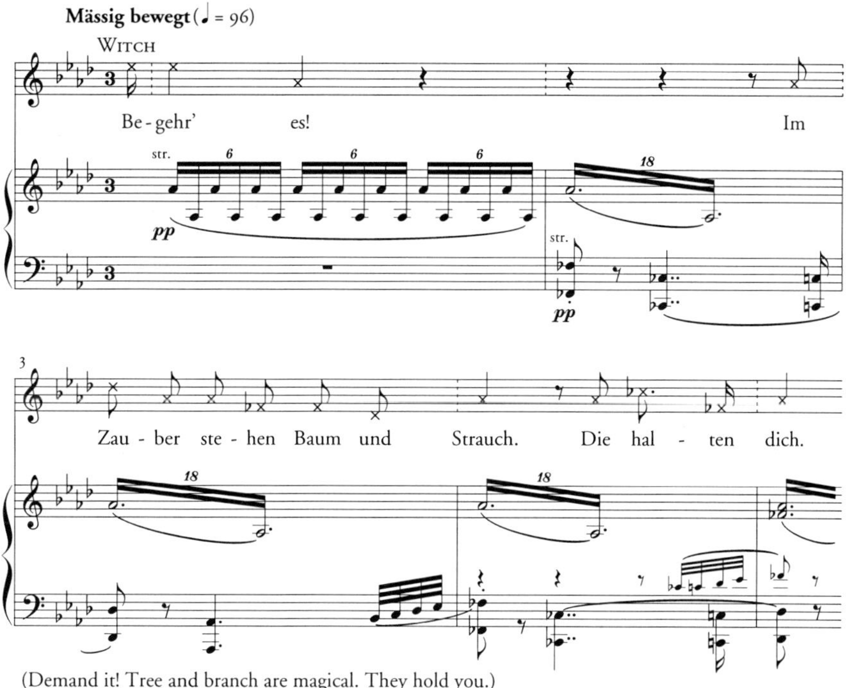

(Demand it! Tree and branch are magical. They hold you.)

a "failed experiment." The problem of a naturalistic music drama, which will have to be a melodrama shaped and spoken according to naturalistic principles, is "still unresolved."

In his essay on naturalistic melodrama, Nodnagel does not mention the recent effort in the genre by Richard Strauss, *Enoch Arden,* op. 38, composed for piano and speaker in 1897 in the wake of Humperdinck's *Königskinder.* But he does address the Strauss work at length in his article-profile on Strauss included in the same volume, *Jenseits von Wagner und Liszt* (Beyond Wagner and Liszt, an obvious reference to Nietzsche's *Beyond Good and Evil).* Although today, and for much of Strauss's career, *Enoch Arden* was considered a sport among his works, Nodnagel devotes almost five pages to an analysis of it, as much or more than he does to major pieces like *Guntram, Till Eulenspiegel,* and *Also sprach Zarathustra.*

Nodnagel claims to have discussed the work with Strauss in May 1897, when the composer made clear that *Enoch Arden* was an "occasional piece" *(Gelegenheitsarbeit),* and that "the whole genre of melodrama was unsym-

Example 3. Strauss, *Enoch Arden*

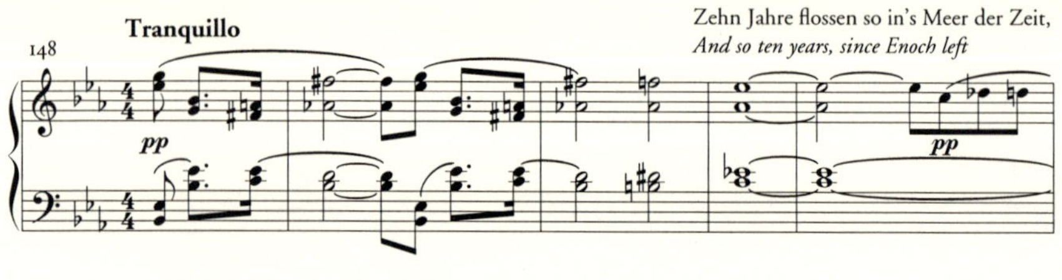

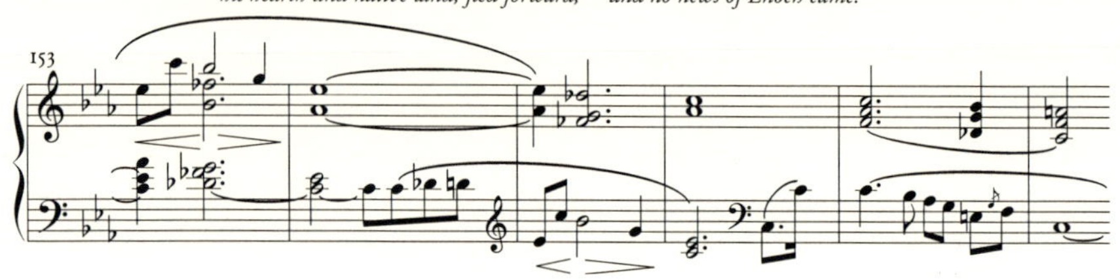

pathetic to him."[42] Nonetheless, Nodnagel notes, Strauss has created an almost perfect example of the genre. The goal of melodrama, according to Nodnagel, should be to enhance the effect of the poetry through compositional means. Strauss's *Enoch Arden* is especially effective in that he does not give in to tone-painting at moments where we might expect it (such as the storm and Enoch's shipwreck), but rather seeks to evoke the shifting feelings and moods of the characters in Tennyson's text. Strauss does so by using a recurring group of basic motives or thematic ideas, which Nodnagel calls "symbols," a term he prefers to the more customary Wagnerian "leitmotive."[43] Example 3 excerpts the passage relating Enoch's long absence at sea. The motive at mm. 156ff., with an octave leap from C to C, followed by a descent through the scale, is just such a symbol; it has been heard earlier as "allegro appassionato" and associated with the moment when Enoch departed soon after his marriage to Annie. As can be seen in the example, Strauss specifies no rhythms or pitches for the speaker. When there is text above the music, speaker and accompanist must pace their parts to coincide. Often in *Enoch Arden,* the text merely alternates with the piano part.

The successful premiere of Strauss's *Enoch Arden* on March 24, 1897, was followed by many enthusiastically received performances in Germany and England.[44] Other composers sought to capitalize on the popularity of musically accompanied recitations, and the practice spilled over into the

Example 4. Schillings, *Das Hexenlied*

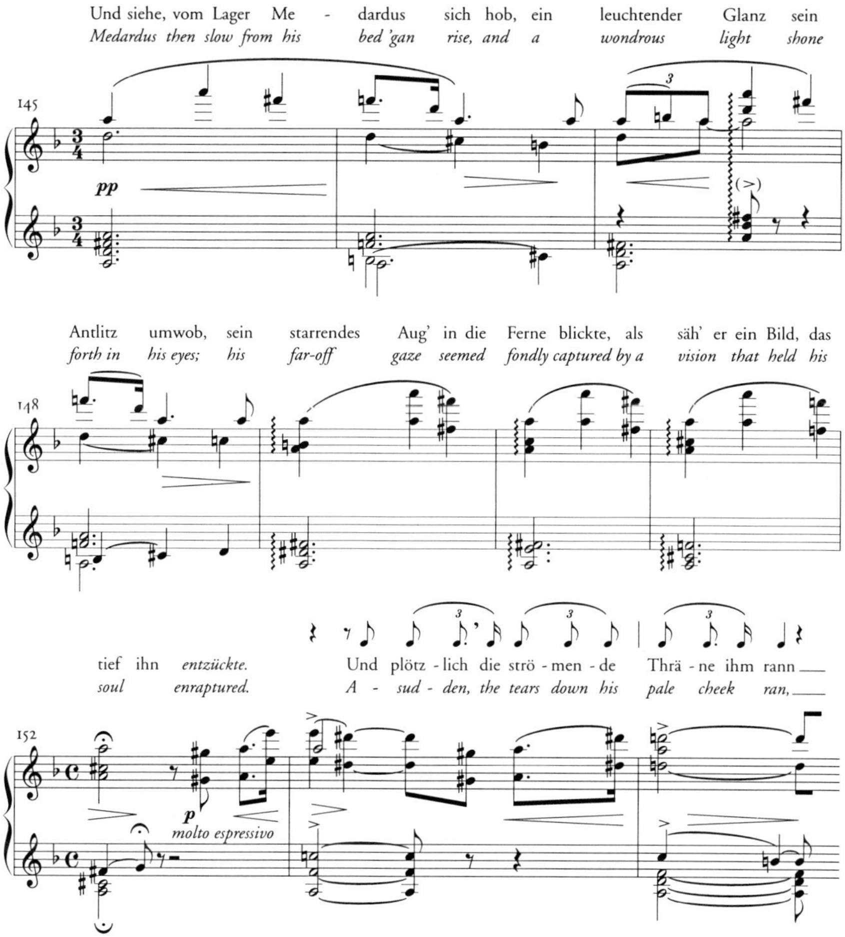

cabaret world of Munich and Berlin (and eventually, of course, into Schoenberg's *Pierrot lunaire* of 1912). After Strauss's effort (followed in 1899 by his second and only other melodrama, *Das Schloss am Meere* [The Castle by the Sea], which uses a text by Uhland), the most successful melodrama was unquestionably Max von Schillings's *Hexenlied* (Witch's Song) of 1902. This melodrama was based on a poem by Ernst von Wildenbruch about the last confession of a dying monk named Medardus. He admits that as a young priest he seduced a girl accused of witchcraft, whose soul he was supposed to save. In terms of fixing the speech-song, Schillings seems to take a middle ground between Humperdinck and Strauss. As noted above,

Humperdinck actually writes out the *Sprechnoten,* replacing note heads on the staves with ×'s, whereas Strauss provides no musical notation at all for the vocal part. Schillings normally follows the Strauss route, which is also that of traditional melodrama. But in some instances he notates the rhythm of the spoken part (example 4).

It is in connection with Schillings's *Hexenlied* that today a remarkable document survives of the kind of "elevated speech" that Kravitt identifies and that Humperdinck, Strauss, Schillings, and their contemporaries must have had in mind. This is a 1933 recording of an orchestral version of *Hexenlied,* conducted by Schillings and recited by Ludwig Wüllner (reissued on CD as Preiser MONO 90294). Wüllner (1858–1938), son of the conductor Franz Wüllner, was recognized as one of the greatest and most versatile reciters, actors, and singers of his day. Although he was seventy-four at the time of the *Hexenlied* recording, he had clearly lost none of his abilities to deliver a text, which is declaimed in a riveting and highly inflected manner that at some moments approaches a hushed whisper and at others articulates distinct pitches.

After Schillings's *Hexenlied,* melodrama made its two most famous appearances in Schoenberg's *Gurrelieder* (composed mainly in 1901–3, but premiered only in 1913) and *Pierrot lunaire* of 1912, which was written for one of the best-known singing actresses of the time, Albertine Zehme. In *Gurrelieder,* melodrama appears to magnificent effect near the end of Part II, in the segment called "Des Sommerwindes wildes Jagd" (The Wild Hunt of the Summer Wind), where over a rich and illustrative orchestral part a *Sprecher* intones the German translation of the poetry by the Dane Jens Peter Jacobsen. Schoenberg follows Humperdinck's method of notating actual pitches and rhythms throughout, but replaces the note heads with ×'s in the full published score and hollow diamond shapes in the piano-vocal score. The melodramas of *Pierrot lunaire* are certainly the most famous of the early modern period (and, indeed, of the twentieth century). As in *Gurrelieder,* Schoenberg specifies pitch and rhythm, but in this case the note heads are conventional and an × appears on the stem. In his preface to the score, Schoenberg asks the vocalist to attack the pitch but leave it immediately by rising or falling. "However, the performer has to be very careful not to adopt a *singsong* way of speaking," Schoenberg continues. "In no way should one strive for realistic, natural speech. . . . But at the same time it must never be reminiscent of singing."[45] Schoenberg's careful, almost obsessive instructions suggest how variable the rendering of melodramatic speech-song could be, and how difficult it was for any composer to regulate the outcome.

Despite Nodnagel's advocacy and imaginative examples from composers as prominent as Strauss, Schillings, and Schoenberg, melodrama was to prove a dead end, or ancillary activity, for most composers of early German modernism. Aspects of declamatory naturalism appeared more consistently in the Lied. Hugo Wolf's songs, most written between 1886 and 1890, encompass a wide range of vocal styles. The poetic text was the driving force behind Wolf's Lieder. The Mörike songs were published, at Wolf's insistence, as *Gedichte,* or poems, not as Lieder or *Gesänge.* Wolf organized Lieder recitals around the work of a single poet, and often he would read the poems, or have them read, before the settings were performed. In some of the Goethe songs, Wolf uses a style of what Kravitt calls "grandiloquent" recitation that is more theatrical than everyday speech.[46] Lyrical or melodic gestures can alternate with, or pervade, a more declamatory phrase. A vocal part like that of *In der Frühe* (In the Early Morning), no. 24 from the Mörike songs, is declamatory yet lyrical; its metrical freedom works against the regular pattern of the accompaniment. The last of the Mörike songs, *Abschied* (Farewell, no. 53), tends toward a more purely dramatic recitative style at the opening.

Wolf has been seen by both contemporary and modern commentators as deriving his attitude toward text-setting from Wagner.[47] No mention is made in the Wolf literature of any association with naturalism, although he wrote many of his Lieder concurrently with the first flush of German naturalist theory. Wolf preferred to set Romantic poets; he showed little interest in the verses by contemporary naturalists. And yet, one might see in *Abschied* a striking similarity to the naturalists' second-by-second style. Wolf conveys an almost stream of consciousness flow in which the musical setting changes rapidly in response to the text.

It was Richard Strauss who took up Wolf's approach toward declamatory naturalism and then seems to have integrated it into a musical technique more consciously based on contemporary theories. Strauss turned decisively toward contemporary poets. In a nuanced investigation of the Lieder written by Strauss during the late 1890s, Suzanne Lodato has argued that the composer was strongly influenced by the theories of the Berlin naturalists, in particular Arno Holz. Lodato analyzes three songs: one set to a text by Richard Dehmel, *Der Arbeitsmann* (The Laborer, op. 39, no. 3; 1898); one to a text by Karl Henckell, *Lied des Steinklopfers* (Stonebreaker's Song, op. 49, no. 4; 1901); and one to a text by Detlev von Liliencron, *Bruder Liederlich* (The Rake, op. 41, no. 4; 1899). The Dehmel and Henckell texts are prime examples of the *Soziallyrik,* the socially conscious strain of naturalism as reflected in poetry. More specifically, they are *Arbeitsgedichte,* poems that show the plight of urban workers. Strauss was the first of his generation to set such poems to music, at least in an art music context.

The text of the *Lied des Steinklopfers* is a litany of workers' resentments:

I am no minister,
I am no king,
I am no priest,
I am no hero;
No honor,
No title
Has been bestowed on me
And no money either.

I will battle you,
You hard block of stone,
The splinters fly,
The sand whirls up like dust—
"You poor lout,"
My father grumbled,
"Take my hammer";
And thereupon died.

Today I, a poor man,
Have not yet had anything to eat,
The All-Merciful
Has not sent anything;
Of golden wine
I dreamt
And break stones
For the Fatherland.

[Ich bin kein Minister, / Ich bin kein König, / Ich bin kein Priester, / Ich bin kein Held, / Mir ist kein Orden, / Mir ist kein Titel / Verliehen worden / Und auch kein Geld. / Dich will ich kriegen, / Du harter Plocken, / Die Splitter fliegen, / Der Sand stäubt auf— / "Du armer Flegel!" / Mein Vater brummte— / "Nimm' meinen Schlägel!" / Und starb darauf. / Heut' hab' ich Armer / Noch nichts gegessen, / Der Allerbarmer / Hat nichts gesandt; / Von gold'nem Weine / Hab ich geträumet / Und klopfe Steine / Für's Vaterland.]

Henckell's poem touches on virtually all the themes of naturalism examined above: the laborer's low social status, his poverty, his exhausting phys-

Example 5. Strauss, *Das Lied des Steinklopfers,* op. 49, no. 4

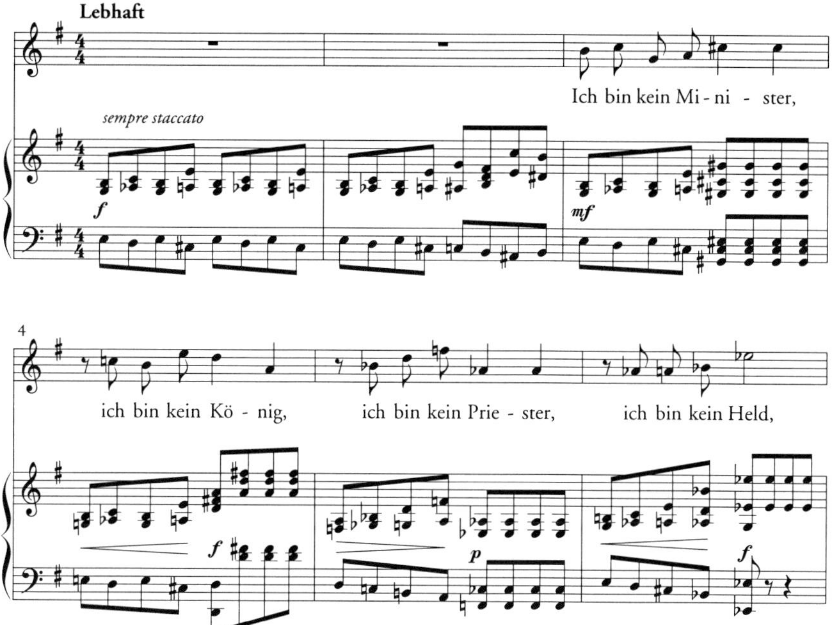

(I am no minister, I am no king, I am no priest, I am no hero.)

ical work, his hunger, and his resentment of the imperial crown. Additionally, the second-by-second style can be observed in the stonebreaker's free-flowing train of thought, perhaps especially in the way he switches suddenly at the end of the poem from the past tense of an idealized dream of wine to the all-too-present task of breaking stones. Henckell clearly avoids a comma where we might expect one, between "dreamt" *(geträumet)* and "and" *(und).* With the stonebreaker we thus plunge suddenly from fantasy back to reality.

In his setting of the poem Strauss makes use of a musical analogue to the naturalistic poetic techniques of second-by-second style and obligatory rhythm. The *Lied des Steinklopfers* is characterized by an episodic, quickly shifting style, which creates, in Lodato's words, a "disjunct surface" made up of "disparate elements."[48] The song begins in an almost manic tonal style, as the stonebreaker at first rattles off all the exalted things he is not (example 5). E minor, although the starting point of each measure in the example except m. 5, gives no firm sense of being the tonic. The proper noun on the second half of each measure is accompanied by a radically different harmony: C♯ major ("Minister"), D major ("König"), F half-diminished seventh ("Priester"), and E♭ major ("Held"). The sonority with "Priester" happens to be Wagner's "Tristan" chord in its original transposition and voicing—and as such is probably no coincidence. The harmonization of "Held" ("hero") is a clear reference to Strauss's own tone poem *Ein Heldenleben* in E♭, as well as to the work in the same key to which *Heldenleben* itself alludes, Beethoven's "Eroica" Symphony. These references are fleeting and succeed each other rapidly, very much in the stream-of-consciousness mode that we might expect in a musical second-by-second style.

Strauss's song becomes far more than a faithful musical transcription of the poem. The composer does not end the song with the last phrase of the text, "for the Fatherland," although the music arrives at a strongly cadential E major (m. 43) that could serve as conclusion. Instead, Strauss launches into an extended but muted and splintered recapitulation of the entire song. The singer, directed by the composer to perform *pianissimo* and "increasingly with half voice, as if humming to himself," reiterates phrases from the preceding three stanzas in their original order but in fragmentary form. At the phrase "and break stones," he rises to a final *fortissimo* and, according to Strauss's indication, sings "as if in despair." He then repeats twice more the phrase "for the Fatherland," as the music dies away to *ppp* and a somber, attenuated cadence to E minor.

The recapitulatory portion of the song, which lasts thirty-five measures, represents Strauss's attempt at a psychological naturalism that incorporates aspects of second-by-second style. Henckell's poem displays what Holz called the "fetters" of rhyme, meter, and stanzaic construction. Strauss dismantles these features in his setting, which becomes virtually a dramatic *scena.* In the *Lied des Steinklopfers* the psychology of the moment breaks the traditional boundaries of the Lied. The effect could be described as follows: after performing the song as a Lied (mm. 1–43), the singer steps outside that form and its conventions; he recalls, in agitated reflection, the main ideas, which inevitably and "naturally" keep running through his head, as they would for anyone in this state of mind. In a final outburst of despair he reiterates his bitterness, then sinks into the quiet misery that is the reality of his situation. The recapitulatory portion of the *Lied des Steinklopfers* is probably as refined an example of Bahr's art of nerves and sensations, and of declamatory naturalism, as can be found in the turn-of-the-century Lied.

The powerful psychological naturalism and outsized emotional rendering of the workers' plight in Strauss's *Lied des Steinklopfers* are well suited for an operatic work. Yet in 1901, when the song was composed, there was no context in Austria or Germany for naturalist music drama along these lines, even though the plays of Gerhard Hauptmann would seem tailor-made for such treatment. In the decade of the 1890s, the period of Hauptmann's soaring success, no major (and, it seems, no minor) German composer attempted to create an opera from one of his naturalist plays. There is no equivalent among Austro-German modernists to the operas composed by the Frenchman Alfred Bruneau between 1892 and 1902, either in direct collaboration with Émile Zola or based on Zola's works. Nor is there anything in Austria or Germany analogous to Gustave Charpentier's *Louise* (1900), the realist *roman musical* about Parisian life among artists and workers.[49] In the 1890s, the three leading young German composers of musical theater, Richard Strauss, Hans Pfitzner, and Max von Schillings, showed no inclination toward naturalist music drama in the manner of Hauptmann. Their major operatic works—Strauss's *Guntram* (1893), Schillings's *Ingwelde* (1894), and Pfitzner's *Der arme Heinrich* (1895)—remain firmly in the grip of the Wagnerian *Erlösungsoper* (opera of redemption) or *Heldenoper* (heroic opera).[50]

A provisional answer to the desire for naturalist opera came with the arrival on the German scene of the works of Mascagni and Leoncavallo in the early 1890s. Their first operas struck Germans like a thunderbolt and unleashed an earnest discussion in the pages of *Die Gesellschaft* and *Freie Bühne* about naturalism, opera, and the role of the Wagnerian inheritance. *Cavalleria rusticana* was taken up in German opera houses not long after its Rome premiere in May 1890; the first performance in Germany was in Hamburg on January 3, 1891, followed by the Viennese premiere on March 20.[51] Hans Merian, one of the broadest-minded of those who wrote about music for *Die Gesellschaft,* contributed a glowing article about the opera. He saw it as an answer, if not *the* answer, to the post-Wagnerian dead end in which opera (in his view) found itself: "One cannot look in Mascagni's music for what has been so beloved in post-Wagnerian Germany: so-called 'profundity' or symbol-laden mysticism touched with a gentle breath of pietism. Mascagni has buried no mysteries within his score."[52] Merian directly attacks "all the grunting, muttering, and bass-singing mystic-symbolic horror" of the works of Wagner and his followers and praises the melodic richness and "vibrant inner glow" of Mascagni. Merian concludes by assuring readers of the journal that they will find *Cavalleria* to their taste and explains why Mascagni's photograph appears as the frontispiece for the issue: "The friends of *Die Gesellschaft* will enjoy this opera; it cannot be otherwise. For *Cavalleria rusticana* is the first real modern-realistic opera. That is why—and not just because the opera is fashionable at the moment—the portrait of Mascagni ornaments the present issue of our monthly journal. Mascagni belongs to us; he is in the full sense of the word a 'modern' artist."[53] Neither the libretto nor the music comes in for much praise from Merian. The libretto, he admits, has all the old requisites of drama: "love, faithlessness, betrayal, jealousy, a duel, death." Mascagni has included drinking songs, folk songs, church choruses. The action is concise, unfolding in a single act. "But everything lives and breathes truth." Merian finds the characters to be not traditional "opera characters," but "complete men, characters full of power and energy." As far as the music: it is dominated by melody.[54]

Merian's comments about *Cavalleria* make clear his understanding that the opera did not conform literally to the tenets of German naturalism. Although *Cavalleria* is often viewed as the archetype of veristic opera, as Dahlhaus has observed, "the number of criteria of naturalistic style which the opera still observes is remarkably small."[55] Among Dahlhaus's points: the libretto is in verse, not prose; the opera is dominated by melody, not declamation; any social criticism in the original Verga play is replaced by more generalized human emotions and situations; and Mascagni uses no Sicilian-style melodies, but instead traditional closed operatic forms. Merian surely understood all this; yet what he liked about *Cavalleria* was its freshness and its non-German, non-Wagnerian nature. These aspects, probably more than any individual feature, led him to praise it as "modern" and "realistic."

Two years later Merian wrote a still more extensive article on "modern-realistic" opera, now in praise of Leoncavallo's *Pagliacci.* Here, in what is probably the first extensive discussion in German of the topic of naturalist opera, Merian goes even more deeply into the question of what such a thing can or should be: "A modern-realistic opera! Isn't there already a contradiction in that expression? Can an opera be genuinely realistic? . . . When one speaks of a 'modern-realistic' opera, images arise of something like sung Ibsen or orchestrated Gerhart Hauptmann. . . . And yet why should realism, which up to now has been able to succeed in all areas of art, exclude the domain of opera?"[56] With the mention of Ibsen and Hauptmann, Merian introduces two of the leading contemporary naturalists in the realm of theater, whom he seems to see as inappropriate models for opera. Like Ehrenfels, Merian questions the transferability of an aesthetic from one medium to another. Verbal and music drama have different orientations: "Music drama gravitates by its nature toward the side of mood, the drama of words toward the side of intellect." And they have different ways of presenting material: "The composer requires an entire aria to express what the poet says in one short sentence" (p. 735).

Like Ehrenfels, Merian points to Wagner as the pathbreaker of modern-realistic opera, because of the dismantling of the traditional number structures and the use of leitmotives. Yet the naturalistic strivings led not to a truly realistic opera, but to a neo-Romantic one, elaborately decorated and staged. Today, says Merian, opera needs to shed the Wagnerian influence: "Opera hungers after modern material; after the long and shining period of Romantic dreams conjured up by Wagner, it thirsts after daylight. It wants to get free of fantastic gods and heroes. . . . German music, however, could not break this spell; it could find no way out of the magic garden in which the great magician of Bayreuth had kept it" (p. 739). It is only in Mascagni and Leoncavallo that Merian sees the "magic word that has broken the spell." The features Merian admires about *Pagliacci* include its powerful melodic style and harmonic language, and the polyphonic nature of much of the orchestral writing, which leads to a constant interchange between the sphere of feeling embodied by the orchestra and the sphere of intellect embodied by the singing voice (p. 748). In fact, as with *Cavalleria,* there is little "naturalistic" about the things Merian praises in *Pagliacci.* It is the non-Wagnerian nature of Leoncavallo's style that is most attractive to him.

Merian's phrase "modern-realistic" and his anti-Wagnerian stance seem to have provoked a strong response among other critics. The Berlin critic and composer Max Marschalk, who wrote in *Freie Bühne* for a time in the early 1890s (and is best known to music historians for his association with and advocacy of Mahler), cast what he called a "skeptical glance" at the "Mascagni cult." Like Merian, Marschalk found much to admire in *Cavalleria:* "But the opera as a whole, as a self-contained art work? I could discover nothing new, epoch-making. I can't understand what is really meant when one asserts that Mascagni is the man who will show opera new paths." Marschalk then takes up the question of Wagner: "I'm far from proposing *Parsifal* or *The Ring* as the final stage in the development of opera or from wishing that opera must everywhere be extended in the same direction. One can set out on side paths, which lead to other goals and eventually bring to light an artwork that in form and manner is an original creation. But Wagner must always be the starting point."[57] Marschalk's remarks suggest that many Germans tended to close ranks around Wagner. For all the excitement created by Mascagni, he was not a German and did not move forward on the Wagnerian path.

A year later Marschalk returned to the topic of *Cavalleria* and realistic opera, on the occasion of Mascagni's next opera, the comedy *L'Amico Fritz.* For Marschalk, opera could or should not be "realistic." Modern subjects do not make for a realistic opera, Marschalk says. The only thing modern and realistic about *Cavalleria* is the peasant life; Mascagni's manner of handling it is, however, unmodern and unrealistic. What might a realistic opera be?

> If one wanted to make a modern-realistic drama fruitful for composition, one must choose an entirely different form; one must transform the natural, plain everyday language into a rhythmicized one; one must reach for the euphoniousness of the poetic style, for the music of rhyme. But then where is the realism? A modern conversation at a dance, any old chit-chat at the beer table, and a serious speech at the Reichstag, with excited injections as chorus, turned into verse and composed, either would be laughable or would make for unbearable, screaming disharmony.[58]

For the Wagner-leaning Marschalk, everyday subjects are not appropriate for opera. Rather, opera must "seek out subject areas that lie distant from not only modern reality, but from any reality whatsoever. It must take refuge in sagas or tales; it must draw into its realm events that are remote, magical, imaginary."[59] In other words, Marschalk pretty much rejects naturalism as a feasible operatic aesthetic and reinforces the Wagnerian approach. Like Ehrenfels, he sees modern naturalism and Wagnerism as incompatible.

Although it did not include the post-Wagnerians Strauss, Schillings, or Pfitzner, there was a group of composers in Austria and Germany who jumped directly on the *verismo* bandwagon and produced one-act operas that were in many cases direct imitations of Mascagni and Leoncavallo. Symptomatic of this development was a competition for a one-act, tragic German opera announced in 1893 by Duke Ernst II of Saxe-Coburg and Gotha. The Duke was seeking, as Josef-Horst Lederer has suggested, a "German *Cavalleria.*"[60] Among the approximately 120 entries, the one selected for the prize was Josef Forster's *Die Rose von Pontevedra* (The Rose of Pontevedra), which has an almost one-to-one correspondence with *Cavalleria* in plot and characters. Virtually all the other submitted operas also follow the veristic archetype: they are set in southern, normally Mediterranean locales; they involve the rural lower class, such as farmers, fishermen, and hunters; and the basic motives of the plot are love, hate, and jealousy. After examining five examples, by Forster, Ferdinand Hummel, Leo Blech, Karl von Kaskel, and Gottfried Grünewald, Ulla Zierau concludes, "Despite some obviously veristic elements, the German one-acters did not succeed in coming out of the shadow of the Italian operas . . . The public, critics, writers, and managers could not be convinced by simple, superficial instances of plagiarism—and apart from that the German one-acters had nothing to offer."[61]

TIEFLAND

The true inheritance of the modern Italian style in Germany comes after the turn of the century in two works, Eugen d'Albert's *Tiefland* (Lowlands, 1903) and Max von Schilling's *Mona Lisa* (1915). *Tiefland* had the greatest success of any German dramatic opera since Wagner; it became one of the most frequently performed operas in the repertories of Hamburg, Vienna, and Berlin. Though not a runaway favorite like *Tiefland, Mona Lisa* was also popular in the major German houses through World War II.[62] Both operas deserve some consideration in any account of musical "naturalism" in the period of early German modernism.

From the beginning, both the libretto and music of *Tiefland* were understood in relation to Italian verismo. The libretto is an adaptation by Rudolph Lothar of the play *Terra baixa* by the Catalan playwright Angel Guimerà. The setting and plot could come out of an Italian verismo opera or one of its early German imitators. The action unfolds around 1900 in two places: on the rocky slopes of the Pyrenees and in a Catalonian village in the foothills or lowlands. In the opera, the two locales become symbolic: the mountains represent freedom, life, and innocence; the lowlands, intrigue, deceit, and death. Pedro, who lives on the mountain tending sheep, is persuaded by the landowner whom he serves, Sebastiano, to come down into the town, marry a young woman, Marta, and take over the mill. What Pedro does not realize is that Marta has been enslaved in a sexual relationship with Sebastiano, who wishes to marry her off only to restore his own reputation. Sebastiano, who has been having financial difficulties, hopes to marry a rich woman, but can only do so (according to the character Tommaso, who relates the situation in act 1, scene 5) if he "can silence the wicked tongues" about his relationship with Marta, which, however, he has no intention of ending. The innocent Pedro agrees to the marriage with Marta, which occurs at the end of act 1. In act 2, Pedro learns the truth about Marta's situation, confronts Sebastiano, and kills him in a fight. As the villagers mutter "Gottes Gericht" (God's judgment), Pedro and Marta, who have in the meanwhile fallen in love with each other, leave to return to the mountains, "up to light and freedom."

The parallels to Italian verismo plots are clear. The relationship between Sebastiano and Marta recalls that of Canio and Nedda in *Pagliacci,* with the important exception that Marta is entirely a victim (Nedda is, in fact, engaged in an affair). The confrontation between Pedro (tenor) and Sebastiano (baritone) recalls that between Turridu (tenor) and Alfio (baritone) in *Cavalleria.* As in *Cavalleria,* the religious piety of certain characters, especially Marta and Pedro, is a central theme of the opera. At moments a church service takes place in the background (in *Tiefland* a wedding service, in *Cavalleria* an Easter mass). The religious element is an important one in most veristic operas, where it acts as backdrop or foil to the tragic personal drama. Sebastiano bears some resemblance as well to Scarpia in *Tosca,* a work that d'Albert must have known by 1903.[63]

Tiefland has little in common with either the plots or the narrative techniques of German naturalists like Hauptmann or Holz. But it can be understood in light of the so-called *Heimat* (homeland) movement that flourished in the years around 1900. The homeland movement was an outgrowth of the antimodern strains of German nationalism of the later nineteenth century examined in chapter 1, such as those of Wagner, Lagarde, Tönnies, and other "cultural pessimists." These writers abhorred the urbanization, industrialization, and mechanization of the *Gründerzeit;* they called for a return to more authentic German values—those associated with the "folk," the countryside, the small town, the farm, handmade products, and so forth.[64]

Guimerà's play originated well outside the orbit of the German homeland movement. Nor was the translator/adaptor, Rudolf Lothar (1865–1943), associated with it; he was a practicing journalist who provided light comedies for the theater. Lothar's intent, as well as d'Albert's, was mainly a work within a German verismo framework modeled on Italian opera. But the homeland sensibility is evident in *Tiefland* in the way that the pure, innocent mountain life is set against the darker intrigue of the village. Pedro is a figure imbued with homeland values; he is willing to work hard and is completely comfortable in a natural setting. Sebastiano is a scheming capitalist landowner. One could without much difficulty alter the characters' names and situations to make Pedro a rural Aryan youth and Sebastiano an urban Jew.

Tiefland also may be said to anticipate a later outgrowth of the homeland movement, the genre of the German mountain film *(Bergfilm)* of the 1920s. In these early (presound) movies, rugged, glacier-laden mountain landscapes, as always associated with something quintessentially Nordic/Germanic, form the backdrop for dramatic adventure and rescue stories. In their most basic form the mountain films valorize individual heroism and raw nature over the comforts and mechanization of urban society.[65]

Tiefland and the mountain film genre actually come together in the movie of that name created by Leni Riefenstahl. Notorious for being Hitler's favorite filmmaker *(Olympia, Triumph of the Will),* Riefenstahl was attracted as early as the mid-1930s to the idea of making a film based on d'Albert's opera. The filming was begun in 1940 and continued across the war years until 1944. After the war the film was confiscated by the French government and was returned to Riefenstahl, with footage missing, only years later. She completed *Tiefland* in 1953.[66] The film, which uses passages from d'Albert's opera only as instrumental background, basically follows the Lothar adaptation but gives greater prominence to the role of Marta, who is now a seductive gypsy dancer played by Riefenstahl herself. Marta is at first attracted to the Sebastiano (here ennobled to the level of a marquis), but then turns against him because of his cruel, sadistic treatment of the peasants who serve him. In the film, Pedro, who strangles Sebastiano and goes off with Marta, is played by the blond, handsome, Germanic Franz Eichberger. He is the natural man, innocent and strong. Riefenstahl's *Tiefland* is, however, no simple example of propaganda, homeland art, or mountain film. Scholars now interpret it as Riefenstahl's "inner emigration" in Nazi Germany, a form of protest against Hitler (represented by the tyrannical Sebastiano).[67]

To return to d'Albert's opera and the years around 1900: *Tiefland* is essentially through-composed, and continuity is carried by the orchestra. D'Albert relies much less than Mascagni on conventional number structures, although they play a dramatic role in the more rustic or folkish aspects of the opera, and in the large duet between Marta and Pedro in act 2, scene 6. Sebastiano's dance song in act 2, "Hüll in die Mantilla" (Wrap Yourself in the Scarf) which he accompanies on the guitar, has a clear ancestor in Alfio's "Il cavallo scalpita" from *Cavalleria.*

The music of *Tiefland* is a fusion of Italian and German styles.[68] Broad, Puccini-like melodies sweep out of the orchestra at moments of high drama,

Example 6. D'Albert, *Tiefland,* act 1

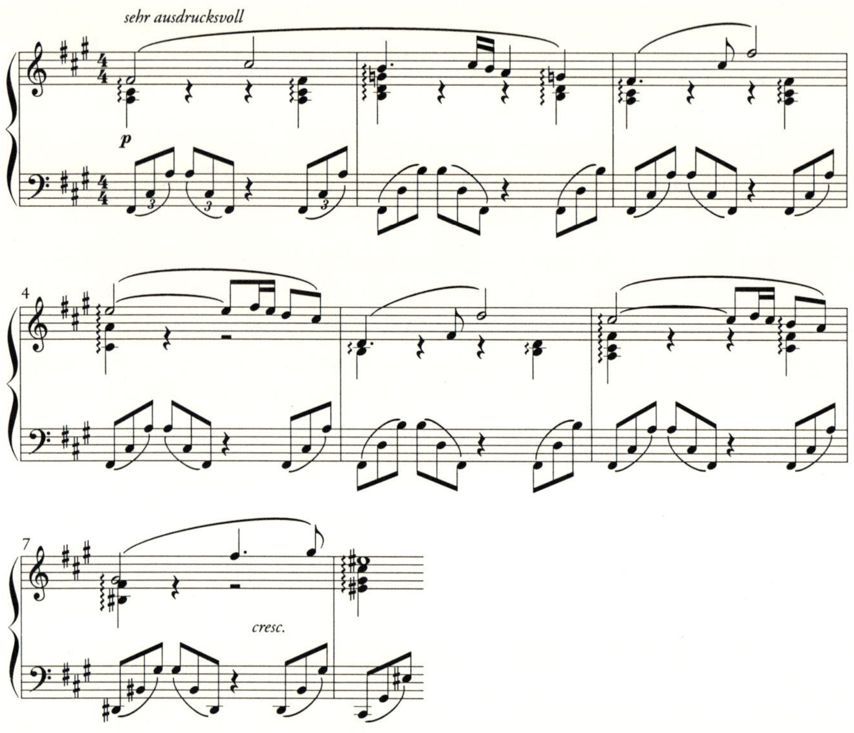

such as the theme that dominates scenes 9–11 of act 1 and seems to capture the tragic sadness of Marta's situation (example 6). This and other themes are treated leitmotivically in *Tiefland,* though less in the manner of Wagner than in that of the Verdian or Puccinian reminiscence motive. This theme, which begins in F♯ minor and eventually moves to F♯ major, starts within a fairly narrow harmonic range, touching upon the Neapolitan G major and the mediant, A major, all over a tonic pedal. The sudden move to the bright, even glaring, secondary dominant V/V, then the dominant V, in mm. 7–8, comes as something of a shock. One would be more likely to find such a harmonic gesture in Puccini than in Wagner or Strauss. The love theme for Cavaradossi and Tosca in act 1 of *Tosca* is characteristic (example 7). Here Puccini moves immediately from the tonic E to V/V/V (C♯), three steps away on the circle of fifths. Two measures later, he moves from vi (C♯ minor) directly to V/V, F♯ major, where we would normally expect ii, or F♯ minor; and then to V.

Example 7. Puccini, *Tosca,* act I

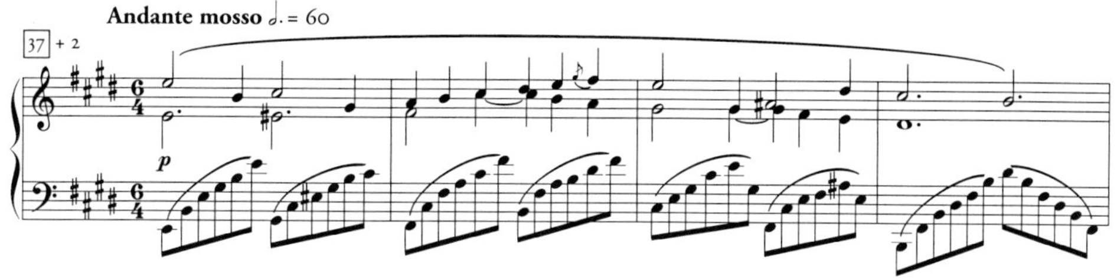

Marta's soliloquy in act I, scene 4 (example 8), where she laments her relationship with Sebastiano, reveals d'Albert's language at its most Wagnerian. The opening harmony is Wagner's beloved half-diminished seventh, in its most famous form the "Tristan" chord. D'Albert's scoring of the opening phrase for low strings, woodwinds, and brass, and timpani recalls some of the darker moments in *Parsifal.* The tonal center of Marta's soliloquy hovers around A minor and A major, but these keys are never confirmed. The first two measures prepare a dominant seventh of A, but in m. 3 the music shifts suddenly to F minor, which initiates a cadential progression toward C minor, reached in m. 4. The whole four-measure unit is then treated in sequence, beginning up a half step. The sequence is modified but still recognizable in its third leg (m. 9). The sequential treatment is clearly Wagnerian in inspiration.

Marta's vocal writing is mainly declamatory, and the orchestra carries the musical continuity. Marta often begins her phrases on weak parts of the measure. As a reflection of her anguished emotional state, her vocal part goes back and forth between a broken, discontinuous style ("Sein bin ich . . .") and more outburst-like melodic fragments ("Ach, ich bin ein schwaches Weib . . ."). At one point ("Heil'ge Jungfrau," m. 9), as she prays to the Virgin Mary, she sings a motive that had previously been heard only in the orchestra.

Tiefland is an extremely well-constructed opera, composed to a skillful libretto. In *Tiefland,* as Zierau puts it, "the German public finally had an opera at the center of which were men of flesh and blood, who had to grapple with everyday problems, and who did not move as unconquerable heroes in an unreal world."[69] That it has failed to hold the stage since World War II is perhaps because the characters are rather thinly drawn, and the mélange of German and Italian styles never quite adds up to more than the sum of its parts. For all its initial enthusiasm for German verismo in the 1890s,

Example 8. D'Albert, *Tiefland,* act 1, Marta's Soliloquy

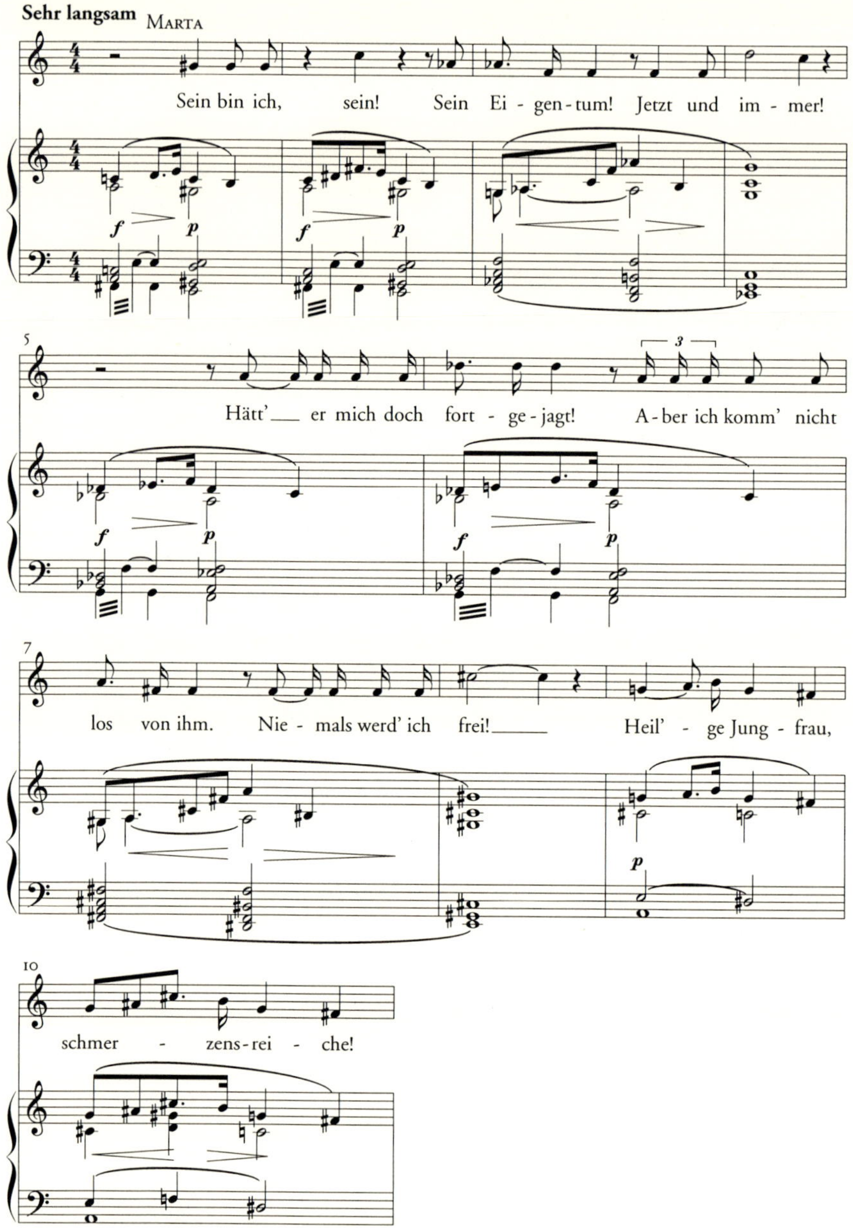

(I am his! His property! Now and forever! If only he had cast me off! But I cannot escape from him. I will never be free! Holy Virgin, full of sorrows!)

the German public by 1903 was ready for something more sophisticated and colorful, as the raging success of Strauss's *Salome* two years later suggests (and to which I turn below).

MONA LISA

Max von Schillings's *Mona Lisa,* composed between 1913 and 1915 and premiered at Stuttgart in 1915, is the other principal German opera of the early modern period that has been directly associated with verismo-oriented naturalism. Unlike d'Albert, Schillings (1868–1933) may be said to come directly out of the same Wagnerian framework as his friend and frequent correspondent Richard Strauss.[70] Each of Schillings's first three operas, *Ingwelde* (1894), *Pfeifertag* (1897), and *Moloch* (1907), has its clear antecedent in Wagner—the first in *The Ring,* the second in *Die Meistersinger,* the third in *Parsifal.* But with *Mona Lisa,* Schillings stepped outside the realm of myth, fairy tale, and biblical history.

The libretto of *Mona Lisa,* written by Beatrice Dovsky as a prologue and two acts (a structure shared by *Tiefland*), is set in Florence in both the present and the Renaissance. In the prologue, a lay brother shows a couple—an older man and a younger woman—around an old palazzo in Florence, explaining that among its former occupants were Fiordalisa Gherardini, the subject of Leonardo's renowned portrait, and her husband Francesco Giocondo. As the brother tells his story, the scene fades into act 1, set in Florence at Carnival in 1492. Francesco, played by the singer who plays the older man in the prologue, is intensely jealous of his younger wife, played by the woman of the prologue, especially because he cannot fathom the mysterious smile she wears in Leonardo's portrait, which is so unlike her everyday serious demeanor. Francesco discovers that Fiordalisa had earlier been in love with Giovanni de Salviati, who appears in Florence that evening (to be performed by the same singer as the lay brother in the prologue) on a mission from the Pope to purchase one of Francesco's rare pearls. Fiordalisa and Giovanni rekindle their love and agree to elope that night. Francesco foils their plan by trapping Giovanni inside a small room set up as a shrine for his pearls. Giovanni suffocates. The next day, Fiordalisa tricks Francesco into going to fetch the pearl, and she locks him in the shrine, where he too perishes. In the final scene, we return to the present as the lay brother completes his narration. As the couple departs, he thinks he recognizes Mona Lisa in the woman.

Schillings's opera was immediately recognized by critics as a departure from the Wagnerian tradition. In his "Introduction" to the opera, published in 1915, Karl Mennicke remarked that in *Mona Lisa,* Schillings "energetically renounces his preference for old, dark tales; he places before our eyes a mirror image of real life, which seizes us more strongly than any mythology."[71] A number of features bring *Mona Lisa* clearly into line with verismo opera. The basic plot motives that lead toward catastrophe are love, jealousy, betrayal, despair, and revenge. As in *Pagliacci,* despite a large number of characters, the action focuses on a single marital relationship, here between Francesco and Fiordalisa. The confrontation between the two at the end of act 1, which lasts almost twenty minutes, is by far the longest segment of the opera (which as a whole lasts about seventy minutes) and is certainly its dramatic highpoint. Mennicke writes of the "realism" in this scene.[72] The "evil" baritone and "good" soprano recall dozens of operas in the Italian tradition. But Scarpia and Tosca certainly come more specifically to mind, as do Sebastiano and Marta in *Tiefland.* Unlike Scarpia or Sebastiano, but like Canio, Francesco has some cause for jealousy.[73]

In musical style and structure, Schillings's *Mona Lisa* is much less beholden to Italian verismo than d'Albert's *Tiefland.* Certain aspects, such as the doubling of the voices by the orchestra (as in Fiordalisa's mad scene at reh. 63), recall Puccini. The use of offstage church choir and church bells—suggesting a pious backdrop to the onstage passions—is reminiscent of both *Cavalleria* and *Tosca. Mona Lisa* is virtually through-composed, and the two main acts are not explicitly divided into scenes. The love duet between Giovanni and Fiordalisa is interrupted at its Tristanesque climax by the entrance of Francesco, a clear gesture toward act 2 of *Tristan und Isolde,* where King Mark breaks in on the lovers (example 9).

But *Mona Lisa* also owes much to Schilling's friend Richard Strauss. The presence of Savonarola and his monks, who burst in with their moralizing Latin chant "Fuge, Zion, fuge" (Flee, Zion, flee) in the Carnival scene of act 1, recalls Jokanaan in *Salome* (although the monks' music lacks the broad diatonicism of Jokanaan's). Fiordalisa's mad scene, after she has locked Francesco in the shrine, has echoes of the final monologues of both *Salome* and *Elektra.* As in Strauss's two operas, the object of the heroine's obsession is now dead, and like them she sings what Mennicke calls her "aria of revenge."[74]

Another striking, though less obvious, influence is that of Strauss's *Ariadne auf Naxos,* a work with whose premiere Schillings had been actively involved in Stuttgart in 1912.[75] Schillings began his *Mona Lisa* in the summer of 1913, less than a year after the *Ariadne* premiere. The four young

Example 9. Schillings, *Mona Lisa,* act 1

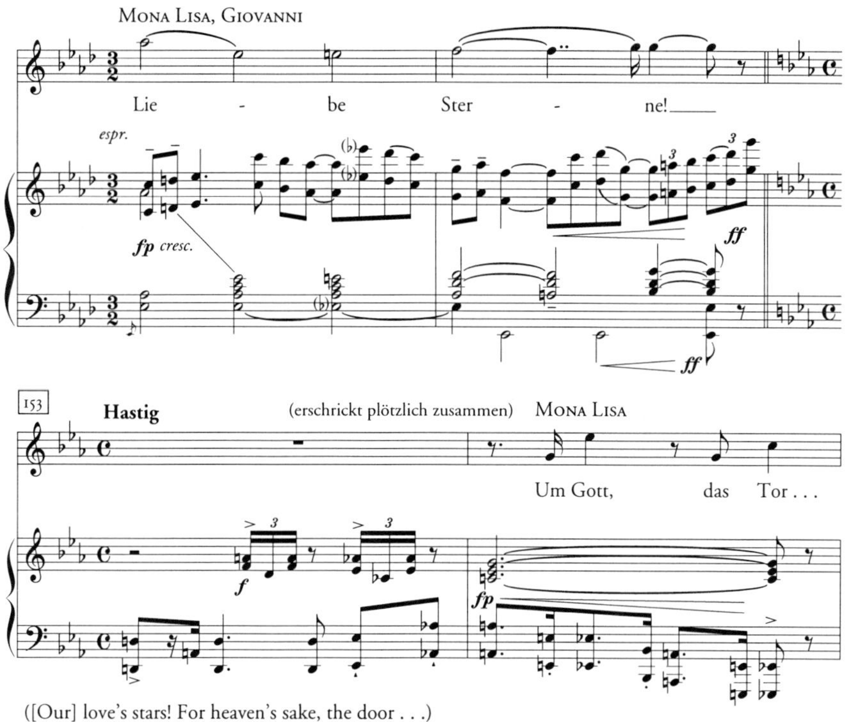

([Our] love's stars! For heaven's sake, the door . . .)

noblemen (Alessio, Masolino, Pietro, and Sandro) who sing a Carnival song, "Jugend ist so hold und süß" (Youth is so lovely and sweet, to words by Lorenzo de Medici), near the beginning of act 1 of *Mona Lisa* bring to the mind and the ear the four commedia dell'arte players in Strauss's opera (example 10).[76] The vocal disposition of Schillings's four singers (two tenors, one baritone, one bass) is identical to that of Strauss's Brighella, Scaramuccio, Harlequin, and Truffaldin; and like them, Schillings's men tend to sing as a group. Although the plots of *Ariadne* and *Mona Lisa* are obviously very different, in both, the light-hearted male singers, with their popular-style songs, serve as a dramatic and musical foil to the more serious main plot. In *Ariadne,* the commedia players poke fun at the mournful Ariadne; in *Mona Lisa,* the quartet contrasts starkly with the serious drama involving the main characters, Francesco, Fiordalisa, and Giovanni. The little ditty about "Jugend" returns (though now sung by two females, Piccarda and Sisto) at the height of the confrontation between Francesco and

Example 10. Schillings, *Mona Lisa,* act 1

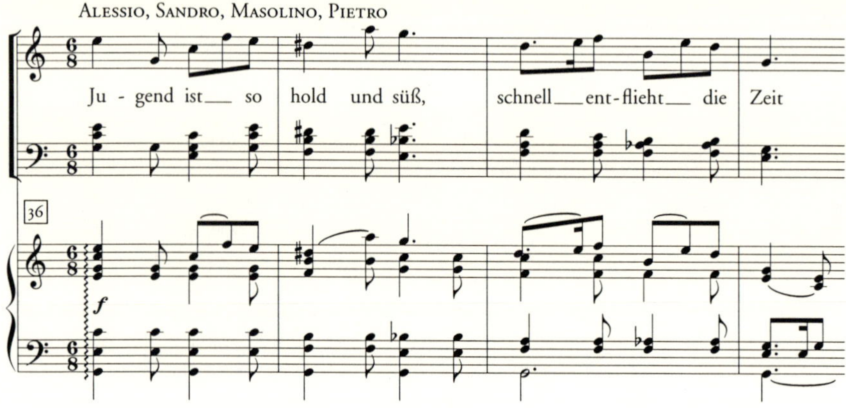

(Youth is so lovely and sweet; time passes quickly.)

Fiordalisa, near the end of act 1. It was in Strauss's *Ariadne* (though obviously not in that opera alone) that Schillings would have found this direct juxtaposition of the popular/light-hearted with the tragic/pathetic.

DER FERNE KLANG

In the realm of serious opera, Italian verismo and Wagnerian music drama were the two most attractive paths for composers in Austria and Germany during the 1890s. The former came the closest to "naturalism" as envisioned by the German literary naturalists, but in the end, as we have seen in looking at even the best examples, *Tiefland* and *Mona Lisa,* the results were disappointing. A better reflection of the naturalist agenda appears in three operas not specifically associated with the phenomenon, Franz Schreker's *Der ferne Klang* and Strauss's *Salome* and *Elektra.*

Although the exact date of the genesis of *Der ferne Klang* (The Distant Sound) remains unclear, Schreker probably began work on it in 1903 or 1904, and completed it shortly before the premiere in 1912. He had originally sought a libretto from Rudolf Lothar, who had provided d'Albert with the translation and adaptation of *Tiefland.* It is not known what work by Lothar he had in mind; in any case, this subject (not *Tiefland* itself) turned out also to be d'Albert's property. Schreker resolved to write his own libretto.[77] It is, of course, intriguing to wonder whether Lothar might have provided Schreker with a verismo-style libretto anything like *Tiefland*—and what Schreker would have done with it. In the event, his own libretto for *Der ferne Klang* is a departure from both Mediterranean verismo and traditional Wagnerian myth or legend.

In *Der ferne Klang,* a young composer named Fritz is obsessed with finding the "distant sound" he feels holds the key to artistic inspiration and success. In the quest he abandons his girlfriend Grete, who is then bartered away in marriage by an alcoholic father needing to pay his drinking debts. Grete escapes and leads a life of prostitution. At the end of the opera, Fritz realizes that the distant sound is really contained in Grete's love for him, and he dies in her arms.

Schreker himself acknowledged in later years the naturalistic traits that distinguish *Der ferne Klang* from its operatic contemporaries: "About thirty years ago, this was a daring venture: the first attempt to break with any kind of Wagnerian imitation. I put on the stage simple bourgeois, everyday people who sometimes speak in an ordinary manner."[78] Indeed, portions of *Der ferne Klang* come much closer to the ideals of German naturalism than any other contemporary opera in Austria or Germany. The socially grounded realism bears some relation to that of Charpentier's *Louise,* which Schreker heard in Vienna in 1903.[79]

The first scene of *Der ferne Klang* presents a family drama much closer to the kind that one might encounter in a play by Hauptmann, Ibsen, or Strindberg.[80] Schreker's stage directions for the first scene bring us directly into a middle-class home of the late nineteenth or early twentieth century:

> Living room in Graumann's house. Sparsely furnished. The remains of a modest elegance. At the back a door and a closed window, through which can be seen the inn that is located across the way. At the side, another window, this one open; it is at an angle to a door that leads into a second living space. As the curtain goes up, Fritz is standing outside the window (the side one), visible to the audience. Grete is next to him, inside at the window. At first both speak in a very hushed manner.[81]

This realistic setting could come from a Hauptmann play, for example *Einsame Menschen* mentioned above (and adduced by Ehrenfels and Nodnagel). The Hauptmann set is described as

> A public-style room—both living and recreation room—furnished in a good bourgeois style. There is a little piano and a bookcase; the walls are hung with portraits. . . . At the left one door, at the right, two. The left door leads into Johannes Vockerat's study. The doors on the right lead to the bedroom and out into the field.[82]

The plot of *Der ferne Klang* is also reminiscent of Hauptmann's, perhaps especially of *Vor Sonnenaufgang* (Before Sunrise), where the story is generated (and consumed) by troubled family relationships. As in *Vor Sonnenaufgang,* one finds in *Der ferne Klang* an alcoholic father, whose wife is eager to marry the daughter off and remove her from the deteriorating domestic situation. In Hauptmann, a young scientist named Loth enters the scene as the potential husband, falls in love with the daughter Helen, but then refuses to marry her out of concern for the genetic implications of her father's illness. In the final moments of the play, Helen commits suicide. In Schreker, Fritz is the outsider who breaks into the family situation and contemplates marriage with the daughter, Grete. But like Loth he is pulled in another direction by his own principles, in this case the "distant sound" that represents an artistic calling. Grete is driven not to suicide, but to a life of prostitution.

Schreker's libretto is distinctive for plunging us immediately into the drama of the Graumann family and of Fritz, without any traditional exposition. As Ulrike Kienzle notes, Grete's first words—"Du willst wirklich fort?"—"confront the listener with a conversation that apparently has been going on for some time" (example 11). Kienzle also observes that the language used by Grete and Fritz "is simple and prose-like; it is the spontaneous, unstylized conversational tone between two people who are intimate with each other."[83] Some sentences are fragmentary or incomplete.

The style of the text is closely mirrored by that of the music, which unfolds in a prose- or recitative-like fashion. Grete begins on the weak part of the measure, and the rhythm of her part closely follows the implied rhythm of the text. The singing voices remain essentially in the middle of their register, except for a few special moments of heightened expression, like Fritz's "zu schwer, Süße!" The musical accompaniment is richer than in much recitative, even that of the late nineteenth century. Yet Schreker keeps it "neutral" in significant ways. The first violins maintain a rhythmic ostinato in triplets, with syncopation; underneath this the other strings play successions of mostly parallel triads. The key signature of three flats indicates E♭ major or C minor, and Grete indeed begins to sing above a dominant seventh chord of E♭. But the harmonic syntax supports no clear tonic. There is a quality to the accompaniment that is at once static and restless; it moves but goes nowhere. Schreker is clearly seeking to create a naturalistic atmosphere with all the musico-dramatic means at his disposal: milieu, libretto, text-setting, and accompaniment.

Other portions of *Der ferne Klang* confirm that it represents the most

Example 11. Schreker, *Der ferne Klang,* act 1

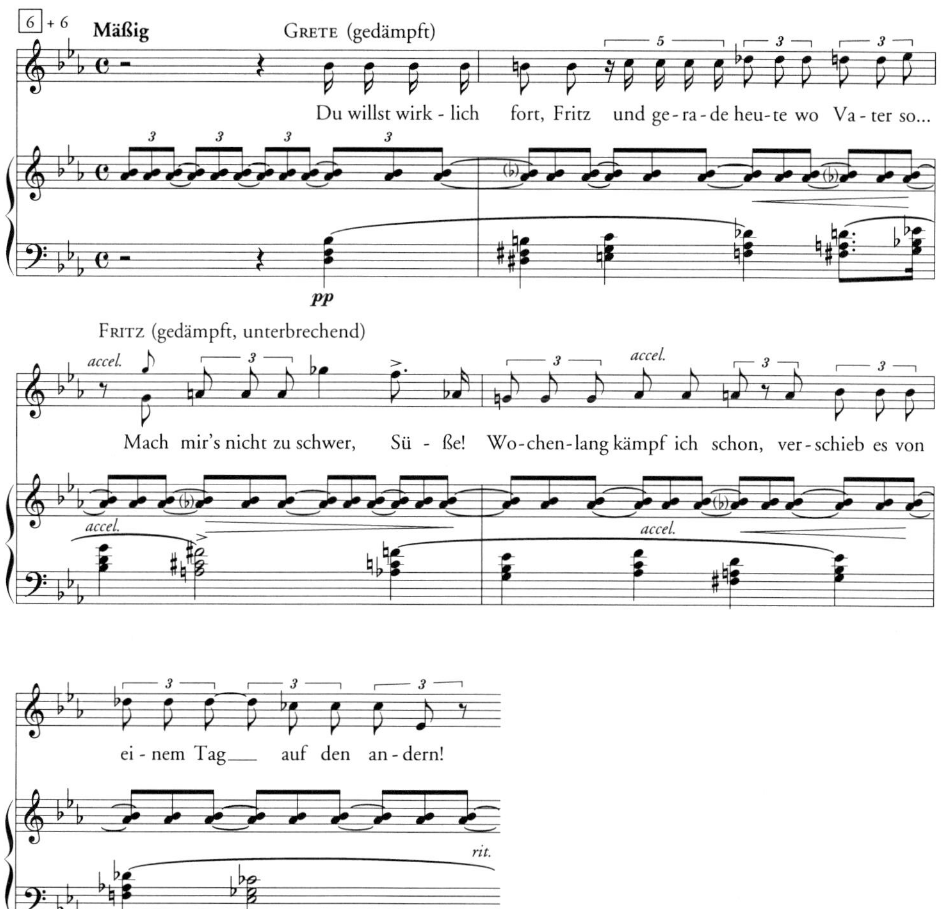

(Must you really go, Fritz, and especially today when Father so . . .
Don't make it too hard for me, dearest! I've been struggling for weeks, postponing it from one day to the next!)

thoroughgoing attempt at German operatic naturalism in the years around 1900. The dialogue between Grete and her mother in act 1, scene 3, is entirely spoken; it unfolds, without notated pitch or rhythm, over sparse orchestral accompaniment, in a fashion that recalls the older melodrama. In the following scene (after reh. 45) the exchanges between Grete, her father, the Actor, and the Innkeeper are written in a fluid, declamatory recitative style.

Act 2, which takes place at a dance hall–cum–bordello in Venice, contains a different kind of naturalism—an attempt by Schreker to capture simultaneously different strands of instrumental music, song, and conversation. These include, at the opening (before the curtain rises), an offstage orchestra playing "Venetian" music, an on-stage Hungarian band, and two women's choruses, one singing a vocalise on "Ah!", another singing a love song. In scene 2, a baritone sings a lyrical melody, against which the earlier vocalise continues and four women converse in a declamatory fashion. Some commentators have heard in this act an innovative collage technique parallel to what was happening at around the same time in the works of Picasso and Braque. Schreker would undoubtedly have known Puccini's *La Bohème* (1896), where the Café Momus setting of act 2 offers perhaps the first modern operatic collage. In a similar way to Schreker's Venetian scene, Musetta's aria is sung against an expanding real-life polyphony of chatter, arguments, a children's chorus, on-stage bands, and more. Verismo and naturalism may be said to meet at this juncture. Schreker comes at his collage from the German naturalist perspective, Puccini from Italian verismo. But the sonic and visual results are not fundamentally different.

Declamatory and collage-like naturalism is only part of the picture in Schreker's *Der ferne Klang,* which moves into the realms outlined by Hermann Bahr in his "Overcoming of Naturalism," as discussed above—that is, in the direction of the psychology of the un- or preconscious, the psychology of nerves and sensations. Kienzle calls this approach "psychological perspectivism," which is to be distinguished from earlier operatic dramaturgy, including Wagner's. Schreker "abstains from any epic commentary on the action. . . . Instead he transmits to the listener those impulses of feeling and those perceptions of consciousness as they occur in the psyche of his characters." What we are shown is not the result of the processes of consciousness (as Bahr suggested was characteristic of the "old" psychology), but rather "the complex development of the facts of consciousness themselves as determined by the mind's manifold wanderings and associations."[84] Kienzle suggests that Schreker achieves this psychological perspectivism through a kind of hierarchy among sonority *(Klang),* motive, and theme. These aspects of Schreker's opera bring them closer to what Bahr saw as the transcending of naturalism in Maeterlinck and what was closer to symbolism than naturalism per se. The actions and thoughts of Schreker's characters are the symbolic manifestations of deeper unconscious motivations.

The Forest Scene at the end of act 1 is the first place in the score where

Example 12. Schreker, *Der ferne Klang,* act 1

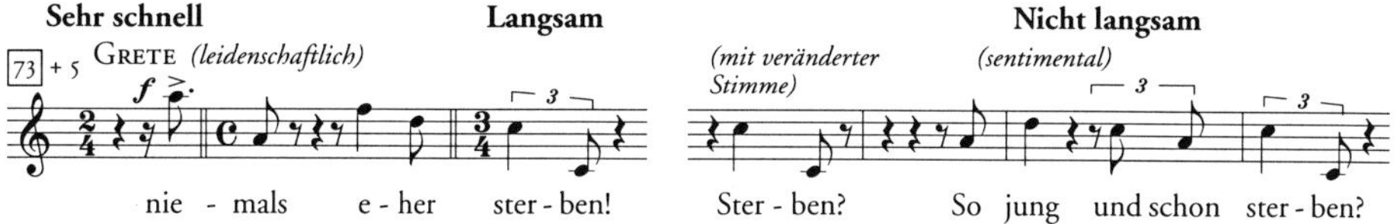

(Never. I'd rather die! Die? Die so young and soon?)

Schreker goes beyond realistic naturalism into the depths of the psyche. Grete has left her family and seems to be searching for Fritz, whom she cannot find. She contemplates suicide, but then, charmed by what Schreker describes in the stage directions as the *Waldzauber* (Forest Magic), falls asleep. An old woman appears mysteriously, wakes Grete, and offers to help her find Fritz; they go off together. Kienzle describes Schreker's portrait of Grete in this scene as a "psychogram," a diagram or summary of her personality: Schreker "shows the inner transformation of his protagonist, whose altered consciousness demands a new technique of scenic, linguistic, and musical representation." Kienzle suggests that the emotional states experienced by Grete correspond exactly to the three possible types of consciousness that Breuer and Freud described in their *Studies on Hysteria* of 1895: waking, "hypnoid" (a kind of transport or *Entrückung*), and sleep.[85] Grete's vocal line as she searches for Fritz is disjunct in a proto-expressionist fashion (example 12). Motives are not grouped into any coherent vocal line, but "appear fleetingly and disappear again, in a way that corresponds to the associative processes" of Grete's consciousness.[86] In the accompaniment, Schreker makes use of several leitmotives introduced earlier in act 1. As well, Schreker employs tone-painting: one of the main orchestral figures recalls the *Waldweben* (Forest Murmurs) from Wagner's *Siegfried.*

Kienzle's assessment of the Forest Scene is sensitive, and yet one comes to question whether Schreker really pioneered a kind of psychological naturalism. To put it more bluntly, we might ask whether Schreker's musico-dramatic skills in this scene are as advanced as Kienzle claims—whether we really find new principles of musical, linguistic, and scenic representation. Kienzle makes a comparison between *Der ferne Klang* and Schoenberg's monodrama *Erwartung* (Anticipation) of 1909, pointing to the similarities of the young woman lost in the woods at night searching for her lover. Schoenberg's *Erwartung* explores the anxious inner states of mind of the woman in a way that, as is often pointed out, parallels contemporary psychoanalytic theory. The musical language is that of free atonality, which perhaps because of *Erwartung* has become indelibly associated with a psychological realism in music. As Kienzle points out, free atonality has no absolute claim to be "the means of expression for psychic deformation."[87] Nonetheless, Schreker's musical language for the "psychogram" of Grete's Forest Scene seems too anodyne to be as path-breaking as Kienzle asserts. Adorno, even while admiring Schreker's musico-dramatic achievement, notes wryly that the composer's stage directions for the Forest Magic music of *Der ferne Klang* "drag Wagner's cautious note on the Good Friday Magic into a realm lying between the oleograph and Jugendstil."[88] Schreker makes too garishly explicit what Wagner had only suggested.

SALOME AND *ELEKTRA*

A middle ground for naturalistic opera, falling between the styles of Schreker and Schoenberg, is found in Strauss's stage works of the first decade of the twentieth century, *Salome* (1905) and *Elektra* (1909). *Salome* and *Elektra* are among the first examples—along with Debussy's *Pelléas et Mélisande* of 1902—of what has more recently been called "literature opera" *(Literaturoper),* which uses a preexisting text without the normal mediating stage of a libretto. In the case of *Salome,* Strauss rejected the offer of a libretto by the Viennese playwright Anton Lindner, in favor of working directly with Hedwig Lachmann's translation of Oscar Wilde's play. For *Elektra,* Strauss used Hofmannsthal's play of 1905, which was shortened and adapted (with some additional lines by the playwright). The conditions of a literature opera make a "naturalistic" label all the more feasible, since with no "libretto" the composer comes into direct contact with the thing itself, the play.

Already in their own day, both *Salome* and *Elektra* were recognized to be in the tradition or trajectory of naturalism. In 1913 Walter Niemann classified them under the rubric of "painterly naturalism." He saw their greatest strengths in Strauss's ability to "illustrate the scene musically by clarifying and intensifying the dramatic events with sounds and musical colors." Niemann continued: "The painterly and the painterly points of view are decisive for the composition of the music. The appeal and contrast of color are everything." Niemann was no fan of Strauss, whom he (like so many critics to this day) found a fine technician, but no "searcher of men's hearts."[89]

Salome and *Elektra* are one-act operas that deviate fundamentally from the one-act German verismo works discussed above. *Cavalleria* has been left far behind. *Salome* is a highly compressed variant of the biblical or Old Testament opera, a genre that includes works as diverse as Verdi's *Nabucco,* Saint-Saëns's *Samson et Dalila,* and Schoenberg's *Moses und Aron.* In Strauss's *Salome* the themes of verismo—love, jealousy, revenge—become magnified into nightmarish obsession. *Elektra* is a similarly compressed, interiorized version of a different genre, Greek tragedy.

Wilde and Hofmannsthal—and Strauss in turn—respect the naturalistic Aristotelian unities of time and place: the operas, each lasting just over ninety minutes, unfold in real time and in a single location. In both, Strauss dispenses with an overture or prelude and plunges us directly into the action. But in both operas—and here is where the musician comes into play—Strauss also may be said to stretch clock time, especially in the long monologues for the heroines. This is especially true in Salome's final scene, where we are pulled inexorably inside her mind in what Kienzle would consider a musico-dramatic psychogram.[90] Here clock time recedes behind extended, distorted psychological time.

Like almost all Strauss's works before *Der Rosenkavalier,* especially the tone poems, *Salome* and *Elektra* have their share of tone-painting. When Herod sings on two occasions of feeling a wind and of hearing birds (reh. 165 and 233), Strauss complies with rushing chromatic scales in the violins, and tremolos in the lower strings and woodwinds. In *Elektra* we hear the cracking of whips, the trudging of beasts, and the scurrying of servants (at reh. 127). These are examples of the "painterly naturalism" that Niemann identified in the operas. But the naturalistic psychological component far transcends simple tone-painting.

In her analysis of Salome's listening at the cistern for the sounds of Jokanaan's decapitation (reh. 304ff.), Carolyn Abbate has shown that Strauss in fact avoids conventional tone-painting. We seem rather to hear directly Salome's anxiety.[91] Strauss writes one of his most famous orchestral effects, in which the double basses are divided. The lower ones play a tremolo on E♭, while a solo bass plays isolated B♭'s in *sforzando* eighth notes. Strauss directs that the string is to be held firmly between the thumb and index finger, then played with the bow in a very short, sharp stroke, "so that a tone is produced that resembles the suppressed moaning and groaning of a

Example 13. Strauss, *Salome*

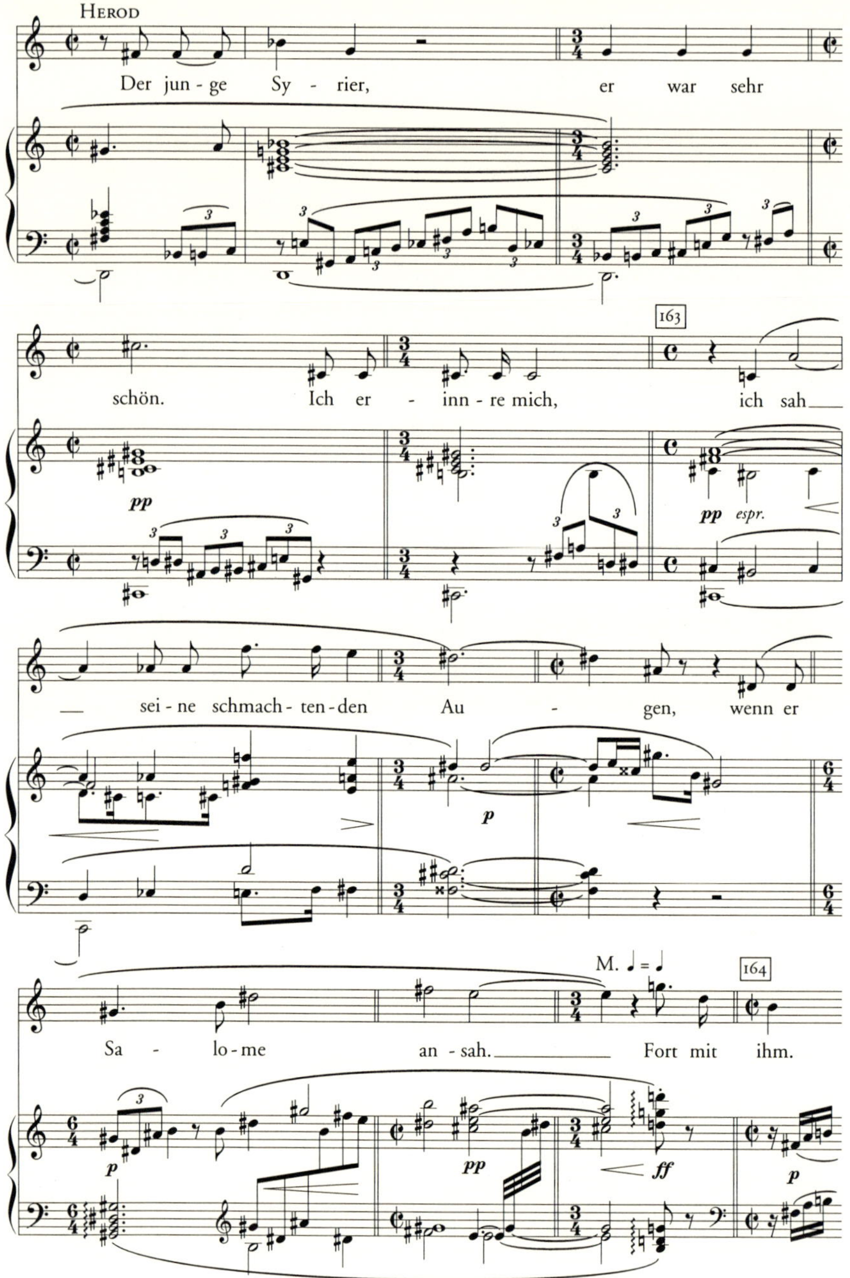

(The young Syrian, he was very fair. I remember, I saw the longing in his eyes when he gazed at Salome. Away with him!)

woman." The only moment of realistic tone-painting comes just before reh. 307. A sudden *fortissimo* in the cellos and double basses evokes a response from Salome: "Es ist etwas zu Boden gefallen. Ich hörte etwas fallen" (Something fell to the ground. I heard something fall). She first assumes that this sound is the executioner dropping his sword as he loses courage to carry out his orders. In fact (if "fact" is the appropriate word here), the sound most likely does represent Jokanaan's head falling, as Salome sees a few moments later when it is offered up to her on a silver tray.

For Paul Bekker, writing in 1909, the musical characterization of Herod was "the crown" of Strauss's *Salome.* Herod "signifies even for Strauss something entirely new. This neurasthenic weather vane is a unique example of impressionistic art, an attempt, until now unmatched, to capture all neural stimulations in a musical mirror, to mix up keys and rhythms capriciously among one another and to create a new style out of shapeless elements that are dissonant with one another."[92] For Bekker, Strauss's portrait of Herod even surpasses that of Salome, whose presentation is "half diluted with conventionalities."

Herod's first appearance, in scene 4, probably counts as one of the most advanced psychodramatic portraits in opera up to this point in history. It is here that we see clearly the kind of "new psychology," located in the realm of the senses and nerves, of which Bahr wrote in "The Overcoming of Naturalism." When he accidentally steps in the blood of his captain, Narraboth, who has just committed suicide onstage, Herod immediately becomes anxious. As he wonders why Narraboth killed himself, then recalls how he looked longingly at Salome, Herod's vocal line is a confused mixture of lyrical and declamatory expression (example 13). It alternates between bare-as-bones declamation ("Der junge Syrier," "Ich erinnere mich," and "Fort mit ihm") and more melodic, though fragmentary, utterances ("er war sehr schön" and "wenn er Salome ansah").

Something similar occurs later when Herod is persuading Salome to dance. He spins out a broadly lyrical, rounded melody in C major (reh. 232). But he is at once overcome by a feeling of cold; he claims he senses an "icy wind," which blows up obligingly through the strings and woodwinds. Herod then imagines that the rustling sound is like that of a "horrid black" bird, which, however is nowhere to be seen. Strauss certainly indulges in some tone-painting here, but far more striking is the naturalism of the vocal part, which it is broken up into short phrases that must be among the most metrically-rhythmically fluid written up to this time (example 14). Strauss notates a succession of mixed meters that essentially

Example 14. Strauss, *Salome*

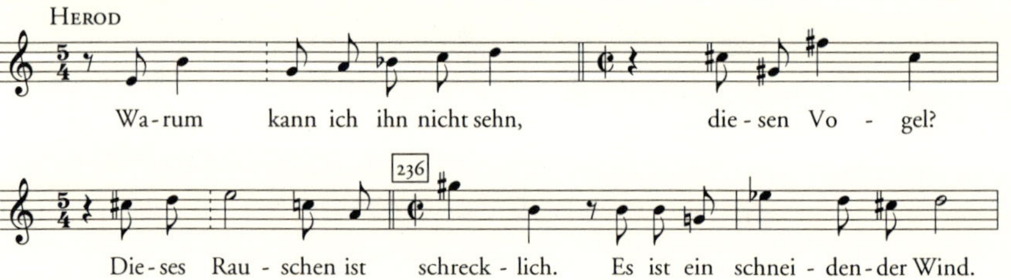

(Why can't I see it, this bird? This rushing is terrible. It is a biting wind.)

alternate duple and triple: $\frac{5}{4}$ (divided as 2+3), ¢, $\frac{5}{4}$, ¢. Even more than in Strauss's *Lied des Steinklopfers,* one may speak here of a vivid musical second-by-second style.

Herod's style is revisited in the music Strauss created for another deficient parental figure, Elektra's mother, Clytemnestra. Like Herod's account of his wild fantasies, Clytemnestra's report of her dreams in *Elektra,* "Ich habe keine guten Nächte" (I have no good nights, reh. 177), is conveyed with a high degree of dissonance, an atomized or fragmented musical discourse, and stark declamatory naturalism. In this case, especially at "Und doch kriecht zwischen Tag und Nacht . . . ein Etwas hin über mich" (And yet, between day and night . . . a something crawls over me, reh. 186), the effect is hauntingly understated or sublimated. Clytemnestra is more profoundly disturbed than Herod; the musical psychogram thus reaches deeper into the unconscious. For many measures, the orchestra plays only *pp* or *ppp.* Under sustained chords in the high strings, brief motives are murmured indistinctly at the very bottom of the texture in the contrabassoon and low tubas. Soon (at reh. 188) this texture gives way to chromatic figures that slither among the different instruments. This part of *Elektra* is virtually atonal. In this respect it is certainly the most "advanced" music Strauss had written up to this time.

Strauss's musico-dramatic techniques in Clytemnestra's dream narrative and Herod's fantasies are much closer to those Schoenberg used for the Woman in *Erwartung* than they are to Schreker's depiction of Grete's forest ecstasy in *Der ferne Klang.* Such techniques are often associated with expressionism in music. In expressionism as classically formulated, music unfolds without regard to standard logic or patterns. Rhythm, meter, melody, harmony, and phrasing all reflect the innermost psychological state of a character; they are the result of "inner necessity," as Kandinsky put it.[93] Naturalism in its "overcome" state as articulated by Bahr—that is, a deeply psychological, nerve-sensitive naturalism—is an obvious precursor to, or perhaps even a form of, expressionism. It is clearly encountered in *Salome, Elektra,* and to a lesser extent, *Der ferne Klang.* As I have tried to suggest in this chapter, naturalism might thus be the best concept through which to understand the goals and achievements of many composers in the Austro-German sphere in the decades after the death of that first great naturalist, Wagner.

THREE

Convergences

Music and the Visual Arts

AS WE HAVE SEEN, the extent to which music was or could be naturalistic occupied writers, thinkers, and composers in the years around 1900. In the end, many realized that music and naturalism were perhaps not well suited for each other, largely because of the prevailing idea—very hard to shake off, at least in German-speaking realms—that music was in essence abstract, absolute, nonreferential, metaphysical, and thus ultimately not connected with the "real world." These qualities had been attributed to music since the rise of German idealist philosophy in the late eighteenth century and were reinforced by the early Romantics, Schopenhauer, and Wagner. Carl Dahlhaus suggested that the aesthetics of absolute music persisted well into the later nineteenth century, making music "neo-Romantic" in an "un-Romantic" age characterized by positivism and materialism. Dahlhaus also argued plausibly that a Schopenhauerian-Wagnerian aesthetics still held sway well into the early modernist period. Even heavily literature- or text-based works like music dramas and programmatic tone poems relied on "self-contained musical logic with no need of extramusical props."[1]

This ideology of music's purity, if not ultimately well suited to naturalism, was perfectly adapted to other movements that emerged in the wake of the "overcoming" of naturalism. This was especially true in the visual arts, which also struggled with issues of naturalism and realism. In music, or in the *idea* of music, some visual artists in the early modern period found a way out of the naturalist bind. Symbolism, Jugendstil, and abstraction, the three most significant trends in early modern art in the German sphere, each owed something to, or would demonstrate a strong tie with, music.

ADORNO'S "CONVERGENCE"

Theodor Adorno's remarks in a 1965 essay about "some relationships" between music and painting can serve as a point of entry into the subject. Adorno, like many commentators before and since, observes that music is essentially a *Zeitkunst,* an art based on time. It can nonetheless achieve a degree of spatialization (*Verräumlichung*) through musical notation, through the concept of "form," and through the ability—evident, as Adorno pointed out, in the electronic music that was in its heyday as he wrote—to treat time in a spatial manner. Inversely, painting is a *Raumkunst,* an art of space, which at certain moments can assume a temporal dimension, because "those pictures seem the most successful in which what is absolutely simultaneous seems like a passage of time that is holding its breath."[2]

Adorno proposes the category of convergence (*Konvergenz*) to describe the way that music and painting can be said to relate to each other most authentically and convincingly. Convergence is not achieved when music or painting attempts to resemble the other art through what Adorno calls pseudomorphosis, or false transformation. "The moment one art imitates another," he observes, "it becomes more distant from it by repudiating the constraint of its own material, and falls into syncretism, in the vague notion of an undialectical continuum of arts in general" (p. 67). Adorno has little sympathy for experiments in synesthesia (hearing colors, seeing sounds) or in what he calls "dubious analogies" between phenomena in the arts of painting and music (p. 74). The arts can converge, Adorno says, only where each one "pursues its immanent principle in a pure way" (p. 67). Adorno admits that in the hands of certain talented artists these principles do seem to allow, or even generate, points of contact. In music one can "inevitably" speak of "line"; and in painting notions like harmony and dissonance of color are "not mere metaphors" (p. 74).

The language of dialectic and immanence betrays Adorno's own philosophical reflexes. For him, painting and music would necessarily stand in a dialectical relationship; they could not just be points on some "vague" continuum. Each art form would moreover also need to retain the integrity of its own inherent techniques. There is much to be said for Adorno's notion of convergence as involving not one art seeking to imitate another, and not synesthesia, but more basic structural connections among the artistic "materials." Convergence, though not ironclad as a category of music-art relations, is thus a useful heuristic construct. It is more powerfully suggestive than affinity or analogy, and it implies a deeper connection between arts than parallelism. Convergence can reveal points of contact between two (or more) arts without necessarily imputing anything as concrete as influence or intention.[3]

Characteristically, Adorno does not historicize his argument about convergence. He is writing not about specific epochs, composers, or painters (although they come up in passing), but rather at a more theoretical level. Yet his comments imply that the years around 1900 in Europe are a very promising place to look for convergence. For Adorno, the Wagnerian *Gesamtkunstwerk* (total artwork) and its "derivatives" in the later nineteenth century represented only a "dream" of convergence as an "abstract Utopia" (p. 74). These attempts failed because the mingling of media did not yet permit true convergence. More propitious circumstances for convergence arose after 1900 with the advent of abstraction in art and atonality in music. Adorno suggests that abstraction occurs in art through the renunciation of object-relatedness, and in music "through the mortal contraction of all its imitative moments, not only its programmatically descriptive elements, but its traditional expressivity, as well, which requires firm conventions linking what is expressed with its signifier" (p. 71). Adorno sees convergence between nonobjective painting and "tonality-free" music, which both yield to their impulses of "pure expression" (p. 72).

Two figures that Adorno mentions in this context, not surprisingly, are Wassily Kandinsky and Arnold Schoenberg, whose names are often linked in histories of early modernism and who are, respectively, the early-twentieth-century masters of nonobjective painting and atonal music in the German sphere. Adorno recognizes them as convergent artists but is nonetheless skeptical about some of the synesthetic implications of their work and thought. He views Kandinsky's notion of visual "sounds" *(Klänge)* with suspicion, and he finds Schoenberg's concept of *Klangfarbenmelodie* (tone-color melody) in part "apocryphal" (p. 74).

Although he does not refer to Kandinsky's 1912 treatise *Über das Geistige in der Kunst* (On the Spiritual in Art), Adorno's arguments about convergence are strikingly similar. Kandinsky suggests that the arts "have never in recent times been closer to one another" than in his day, and that it is the tendency toward nonobjectivity (and "spirituality") that has brought them together.[4] He argues too for something like Adorno's immanence: one art borrowing methods from another "can only be successful and victorious if not merely the externals, but the principles are learned." One art must learn how another "tackles its own materials and, having learned this, use in principle the materials peculiar to itself in a similar way, i.e., according to the principle that belongs to itself alone" (p. 154).

In this chapter I will examine how certain creative artists in the Austro-German sphere in the early modernist period from about 1885 to 1915 strove toward convergence. The goal was reached—perhaps only *could* be reached—with the emergence around 1910 of abstract or nonobjective art, which was in itself strongly influenced by ideas of music. The phenomenon of symbolism, adumbrated briefly in the last chapter as a successor to naturalism, forms a key intermediary step in the move toward abstraction. It too is allied with musical thought.

My investigation is framed by consideration of two remarkable artist-musician pairs: Max Klinger and Johannes Brahms, and Kandinsky and Schoenberg. Klinger sought to bridge the gap between art and music with his cycle of engravings entitled *Brahms-Phantasie* (Brahms Fantasy), created in 1888–94 out of his experience of Brahms's music. The cycle, which is essentially symbolist in orientation, uses images that have strong musical associations; it also links visual narrative with musical notation. Kandinsky's most compelling moment of convergence comes with his painting *Impression III (Concert)* of 1911, which was stimulated by a concert of Schoenberg's music.

In this chapter I do not discuss Schoenberg's own paintings, which might be another logical source for investigating convergence. As is well known, Schoenberg painted actively in the years around 1910. His visual works were admired by Kandinsky, who included four of them in the first *Blaue Reiter* (Blue Rider) show in December 1911. Schoenberg's paintings have been recently (and at long last) been given important critical treatment by art historians, including Thomas Zaunschirm and Esther da Costa Meyer.[5] Yet Schoenberg always considered himself an "amateur" in painting, despite his considerable "ability."[6] Therefore I may be justified in focusing in the present study on the areas of endeavor where Schoenberg and Kandinsky were fully "professional."

THE TOTAL ARTWORK

In his essay, as we have seen, Adorno denigrates late-nineteenth century attempts at the total artwork as mere "dreams" of convergence, although he gives no names or specific works.[7] The concept of the total artwork is at once powerful and vague. The term itself was coined by Richard Wagner, in his 1849 essay "Artwork of the Future," to characterize the kind of modern artwork that he hoped would unite the various arts that had fallen asunder since their original state of togetherness in the ancient world.[8] But Wagner did not invent the concept. As Adorno implies, the idea of the total artwork had long been closely linked with utopian visions. A large and widely noted art exhibit of 1983, entitled "Der Hang zum Gesamtkunstwerk" (The Tendency toward the Total Artwork), was subtitled "Europäische Utopien seit 1800" (European Utopias since 1800).[9] In the catalog, there are, in addition to introductory essays on various intellectual, cultural, and artistic manifestations of the "tendency," fifty individual segments on philosophers, painters, composers, architects, poets, filmmakers, and the like. A more recent collection of writings, *Gesamtkunstwerk: Zwischen Synästhesie und Mythos* (Total Artwork: Between Synaesthesia and Myth), includes, in addition to the obligatory essays on Wagner, essays on the Third Reich and Madonna as total artworks.[10] Clearly, this is a big-tent concept.

The artists Philipp Otto Runge (1777–1810) and Moritz von Schwind (1804–71) created important precursors of the total artwork within the German sphere in the earlier nineteenth century, especially in their attempts to give musical dimensions to their paintings. Runge had a very holistic view in which "an artwork requires the whole person, and art all of humanity. . . . One should view one's own life like a work of art." He set out a theory in which there are ten requirements for an artwork, including "our perception of God," "our feelings about ourselves in connection with the whole," and "religion and art."[11] Runge was interested in realizing the musicality of the visual arts. He wrote of some of his works as having "movements" and as being in the form of a fugue. He reported that he had in mind a symphony when in 1803 he began to create his renowned cycle of the *Vier Zeiten* (Four Times, Hamburger Kunsthalle), engravings and paintings that represented the four times of the day. Tieck saw this cycle as reflecting a continuity of mathematics, music, and colors.[12]

Schwind's painting *Eine Symphonie* (A Symphony, 1852, Neue Pinakothek in Munich) is based, according to the artist himself, on Beethoven's Fantasy for Orchestra, Chorus, and Piano, op. 80.[13] The painting is divided into four panels that Schwind claimed to be "analogous" to the movements of a symphony. The story, as he relates it, begins with a performance of the Fantasy, represented in the lowest panel, in which a solo soprano catches the attention of a young man in the audience. In the next panel (slow movement), he sees her walking in the woods. In the next (scherzo), they meet at a masked ball and (in a cameo insert) mutually declare their love. The uppermost panel (finale) shows the pair setting off on their honeymoon journey.[14]

There is no question that the idea of a total artwork, as well as a utopian framework, influenced early modernists in the German sphere. The program of the artistic movement Jugendstil (to which I return below) manifests a clear "tendency" toward the total artwork. Jugendstil was intended as a complete "style." Life itself was to be a total artwork uniting the various arts, fine and applied, including architecture, painting, book design, typography, textiles, clothing, furniture, and dishware. Underlying Jugendstil and allied phenomena like Art Nouveau in France and Belgium, and the Arts and Crafts movement in England, was, as Peg Weiss has observed, the goal of "the ultimate creation of a socially viable total aesthetic environment."[15]

MAX KLINGER

One of the most important "total" artists of the later nineteenth century in Germany was Max Klinger (1857–1920), the graphic artist, painter, and sculptor perhaps best known today for his powerful statue of Beethoven that formed the centerpiece of the Vienna Secession exhibit of 1902. In his cycles of engravings and etchings, produced mainly between 1880 and 1895, Klinger sought to produce a new kind of artistic synthesis.

Some of Klinger's goals are adumbrated in his short but suggestive treatise *Malerei und Zeichnung* (Painting and Drawing) of 1891, which contains a compelling association between the graphic arts and music. Klinger proposes that the graphic arts offer richer possibilities than painting for unleashing fantasy and "the darker side of life." Painting is too likely to fix images; the graphic arts (which he dubbed *Griffelkunst,* roughly "stylus art") have greater indeterminacy and subjectivity. These qualities, according to Klinger, also bring the graphic arts closer to music and poetry, especially to piano music and lyric verse, where a creator is "free from the strict demands of stage and orchestra" and can give free rein to "his most characteristic joys and sorrows, his most fleeting and profound feelings." Elsewhere in his book, Klinger calls for a "Gesamtwirken aller bildenden

Künste" (total effect of all the visual arts) in a way that would parallel Wagner's total artwork.[16]

Klinger's graphic cycles show an extraordinary commitment to the medium and a command of engraving techniques that Kirk Varnedoe and Elizabeth Streicher have characterized as "virtuoso."[17] Klinger's first major cycle, *Der Handschuh* (The Glove) of 1881, presents a series of images that move from the world of everyday bourgeois life (a glove found in a Berlin skating rink) into bizarre fantasies of fetishism and sexual obsession that seem to anticipate the theories of Freud and Krafft-Ebing.[18] Klinger's images also partake fully of symbolist principles and anticipate surrealism by several decades. (Klinger was one of the heroes of Giorgio De Chirico.)

Musical analogies run deep in Klinger's graphic work. His cycles have opus numbers; they are described in their titles as being "composed"; and their component parts are often names adopted from musical character pieces like "Capriccio," "Intermezzo," and "Fantasy." Klinger's Opus I and IV are groups of engravings inspired by the piano music of Robert Schumann.[19] (Klinger was an accomplished pianist, and kept a grand piano in his studio.) Above all, Klinger adored the music of Brahms, and already as a twenty-year-old (in 1877) inscribed and sent to the older composer a printed collection of poetry illustrated with his engravings. Two years later Klinger hoped to dedicate his Opus I to Brahms, but his publisher refused to include the dedication, apparently on grounds of cost. In 1880 Klinger succeeded in publishing his graphic cycle *Amor und Psyche,* Opus V, with a dedication to Brahms. Several years later Klinger asked Brahms's publisher Simrock if he might prepare title pages for the first editions of Brahms's song collections, opp. 96 and 97. These appeared with Klinger's artwork in 1886. Klinger also sketched title pages (ultimately never used) for several other works, including the First Cello Sonata, op. 38, and four-hand arrangements of orchestral works.[20]

Brahms, who admired the work of Klinger and was genuinely flattered by the artist's numerous tributes, wrote Klinger complimenting him on his "rich invention, full of fantasy, which is at once of such splendid seriousness and such profound meaning, and at the same time invites further thought and reflection."[21] Brahms is clearly picking up on, and responding positively to, the symbolist aspects of Klinger's works. But he expressed some discontent over an illustration Klinger had prepared for the song *Feldeinsamkeit* (op. 86, no. 2), which appeared on the cover of an entirely different collection of Lieder, op. 96, where it was (for Brahms) "too puzzling and incomprehensible."[22]

Klinger was mortified by Brahms's relatively mild criticism of the *Feldeinsamkeit* illustration and sought to make amends—and especially to show the composer what Brahms's music really meant to him—in his cycle *Brahms-Phantasie* (Brahms Fantasy), Opus XII, on which he began to work actively in 1888. Klinger had the intention of presenting the work to Brahms on the latter's sixtieth birthday (May 7, 1893) but missed the deadline. He sent proofs to Brahms in December of that year, and Brahms received the completed work on New Year's Day 1894.

The *Brahms Fantasy* is perhaps the closest Klinger, or any Austro-German artist of his period, came to creating a convergent total artwork that incorporates music. The *Brahms Fantasy* is subtitled by Klinger "Einundvierzig Stiche, Radierungen und Steinzeichnungen zu Compositionen von Johannes Brahms" (Forty-one Engravings, Etchings, and Lithographs on Compositions of Johannes Brahms). It presents the musical scores of five Brahms Lieder (*Alte Liebe,* op. 72, no. 1; *Sehnsucht,* op. 49, no. 3; *Am Sonntag Morgen,* op. 49, no. 1; *Feldeinsamkeit,* op. 86, no. 2; and *Kein Haus, Keine Heimat,* op. 94, no. 5) and a piano-vocal reduction of his *Schicksalslied,* op. 54. The selection and ordering of the music is entirely Klinger's. Preceding and appearing alongside the music are different kinds of images: border decorations, larger pictures on the same page, and full-size independent graphic works.

The *Brahms Fantasy* has been recognized as a highpoint of Klinger's engraved work. Streicher has suggested it is "technically the most complex and varied," making use of the broadest range of media and techniques, including lithography, etching, engraving, mezzotint, and aquatint. Klinger's vision of the total artwork, as reflected in the *Brahms Fantasy,* is in some sense paradoxical, as Thomas Nelson has pointed out, since the cycle is at once "monumental" and yet intended "for quiet contemplation in the privacy of the parlour."[23] Klinger had only five copies of the deluxe first edition printed, and 150 copies of the second.

Klinger's cycle represents more than mere analogy or parallelism with music. In a letter to Brahms, with which he sent some proof pages of the *Brahms Fantasy* in December 1893, Klinger explained his basic goal: "Above all, I had no thought of making 'illustrations' with these things. Rather, I wanted to move outward from the judgments into which we are led—led blindly—by poetry and above all music; I wanted to cast a glance over the range of feeling, and from there look around, continue, connect, or complete."[24]

The gist of Klinger's remarks is that he is seeking through his artwork to extend the range of reactions which poetry and music can evoke in us but of which we may not be aware because we are normally led to them "blindly." Klinger goes on to tell Brahms, in the next sentence, that in the *Brahms Fantasy* he sought to capture the *Stimmungsgehalte,* or mood content, that is present in Brahms's works but remains unexpressed.[25]

Brahms was delighted with the *Brahms Fantasy,* and he responded to Klinger in much the same terms, implying that Klinger's art realized or expressed things more clearly than was possible with music alone. Brahms wrote in December 1893:

> Perhaps it has not occurred to you to imagine what I must feel when looking at your images. I see the music, together with the nice words—and then your splendid engravings carry me away unawares. Beholding them, it is as if the music resounds farther into the infinite and everything expresses what I wanted to say more clearly than would be possible in music, and yet still in a manner full of mystery and foreboding. Sometimes I am inclined to envy you, that you can have such clarity with your pen; at other times I am glad that I don't need to do it. But finally I must conclude that all art is the same and speaks the same language.[26]

This kind of aesthetic credo is rare for Brahms, who was notoriously reticent about communicating on such matters. He seems to concur with Klinger's idea of how one artwork can provide an *Ergänzung,* a completion or extension, of another.

The nature of the overall structure of the *Brahms Fantasy* has been much debated. For many commentators, the cycle is fundamentally in two parts, each oriented around Brahms's music—five songs in the first part, and the piano-vocal score of the *Schicksalslied* in the second. In this scheme, the image *Accorde* is said to open the first part, *Evocation* the second.[27] In fact, *Evocation* is followed directly not by the *Schicksalslied,* but by a minicycle of six full pages devoted to images of the Prometheus legend. Thus, a three-part division is also plausible, in which the Brahms musical units flank the central Prometheus cycle. Yet following the *Schicksalslied* score is another Prometheus image, *Der befreite Prometheus* (Prometheus Unbound), whose placement at the end of the *Brahms Fantasy* complicates any simple two- or three-part plan.[28] Perhaps the most reasonable position to take is that there is no single unifying perspective on the cycle: the overall design of the *Brahms Fantasy* is intentionally multifarious and "messy."

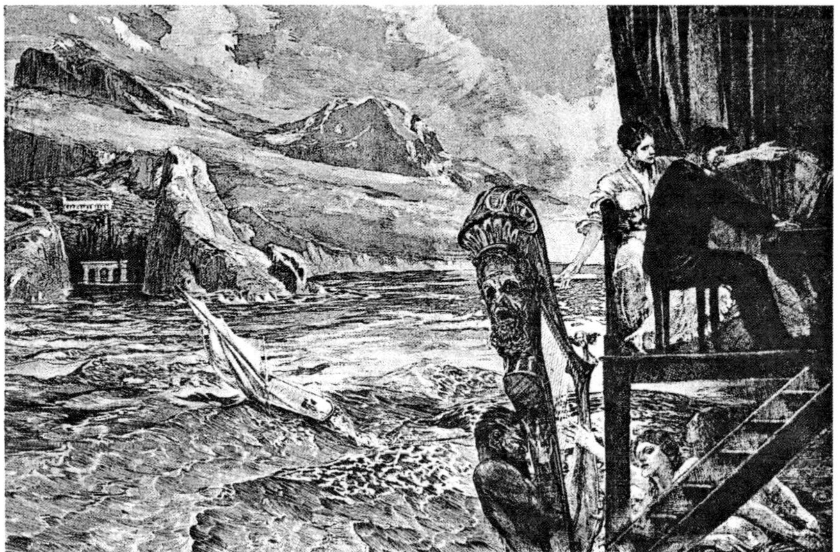

Figure 1. Max Klinger, *Accorde* (Chords), from *Brahms Fantasy.* Courtesy of Avery Architectural and Fine Arts Library, Columbia University in the City of New York.

The full-page images *Accorde* and *Evocation* (figures 1 and 2) may be said to frame the Brahms song cycle that Klinger assembles between them. Both celebrate the power of music to conjure up imaginary worlds. Nelson has further interpreted these two engravings as a statement within what he calls the "cultural politics of absolute music," specifically as an "allegorical ode" to liberal bourgeois values of the German idealist tradition and a pure, abstract music embodied in the works of Beethoven and Brahms. These values, shared by Klinger and Brahms, were under siege in the later nineteenth century by Wagnerism and right-wing politics.[29]

Jan Brachmann, in a very thoughtful monograph, takes a more sociological perspective, arguing that the *Brahms Fantasy* is essentially Klinger's way of entering into a "dialogue" with the works of Brahms. It is a dialogue that as a somewhat solitary bourgeois artist (like Brahms), Klinger preferred to a direct contact with the composer himself.[30] Brachmann points out that both Klinger and Brahms seem to view art in terms of communication and of language. As we have seen, Klinger writes of attempting to capture moods that remain "unexpressed" in music alone, and Brahms notes that "all art speaks the same language." Both Nelson's and Brachmann's perspectives help

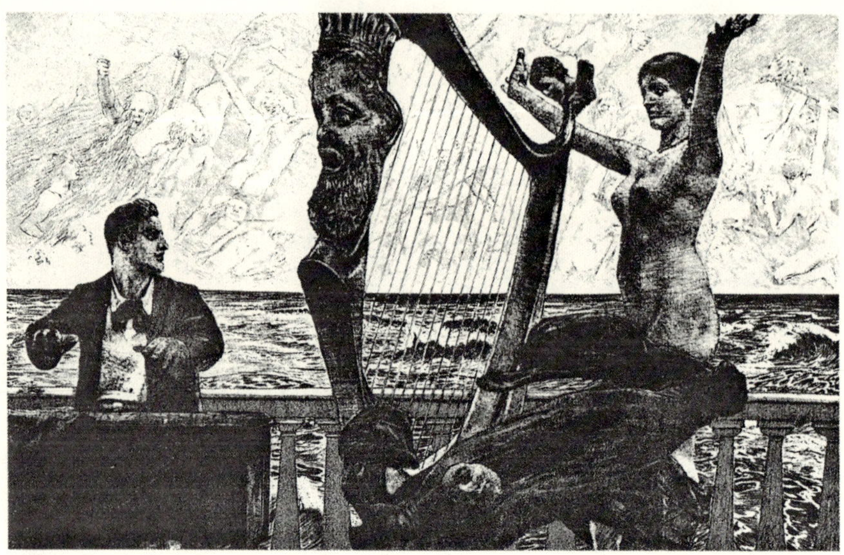

Figure 2. Max Klinger, *Evocation,* from *Brahms Fantasy.* Courtesy of Avery Architectural and Fine Arts Library, Columbia University in the City of New York.

confirm Klinger's *Brahms Fantasy* as a work of convergence, or at least near-convergence.[31]

It seems no coincidence that in *Accorde,* the first image of the *Brahms Fantasy,* it is piano music that releases its power, the very kind of music that Klinger, in his *Malerei und Zeichnung,* saw as the most open to fantasy and unfettered emotions. The pianist conjures a world of moody landscapes and stormy seas inhabited by nereids and tritons. These "chords" emanate directly from the bourgeois parlor so familiar to both Brahms and Klinger. As many commentators have pointed out, the pianist is a self-portrait of Klinger, who seems thereby to be making still more explicit the connection between a graphic artist and a musician, especially a composer for piano.

Sitting beside the pianist is a woman dressed in white who, with her arms pointing in opposite directions, seems to act as the link between his playing and the worlds it evokes. Although the image is followed in the *Brahms Fantasy* by a song cycle, the woman appears to be more muse than singer. The piano, the pianist, and his companion have their counterparts in the fantasy world: the harp, which is played by a nereid and being grasped intensely by a triton. The fantasy world brings a gender reversal: the player is now female, the listener male.

The fantastic images in *Accorde* allude to the world of Böcklin, to whom Klinger had dedicated the graphic cycle *Eine Liebe* (A Love) of 1887. The island to which the boat is sailing is a visual reference to Böcklin's most famous painting, *Toteninsel* (Isle of the Dead, 1880).[32] The triton and nereids resemble those in some of Böcklin's well-known canvases, like *Triton und Nereide* (Tritons and Nereids, 1875) or *Im Spiel der Wellen* (At Play in the Waves, 1883).[33] However, there is a significant difference: unlike in Böcklin, they are not involved in some kind of erotic play, but are focused on or around musical expression.

In the image *Evocation,* which appears in the *Brahms Fantasy* after the end of the group of Brahms songs, Klinger radically changes perspective or viewpoint to bring together the two worlds that were linked but separate in *Accorde.* In *Accorde* we looked at the pianist and his instrument in profile; the bourgeois and fantasy worlds are divided, respectively, into the right and left portions of the image. Now, in *Evocation,* the viewer seems to be on the pianist's platform, looking at him head-on. The harp-playing nereid and her instrument are on the platform beside the pianist, roughly in the spot occupied in *Accorde* by his companion, who has now disappeared from our view. In the background, etched faintly on the sky (and not visible in most reproductions), are many writhing bodies engaged in a powerful struggle. This is most often interpreted as the battle of the Titans, and it foreshadows the engravings in the next part of the cycle. The pianist, who in *Accorde* was looking straight ahead earnestly, his eyes fixed on the music, now looks up, seemingly astonished at his power to have called forth the nereid and her harp (and perhaps the battling Titans).

The song cycle that Klinger assembles in the first part of the *Brahms Fantasy* presents something of a trajectory from the wistful thinking on "old love" to a bitter tone of resentment. Klinger himself told Brahms in December 1893 that he wished he had labeled the entire cycle *Alte Liebe,* the actual title of the first song, but that he realized only too late how appropriate this name would be. Klinger explained how his basic idea for this section of the *Brahms Fantasy* was to capture something of how a "tender, too tender, reflection on what is past and what is lost" is overcome "through powerful, energetic pulling together of oneself." The process is complete, he implies, in the song *Kein Haus, keine Heimat* (No House, No Home), the final one in Klinger's group, which, the artist says, he has left "standing alone," a comment I take to refer to his decision to include that song without any visual component.[34] This is the only page in the entire *Brahms Fantasy* that contains musical notation but no engraving.

Klinger clearly wanted a sense of continuity in the five Brahms songs. Although the titles, poets, and opus numbers of the individual songs are given in the table of contents, they are omitted in the actual body of the *Brahms Fantasy.* Yet the initial tempo-mood markings for each song are hand-lettered in large characters. These may almost be said to serve as substitute titles; and their prominence lends credence to Klinger's claim, in his letter to Brahms, about wanting to capture the "mood content" of the songs. From the avoidance of printed titles and the use of hand-lettered tempo indications, it is clear that Klinger viewed the musical scores as a fundamental part of the overall design of the *Brahms Fantasy.* The integration of score and image is probably unique in the history of art or music up to this time. There is a fundamental difference between Klinger's *Brahms Fantasy* and earlier printed scores with decorative title pages or borders. Klinger's is really a separate work of art in which musical notation is but one component.

There is one page of the *Brahms Fantasy,* the third and final page of the first song *Alte Liebe,* that makes clear how Klinger treats the musical notation as a visual element and how he is able to integrate it with the artwork (figure 3). The right-hand part of the page has a two-tone lithograph of a tower around which a flock of swallows is flying off into the distance. The distinctive aspect of the image is how the end of the swallows' formation lies outside the frame of the lithograph: the birds are represented as flying literally into the image from a measure of the Brahms song. This is the only place in the *Brahms Fantasy* where such a direct physical connection is made between music and visual image. The birds themselves would have been suggested to Klinger by the very first image of the Candidus poem: "Es kehrt die dunkle Schwalbe aus fernem Land zurück" (The dark swallow is returning from a distant land). But Klinger's birds appear near the end of the song, on a different page, which sets the last line of the poem, "ein alter Traum erfasst mich und führt mich seine, seine Bahn" (an old dream grips me and takes me along its path). What seems to have inspired Klinger here, as Brachmann points out, is the *visual* aspect of the downward arpeggiated quarter notes in the piano part and of the more extended arpeggio in the vocal part. The swallows appear to flow directly out of the slur over the piano arpeggio.[35] Klinger's engraving is not pseudomorphosis in Adorno's sense: this is not art attempting to be musical (or vice versa). Rather, in what seems to me a small but stunning moment of convergence, the artist has actually recreated in visual terms—with the "immanent" materials of his art—an essential aspect of the music.

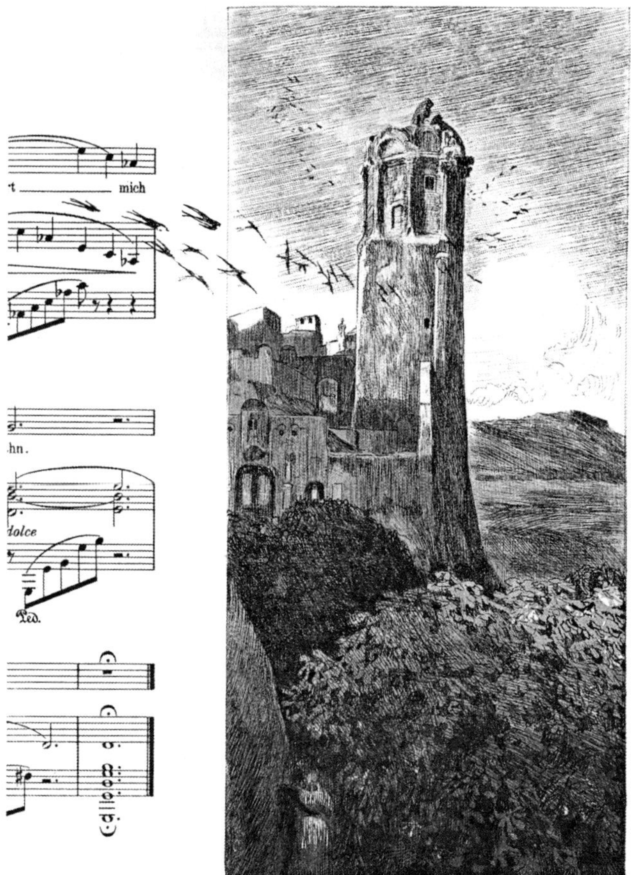

Figure 3. Max Klinger, *Turm* (Tower), from *Brahms Fantasy.* Typ 820.94.4895 P, Department of Printing and Graphic Arts, Houghton Library, Harvard College Library.

Klinger may have been the first artist, at least in the early modern period, to use musical notation as a visual device. In his wake came some of the important Jugendstil periodicals like *Pan* and *Jugend* itself, which sometimes incorporated music as part of the total artistic effect being sought. One important example that might well owe its origins to Klinger's practice is the song by Richard Strauss *Wir beide wollen springen* (We Tend to Spring Apart; WoO 90, TrV 175), which he contributed specially to the periodical *Jugend* in 1896.[36] The elegantly flowing aspect of Strauss's notation, set into the frame of a drawing by Julius Dietz, was clearly understood (at least by the composer and the editors) as a musical evocation of the Jugendstil aesthetic of the graceful line. Klinger's engravings may also have inspired Max Slevogt's forty-seven drawings in the margins of facsimile pages from the manuscript of Mozart's *Magic Flute,* published in 1920.[37] Though Slevogt interweaves notation and image attractively, his drawings differ from Klinger's in being actual illustrations of scenes from Mozart's opera. The relation of Klinger's engravings to Brahms's music is far more abstract and symbolic.

After *Evocation,* the *Brahms Fantasy* moves out of the world of Lieder and the bourgeois parlor, into the world of classical myth, with six graphic representations of the Prometheus story. These are followed by the text of Hölderlin's "Hyperions Schicksalslied" (Hyperion's Song of Destiny), which is illustrated with an image of Homer; the piano-vocal score of *Schicksalslied;* and a final image of Prometheus's being liberated. The thematic connections between the Prometheus story and Hölderlin's poem are obvious enough, though it took an artist like Klinger to realize them so suggestively. Hölderlin's poem, which is sung by the eponymous character in his novel *Hyperion,* points up with bitterness the contrast between the blissful, untroubled life of the gods on high and the suffering, tormented existence of human beings on earth. It was awareness of just this miserable existence that led Prometheus to steal fire from the gods and bring it to mankind. One might say that an empathetic Prometheus sought to act on the feelings expressed in the *Schickalslied* poem.

Klinger's *Brahms Fantasy* includes the entire piano-vocal score of Brahms's *Schicksalslied,* which extends over fourteen pages, most of which are decorated not with full illustrations but with narrow border images. As has often been noted, Brahms's setting of the Hölderlin seems to reverse or revise the poem's pessimistic ending, in which an oppressed humanity is slipping "ins Ungewisse hinab," downward into oblivion. Brahms sets the final stanza in a dark turbulent C minor, but then concludes the *Schicksalslied* with a long, serene orchestral postlude in C major that returns to the opening material of the work but not the original key of E♭ major. John Daverio has suggested that in overriding Hölderlin's own gloomy ending Brahms conveys what in his theoretical writings Hölderlin called the "Wechsel der Töne," an alternation of poetic tones or styles. For Daverio, Brahms's postlude appropriately "imparts an open-ended, spiral shape to the whole."[38]

The margin illustration that Klinger provides for the final page of Brahms's score would not seem to capture that optimistic spirit. It shows what an authoritative catalog of 1909 described as "the farmer whose seed sows disaster" (Der Bauer dessen Saat in Unheil aufgeht) (figure 4).[39] The imagery is complex, to say the least. In the middleground the farmer trudges away from us, bending wearily over his plough. Behind him, in the foreground of the engraving, swords and sabers sprout from the ground he has sown, suggesting, as one early commentator put it, that "a brief peace is followed by murderous war."[40] To the left in the middle- and background, a farmhouse is enveloped in a dark rainstorm. Above, in the sky, appears a radiant equilateral triangle—normally a symbol of benign divine power and of prosperity within the Judeo-Christian tradition (as in the iconography of the Freemasons and on our dollar bills).[41] Klinger's triangle is also a measuring tool; in the middle hangs a plumb line, which is being yanked off by a hand reaching in from the right. In both the 1909 catalog and an earlier article about the *Brahms Fantasy* from 1895, the hand is described plausibly as the hand of Fate; it "tears away the plumb and thus destroys every norm."[42]

This illustration seems far more suited to Hölderlin's ending than to Brahms's. But Klinger wanted to represent both endings, and he does so by following the marginal engraving with a full-page one, *Der befreite Prometheus*, which serves as the final image in the *Brahms Fantasy* (figure 5). Klinger imported this image into the *Brahms Fantasy;* it dates from 1885 and was apparently the very first one sketched for what became the Brahms cycle.[43] In it we see Prometheus, head in his hands, having been freed by Hercules, who stands solemnly beside him with the bow used to kill the eagle that had tormented him. From below, ocean nymphs look on sympathetically and expectantly. Klinger captures the moment of Prometheus's liberation not with triumph or jubilation, but with that all-too-human mixture of disbelief and relief—just the kind of reaction one might expect someone to have at such a moment. What Klinger seems to suggest is that the freeing of Prometheus, although it in one sense ends the story, will not return Prometheus to an original state. There is no going back. Mankind will still have its gift of fire, and Prometheus, although free, can never return to a condition of innocence. The future may look bright, but it is not the same as the past.

Klinger's *Der befreite Prometheus* may be said to be the real rendering of the conclusion to Brahms's *Schicksalslied.* As suggested above, Brahms's orchestral postlude returns to the opening material of the work, but not to the original key: the piece ends in C major, not the initial E♭. The scoring

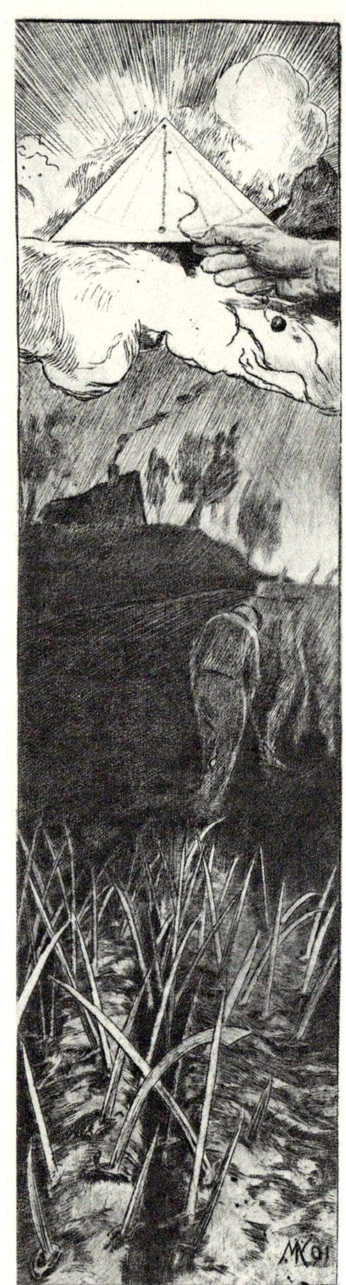

Figure 4. Max Klinger, *Der Bauer dessen Saat in Unheil aufgeht* (The Farmer Whose Seed Sows Disaster), from *Brahms Fantasy.* Typ 820.94.4895 P, Department of Printing and Graphic Arts, Houghton Library, Harvard College Library.

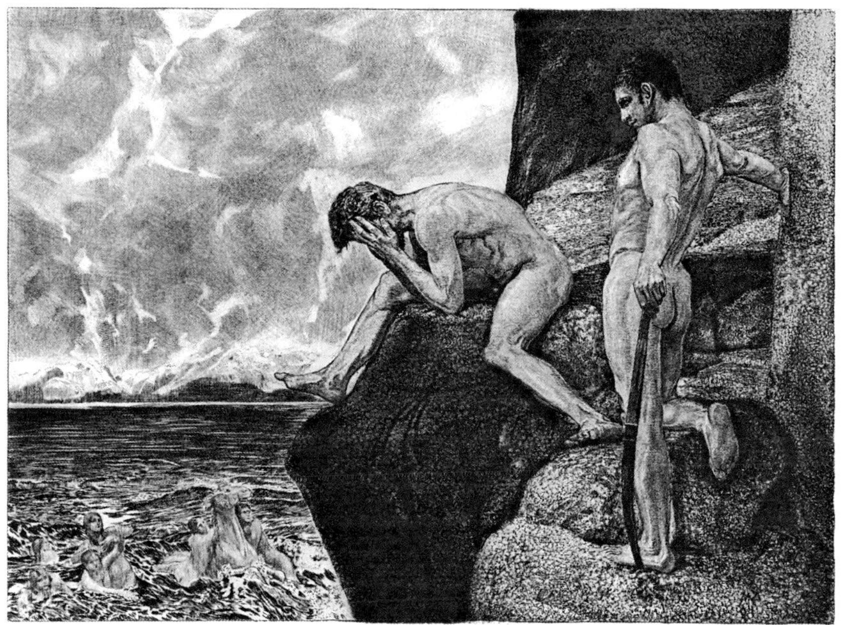

Figure 5. Max Klinger, *Der befreite Prometheus* (Prometheus Unbound), from *Brahms Fantasy.* Typ 820.94.4895 P, Department of Printing and Graphic Arts, Houghton Library, Harvard College Library.

of the main theme is also different. As Daverio points out, although Brahms takes over his opening twenty-nine measures intact, the scoring is altered. In the postlude, the texture is less transparent than at the opening; the strings have more complex figuration, and the higher woodwinds are featured more prominently.[44] These changes are even apparent in the piano-vocal score used by Klinger in the *Brahms Fantasy.* The import of Klinger's freed Prometheus is similar to that of Brahms's postlude: for Brahms as for Klinger there is no simple return. Time, experience, life move forward. Resolution does not imply recapitulation.

Brachmann has proposed a bolder interpretation of the *Der befreite Prometheus* image and its relationship to the *Schicksalslied.* He points out that Klinger may have been aware of Nietzsche's interpretation of the freeing of Prometheus as adumbrated in *The Birth of Tragedy,* where the liberator of Prometheus is the "Hercules-like power of music" that rescues tragedy. For the Nietzsche of 1872, of course, it was Wagner's music that would achieve the rescue. Brachmann suggests that Klinger is asserting Brahms as the one who will fulfill that role. He also points out that in *Der befreite Prometheus* the figure of Prometheus, though his hands hide his face, appears to be a self-portrait. It is a logical notion that Klinger might round out the cycle with his own image, just as he began it with the pianist in *Accorde* and articulated its midpoint with *Evocation.* It is striking that the other depictions of Prometheus in the *Brahms Fantasy* are distinctly unlike Klinger's own physiognomy: in *Raub des Lichtes* (Theft of Light) and *Entführung der Prometheus* (Abduction of Prometheus), Prometheus seems to be an older man with longer hair and a long beard. But in *Der befreite Prometheus* the similarity to Klinger is much more obvious.

The ending of Brahms's *Schicksalslied* involves only the orchestra; the chorus remains silent in the postlude—a gesture Brachmann takes to represent an assertion of the primacy of "absolute" music.[45] Working from that premise, together with the likeness of Klinger and the possible Nietzsche connection, Brachmann suggests that what Klinger is representing in this final engraving is the role that music can play in liberating the visual arts. Even more, Brachmann sees the image as reflecting the relationship between Klinger and Brahms as men and artists. Hercules might be a representation—not literal, of course—of Brahms himself. *Der befreite Prometheus* is for Brachmann an image of friendship, "which seeks to unite pathos and intimacy, which reveals itself as a symbol for that great longing . . . to finally find a partner with whose help he [Klinger] could break out of his communicative isolation as artist, another artist with whom he aspired through artistic dialogue to satisfy himself about the meaning of his own artistic activity."[46]

SYMBOLISM, ABSTRACTION, JUGENDSTIL

Klinger was not alone among German symbolists in manifesting a strong relationship to music. One of the key influences on Klinger, as already suggested above, and in some ways the originator of German symbolism, was Arnold Böcklin (1827–1901), whom the art historian Max Schneider dubbed, with a Nietzschean innuendo, "a painter from the spirit of music."[47] Böcklin had a deep personal interest in music; he composed a bit, and like Klinger kept an instrument (in this case a harmonium) in his studio. His two most famous canvases involving music are one of a violin-playing hermit (*Der Einsiedler,* 1884) and his self-portrait with Death playing the fiddle (*Selbstbildnis mit fiedelndem Tod,* 1872). There are also

Arcadian images like the flute-playing Pan (*Idyll,* 1875) or the harp-playing Flora (in *Flora, die Blumen weckend* [Flora Awakening the Flowers], 1876).[48]

Schneider argues that Böcklin "created from the very source of music, and in that his painting is unique in the art of the nineteenth century."[49] This may be an exaggeration. Schneider does not explain what that "very source" would be and how it makes Böcklin "unique." But there is no question that Böcklin in turn stimulated many composers. His paintings, especially *Toteninsel,* which has no explicit musical imagery, inspired more musical works around 1900 than those of any other German modernist artist. These compositions include Reger's *Four Tone Poems after Böcklin,* op. 128 (1913), and Rachmaninoff's tone poem *Isle of the Dead,* op. 29 (1909).[50] In act 3, scene 9, of Schreker's *Der ferne Klang* (premiered 1915), the wall of Fritz's room—the room where he has presumably created his opera—is decorated with a "clearly visible" copy of Böcklin's painting of the hermit.

Beside Klinger and Böcklin, the leading symbolists in Germany, Austria, and Switzerland during the later nineteenth and early twentieth centuries include Hans Thoma (1839–1924) and Ferdinand Hodler (1853–1918). However different in style and subject matter, all of these artists share the desire to "spirit us into the equivocal world of the indeterminate," which is how the French painter Odilon Redon concisely identified the symbolist principle.[51] Or, as expressed by the poet and writer Jean Moréas, who gave symbolism its name and something of a definitive profile in 1886: "The essential trait of symbolist art consists in never conceptually fixing or directly expressing an idea. And this is why the images of nature, the acts of men, all concrete appearances in this art, must not themselves be made visible, but instead should be symbolized through sensitively perceptible traces, through secret affinities with the original ideas."[52] In most symbolist art, objects, landscapes, and figures are indeed "visible" and identifiable but are made to resonate beyond their immediate context, to suggest meanings that lie beyond what is present.

Music's ineffability, its incorporeality, and its ability nonetheless to communicate directly appealed to the symbolists, as it had to many artists and thinkers since the late eighteenth century. Within France—not the primary subject of our investigation here—the music of Wagner was a direct inspiration for many symbolist writers, who sought to imitate closely in prose certain qualities of his scores.[53] Music may be said to have reinforced the tendency of symbolism toward abstraction. Stripped of their apparent or everyday meaning, objects lose their object-relatedness. In this sense symbolism was an important precursor to the nonobjectivity that entered the visual arts in the years around 1910 in the work of Kandinsky, Malevich, Mondrian, and some other painters. Indeed, one might say that these figures were themselves symbolists. Ingrid Ehrhardt has pointed out that symbolism corresponds less to a specific group of artists than to a widespread "attitude that involved a rejection both of the academic naturalism of dominant salon art and of Impressionism, both of which focused primarily on representing the visible world."[54] Understood in this way, the symbolist tent is indeed a large and inclusive one in the years around 1900.

The symbolist aesthetic must also be seen as part of a still broader impulse toward abstraction that was shared with the decorative or applied arts at this time. Central to the this development was the way in which the view of ornament changed across the later nineteenth century in the Austro-German sphere. This process has been well outlined by David Morgan, who shows that beginning with Kant, and continuing through Herbart, Vischer, Lipps, Riegl, and Worringer, the ornamental or decorative in art came to be prized as something independent from, and even prior to, naturalistic representation. The result was, Morgan says, a "formalist aesthetics which disregarded imitation as the basis of art."[55] Writing in the 1890s, Lipps and Riegl—the one an aesthetician and psychologist, the other an art historian—argued that techniques of representation could be modified by stylization, which for Lipps meant "to make forms of reality detached from their concrete contexts in reality."[56] Riegl wrote famously of a "will to art" *(Kunstwollen)* that in a number of cultures (including late Roman, the subject of his main monograph) led to stylized ornament.[57] Worringer's influential treatise *Abstraction and Empathy* of 1908 built upon both Lipps and Riegl to argue that the urge toward abstraction is a "primal artistic impulse" that "has nothing to do with the rendering of nature." Abstraction is "the consummate expression . . . of emancipation from all the contingency and temporality of the world-picture."[58]

As Morgan points out, the German discourse surrounding ornament and abstraction remained on the more theoretical level of aesthetics and history through much of the nineteenth century. But in the years around 1900, some of the writers, artists, and architects involved with the movement known as Jugendstil sought to put these ideas into the practice of a genuine artistic program. In turn, as Peg Weiss and Werner Hofmann have shown, modernists like Kandinsky and Klee were strongly influenced by Jugendstil in their own evolution toward abstract or nonobjective art.[59] Hofmann goes further in suggesting that Jugendstil is really at the root of modernist abstraction.

Jugendstil, which took its name from the Munich periodical *Jugend,* was one of the most significant movements in the arts in the years around 1900.[60] Historians of art and design seem to agree on at least three elements basic to Jugendstil: the primacy of the dynamic, flowing line, flatness or two-dimensionality (Jugendstil has been called a *Flächenkunst,* or surface art), and the profuseness of ornament. All these features are neatly embodied in a drawing by Thomas Theodor Heine (1867–1948) of 1900 called *Serpentinentänzerin* (Serpentine Dancer; figure 6), in which the ostensible subject matter, the dancer Loie Fuller, is virtually dissolved into the motion created by the linearity of her dress and the swirling incense. This drawing is a good example of how the representational elements can recede through the impulse of abstraction, of "pure" design. A painting by the Munich painter (and teacher of Kandinsky) Franz Stuck, *Tänzerinnen* (Dancers) of 1896, and a wall relief based on it (1897–98), already hint at Heine's techniques. The two dancers are presented against a flat background—this is especially clear in the relief version—and everything is in linear motion, as their diaphanous dresses billow in the air.[61]

Another celebrated example of Jugendstil is the *Cyclamen* tapestry created by the Munich artist Hermann Obrist (1862–1927) in about 1895, in which line and ornament are largely liberated from their representational obligations.[62] As Schmutzler has remarked, the tapestry is "on the borderline dividing the symbol and the ornament, between abstract dynamism and the representation of a distinctive organism."[63] This aspect of Obrist's tapestry was realized as early as 1895 by the critic Georg Fuchs, who wrote in the journal *Pan,* "These embroideries do not intend to 'mean' anything, to say anything." He went on to describe the dynamic motion of the image in terms that have nothing to do with cyclamens: "This racing movement seems like the abrupt, powerful convolution of the lash of a whip. One moment it is a lightning bolt. Another moment it resembles the defiant signature of a great man, a conqueror, an intellect who decrees new laws through new documents."[64] Fuchs's metaphor of the whiplash, or *Peitschenhieb,* proved very persuasive: Obrist's tapestry is known today principally by that name.

Adolf Hölzel (sometimes also spelled Hoelzel; 1853–1934) was another important Munich artist experimenting with organic forms that took on an abstract appearance. Even before 1900, probably at around the same time as Obrist, Hölzel created drawings that bore no resemblance to natural

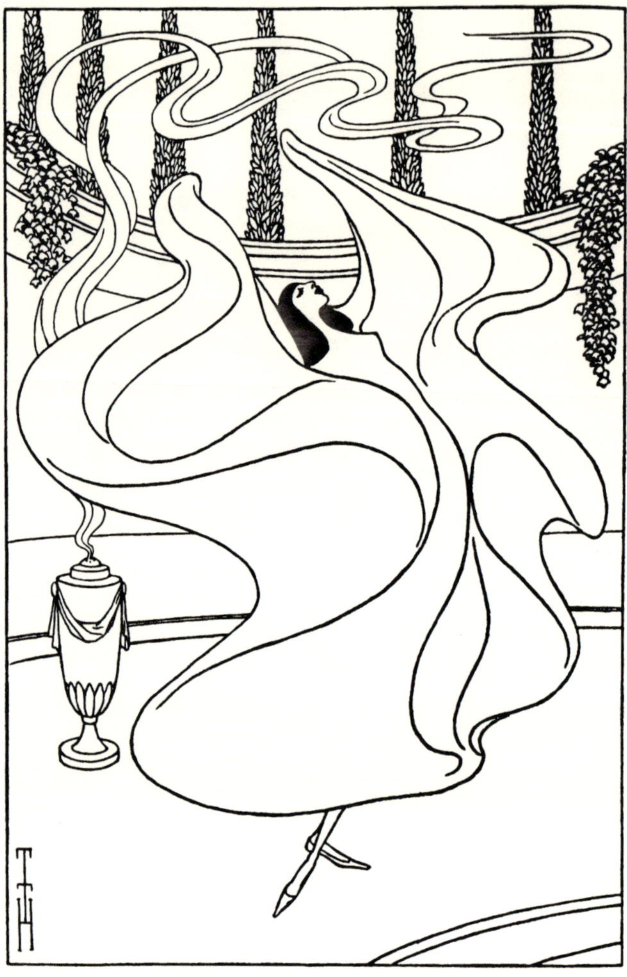

Figure 6. Thomas Theodor Heine, *Serpentinentänzerin* (Serpentine Dancer), 1900.

objects; these were published in 1905 with the title *Abstract Ornaments.*[65] In his own writings at the beginning of the decade, in 1901 and 1904, Hölzel emphasized the role of design and abstraction over that of imitation in the visual arts. Like Riegl and (later) Worringer, he saw in the art of earlier eras a strong urge to abstraction, as manifested in the manipulation of line, color, and form. Titian, for example, is understood by Hölzel as being interested not in a "purely objective" representation, but rather in "a unification of the most simple contrasts and harmonic combinations of object-form, spatial distribution, chiaroscuro, and color movement."[66]

There is a close historical link between the artists and the styles normally characterized as Jugendstil and those classified as symbolist. Indeed, Jugendstil and symbolism might be said to be two sides of the same coin. A painting like Stuck's *Frühling* (Spring, versions from 1902 and 1909) shares certain stylistic elements with Jugendstil, including the subject—a young maiden with flowing hair—and its theme of springtime and renewal.[67] Yet the suggestive voluptuousness of the image, and the mystery of the girl's gaze, which engages the viewer directly, are characteristic of symbolism. In Kandinsky we also see elements of both Jugendstil and symbolism at work. Ornament plays a significant role in some of Kandinsky's canvases of the early 1900s, painted just after his period of study with Stuck, such as *Reitendes Paar* (Riding Couple) and *Buntes Leben* (Colorful Life) of 1906–7.[68] Kandinsky's interest in spirituality played an important role in his transition to nonobjectivity. In his treatise *On the Spiritual in Art* of 1912, colors, forms, and lines have meaning beyond their immediate physical incarnations. Kandinsky's may be said to be in many respects a symbolist agenda.

MUSIC AND JUGENDSTIL

The affinities between music and Jugendstil have been explored in what is by now a large literature. Many critics have sought—with mixed results—to read the linear abstractness of Jugendstil art into music composed around 1900. Hans Hollander finds elements of Jugendstil in works by a suspiciously wide range of composers, including Schoenberg, Strauss, Mahler, Berg, Zemlinsky, Schreker, and—quite remote from the Austro-German milieu—Debussy, Scriabin, Delius, Vaughan Williams, and Holst.[69] Almost any piece with a flowing line, decorative surface, or rich orchestral color is potentially linked to Jugendstil. Richard Hamann and Jost Hermand develop from Jugendstil the notion of "dancelike, linear motion," which they then find in the "dance-and-reel" *(Tanz-und-Taumel)* atmosphere of operettas of the fin de siècle.[70]

For Adorno, and for the present author, the commentaries of Hollander and of Hamann and Hermand would smack of pseudoconvergence. The unsatisfactory nature of this and much other literature on music and Jugendstil stems from the assumption (often unspoken) that such terms as *line, ornament, color,* and *symmetry* are readily transferable to music. In musical commentary these are metaphors that we borrow from the visual arts.

But line in music, by which we usually mean a coherent succession of tones, might not fulfill the same technical or aesthetic function as line in a drawing or painting.

Dahlhaus and Brinkmann have sounded cautionary notes about attempts to link music and Jugendstil. Dahlhaus asserts that no possible categorical analogy or mediation can be found between the primacy of sonority *(Klang)* in music around 1900, as manifested primarily in harmony and orchestration, and the primacy of line in Jugendstil.[71] Brinkmann suggests that musical Jugendstil (if it exists) may be recoverable less in compositional techniques than in the settings in which music was performed and heard. He problematizes the issue by examining the large role that music played in the first exhibition prepared by the Darmstadt artists' colony in 1901. The exhibition was an attempt by prominent architects/designers, including Peter Behrens and Josef Maria Olbrich, to create a total artwork in the form of an integrated living environment. Building and room design, furniture, decorations, clothing—all these were part of the project. The presentations included music by a wide range of composers who, as Brinkmann implies, cannot be meaningfully grouped under Jugendstil: Richard Strauss, Johann Strauss, Wagner, Bizet, Dvořák, and Offenbach, as well as many contemporary figures today forgotten, including Willem de Haan, Ernst Otto Nodnagel (discussed in chapter 2 above as a critic), Arnold Mendelssohn, and the Grand Duke Ernst Ludwig. Their works were performed in a variety of settings, ranging from a small music room, to a larger playhouse, to an outdoor orchestral pavilion.[72] These events, Brinkmann implies, might be as close to a musical Jugendstil as we can get.

In my own work, I have postulated that a musical Jugendstil might be located most persuasively in Austro-German Lieder composed around 1900 to texts that in themselves bear traits of a Jugendstil aesthetic.[73] These include especially songs by Arnold Schoenberg and Alexander Zemlinsky. I will return to this topic below in my discussion of Schoenberg's music set to the poetry of Richard Dehmel and Stefan George. For the moment, however, I suggest that one path around the critical impasse of a musical Jugendstil is to ask not what Jugendstil could do for music (as have writers like Hollander and Hamann and Hermand), but the reverse—what music can or did do for Jugendstil. As we have seen above, ideas about music provided models for symbolist and abstract art. The writings of August Endell, one of the leading architects and architectural thinkers of the years around 1900 in Germany, can help us understand the role that music played in the development of both the theory and practice of Jugendstil.

THE THEORIES OF AUGUST ENDELL

August Endell (1871–1925) studied philosophy, psychology, and mathematics in Munich, but was self-taught as an architect and applied artist. He became best known for his work in Jugendstil design, especially the pioneering Atelier Elvira in Munich (1896–97), and for his book *Die Schönheit der großen Stadt* (The Beauty of the Large City) of 1908. Endell was one of the first German artists to argue against naturalism and realism in the visual arts. In his essay "Um die Schönheit" (On Beauty) of 1896, subtitled "a paraphrase on the Munich art exhibitions of 1896," Endell called directly for what would later be considered abstract art. He emphasized that nature is no "pattern book" for an artist. Art is "not at all nature, but something completely different."[74] Art should be based on a "feeling of pleasure" and on "the pure joy of form and color" (pp. 31, 55).

In his article Endell goes in detail through many of the paintings he saw in Munich in 1896, presumably at the shows of both the older Artist's Society and the newer Secession.[75] He criticizes those canvases that are more purely naturalistic, because "not everything that strikes the eye should be painted" (p. 38). Endell tends to reserve his praise for those artists who move in the direction of what today we would identify as symbolism and impressionism, as well as expressionism. These include Franz Stuck, Lovis Corinth, and Ernst Kirchner, in whose canvases, drawings, or watercolors any realism recedes behind just the kind of color and form for which Endell called. These artists gradually eclipsed in critical and public taste more traditional naturalists like Max Liebermann.

A year later, in 1897, Endell wrote another important essay, "Formenschönheit und dekorative Kunst" (Beauty of Form and Decorative Art), which focused on architecture and decorative art and went much further in the direction of calling for abstraction. Music now becomes a specific model. Endell again stressed the "joy of form" to which artists must aspire. He argued that "we stand at the beginning of not only a new style period, but also of a development of an entirely new art—the art of using forms that mean nothing and represent nothing and recall nothing, forms that stir our souls as deeply and as powerfully as only music is capable of doing with notes."[76] Endell seeks for art to exploit "the power of form on our feelings, a direct, immediate influence, without any mediation" (p. 149). Music, he says, can be enjoyed "without knowing why chords and progressions are in a position to stimulate us so powerfully" (p. 151).

Endell then goes on to provide a demonstration of how in architectural

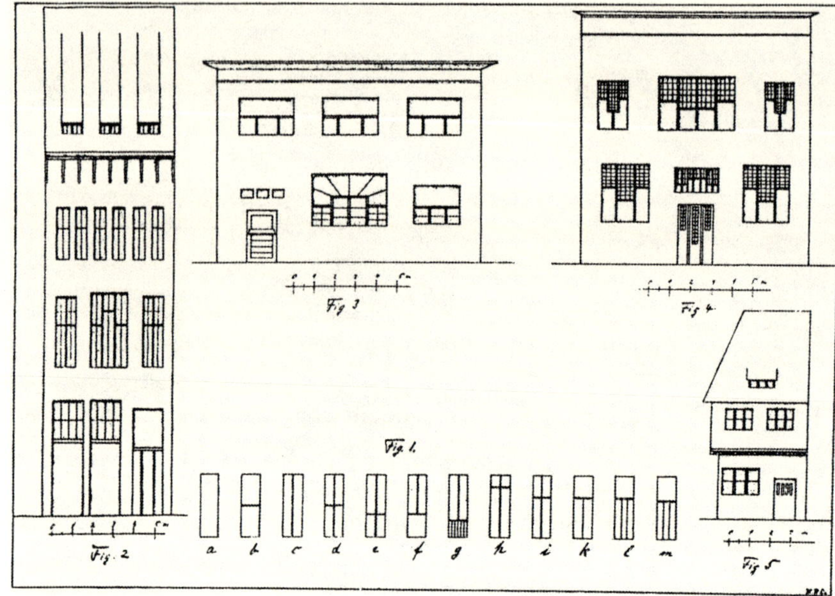

Figure 7. August Endell, Window Forms (1897). Courtesy of Avery Architectural and Fine Arts Library, Columbia University in the City of New York.

design a straight line can have musical effects upon our feelings and perceptions through direction and tempo. He presents a series of rectangular window designs that he analyzes for their tempo and their tension *(Spannung)* (figure 7). When the vertical axis of the window is subdivided by a horizontal line, the tempo becomes slower. The level of tension depends on whether one is viewing the window from top to bottom or bottom to top; the latter creates greater tension.

Endell places these windows in actual facades and analyzes the results. Certain facades will have a slower tempo and less tension, others greater. In one facade of a two-story house, the lower windows are larger and wider, the upper ones narrower. This makes for greater tension and tempo as one moves upward. The upper windows "moderate the tempo" by having their upper borders all on the same level. But the gaps above the top story once again speed up the motion, which then "fades away" *(verklingt)* in the broadness of the roof. Thus, says Endell, "a crescendo is followed by a double decrescendo" (p. 159). Endell tends to mix up here metaphors of musical time with those of dynamics: where he mentions crescendo and decrescendo, he should have said accelerando and ritardando. But the meaning is clear, as is the import.

A year later still, in 1898, Endell repeated forcefully the analogy between form-art and music. In his essay entitled "Formkunst" (Form-Art), he wrote, "There is an art that no one seems to know about: *Formkunst,* which bubbles up out of the human soul only through forms, which are like nothing known, that represent nothing and symbolize nothing, that work through freely found forms, as music does through free tones."[77] Endell certainly did not invent the interpretation of architecture or of visual linear motion in musical terms. But what is significant is how forceful this kind of critical language and program for art became in the years around 1900 in the German-speaking world, and how closely it became linked with a move toward nonobjective art.

THE BLUE RIDER

It is in the work of the artists associated with the *Blaue Reiter* (Blue Rider) group—also centered on Munich—that music comes to play a still more central role in the formulation of artistic theory and practice. In his "Reminiscences" of 1913, Kandinsky pointed to two important artists, Monet and Wagner, whose works "stamped my whole life and shook me to the depths of my being" (p. 363). He reports being struck by one of the Haystack paintings of Monet at an exhibit in Moscow, probably in 1896. And a performance of Wagner's *Lohengrin* that Kandinsky attended in Moscow seems to have unleashed a moment of synesthetic apotheosis:

> The violins, the deep tones of the basses, and especially the wind instruments at that time embodied for me all the power of that pre-nocturnal hour. I saw all my colors in my mind, they stood before my eyes. Wild, almost crazy lines were sketched in front of me. I did not dare use the expression that Wagner had painted "my hour" musically. It became, however, quite clear to me that art in general was far more powerful than I had thought, and on the other hand, that painting could develop just such powers as music possesses. (p. 364)

In a sense it could be said that Kandinsky's goal became the development of these "powers." Synesthesia was certainly a part of Kandinsky's makeup. Wagner's music called forth colors, and much in Kandinsky's later life and writings confirms that he had synesthetic leanings, including his set of illustrated prose poems, *Klänge* (Sounds, 1912); his stage drama *Der gelbe Klang* (The Yellow Sound, 1909–12); and the numerous color-sound associations proposed in *On the Spiritual in Art,* published in 1912 (though largely drafted by 1909).

Yet Kandinsky was ultimately not interested in what Adorno called pseudomorphosis. "I do not want to paint music," he wrote in 1914 (p. 400). In *On the Spiritual in Art* he made clear (as Adorno would) that each of the arts—he is addressing in particular music and painting—has its own unique qualities such that "the exact repetition of the same sound by different arts is not possible." Kandinsky called for a kind of total artwork in which the arts could function together: "Each art will display that extra element which is essential and peculiar to itself, thereby adding to that inner sound which they have in common a richness and power that cannot be attained by one art alone." This working together can help overcome, but not mask, the differences between the arts: "The forces that are hidden within the various arts are fundamentally different, so that the result to be achieved (even in the case of the same person) will be more intense than if each of the different arts were to work independently, in isolation" (pp. 191–93).

Kandinsky seems to accept without question that painting can have "voices" and "harmonies." Here music becomes the model for abstract or nonobjective art:

> An artist who sees that the imitation of natural appearances, however artistic, is not for him—the kind of creative artist who wants to, and has to, express his own inner world—sees with envy how naturally and easily such goals can be attained in music, the least material of the arts today. Understandably, he may turn toward it and try to find the same means in his own art. Hence the current search for rhythm in painting, for mathematical, abstract construction, the value placed today upon the repetition of color tones, the way colors are set in motion, etc. (p. 154)

One can read echoes here of the thoughts of Endell about the relationship between music and art as form-arts.

Much of *On the Spiritual in Art* develops the musical analogies or qualities of the visual arts in great detail. In his chapter on color, Kandinsky asserts that certain colors or color combinations produce effects on viewers much like those of music. Thus, yellow is "a color that inclines considerably toward the brighter tones"; it "can be raised to a pitch of intensity unbearable to the eye and to the spirit. Upon such intensification, it affects us like the shrill sound of a trumpet being played louder and louder, or the sound of a high-pitched fanfare" (p. 181). Of white, Kandinsky writes that "its inner sound is like the absence of sound, corresponding in many cases to pauses in music. . . . It is a silence that is not dead but full of possibilities. White has the sound as of a silence that suddenly becomes comprehensible" (p. 185).

Well before their encounters with Kandinsky, two painters who would become members of the Blue Rider group, August Macke (1887–1914) and Franz Marc (1880–1916), likewise displayed a strong interest in the structural relationships between painting and music. Macke and Marc, who were both to die in battle in World War I, met in January 1910 and formed a close friendship. Macke, the younger of the two, was particularly intrigued by color theory. As early as 1907 he had expressed the desire to bring colors into a system like those of musical notes. His synesthetic leanings are clear from his musings about a scent-keyboard *(Geruchsklavier)*.[78] In December 1910, Macke wrote to Marc about having asked a pianist to play him on the piano three chords that "in her opinion play the same large role in music" as three primary colors, red, yellow, and blue.[79] Macke does not say what the chords were—one suspects they may have been the tonic, subdominant, and dominant—but he goes on to propose a "parallel appearance" *(Parallelerscheinung)* between colors, emotions, and these chords. Thus blue is sad, yellow cheerful, and red violent. He continues: "The sequence of colors (or chords) determines the lines (or melody). Rising, falling melodies, which sink contentedly like sisters into each other's arms. Thus the falling melodies can be contained in part within the rising ones, and vice versa. The color complex that is conveyed by the lines (melodies) is the question that is answered by the opposing complex" (p. 26).

In his letter, Macke constructs a color wheel divided into six even parts or slices, each occupied by a single color. Each slice is then further divided according to shade, moving concentrically outward from the dark center to the bright edge of the circle. In Macke's wheel, the direction toward brightness "corresponds to the rise in register of piano notes." (Here Macke writes out the letter names of a scale from C to "H" or B♮.) The number of octaves on the piano (eight) corresponds to the number of concentric rings that radiate out from the center in Macke's design (p. 26).

Marc, the elder of the two painters, was receptive to many aspects of Macke's ideas and, indeed, countered with his own color theory, in which blue is "the *male* principle, rough and spiritual"; yellow is the "*female* principle, gentle, cheerful, and sensuous"; and red is "the *material,* violent and hard" (p. 28). But Marc is "skeptical" about carrying over what he calls "musical-technical laws" into painting:

> I think that musical, theoretical technique—counterpoint, for example—was created by people specifically for musical processes. Rising and falling melodies are such a thoroughly musical concept, almost an "instrumental" one (insofar as our voice is really an "instrument"), that the application of them to painting is somewhat vague and in a practical sense does not really rise above analogies that are sensed mysteriously. What you say about melodic progress through light and dark, etc., I find very fine. Surely melody and line grew out of the same ancient trunk of artistic sensibility, but they are two different shoots, siblings that have become from a technical viewpoint widely separated from each other. (p. 29)

Marc's cautionary response to Macke's somewhat jejune synesthesia may recall Adorno's and Kandinsky's more sober attitudes toward music-painting relationships. In developing his own analogies, Kandinsky never goes so far as to propose the kind of precise pitch-to-color correspondence that Macke depicts in his wheel. Kandinsky is more interested in sound as reflected in timbre or instrumental color. For Adorno, Macke's ideas of color chords and linear melodies might be pseudomorphosis and would smack of the "apocryphal." Marc, like Adorno and Kandinsky, warns that though there are certain principles in common, the technical aspects of music and of art are fundamentally separate. For Marc as for Kandinsky, any Adornian convergence must occur at a level, or in a fashion, different from what Macke has proposed.

THE SCHOENBERG CONCERT OF JANUARY 2, 1911

Just a few weeks after this exchange of letters, which took place in December 1910, Marc attended the January 2, 1911, concert devoted exclusively to Schoenberg's music in the Jahreszeitensaal (Hall of the Seasons) in Munich. The program included Lieder; the First and Second Quartets, opp. 7 and 10; and the Piano Pieces, op. 11.[80] Kandinsky also attended this concert and depicted it in his painting entitled *Impression III (Concert)* (to which we return below). The event also prompted him to write to Schoenberg, initiating what was to become one of the most renowned correspondences between creative artists in the twentieth century.

In his often-cited letter of January 18 to Schoenberg, Kandinsky wrote: "In your works, you have realized what I, albeit in uncertain form, have so greatly longed for in music. The independent progress through their own destinies, the independent life of the individual voices in your compositions, is exactly what I am trying to find in my paintings."[81] Kandinsky goes on to describe a new kind of "harmony" in painting, which is to be founded not on a schematic or "geometric" structure, but rather on something "antilogical."

On the poster for the evening the concert producer Emil Gutmann had included a passage from a chapter of Schoenberg's *Harmonielehre* (Theory of Harmony) that had appeared, in advance of the book's publication, in the Berlin periodical *Die Musik.* The passage included sentences about dissonance and consonance that had an impact on both Kandinsky and Marc: "Dissonances are only different from consonances in degree; they are nothing more than remoter consonances. Today we have already reached the point where we no longer make the distinction between consonances and dissonances."[82] Kandinsky wrote Schoenberg: "And 'today's' dissonance in painting and music is merely the consonance of 'tomorrow.' . . . It has given me immense joy to find that you have the same ideas." Kandinsky signed his letter, as he did in several cases during the early correspondence with Schoenberg, "With feelings of real affinity."[83]

Kandinsky's remarks in the letter (as in his treatise) would seem to be prime instances of the recognition of convergence between painting and music. But it is also worth turning our attention to the letter about the Schoenberg concert that Marc wrote to Macke on January 14, 1911—thus four days before Kandinsky's letter to Schoenberg. Marc reports that after the concert he joined Kandinsky and members of his circle for a drink. Undoubtedly at that occasion the mutual enthusiasm for and empathetic recognition of Schoenberg's music was discussed. Although Kandinsky's letter is far better known, Marc's is equally thoughtful and even more detailed in communicating the convergent excitement that must have been shared over the postconcert drink. He even proposes a hypothetical painting based on these ideas. Marc's letter deserves citation at length:

> A musical event in Munich gave me a strong shock; a chamber music evening by *Arnold Schoenberg* (Vienna). Two quartets, piano pieces, and songs. . . . Can you imagine a music in which tonality (that is, the adherence to any key) is completely suspended? I was constantly reminded of Kandinsky's large *Composition,* which also permits no trace

of a key . . . and also of Kandinsky's "jumping spots" in hearing this music, which allows each tone sounded to stand on its own (a kind of *white canvas* between the spots of color!) Schoenberg proceeds from the principle that the concepts of consonance and dissonance do not exist at all. A so-called dissonance is only a more remote consonance.—This is an idea that today occupies me incessantly and that I apply in painting as follows: It is absolutely not obligatory that complementary colors be made to appear next to each other as in a prism; they can, insofar as is possible, be "kept apart." The partial dissonances that thereby arise will be cancelled out in the appearance of the entire picture; they will seem consonant (harmonic) insofar as they are complementary in their distribution and intensity. Suppose, for example, I paint a forest scene. Instead of painting the trees in a complementary way, from the angles of light, interior *[Kern-Seite]*, and shadow, and in their relationship to the ground and background, I paint one a pure blue, the next pure yellow, green, red, violet, etc. (as many colors as appear to me in my image of nature, but now mixed up and juxtaposed). Likewise I separate the color of the earth and of the foliage into individual, separated pure elements of color, which I spread out over the whole painting with artistic taste and instinct (but without precise regard to the juxtaposition of complementary colors). (p. 40)[84]

Like Kandinsky, Marc seems to have felt instinctively that Schoenberg was attempting (and achieving) in music something toward which he was striving as an artist. He too was struck by the statement from Schoenberg's *Theory of Harmony* that had been included on the program for the concert: that the difference between consonance and dissonance is relative, not absolute; that dissonances are only more remote consonances. But Marc goes further than Kandinsky in immediately exploring this notion with respect to painting. Like Macke, Marc is going forward from color theory. But he makes a more precise analogy between the treatment of colors and the treatment of harmony in music. Colors can be juxtaposed in ways that are consonant (according to complementarity) or dissonant. An overall unity or coherence can result even if there is "dissonance" on a more local level. In Marc's scheme, musical chords would seem to be roughly equivalent to colors. There is something of a disjunction here in that chords are made up of individual notes, while primary colors are unitary. Yet, mutatis mutandis, we can, I think, understand and appreciate Marc's suggestions.

Marc claims to have been "constantly reminded," while listening to Schoenberg's music, of Kandinsky's painting *Composition,* which likewise has "no trace of a key." Marc would likely have been referring to Kandinsky's *Composition II* or *III,* painted in 1910. Both these canvases were destroyed in World War II and survive only in black-and-white photographs. For *Composition II* a large color sketch survives, in which there are elements that one can clearly take as representational, such as four human figures standing, reclining, or with arms in the air; two men on horseback; a sheep; and landscape features like boulders and trees.[85] But Marc is right that there is no unifying theme or "key" to these shapes. This is also true of the colors (which is perhaps closer to what Marc meant). The pure Fauvist shades, especially red, blue, yellow, white, and black, have a bold presence that is divorced from any functional or conventional association. Somewhat like *Composition II,* the hypothetical painting Marc describes in his letter, a "forest scene," is not fundamentally abstract. What is abstract, or divorced from standard categories of representation, is the treatment of colors. Marc makes it clear that he is using colors in the way that (to his ears) Schoenberg is using harmonies—that is, isolated and juxtaposed, displaced from their "natural" state in a prismatic presentation.

It is worth stressing here that, for Kandinsky and Marc, abstraction was never a goal in and of itself, at least at this period. Even though in his *On the Spiritual in Art* Kandinsky took a stance against "materialism" in art, he did not renounce the object. He observes, and applauds the fact, that "the abstract element in art has come increasingly to the fore," a process he sees as "natural" when "the more organic form is pushed into the background" (pp. 167–68). But Kandinsky sees no reason to give up "material objects," which as much as purely abstract forms can arouse "inner vibrations" in the viewer. It is the arousal of those inner vibrations that should be the goal of art, no matter what outward form the image assumes (p. 169).

One can understand the empathetic response of Kandinsky and Marc to Schoenberg's compositions and ideas. For Schoenberg as for them, abandonment of the material object—in his case, tonal harmony—was no absolute necessity. In the compositions played on the January 2 concert, spanning the years from 1899 to 1909, we can hear the "abstract" element "coming to the fore," in the form of more frequent harmonies that are nonfunctional in a traditional sense. Yet even the most advanced pieces of op. 11, as commentators have long recognized, contain plenty of triads and other chords with tonal implications. For Schoenberg, as is clear from the passages from the *Theory of Harmony* alluded to by Marc and Kandinsky, consonance and dissonance were relative, not absolute categories. Similarly, for Kandinsky there would be no absolute dividing line between material objects and abstract forms. He may not have formulated his ideas in exactly that way in *On the Spiritual in Art,* but the paintings of this period, from 1909–12, make quite clear how material objects, both animate and inanimate, take on abstract qualities. We can explore the ways in which Schoenberg and Kandinsky each achieve these goals by looking first at some of the music played on the January 2 concert, then at the painting inspired by that music.

SCHOENBERG'S MUSIC

Most commentators who have cited Kandinsky's letter and sought to relate it to the music he heard on January 2 have focused on Schoenberg's Piano Pieces, op. 11, as the works that must have made the strongest impression and on which any discussion of convergence should be based.[86] These are, to be sure, the most technically advanced—and the least tonal—works played at the concert. But we should recall that Kandinsky's first remark to Schoenberg, in the letter of January 18, is about "the independent progress through their own destinies, the independent life of the individual voices in your compositions," which is "exactly what I am trying to find in my paintings." This comment seems to concern *linearity,* the individuality and primacy of line.

At the January concert, the final piece played and also the longest—and thus perhaps the one most likely to stick in the memories of Marc and Kandinsky—was Schoenberg's First Quartet in D Minor, op. 7, which lasts close to fifty minutes in performance. This work, as well as the Second Quartet, op. 10, which opened the concert, would have given Kandinsky and his colleagues an indelible impression of linearity. In op. 7 the four instruments achieve a level of polyphonic independence unprecedented in the quartet literature. More than the Lieder or piano works, the quartets would have reinforced the quality of linear independence visually and spatially: in the physical disposition of the string quartet the linearity would have been *seen* as well as heard.

The D-Minor Quartet has been analyzed extensively elsewhere in the literature, including by myself, but we can summarize here some of the aspects that might have struck Kandinsky and Marc.[87] The opening "theme" of the Quartet is really a thematic complex of three distinct lines unfolded simultaneously. As if to emphasize the individual identity of the lines, Schoenberg inverts their position each time the theme recurs during the quartet.

Linearity would have been especially audible to Kandinsky and his circle in the transitional theme in the exposition of the first movement of op. 7. This is a dense, strict fugato, in which the actual subject begins on G♮. The successive entries of the subject do not alternate at the traditional interval of the fifth—a conventional fugue would proceed G–D–G–D—but spell out successively the pitches of a diminished-seventh chord, G–E♮–C♯–B♭ (example 15). The effect of these entries, combined with the highly chromatic nature of the subject itself, bring this passage to the brink of atonality. There is certainly no more striking passage in the work of the individual lines pursuing their own "destinies."

Two moments in the Second Quartet may also have impressed Marc and Kandinsky. The "theme" of the third movement, which is subject to a set of variations, is—somewhat like the main theme of op. 7—really a complex of themes. In this case the complex is divided among the different instruments not into long lines, but into shorter, more fragmentary gestures. The most prominent example of imitative counterpoint in op. 10, analogous in its way to the transition in op. 7, occurs at the opening of the finale. Here each of the instruments successively takes up a circling or floating subject, which is itself completely atonal (comprising eight different pitches). As in op. 7, the theme enters successively on four different pitches, here organized by ascending perfect fifth, G♯, D♯, B♭, F (example 16).

The vocal music on the January 2 concert, though not specifically mentioned by Marc or Kandinsky in their letters, was all set to texts by modernist poets, including Stefan George, Richard Dehmel, John Henry Mackay, Hermann Conradi, and Friedrich Nietzsche. The first two of these poets, Schoenberg's favorites at this time, wrote in a highly visual style that has been seen as akin to Jugendstil. Volker Klotz adduces examples of the "deactivation of action words" in George and Dehmel, which he sees as analogous to the goalless motion of the Jugendstil line. This effect can be achieved in several ways: first, through the frequent use of modal adverbs, which help to displace "the weight of the bearer of motion, the verb . . . from the goal to the manner"; second, through the use of intransitive or reflexive verbs, "whose subjects have either nothing or themselves as objects, which have no effect, change nothing"; and third, through an emphasis on detailed visual description and a lack of spatial perspective analogous to the surface art of Jugendstil.[88]

One song that was performed at the January 2 concert—and the earliest of all the works played—was *Erwartung* (Anticipation), op. 2, no. 1, composed by Schoenberg in 1899 to a poem by Dehmel. This is a fully tonal work, yet one in which the kind of convergence sensed by Kandinsky and

Example 15. Schoenberg, String Quartet No. 1, op. 7

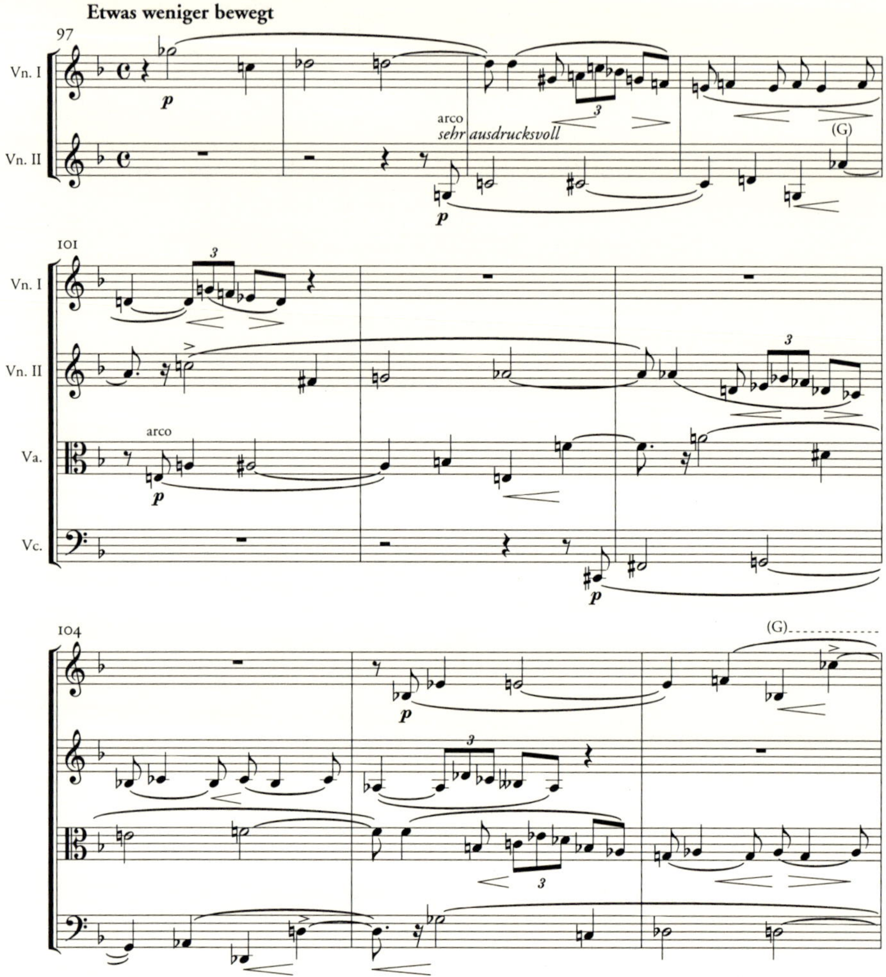

Schoenberg in 1911 is already present to a large degree. The interest in manipulating colors for their own sake or value, rather than their for their more purely representational function—precisely the kind of things Kandinsky and Marc write about—are already evident in Dehmel's poem "Erwartung." In 1894, two years before the publication of "Erwartung" in the volume *Weib und Welt* (Woman and World), Dehmel had called for a closer relationship between the arts, noting in his diary, "Nowadays we aim to make poetic technique more sensuous by incorporating painterly and musical

Example 16. Schoenberg, String Quartet No. 2, op. 10, IV

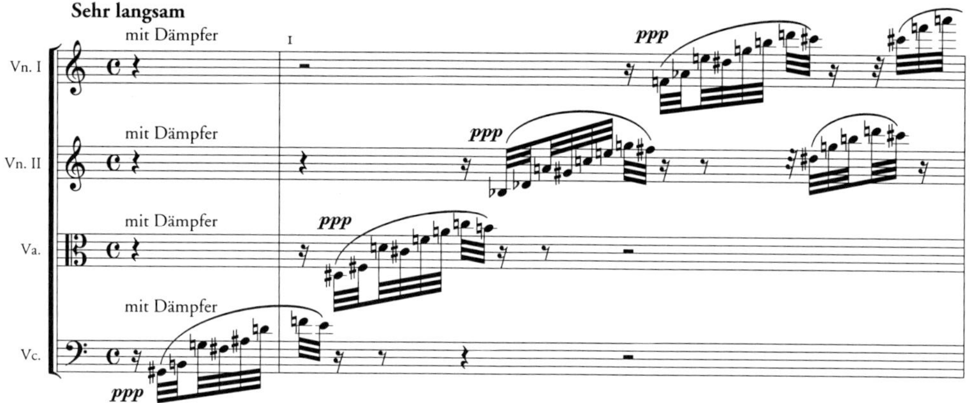

effects, just as painting and music attempt to learn new means of expression from the sister arts." Although Dehmel admits that there are limits to this kind of technical exchange, he suggests, for example, that a poet might "associate a color word with a particularly strong upsurging of a psychological state" or might intensify his verse "through the use of sound symbols."[89]

The poem "Erwartung" might be the perfect demonstration of Dehmel's ideas. Within a basic style of imagery that is close to Jugendstil in inspiration (especially the opals and the woman's white hand), it is a virtual textbook of painterly effects:

Out of the sea-green pond,
near the red villa,
under the dead oak
shines the moon.

Where her dark image
reaches through the water,
a man stands and draws
a ring from his hand.

Three opals glimmer;
through the pale stones swim
red and green sparks
and sink down.

And he kisses them,
and his eyes glow

like the sea-green depths:
a window opens.

Out of the red villa,
near the dead oak,
beckons to him
the pale hand of a woman.

[Aus dem meergrünen Teiche / neben der roten Villa / unter der toten Eiche / scheint der Mond. / Wo ihr dunkles Abbild / durch das Wasser greift, / steht ein Mann und streift / einen Ring von seiner Hand. / Drei Opale blinken; / durch die bleichen Steine / schwimmen rot und grüne / Funken und versinken. / Und er küßt sie, / und seine Augen leuchten / wie der meergrüne Grund: / ein Fenster thut sich auf. / Aus der roten Villa / neben der toten Eiche / winkt ihm eine bleiche / Frauenhand.]

The poem comprises a highly stylized, almost abstract play of color. Each line of the first stanza states or implies a different color: the pond sea green, the villa red, the oak black or dark brown, the moon white. These color images recur throughout the poem and are then recapitulated in the final stanza, where red and "dead" recur, and the color value of white is transferred from the moon to the woman's "pale" hand.

The paired juxtapositions in stanza 1 suggest that Dehmel may consciously have sought to exploit color complementarity. Red and green, and black and white, are considered complementary colors from the standpoint of perception. Indeed, Dehmel seems to endow these colors with associations like those Kandinsky would outline in *On the Spiritual in Art,* where the elements of each such pair are called "opposites." In Kandinsky's scheme green is passive, a color of "self-contented repose"; its opposite, red, is warm, intense, and "turbulent." Black represents a "dead nothingness," an "eternal silence without future"; white, as we have seen, is "a silence that is not dead, full of possibilities" (pp. 183–86). Dehmel's poem is also strongly symbolist in orientation; it is a poem of gestures, allusions, and suggestions, rather than direct description or actions. These features are also typical of what has been deemed Jugendstil poetry.

The language of Dehmel's poem is certainly "deactivated" in the sense discussed by Klotz. The principal verb phrase of the first stanza, "shines the moon," comes only in line 4. The preceding lines are made up of three similarly constructed prepositional phrases that serve to weigh down the syntax and ornament the subject-verb complex. Throughout the poem, any human

Example 17. Schoenberg, *Erwartung,* op. 2, no. 1

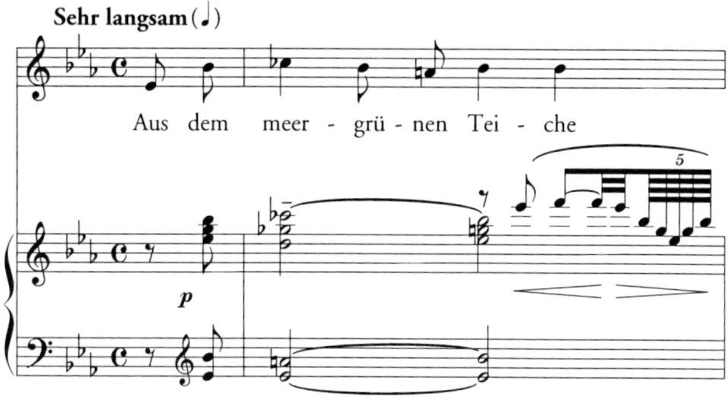

actions (the man pulling the ring from his finger, his kissing it, the woman waving) tend to be surrounded by the delicate play of colors. One could imagine Dehmel's poem depicted in a painting by one of the German symbolists like Böcklin or Thoma, or perhaps the early Kandinsky, all painters who specialized in canvases with a highly decorative sense of color put in the service of an intense but veiled eroticism.

The presence of Schoenberg's setting of *Erwartung* on the concert of January 2, 1911, even amid many later compositions that were more characteristic of Schoenberg's newer directions, should not surprise us: Schoenberg clearly felt *Erwartung* could hold its own. (He often programmed the work in recitals.) In Schoenberg's song, Kandinsky and Marc would have heard a convergent color play. Schoenberg does not aim for text painting in any conventional sense. There is no attempt to create a different harmonic or melodic equivalent for each of the colors or images mentioned in the text; there is no pseudomorphosis. Instead, Schoenberg creates a five-note sonority that we might call a "color" chord, comprising the tonic note E♭ and four neighbor notes dissonant to the tonic triad. The chord, which is heard in the very first phrase of the song at the word "meergrünen" (example 17), stands in place of a conventional dominant, as a pole of tension with the tonic. The fact that the tonic is itself present within the color chord tends to rob it of forward motion. Schoenberg thus manipulates harmonic syntax in a way that mirrors the static modifying phrases of the first stanza of the poem. Throughout the song, Schoenberg reinterprets this color chord in a number of different configurations or inversions, such that it becomes structural as well as coloristic.[90]

At the January 2 concert Kandinsky must also have been pleased to encounter settings of the poetry of George, with whom he had direct contact via George's followers in Munich. Munich was one of the centers of the so-called George Circle *(George-Kreis),* which was especially active and prominent through the George apostle resident there, Karl Wolfskehl (1869–1948). Weiss has documented convincingly the close ties between Kandinsky and Wolfskehl beginning as early as 1907.[91] Kandinsky was (like many artists of the time) struck by George's refined and chiseled features, which he incorporated into one of his early woodcuts. Weiss has suggested that there are a number of "parallels" between George's poetry and some of Kandinsky's pre-abstract paintings.

As suggested above, some of George's poetry also has been characterized as Jugendstil in spirit and technique. George's cycle *Das Buch der hängenden Gärten* (The Book of the Hanging Gardens, 1895), in which a Babylonian king recalls his youth and his discovery of, and then bitter disappointment in, erotic love, is rich in adjectives and nouns that describe places and natural phenomena (especially in the gardens), and short on active verbs. (Here, as so often happens in Jugendstil, we cross paths again with symbolism. Many of the techniques George uses in the *Hanging Gardens* could equally qualify as symbolist.)

Although none of Schoenberg's settings of the *Hanging Gardens* poems (op. 15, 1908–9) were included on the January 2 concert program, they merit mention here in our discussion of convergence. Schoenberg's musical style in op. 15 hovers in a nether region between tonality and atonality. Although the second song, *Hain in diesen Paradisen* (Groves in These Paradises), has no central tonic, harmonic stability is attained by certain recurring sonorities that are "dissonant" by conventional standards, especially the opening chord D–F♮–A–C♯. There are also many vocal appoggiaturas and half-step resolutions that are characteristic of tonal music, as well as an unmistakable cadence to B major in m. 5. All these gestures are, like the visual imagery and literary syntax of Jugendstil and symbolism, defamiliarized. Gestures or procedures recognizable from the past, in this case music of the eighteenth and nineteenth centuries, are placed in unfamiliar contexts.[92]

KANDINSKY'S *IMPRESSION III*

In his *On the Spiritual in Art* of 1912, Kandinsky, thinking as so often in terms of musical analogy, posited "melodic" and "symphonic" as two extremes of technique in painting. Melodic implies a "simple composition" with a "simple form." Symphonic painting is more complex, comprising several forms (p. 215). In the book Kandinsky included some of his own recent paintings as "examples of the new symphonic type of construction, in which the melodic element is used only occasionally, as one of the subordinate parts." He differentiated these into "Impressions," "Improvisations," and "Compositions." "Impressions" were intended to be "the direct impression of 'external nature,' expressed in linear-painterly form." "Improvisations" were "chiefly unconscious, for the most part suddenly arising expressions of events of an inner character, hence impressions of 'internal nature.'" "Compositions" were more developed, elaborate paintings which, Kandinsky said, "I have slowly and almost pedantically examined and worked out" (p. 218).

In 1910–11 Kandinsky painted six Impressions, in which "external nature" encompasses a scene from bourgeois urban society—a concert *(Impression III),* a couple walking in the city *(Impression IV),* a street scene with a gendarme *(Impression VI).* We are, of course, very distant here from traditional naturalism. *Impression III (Concert)* was created the day after the Schoenberg concert, on January 3, 1911.[93] As an artwork conceived by a master at the height of his powers, in response to music by another master, Kandinsky's *Impression III* bears some comparison with Klinger's *Brahms Fantasy,* as much for the differences as the similarities. Klinger fashioned a graphic cycle of technical complexity over a number of years. He did so out of a deep reverence for, and long acquaintance with, a wide range of Brahms's music. Kandinsky painted his canvas in a single day after a brief first exposure to Schoenberg's music. Klinger's work is based in part on the graphic aspects of Brahms's notated music, Kandinsky's on the aural and visual experience of a live concert. Klinger's cycle qualifies as a total artwork in the late-nineteenth-century sense, but does not manifest the kind of convergence outlined by Adorno. Twenty years later, in 1910, the cumulative force of symbolism, Jugendstil, and abstraction had made convergence technically and expressively possible for an artist of Kandinsky's sensibility.

Before turning to Kandinsky's *Impression III,* we should examine one further and highly relevant example of the power that music—specifically abstract musical structures—held for Kandinsky at this time. In the Kandinsky collection in the Centre Pompidou is a charcoal sketch almost certainly from 1911 and never before reproduced, to my knowledge (figure 8). It appears to be a preliminary study for Kandinsky's 1911 painting *Improvisation mit Pferden* (Improvisation with Horses).[94] No horses are apparent in the

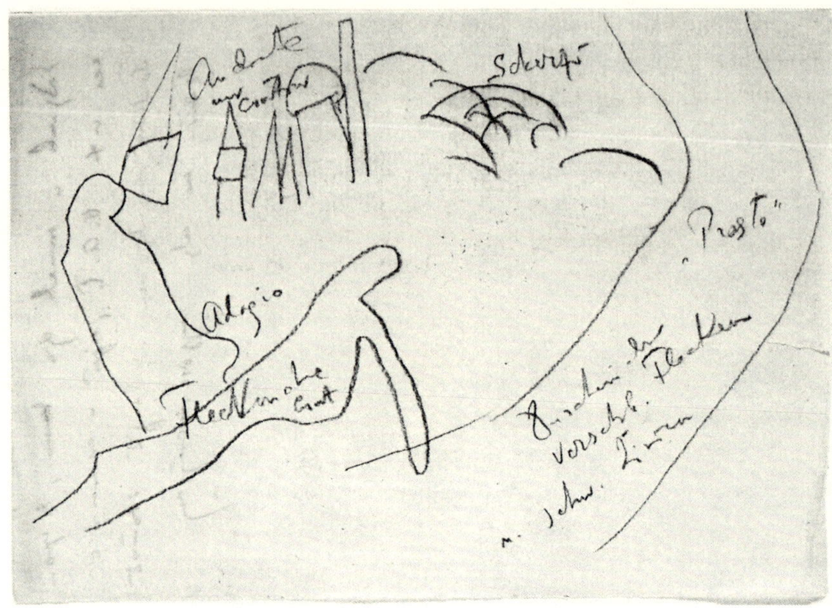

Figure 8. Wassily Kandinsky, charcoal sketch, 1911. Musée National d'Art Moderne, Centre Georges Pompidou, Paris. © 2004 Artists Rights Society (ARS), New York / ADAGP, Paris. Photo: CNAC/MNAM/Dist. Réunion des Musées Nationaux / Art Resource, NY.

sketch, where the artist constructs a tiny symphonic landscape, a modern analogue to Schwind's *Symphonie.* The four areas are labeled by Kandinsky "Andante," "Adagio," "Scherzo," and "Presto." Each corresponds to a different kind of formal and visual pattern. As he would do in one of the sketches for *Impression,* he includes verbal indications of color and of details to be filled in later.

The "Andante" segment is composed of geometrically conceived vertical figures or elements that closely resemble some of those in *Composition II* and other canvases of this time. They might represent landscape elements like mountains or hills, or possibly some of the buildings of Murnau, the village outside Munich where Kandinsky spent much time. The annotation below "Andante," though difficult to decipher, suggests that these forms are to be depicted only in contour *(nur Contour),* something that in fact happens in the painting *Improvisation mit Pferden.* The "Adagio" is more amoeba-like, constructed as two more or less perpendicular shapes that are broad and flat. Kandinsky indicates—again, the German is difficult to decode—that the shapes are to be filled with spots without contour *(Flecken ohne Cont[our]).* The "Scherzo" is composed of a series of tightly interlocking or overlapping curves. (These do not appear in the final painting.) Two of the curved lines seem to link the "Andante" to the "Presto." The "Presto" is less formally delimited than the other "movements"; like a river, it flows from the lower middle part of the sketch up to the right and off the edge. (One could say it flows in the other direction, from above to below, but I sense a left-to-right motion, which is also more natural for the eye.) Here Kandinsky marks that the area is to be filled with interwoven spots *(verschl[ungenen] Flecken)* and black lines *(schwarz[en] Linien).* (Large spots and black lines are used in the painting.)

Unlike the "symphonic" sketch of 1911, the two sketches for *Impression III* (figures 9 and 10) contain no references to musical forms; they seek to capture directly an actual musical event or experience. We can trace a process of transformation from representation to something far more abstract.[95] From the first, the image is dominated by the piano, at which is seated a performer, presumably Etta Werndorff, who played at the concert. What is especially striking about the first sketch is the informality and unconcert-like feel of the moment; the piano is surrounded here by what appear to be audience members, some sitting, some standing, and some conversing. All the activity seems to take place in the corner of a room, with a large chandelier hanging overhead. The figure seated at the left with his left arm raised in the air might be a violinist or cellist, yet there are surely far too many figures here to account for the Rosé Quartet and the soprano Marie Gutheil-Schoder.

To what extent does Kandinsky's sketch render a real event at a real place? The January 2 concert took place in the Jahreszeitensaal of the Hotel Vier Jahreszeiten, which is still today Munich's leading hotel (under the name Hotel Kempinski Vier Jahreszeiten). The room also still exists, though it has been many times remodeled and is now called the Cherubin-Saal. Figure 11 is a photograph of the room at around the turn of the century, as it would most likely have looked at the time of the Schoenberg concert. We can see that it was not a fixed-seat hall, but a large, open, multipurpose space with a dance floor in the middle. There appears to be a small elevated stage area in the back (perhaps intended for a dance orchestra). In the photograph the room is set up for a banquet. Given the structure of the Jahreszeitensaal, it is indeed possible that audience and performers at the Schoenberg concert would have come into the kind of close proximity indicated in the first sketch. We note, however, that the room seems to have no corners of the kind depicted by Kandinsky.

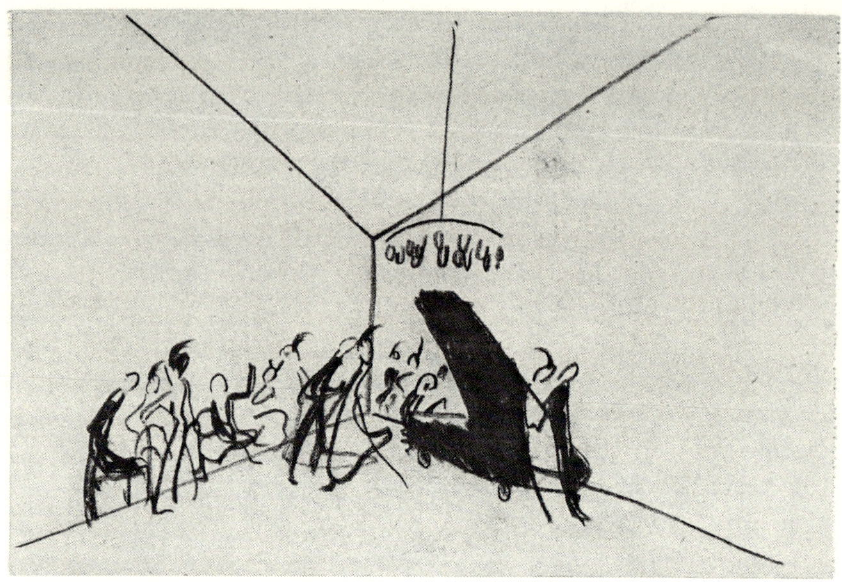

Figure 9. Wassily Kandinsky, charcoal sketch for *Impression III (Concert),* 1911. Musée National d'Art Moderne, Centre Georges Pompidou, Paris. © 2004 Artists Rights Society (ARS), New York / ADAGP, Paris. Photo: CNAC/MNAM/Dist. Réunion des Musées Nationaux / Art Resource, NY.

In the second of the two sketches for *Impression III* (figure 10), the level of abstraction is greater in that the perspective and vanishing point of the first sketch have been largely dissolved. Yet we have a much clearer sense of an actual concert. Rows of heads incline toward the piano, where the pianist is still recognizable, leaning over the keyboard. Several details seem even *more* realistic here than in the first sketch. The long hair indicates the pianist to be a woman. Two bulbous globes in the upper part of the sketch seem to represent the distinctive chandeliers that hang from the ceiling of the Jahreszeitensaal. In the earlier sketch the chandelier bore no resemblance to those of the room. In the second sketch, Kandinsky also begins to map out the color scheme of the painting, marking certain areas for white, yellow, and black.

The two pairs of standing figures from the first sketch, at the foot of the keyboard and to the left of the piano (from the viewer's perspective), have metamorphosed into long strips, which are marked by Kandinsky to be colored white ("w" for *weiss*). These might seem to be actual columns, but as we see in the photograph, the Jahreszeitensaal had none. Kandinsky's

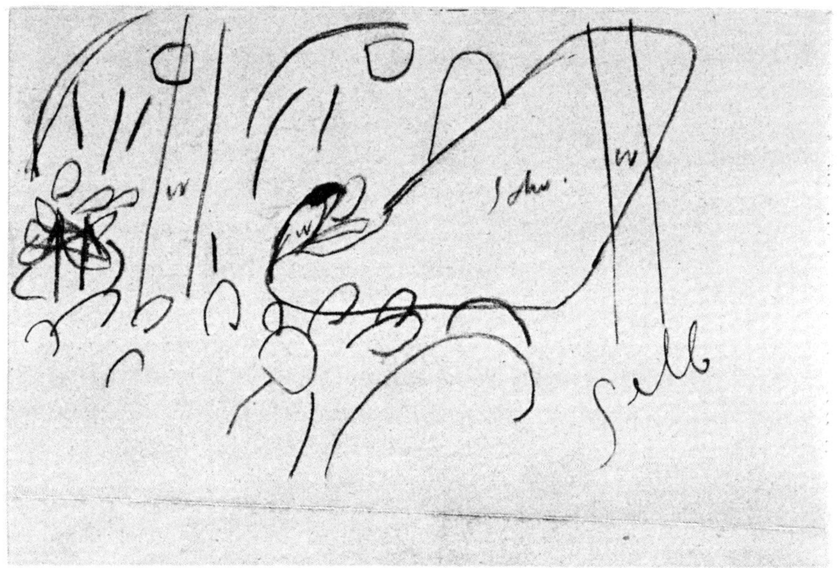

Figure 10. Wassily Kandinsky, charcoal sketch for *Impression III (Concert),* 1911. Musée National d'Art Moderne, Centre Georges Pompidou, Paris. © 2004 Artists Rights Society (ARS), New York / ADAGP, Paris. Photo: CNAC/MNAM/Dist. Réunion des Musées Nationaux / Art Resource, NY.

"columns" derive from human forms. The piano cover is now a triangular shape occupying a large portion of the image and is indicated to be colored black ("schw." for *schwarz*). The lower right-hand corner of the image, essentially a blank area devoid of color, is to be yellow *(gelb).*

The original group of figures along the left-hand wall of the first sketch is amalgamated into a kind of composite blob with several heads and a jumble of activity among the arms. There is in this group something of the same active intensity as in the pianist, and their implied faces are turned toward the viewer. Specifically, I believe this cluster on the left represents—or renders, since the purely representational aspect is receding—the Rosé Quartet and, standing in the center as the vertical column, Gutheil-Schoder. At the actual concert the Lieder, the piano pieces, and the quartets were of course performed successively. But in this sketch Kandinsky has collapsed the performance into a single "impression" that includes or implies all the players.

The painting itself (figure 12) is a demonstration of Kandinsky's theories of color and form put in the service of an image that retains strong as-

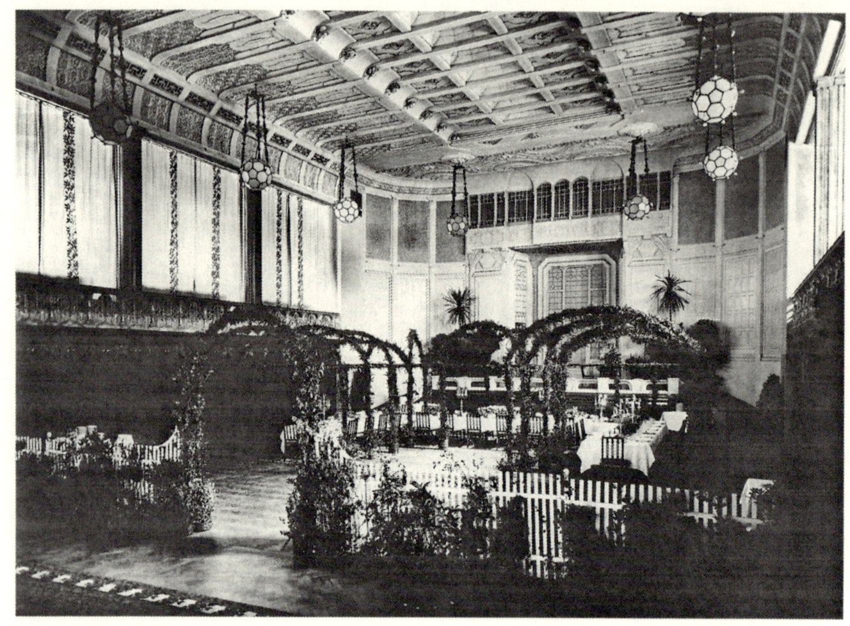

Figure 11. Photograph of Jahreszeitensaal, beginning of twentieth century. Courtesy of Hotel Kempinski Vier Jahreszeiten, Munich.

pects of representation. *Impression III* is a reasonably faithful rendering of the second pencil sketch. As in the second sketch, the Rosé Quartet and Gutheil-Schoder occupy the upper left-hand section of the canvas. The soprano is a white column, outlined in black; her head is a black shape with a purplish halo. Her chest is crossed by a rectangular black bar, an abstract element that seems to reflect the other black shapes that lean toward the right in the canvas and work against the purely vertical.

Of the two chandeliers, only the one on the left remains, a globe of yellow; the one over the pianist is now outside the frame of the image. In a sense, the piano has been pushed upward by the huge yellow triangle that emerges from the lower right and occupies almost a third of the canvas. Jelena Hahl-Koch has rightly called this triangle "the most daring feature" of the painting.[96] Yellow seems to be the color that Kandinsky associates most immediately with sound. It is perhaps not a coincidence that Kandinsky had called his stagework, on which he was working at the time, *Der gelbe Klang.*[97] In *On the Spiritual in Art* Kandinsky observes that there are different kinds of movements in the color yellow: on the one hand a "striving *toward* the spectator" in which, as a "secondary movement," the color "leaps

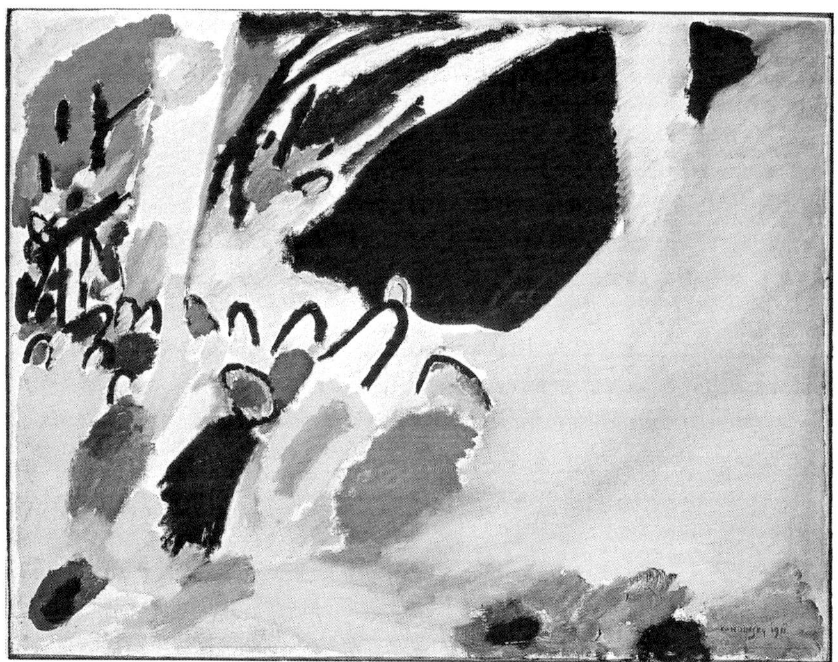

Figure 12. Wassily Kandinsky, *Impression III (Concert),* 1911. Städtische Galerie im Lenbachhaus, Munich.

over its boundaries, dissipating its strength upon its surroundings." A contrasting kind of movement occurs when yellow is "directly observed (in some kind of geometrical form)"; here it becomes "disquieting to the spectator, pricking him, stimulating him, revealing the nature of the power expressed in this color, which has an effect upon our sensibilities at once impudent and importunate" (pp. 180–81).

In *Impression III* the yellow triangle seems to fulfill all those impulses. It certainly strives toward the listeners of the concert (though this is perhaps not what Kandinsky meant) and outward toward the viewer. It also leaps over its "boundaries," spilling across into the left side of the painting. The listeners, who lean forward toward the piano, seem to be enveloped by the yellow, as does even the lower right portion of the piano. At the same time, the yellow is a disquieting element, perhaps both to the listeners "inside" the painting and to the spectator on the outside. The "yellow sound" is a stimulant.

THOUGHTS IN CONCLUSION

The sources or inspirations for Kandinsky's breakthrough to abstraction—certainly one of the major moments of twentieth-century art—have been much disputed in the scholarly literature. In a helpful but hardly even-handed survey of Kandinsky research through 1993, Hahl-Koch examines different theories that have been advanced for the artist's development. She mounts an assault on Sixten Ringbom, whose influential book *The Sounding Cosmos* (1970) argued that the spiritual dimension of Kandinsky's work, as manifested in the paintings and his writings, was strongly shaped by an exposure to theosophy, anthroposophy, and other occult thought.[98] Hahl-Koch claims that Ringbom made the mistaken assumption that texts by such authors as Rudolf Steiner were in Kandinsky's library rather than in that of his companion Gabriele Münter (even though Kandinsky made annotations in many of these writings). Kandinsky's spiritualism, she argues, has its sources in his lifelong Christianity and in his "'abstract' spiritual inclinations," as well as in his documented acquaintance with Sufism.[99] Hahl-Koch has little good to say about the work of Rose-Carol Washton Long, who also investigated Kandinsky's interest in the occult and saw the artist as in some ways "disguising" objects in his abstract paintings in order not to alienate his viewers.[100] Another target of Hahl-Koch is Peg Weiss, who, as we have seen, emphasized the role played in Kandinsky's development by the Munich milieu and its Jugendstil practices. For Hahl-Koch, Weiss ignored facts, misinterpreted primary sources, and engaged in a kind of "pseudo-research."[101]

Hahl-Koch's dismissive remarks about other scholars suggest that much is at stake in how, when, and why Kandinsky developed his abstract style. It is hard to imagine the equivalent debate raging quite so fiercely in musicology about Schoenberg's analogous and contemporaneous turn to atonality. Was it an extension of Wagnerian tonality? A consequence of Brahmsian motivic saturation? A response to inner psychic pressures? A reflection of Freudian theories of the unconscious or his own fascination with mystical Swedenborgian thought?

The most reasonable position to take on these matters, for Kandinsky as for Schoenberg, is to acknowledge many influences on these receptive young artists, who processed them in unique ways. In the case of Kandinsky, these influences would include (but not be limited to) the background of his native Russian art and culture; his decisive encounter with the work of the French Fauvist painters; an acquaintance with symbolist art and theories;

his early period in Munich, both studying with and circulating among Jugendstil artists; a fascination with Bavarian folk painting on glass; contact with the Russian avant-garde; and a dabbling in occult thought.

From the vantage point of the present study, what is most important is the central role played by music and ideas about music in Kandinsky's artistic development, including his move toward abstraction. That one of Kandinsky's major paintings of the period should have been inspired by a musical event, which also precipitated a personal relationship with a composer, is certainly worthy of attention. Yet the biographical circumstances can only contribute to, but not determine or define, the kind of convergence I have sought to explore in this chapter. Only critical and analytical engagement with the artworks themselves can begin to recover that convergence.

FOUR

Bach, Regeneration, and Historicist Modernism

AS SUGGESTED IN THE LAST CHAPTER, the technical and expressive features of the music by Schoenberg played at the January 2, 1911, concert were "convergent" with many aspects of Kandinsky's paintings. However much they appealed to Kandinsky and his circle, the intense polyphony, asymmetrical phrase structures, and dissonant chords made the works hard for the general public in Austria and Germany to swallow. As is well known, Schoenberg's mature compositions provoked hostility from audiences and critics. The premieres of the First Quartet and First Chamber Symphony in February 1907 were hissed. The first performance of the Second Quartet in December 1908 provoked an even worse scene. Still later, the so-called *Skandalkonzert* in March 1913 of works by Schoenberg and his circle was interrupted by fistfights, and the police had to be called in.

The history of early-twentieth-century modernism in music has often focused on the negative reception of the works of Schoenberg and his circle in the first decade of the twentieth century as the main turning point in the formerly harmonious—or at least nonacrimonious—relationship between the public and newer music. Yet there were earlier and different rumblings that had little to do with dissonance per se. In the last decade of the nineteenth century, European culture was perceived by many critics as increasingly decadent and degenerate—and in need of rescuing. As we saw in chapter 1, as early as 1888 Nietzsche used decadence and degeneration as sticks with which to beat Wagner. Wagner's art was "sick," "corrupt," "calculated," and "artificial."[1]

The concept of degeneration, though circulating as early as the 1850s, took hold still more firmly in the 1890s, most famously in Max Nordau's book of 1892, *Entartung* (Degeneration). Here culture (including musical culture) is seen as being in decline because of a physiological decay of the human brain and nervous system.[2] In musical commentary around 1900, certain composers or styles were considered healing or regenerative in a culture prone to degeneration. Within the Austro-German sphere, Bach fulfilled that role most directly, as we will see shortly. He would do so under the aegis of what I call historicist modernism.

Historicist modernism is represented most strikingly by Max Reger and Ferruccio Busoni. Reger gets the lion's share of commentary in this chapter, in part because his music has been vastly underappreciated in Anglo-American musicology. In historicist modernism, musical techniques from the remote past are used prominently and vigorously as a way of achieving a distance from late Romantic styles. Historicist modernism is not nostalgic or conservative in any traditional sense. It represents an attempt to bridge a historical gap without denying it, collapsing it, or retreating over it to return to the past. Perhaps because so much is seen to be at stake, composers of historicist modernism also tend to take themselves seriously; they show little of the wit and detachment that we associate with the neoclassicism that emerged in the years just after World War I in composers like Stravinsky and Hindemith.[3]

BACH AS HEALTHY, BACH AS HEALER

In German musical life around 1900 Bach becomes seen as "healthy" and restorative for a culture—and not just a musical culture—that is perceived as decadent or sick. The emergence of a Bach ideology of health can be seen at its clearest in the pages of the journal *Die Musik,* which began publication in Berlin with the new century, in the fall of 1901. On the title page of the first issue was a musical excerpt from Wagner's *Die Meistersinger,* comprising the first four measures of the "Wach' auf!" chorus from the last scene of act 3. (The words translate as "Awake! A new day is dawning!") The combination of old and new implied by the fusion of this Renaissance text (by Sachs) and Wagner's setting in the Baroque chorale style, together with the resources of Romantic harmony (as in the sustained dominant seventh on the last note), was a perfect emblem for the inclusive goals of the new journal. Another appropriate emblem appeared two pages later, just before the Foreword or "Praeludium." The editors printed Schiller's text as appropriated by Beethoven in the finale of the Ninth: "O Freunde, nicht diese Töne, sondern lasst uns angenehmere anstimmen und freudenvollere!" (O friends, not these tones, but let us perform something more pleasant and full of joy!) The editors and publisher go on to proclaim that their new journal should be free of any factionalism and uncritical hero worship, that German readers need a periodical that takes a broad historical perspective on music.[4]

Given the stated goals, it seems no coincidence that the very first article in *Die Musik,* extending over the first three issues and written by Wilibald Nagel, a critic-historian from Darmstadt, was entitled "Johann Sebastian Bach und die deutsche Musik der Gegenwart" (Johann Sebastian Bach and German Music of Today). Nagel's title is a bit misleading, as he himself observes, because his article in fact deals little with music being composed in the "present." Rather, as he says, his goal is to trace the influence or impact of Bach upon the music that forms the core of the contemporary concert repertory—the music of the nineteenth century.

Nagel proceeds patiently through Mozart, Beethoven, Mendelssohn, Schumann, Wagner, and Brahms, all composers for whom Bach played a significant role. Nagel's may well be one of the first such surveys of Bach's influence on later composers, a topic that Ludwig Finscher has said still remains "virtually unwritten" today.[5] But Nagel's main point seems to be that Bach could and should play a larger role in contemporary musical life. "Bach als Erzieher," Bach as educator, is the proper role for Bach today, says Nagel, in obvious reference to both Nietzsche's essay "Schopenhauer als Erzieher" of 1874 and Julius Langbehn's cultural conservative tract, in turn written with Nietzsche in mind, *Rembrandt als Erzieher* (Rembrandt as Educator) of 1891.

But there is more behind Nagel's rhetoric and his promotion of Bach. He argues that "sensation" dominates the artistic world of the present—the same *Sensation* that we saw championed as an aesthetic category by Bahr in chapter 2. For Nagel, Bach could help provide a *Wiedergesundung,* a regeneration of health.[6] The cultural politics of Nagel's stance, and, by implication those of the editors who placed his article at the head of the new journal, are not hard to divine. Bach had already become a kind of pawn in a struggle against what was seen as degenerate or "unhealthy" in German music at the turn of the century.

Four years later, for all their professed impartiality in the foreword to their first issue, the editors of *Die Musik* were to take an even stronger stance on this issue. In 1905 they conducted a survey or *Rundfrage,* inviting over two hundred composers, performers, scholars, critics, writers, and even poets to respond to the question "Was ist mir Johann Sebastian Bach und was bedeutet er für unsere Zeit?" (What does Johann Sebastian Bach mean to me and what is his significance for our time?). No major living figure in music was omitted in the survey; nor did the editors restrict themselves to German-speaking lands. Gustav Mahler, Max Reger, Max von Schillings, Artur Nikisch, and Guido Adler were among those approached, but also Jean Sibelius, Alexander Glazunov, Claude Debussy, Ruggiero Leoncavallo, Giacomo Puccini, Edvard Grieg, Edward MacDowell, and Edward Elgar.

The very idea of taking such a poll and then devoting seventy-five pages to reporting the results indicates an ideological stance on the part of the editors on the state of contemporary music. "The stimulus for our survey came from our readers," the editors note. "From numerous communications we have formed the impression that the 'Bach of Bachs' still represents a 'problem,' whose solution many a mind is working assiduously to find."[7] The editors go on to say that all the historical, editorial, and philological work on Bach—they presumably mean the recently completed edition of the Bach-Gesellschaft—has not pointed the way to the "Castalian source" from which sprang Bach's "God-filled" soul.

Responses came in from approximately half those people contacted. Comments ranged from a few pages to a substantial essay, and in style from lyric verse to acrostics to confessional prose to serious narrative. (Richard Dehmel contributed a poem.) Of course, none of the responses is negative about Bach. But what is striking is how often the responses evoke the metaphor associated with Bach by Nagel in 1901—that of "health" or restoration. Bach is seen as a healer, a restorative fountain, or a physician, in times that are troubled or "hypernervous." For Max Reger, to whom we return below, Bach represents an "inexhaustible medicine." For Felix Draeseke, Bach counters the "unnatural"; for the conductor Fritz Steinbach, "effeminacy." Several of the respondents emphasize, as did Nagel in 1901, that their era is dominated by "sensations" (Alexis Hollaender), is "neurasthenic" (Frank van der Stucken), or is one of "temptation" (Max von Schillings). Here are remarks from the survey that touch upon aspects of health or restoration:

FELIX DRAESEKE: "Bach is healthy and natural, our present day unhealthy and unnatural." (p. 12)

ALEXANDRE GUILMANT: "The music of Bach is restful, satisfies the heart and the soul; it makes them better!" (p. 13)

ALEXIS HOLLAENDER: "Bach's music signifies, or rather should signify, a healing bath for the music of our time, which could thereby rid itself of overactive sensations, grow, and take possession of itself." (pp. 18–19)

FRITZ STEINBACH: "What does Bach mean for our time? . . . [His music is] fresh and healthy in our era that is threatened by effeminacy *[Verweichlichung]*." (p. 39)

THEODOR MÜLLER-REUTER: "For me Bach is a healthy spring, into which I step when my musical soul has suffered any kind of injury. He is a healthy spring that strengthens and purifies; he gives powers to oppose all shallow, hypernervous, and unhealthy music. Bach is like a physician. Through his works he speaks to me like a father who cautions his son, who sharpens my knowledge and who heals me when musical excesses have endangered the health of fantasy and of artistic practice." (p. 46)

FRANK VAN DER STUCKEN: "Bach's fundamentally healthy art is, for our neurasthenic generation, beneficial nourishment of musicians. . . . The study of Bach's music is a good medicine against the over- or undervaluation of a composer." (p. 47)

WILHELM BERGER: "Bach is the original source of everything that is healthy in music." (p. 61)

LUDWIG THUILLE: "Whoever is in a position to understand fully the spirit of Bach's music has reached a healthy spring, which will never run dry his life long." (p. 62)

WALDEMAR VON BAUSSNERN: "Without Bach there is no health for us." (p. 70)

MAX VON SCHILLINGS: "In our age of 'tempation' *[reizsames Zeitalter]*, no one should miss drinking from the healthy spring of Bach, which offers reinforcement for the heart and the brain." (p. 71)

MAX REGER: "[Bach is] a really powerful, inexhaustible medicine, not only for all those composers and musicians who suffer from 'misunderstood Wagner,' but for all those 'contemporaries' who suffer from spinal tuberculosis *[Rückenmarksschwindsucht]* of any kind." (p. 74)

In his response to the survey (pp. 75–76), Albert Schweitzer stressed the more religious and mystical side of Bach: Bach as *Tröster,* as comforter. Yet a few years later, he may be said to have put in his two pfennige into the discussion reflected in the pages of *Die Musik.* In the German edition of his Bach study, published in 1908, Schweitzer added at the very end the plea that "Bach help our age to attain the spiritual unity and fervour of which it so sorely stands in need."[8] This sentence does not appear in the original French edition of 1905.

In fact, the image of Bach as healer was not a new one. The Bachian counterpoint in Beethoven's late sonatas and quartets—and let us even throw in the more Palestrinian technique of the "Heiliger Dankgesang" from the A-Minor Quartet, op. 132—implies a restorative, a cure. Robert Schumann on several occasions noted the healing powers of Bach's music and techniques. In the summer and fall of 1845, when he was suffering from a bad bout of mental illness, Schumann turned to an intensive study of counterpoint, especially Bach's, which seems to have had a therapeutic effect.[9] Bach was also comforting to the mortally ill Brahms, whose biographer Max Kalbeck reported of his last visits with the composer in March 1897: "He [Brahms] complained about his situation and said: 'It's lasting so long.' He also told me that he was not able to listen to any music. The piano remained closed: he could only read Bach, that was all. He pointed to the piano, where on the music stand, which stood on top of the closed cover, lay a score of Bach."[10]

One could probably find other examples of such attitudes from nineteenth-century composers. (Wagner liked to have parts of the *Well-Tempered Clavier* played to him at Wahnfried in the evenings.) Yet there is a difference between these more individual nineteenth-century views of Bach as healer and the rhetoric evident in the responses to the survey of 1905. For the respondents in 1905, Bach is more than a personal healer; he is a balm for an entire culture that is seen as degenerate, perverted, effeminate, and unhealthy. These writers are taking shots in a culture war, a war whose more famous conservatives included Julius Langbehn and Max Nordau.

The Bach number of *Die Musik* was followed within two months, in December 1905, by the premiere of Strauss's *Salome,* the great *succès de scandale* of early German modernism and a work that unleashed further discussion about musical decadence and degeneration.[11] In turn, there arose a broader dispute about musical and cultural values that extended over several years in the pages of various periodicals. It may be said to have taken wing with a polemic against musical modernism written in October 1906 in the *Neue Musik-Zeitung* by one of the contributors to the earlier Bach survey, the composer Felix Draeseke. Draeske entitled his article "Die Konfusion in der Musik: Ein Mahnruf" (Confusion in Music: A Warning Call). He does not mention *Salome* specifically—in fact, no moderns are mentioned by name—but is clearly tilting at it in certain passages about dissonance, cacophony, and so forth. Draeseke's article elicited a wide range of responses, including an exchange between Reger and his teacher Hugo Riemann on the topic of "degeneration" and "regeneration" in music, to which I return below.[12] Like many critics of the time, Draeske was concerned not just with the technical aspects of modern German music, but with its national identity, an issue that can lead us back directly to our consideration of Bach.

BACH RECEPTION AROUND 1900

Bach reception in German-speaking lands in the period of early modernism is marked by an intensification of what had occupied the nineteenth century since Forkel and had continued with Wagner (as we saw in chapter 1): the image of Bach as an embodiment of the German *Volk*. The goals of the Neue Bach-Gesellschaft (New Bach Society, hereafter NBG) directly reflect that image of Bach. The NBG, which was brought into being on January 27, 1900, proposed to use the advances of the modern world—including travel, music publishing, and professional musical training—to promote Bach among the German public through performances, practical editions, and the integration of his sacred works into the Protestant church service. The bylaws of the NBG stated that the goal of the organization was "to make the works of the great German composer Johann Sebastian Bach a creative force among the German people and in those countries that are open to serious German music, and in particular to make his sacred works useful for the worship service."[13] The NBG initiated a series of "traveling" (*wandernde,* as the bylaws put it) Bach festivals, which would take place in different locales. The first was held in Berlin in 1901, the second in Leipzig in 1904. The Bachfeste continue to this day. The NBG also began publishing the *Bach-Jahrbuch,* which first appeared in 1904.

The populist impulse among many Bach lovers at the turn of the century is well reflected in some comments made to NBG members at their meeting in October 1908 on the occasion of the Bachfest in Chemnitz. A parish priest named Löscher from the nearby town of Zwönitz reminded the group that according its statutes the NBG had a two-pronged goal: to make Bach's works an "animating force" among the German people, and to make his sacred works "useful" for congregations.[14] Löscher admired the high level of performance of large and difficult vocal works that one heard at the Bach festivals, but said that "the center of gravity of the Bach Society does not lie in these large Bach festivals, which are really celebrations for a select community of Bach lovers, but rather in extending Bach's influence into broader circles." The Bach motets and many of the cantatas are too difficult for amateur church choirs, Löscher observes. The NBG could really fill a void by creating practical editions of the Bach chorales, arranged according to the church year, which could be used by parish choirs across Germany. Such a volume could be followed by a second, containing a selection of small, easy choral segments from the cantatas, also arranged according to the liturgy. "In this way," he says, "the Neue Bach-Gesellschaft could really do something to make Bach 'volkstümlich' in the best sense of the word."[15]

In fact, at its October 1908 meeting, the NBG determined to prepare all the sacred vocal works of Bach in performing editions "für den praktischen Gebrauch" (for practical use), to be published by Breitkopf & Härtel. The goal was to publish yearly six to twelve smaller works and one larger work. Even prior to 1908 the NBG had begun to issue such editions. In 1907 Cantata 88 appeared; in the following year, the Violin Concerto in E Major. In 1908 the NBG published Cantata 85 *(Ich bin ein guter Hirt)* and the *Brandenburg Concerto* No. 3 in both orchestral and four-hand arrangements. In 1910 the *Brandenburg Concerto* No. 1 appeared in similar fashion.[16]

There was more than populism and nationalism behind the Bach activities around 1900. Rudolf Stephan has suggested that they represented a counter-movement against the emphasis on *Ausdruck* or expression, which in the late nineteenth century had gradually replaced *Schönheit* or beauty as the leading aesthetic. Stephan argues that the work of Bach, as it became better known, came to represent an *Altklassik* or old classicism alongside the *Klassik* represented especially by Beethoven. At the same time—and this is a key point—Bach's music came to represent the New at the turn of the century. Bach was an important stimulus to composers, says Stephan, less because of any specific structural technique or historical role, but because the *Aussenhalt* or "framework" of his music offered composers around 1900 a way out of the more conventional Classic-Romantic idioms and structures.[17] Bach became an essential stimulus to the creative personalities of several of the important figures of early German modernism, including Reger, Schoenberg, Busoni, and Mahler.

It should not surprise us that in the years after 1900 Bach became important not only in the culture wars, but also in the areas of musical theory, aesthetics, and analysis, disciplines that are never immune to the broader currents swirling around them. August Halm's book of 1913, *Von zwei Kulturen der Musik* (On Two Cultures of Music), was one of the most important studies to feature Bach prominently. This was by no means a study of musical "culture" in any real sociological, anthropological, or even historical sense. Halm's "cultures" do not involve listening behavior, repertory formation, or institutions like the concert hall and opera house. Rather, in what we might call an aesthetically aware book of musical analysis, Halm sought to distinguish two important periods of recent Western art music, one characterized more by what he called "style" and "language," the other by "form." The former he designated as a culture of fugue or fugal process, associated most strongly with Bach; the latter is a culture characterized most powerfully by Beethoven's sonata forms. Halm's only real bow toward a social dimension is when he suggests that fugue carries out the implications of a single theme and thus is "the formula of an individuality." By contrast, the sonata is analogous to many individuals working together. It is an organism on a large scale: "it resembles the city."[18]

In the book Halm actually examines these phenomena in reverse order: first, form as manifested in the sonata, then language as manifested in the fugue. Of the latter he says, "It was Bach who first elevated musical language to the level of a real art, and after him it did not retain this level." Halm analyzes a number of Bach themes for their organic growth and integrity, their "spiritual, biological unity," and their powerful life force.[19] Halm's exalting of Bach's language or style is significant in the context of modernist thought and practice in Austro-German music around 1900, in part because Bach is raised to the level of Beethoven as a compositional model. As Stephan has shrewdly put it, "By placing Bach beside Beethoven, Halm's theory was historically significant above all because it was one of the first to relativize, and thereby restrict, the notion of Beethoven as the unsurpassed and unsurpassable summit of all music."[20]

Halm's work had a direct influence on his friend Ernst Kurth, whose *Grundlagen des linearen Kontrapunkts* (Foundations of Linear Counterpoint) appeared in 1917. Kurth, a professor at Berne, took a psychologically or experientially oriented view of music that differed from traditional approaches to music theory. In his view, melodic tones contain a "kinetic energy" that pushes them forward in a linear, dynamic way. They are not perceived or experienced individually, but as part of a larger shape: "The tones do not exist first and their connection afterwards; rather the dynamic current is the primary element." Or: "The melodic element resides in the motion through the tones, not in the individual tones through which the motion flows."[21] As Lee Rothfarb has pointed out, this aspect of Kurth's thought anticipates some of the fundamental principles of Gestalt psychology.[22]

For Kurth, Bach is the greatest manifestation of the way in which a dynamically flowing melodic line can generate larger polyphonic and formal structures. He follows up on Halm's view of the generative powers of Bach's melodies. Kurth's book is an attempt to demonstrate this through detailed analysis, mostly of individual phrases or passages from Bach's works. Kurth lays out his theories in the opening part of *Grundlagen* before taking up Bach's counterpoint specifically. For Kurth, melody is a primarily linear phenomenon, whose harmonic implications are real but ultimately secondary. Rothfarb has called this a "melodic-genetic" view, and it informs Kurth's entire approach to Bach. For Kurth, Bach's was the purest and most authentic melodic style: "The technique of the monophonic line . . . is to be achieved primarily by taking Bach's melodic style as a model."[23]

Kurth's melodic-horizontal view of Bach was in part a reaction to the emphasis on Bach's harmonic language in more recent music theoretical works, especially perhaps Schoenberg's *Theory of Harmony,* which appeared in 1911. Already in this book, which preceded Halm's study, Bach may be said to be elevated beside (or beyond) Beethoven. As Stephan has pointed out, Schoenberg cites or refers to Bach here more often than any other composer, including Beethoven and Wagner, both of whom one would expect to see heavily represented in a harmony treatise written around 1900.[24] Of course, Schoenberg's *Theory of Harmony* is anything but a book of harmonic analysis or even "theory" in a conventional sense. Very few musical examples are taken from the musical literature; most are created by Schoenberg himself.

For Schoenberg, Bach serves a key ideological purpose that may be said to lie behind the treatise: to show that tonality is not a natural phenomenon, but an artificial one, and concomitantly that "harmony" could mean any group of tones sounding together, not just those that follow rules deemed to be eternally valid. For Schoenberg, famously, "there are no nonharmonic tones, for harmony means tones sounding together." Such a view led Schoenberg to claim, as we recall from chapter 3, that the difference between consonance and dissonance was a relative rather than absolute one. Dissonances are only more distant elements, or "more remote consonances," of the overtone series.[25]

Bach is Schoenberg's principal example of this phenomenon, and in the chapter of *Theory of Harmony* on nonharmonic tones he cites passages from Bach's eight-voice motet *Komm, Jesu, komm* (BWV 229, mm. 14 and 41–43). The simultaneities formed by the voices at these moments would be considered intensely, unclassifiably dissonant by traditional theory, which would argue that the chords produced are incidental, the result of passing tones in a complex contrapuntal texture. But Schoenberg argues that these chords are coherent harmonies in their own right, and that although they may sound "harsh," Bach must have considered them "beautiful," because he used sonorities like them in many works. "He followed his urge to accommodate more complicated harmonies, wherever he thought he could do it without danger to the intelligibility of the whole," says Schoenberg. "But the essential thing, the urge to write harsh harmonies, which I find identical with the urge to include more remote overtones—this urge was there."[26] As has long been realized, Schoenberg was setting down his thoughts on Bach and nonharmonic tones in *Theory of Harmony* just after he had written his own first freely atonal works in 1909. Bach's harmonies provided a noble precedent for Schoenberg's own compositional procedures in emancipating dissonance.

Although he thus had good reason to champion Bach as Harmonist, Schoenberg did not ignore the horizontal dimension of Bach's music. He had little patience with Kurth's theories, at least as transmitted by what he in 1931 called Kurth's "acolytes" (he said he never read Kurth's work itself). Schoenberg felt the phrase "linear counterpoint" was a "contradiction in terms," "a piece of nonsense," because counterpoint implies harmonic progression and vertical relationships between notes.[27] But Schoenberg found in Bach the origin of what he was to deem the most important melodic-thematic principle in Western music, developing variation, through which small motives, intervals, and rhythms are continually reshaped to generate broader structures. Bach was able, wrote Schoenberg in 1946 (in an essay originally drafted in 1933), "to write fluent and well balanced melodies of . . . beauty, richness and expressiveness." He was thereby "the first to introduce . . . the technique of 'developing variation,' which made possible the style of the great Viennese Classicists."[28]

The critic Paul Bekker in an essay, "Neue Musik" (New Music) of 1919, characterized the awareness of Bach as Melodist as a key feature of the modern era: "Our position vis-à-vis Bach is nonetheless a very different one from that of the earlier generations. We see in Bach not only the great master of contrapuntal technique, we see in him not only the powerful tone poet; we also see in him principally the unmatched *shaper of melodies.* His melodic art was founded in an unprecedented power of linear musical sensibility, for which later eras despite their Bach cult had little regard."[29]

For Bekker, Bach's melodic art could show the way to a modern musical language, not by mere imitation or "superficial adoption," but "only through the recognition and readaptation of stylistic elements of older art arising out of the spirit of a new age." Bekker is calling not for neoclassicism, but for a profound historical-structural engagement with music of the past. The one composer he mentions specifically in this context is Max Reger, whom he calls "the first who in his art made reference once again to that past which for us, insofar as we want to connect with a past, is fruitful; he was thus the first to reach beyond the Classic-Romantic models to *Bach.*"[30]

REGER'S HISTORICIST MODERNISM

In his description of adapting older styles "in the spirit of a new age" Bekker provides as plausible a characterization of historicist modernism in music—and of the role of Reger's Bach reception within it—as we might want. The concept of historicism in music requires some explanation. "Was ist Historismus?" (What Is Historicism?) asks Carl Dahlhaus anxiously in the first subhead of his *MGG* article on the topic.[31] For Dahlhaus, musical historicism can be both a *Denkweise,* a mode of thought, for historians, and a *Praxis,* or practice, for composers. As he develops this argument, Dahlhaus proposes, as is his wont, a number of further dialectics that are suggestive for understanding a figure like Reger. One dichotomy is between "tradition" and "restoration." Tradition connotes an unquestioning or "naïve" (in Schiller's sense) appeal to the past, with which there is the implication of an unbroken continuity. "Restoration" acknowledges a gulf between present and past; it seeks to restore something that has been broken off. Restoration is thus reflective and self-conscious—"sentimental" in Schiller's sense.

Another, related dialectic introduced by Dahlhaus is that of "retrospective" versus "relativistic" historicism. The former, like tradition, reaches back to older styles and techniques as if they could somehow be freed from history with impunity and incorporated into the present. Masses in the Palestrina style in the nineteenth century, for example, might be excellent imitations, says Dahlhaus, but they are only "empty husks" of tradition. They manifest retrospective historicism, a kind of naïve traditionalism based on the "belief in the timeless, unchanging substance and validity of an old style." "Relativistic" historicism is, on the other hand, like "restoration," sentimental; it is marked by a desire, in Dahlhaus's word, "to appropriate the past compositionally with a historical consciousness, precisely because it is past and bears the colors of an earlier era" (col. 341). In other words, relativistic historicism exaggerates, even celebrates, the distance with the past, rather than collapsing it.

Many works of Brahms, which impart a sense of identification, comfort, and continuity with masters of the past, would seem to capture this kind of relativistic or sentimental historicism. Brahms showed how techniques of the remote past could be put in the service of a musical language both expressive and original. His a cappella sacred vocal works, steeped in Renaissance and Baroque principles, are prime examples, but the most extraordinary and influential product of his historicist imagination is the finale of the Fourth Symphony from 1885. With its unique fusion of ancient and contemporary practice, this passacaglia had a profound impact on subsequent composers. Schoenberg, Berg, Webern, Reger, and Zemlinsky all wrote pieces modeled after or partially inspired by Brahms's finale.[32]

Reger understood perhaps better than any other composer of his generation that for Brahms the music of the past was not a crutch but a creative stimulus. "What assures Brahms immortality," he wrote in 1896 (and reiterated in later years), "is never and will never be his reliance on old masters, but the fact that he knew how to produce new, unimagined psychological *[seelisch]* moods on the basis of his own psychological makeup."[33] More so than Brahms, however, Reger seems to be reaching back, often obsessively or desperately, to the world of Bach that is acknowledged as past and that must be reenvisioned in contemporary terms. That is what makes his historicism modernist. There is no real trace of nostalgia, as might be characteristic of retrospective historicism; there is no sense of being able to go back to an earlier world, time, or style. As a modern composer, Reger must face up to the historical gap and seek to bridge it, but not cross back over it.

Reger's position is apparent from his response to the 1905 survey in *Die Musik* on the contemporary significance of Bach, which reads in full as follows:

> Sebastian Bach is for me the beginning and end of all music; upon him rests, and from him originates, *all* **real** progress!
>
> What does—pardon, what **should**—Sebastian Bach mean for our era? A really powerful, inexhaustible medicine, not only for all those

composers and musicians who suffer from "misunderstood Wagner," but for all those "contemporaries" who suffer from spinal tuberculosis of any kind. To be "Bachian" means: to be *authentically German, unyielding.*

That Bach could be misunderstood for *so* long is the greatest *scandal* for the "critical wisdom" of the eighteenth and nineteenth centuries.[34]

Reger touches here on virtually all the major themes of contemporary Bach reception—Bach as progressive, Bach as German, Bach as sturdy, Bach as healthy. But his relationship with Bach went far beyond fervent admiration; it approached what Johannes Lorenzen has aptly called "monomaniacal identification."[35] Reger's letters and reported comments are full of references to "Allvater Bach," on whom he would call in times of need. In 1902 Reger described to his fiancée Elsa his work on an arrangement of Bach's Cantata 93 *(Wer nur den lieben Gott läßt walten)* as a "spiritual chalybeate bath *[Stahlbad]*."[36] Bach became an essential companion to a composer who was plagued by self-doubt, was physically and psychically restless, suffered from alcoholism, and composed and performed with compulsive prolixity. Antonius Bittmann relates Reger's personality and his musical style to a fin-de-siècle culture obsessed with, and often characterized by, nervousness—or, as it was often called around 1900, neurasthenia.[37]

Lorenzen has given us what is undoubtedly the most complete picture to date of Reger's Bach-related activities as reflected in the vast array of arrangements and transcriptions. These cover virtually all genres and span almost Reger's entire career, from 1895 to 1916. The numbers are astonishing: Reger edited, arranged, or transcribed 428 individual pieces by Bach. No other composer since Bach himself was so deeply, indeed pathologically, involved with his works.

Reger's activity in this sphere can be summarized as follows:

- Thirty-four arrangements of Bach organ works, for either piano two hands or four hands, or for two pianos. These include larger works like preludes or toccatas and fugues, as well as chorale preludes.
- Thirty-five arrangements for organ of Bach keyboard works. These include some Preludes and Fugues from the *Well-Tempered Clavier,* the *Two-Part Inventions,* and the *Chromatic Fantasy and Fugue.*
- Fourteen arrangements of Bach's orchestral works for four-hand piano or for chamber ensemble, including the Orchestral Suites and the *Brandenburg Concertos.*

- Seven arrangements of solo concertos, often for chamber ensemble, or with piano reduction of orchestral part.
- Two arrangements of Bach's violin sonatas for violin and piano.
- Two arrangements of Bach's cantatas, with realized organ part.[38]

We can add to this list Reger's edition of Bach's keyboard works prepared with August Schmid-Lindner for Schott and his revision of Josef Rheinberger's two-piano arrangement of the *Goldberg Variations.*

Reger's Bach arrangements and transcriptions had varying purposes. Some of the earliest transcriptions of organ works for the piano, from 1895 and 1896, were virtuoso pieces destined for concert use, much in the mode of Busoni (whose transcriptions were a direct inspiration for Reger) or d'Albert. Also intended for the concert hall were some of the arrangements of the concerti and orchestral music for smaller ensembles. The four-hand arrangements of the *Brandenburg Concertos* (and of some of the organ works) were offered as *Hausmusik.* The transcriptions of the *Two-Part Inventions* for organ and of selected chorale preludes for piano were for instructional use. The cantata arrangements and some of the transcriptions for organ of keyboard works were intended for the Protestant liturgy.[39]

Lorenzen locates Reger's Bach-related activities directly under the rubric of historicism, a fundamental aspect of Reger's artistic formation with Hugo Riemann, with whom he studied from 1890 to 1895. That a composer of Reger's ability should have as his principal teacher not another composer, but a musicologist—moreover a musicologist of the status and authority of Riemann—does indeed constitute, as Lorenzen says, a "unique constellation."[40]

But ultimately Reger's Bach was not Riemann's Bach. For Riemann, Bach was part of a formidable past that was being brought to light by historical research and that had to be absorbed into the music of the present. "Behind Beethoven, Mozart, and Haydn, now Gluck, Handel, and Bach have risen again as the first great masters of the most recent past," Riemann intoned in "Degeneration und Regeneration in der Musik" (Degeneration and Regeneration in Music), a broadside of 1907 that formed part of the series of polemical exchanges discussed above. "And behind them in turn rise up Palestrina and Lasso as witnesses of a period that lies still further in the past, and the greatness of whose music, which at first sounds strange to us, must be, and will be, exemplary for the music of the present and future, just as the art of the Renaissance and Antiquity are for the visual arts."[41] All this sounds very much like a musicologist placing a clammy and restrictive hand on the music of his own time. Reger broke publicly with his former teacher over the "Degeneration" article. In a response, he proudly included himself among the "moderns" like Strauss and endorsed a vision of music in which one could revere the older masters and still "ride to the left," a metaphor which he takes from—and turns against—Riemann.[42]

Reger's own compositions give a better picture of this left-tilting, modernist historicism than either his arrangements or his polemical writings. It seems clear that the flood of organ works that issued from Reger for about a decade, from the mid-1890s until 1905, were part of a determined attempt to forge a modernist style in the image of Bach, the composer most closely associated with the instrument. Heinrich Reimann, a leading writer on music and one of the most renowned organists of the time, urged all players and prospective composers for organ to steep themselves in the style of Bach. He wrote in 1894, using the metaphor of health that would dominate the responses to the 1905 survey: "Beyond this style there is no salvation *[Heil]*. . . . Bach becomes for that reason the criterion of our art of writing for the organ."[43]

At this point in his career, Reger steered clear of the genres in which the major musico-political battles of the later nineteenth century were being fought. He avoided the post-Wagnerian symphonic poem and music drama, cultivated by Strauss, Schillings, and Pfitzner. After an initial flurry of chamber music (opp. 1, 2, 3, 5, from 1890–92), Reger created little in that medium until after 1900. He thus may be said to have avoided at this point continuing the tradition strongly associated with Brahms, where figures like the young Zemlinsky, Schoenberg, and countless Brahms epigones (Robert Fuchs and Heinrich von Herzogenberg, for example) located themselves. In organ music Reger found an area that offered rich possibilities because it was largely unplowed.

Most commentators recognize the summit of Reger's Bach reception in the so-called Weiden organ works, written between 1898 and 1901, when he returned to live with his parents and be treated for nervous exhaustion and alcoholism. These colossal pieces include three Chorale Fantasies (opp. 27, 30, and 40); three Fantasies and Fugues (op. 29; the Fantasy and Fugue on BACH, op. 46; the Symphonic Fantasy and Fugue, op. 57); and two sonatas (opp. 33 and 60). I would like to focus on Bach-inspired works composed on either side of the Weiden period: the First Organ Suite, op. 16; the *Bach Variations* for piano, op. 81; and the slow movement of the Piano Concerto, op. 114.

REGER'S ORGAN SUITE, OP. 16

Reger completed his Suite for Organ, op. 16, in E minor, on July 23, 1895, near the end of his formal study with Riemann. He had begun the work in 1894 as a "sonata" in three movements, comprising an introduction and triple fugue; an Adagio based on the chorale "Es ist das Heil uns kommen her"; and a passacaglia. The work evolved into a "suite" in four movements, although the Suite in fact resembles a sonata.[44] The Adagio was expanded to a ternary form, of which the middle part incorporates two more chorales, "Aus tiefer Not" and the Passion chorale "O Haupt voll Blut und Wunden." Between the original second and third movements Reger added an Intermezzo in the form of a scherzo with trio.

Reger dedicated his Suite not, as was to be his practice, to a living figure he admired, but "To the Memory of Johann Sebastian Bach" (Den Manen Johann Sebastian Bachs). The work, which appeared in 1896, was given its premiere by Reger's friend, the virtuoso organist Karl Straube, on March 4, 1897, in Berlin. The strongly historicist orientation of the score was remarked by critics, including one reviewer in the *Monthly Musical Record,* who noted that the "boldness" of the inscription to Bach was "in large measure justified" by Reger's "knowledge of harmony, of counterpoint, canon, and fugue, and of part-writing generally."[45] Reger himself thought the Suite was the best thing he had composed up to that time. Seeking a wider audience for it than it might receive as an organ work, he arranged it for piano four hands, as one might a symphony.[46]

Reger alluded to the significance of the Organ Suite in a letter he wrote to Riemann in August 1895, as the latter was leaving Wiesbaden and as Reger's formal instruction with him came to a close: "As a young musician who, full of the noblest enthusiasm, continued to serve only his masters Bach, Beethoven, and Brahms, and to absorb them within himself, I ask your permission for this young unknown musician to give you and your wife once again the most heartfelt and best thanks. . . . *As your student* I will not bring you any dishonor. As proof you must get to know my Organ Suite (with Passacaglia). (Bach varied the theme 21 times in his; I have done it 32 times.)"[47]

In the spring of 1896, Reger felt sufficiently confident to send a copy of the Suite to his idol, Brahms. This was the occasion of his only direct contact with the older composer, who would die the following April. In his accompanying letter, Reger asked Brahms's permission to dedicate to him a symphony in progress (a work that was never completed). Brahms replied with the following note:

> Dear Sir! Heartfelt thanks for your letter, whose warm, indeed too friendly, words were very sympathetic to me. Moreover, you spoil me with the lovely offer of a dedication.
>
> Permission for that is certainly not necessary, however! I had to smile, since you approach me about this matter and at the same time enclose a work whose all-too-bold dedication terrifies me!
>
> You may then without concern set down the name of your most respectful
>
> *J. Brahms.*[48]

Brahms provided no comments on the Suite, but he did enclose an autographed picture of himself and asked the young composer to reciprocate.[49]

Brahms might have been "terrified" not only by the dedication of the Suite to Bach—one could scarcely imagine him doing something similar—but by the close associations with a work of his own. Reger's Suite concludes with a passacaglia in E minor that bears more than a passing resemblance to the finale of Brahms's Fourth Symphony. Reger's finale is in fact an extraordinary synthesis of past and present, drawing on Bach's C-Minor Passacaglia (the model acknowledged by Reger in his letter cited above) and on the finales of Joseph Rheinberger's Organ Sonata No. 8, op. 132 (1882), and Brahms's Fourth Symphony, both also in the key of E minor.

As Martin Weyer has shown, Reger's Suite follows closely the structure of Rheinberger's Sonata No. 8, which has as its first movement an Introduction and Fugue in E minor; as its second or slow movement an "Intermezzo" marked Andante (in E major); as the third a *scherzoso* in A minor; and as a finale a passacaglia.[50] The similarities extend to numerous details as well. Both introductions begin with tonic pedal points, which are followed by dissonant chromatic chords and scalar flourishes. The principal fugue themes are close in shape. In both works, material from the slow introduction is brought back at the end of the passacaglia.

Besides following the "sonata" model of Rheinberger, Reger might be said to adopt the "symphonic" design of Brahms, as manifested in the first three symphonies, in which the outer movements are the largest and most imposing, while the two interior ones are on a smaller, more intimate scale. The model of Brahms's Fourth Symphony lies—remotely, but significantly—behind the larger plan of Reger's Suite. The key signatures of Reger's four movements match precisely those of Brahms: one sharp in the outer movements, five sharps for the Adagio, and no sharps or flats for the Intermezzo. Three of Reger's movements do in fact share Brahms's keys: E minor for first movement and finale, and B major for the Adagio.

I would like to look in some more detail at two movements from Reger's Suite, the slow movement and finale. The Adagio assai is at once a Classical-Romantic slow movement with a ternary form (ABA) and a composite neo-Baroque chorale prelude. The chorale on which the A segment (the original slow movement of the 1894 sonata) is based, "Es ist das Heil uns kommen her," never appears in a purely melodic form, but is elaborately decorated in the upper voice (example 18; chorale tune added above example). The models for this portion of Reger's movement seem to be the chorale preludes from Bach's *Orgelbüchlein* that have been called "ornamental," where the tune appears in the soprano part complete and continuous, but highly embellished. These preludes would include "Das alte Jahr vergangen ist" (BWV 614), "O Mensch, bewein dein Sünde gross" (BWV 622), and "Wenn wir in höchsten Nothen sein" (BWV 641).[51]

"O Mensch" must have been Reger's primary inspiration. In the Bach-Gesellschaft edition that Reger would have known (volume 25), this chorale prelude is one of the few from the *Orgelbüchlein* to appear with a tempo indication (presumably Bach's own), Adagio assai, precisely the tempo marking Reger gave to the A segment of his slow movement. "O Mensch" seems moreover to have been one of Reger's favorites among Bach's chorale preludes. It took pride of place—as the first—in the edition of thirteen Bach chorale preludes he arranged for solo piano, published in 1900. (It was in the preface to this edition that he called Bach's chorale preludes "symphonic poems in miniature.") In 1915 Reger published two different arrangements of "O Mensch" as an instrumental "aria," one for violin and keyboard and another for string orchestra.[52]

Rudolf Huesgen points to what he calls a "*Parsifal* mood" in the A segment of Reger's Adagio and at the same time identifies an "exalted religious mysticism, such as we sense in the *St. Matthew Passion* and in certain cantatas by Bach."[53] Indeed, Wagner and Bach, who join hands in certain moments of *Die Meistersinger* and *Parsifal,* are both plausible inspirations for Reger's Adagio, which, however, is characterized by a thicker and busier contrapuntal texture than either of his predecessors would have provided

Example 18. Reger, Organ Suite, op. 16, II, with chorale superimposed

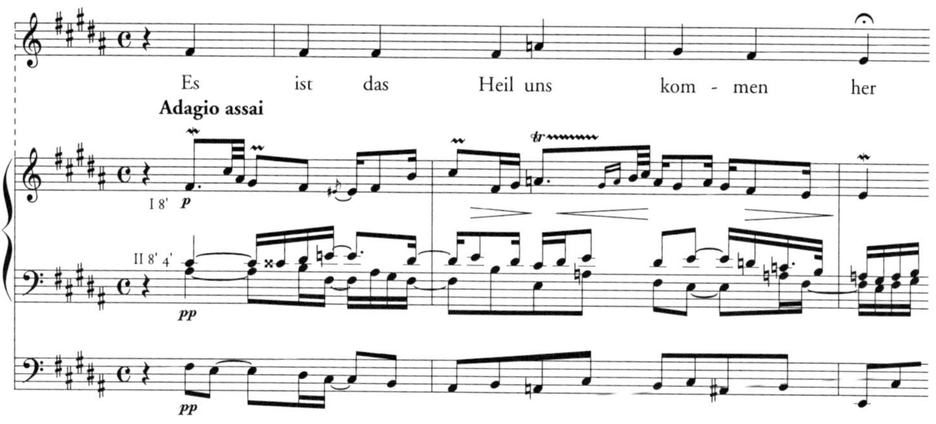

in such an instance. The contrasting B section in B minor is in two parts, each based on a different chorale, "Aus tiefer Not" and the Passion chorale ("O Haupt voll Blut und Wunden"), respectively.[54] The two chorales are developed successively—and in different ways—and are then combined in counterpoint. "Aus tiefer Not" is treated by Reger fugally in as many as six parts (example 19; chorale text added by author). Reger also manages to fit in stretto (m. 16) and augmentation (mm. 17–18). His elaborate treatment of "Aus tiefer Not" alludes unmistakably to Bach's own chorale prelude on the same tune from part III of the *Clavierübung* (BWV 686). This is the most elaborately contrapuntal of Bach's chorale preludes, in which the melody is likewise treated in six-part imitation through the use of a double pedal.

Reger develops the chorale tune "Aus tiefer Not" for sixteen measures, modulating to the dominant, F♯. After this densely polyphonic discourse comes a long fermata, and the Passion chorale begins as a solo line, marked "Adagio (recitativo)" (example 20). Reger has gone from the most "instrumental" of textures and styles to the most vocal. In this section, phrases of the Passion chorale alternate between a recitative manner and fuller five-part writing that clearly is meant to imitate choral style. Just as Reger's treatment of "Aus tiefer Not" brings to mind Bach's six-part chorale prelude, so his use of the Passion chorale reminds us of the *St. Matthew Passion,* where it plays a starring role. In the B section of his Adagio, then, Reger seeks to embrace both sides of Bach—Bach the instrumental composer-contrapuntalist and Bach the composer of sacred vocal music. In the closing

Example 19. Reger, Organ Suite, op. 16, II

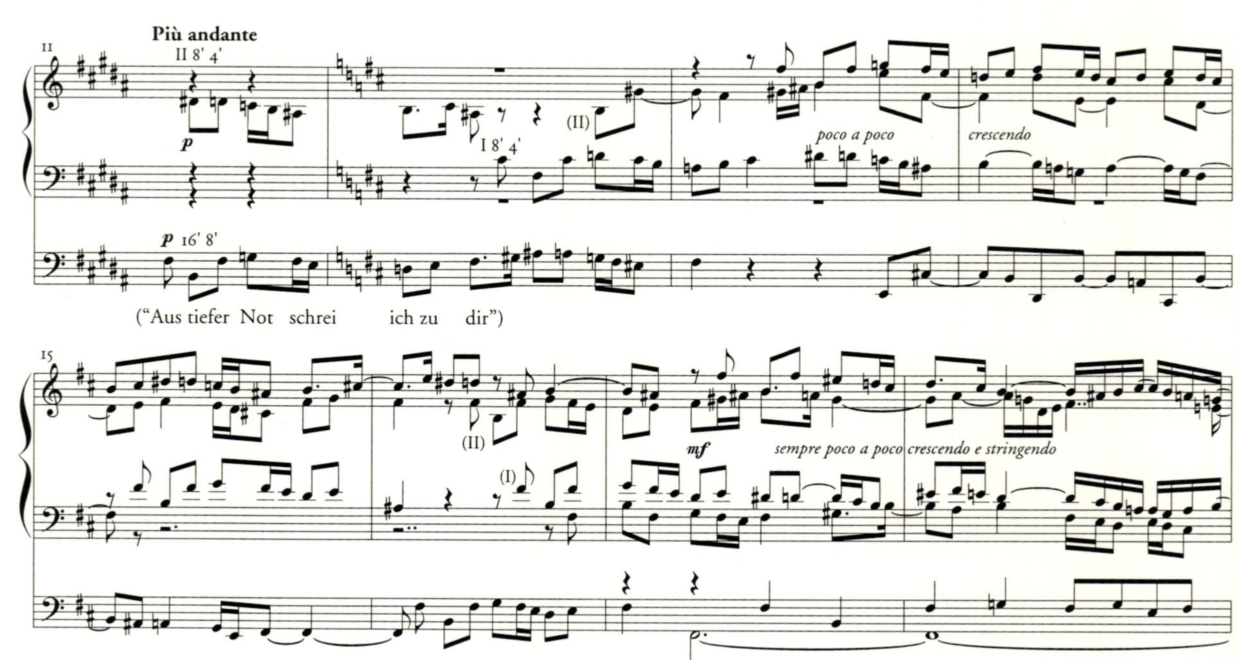

measures of the B section, Reger brings together the two tunes, "Aus tiefer Not" and the Passion chorale, in a final gesture of contrapuntal legerdemain (example 21).

No one could mistake Reger's Adagio for a work by Bach, nor for one by Brahms in his historicizing, Bachian mode, as in the late Chorale Preludes, op. 122 (which were yet to be composed at the time Reger wrote his Suite). The language and the quality of expression are uniquely those of Reger, whom we sense is constructing a modern music by delicately handling the relics of a beloved past. Reger seems to acknowledge a gulf between himself and the past, yet does not wallow in nostalgia. As throughout his oeuvre, he places a high value on craft, especially on counterpoint. The counterpoint leads to a higher level of ambient dissonance than we would find in either Bach or Brahms. The dissonance creates for the listener a level of discomfort that is clearly intentional on Reger's part. The disjunction between the historical technique and the sonority it is manipulated to produce serves to reinforce the presentness—the modernity, as it were—of the music and our reception of it.

The finale of Reger's E-Minor Suite is less strikingly original than the Adagio, but is, if anything, more synoptic, drawing on several previous passacaglias (example 22). The themes by Bach, Brahms, Rheinberger, and Reger all share the triple meter characteristic of the passacaglia genre and follow a standard eight-measure pattern.[55] From Bach and Rheinberger, Reger adapts the contour of large leaps followed by half- or whole-step motion. From Brahms he takes the initial rising stepwise ascent, as well as the introduction of one, and only one, chromatic note (aside from the leading tone), A♯, or the raised fourth. The total number of Reger's variations (29) is closely in line with Brahms (30). (Rheinberger, with twenty-four variations plus a coda, lies somewhere in between.)

As in the Bach C-Minor Passacaglia, Reger's first variation introduces rhythmic syncopation in the upper voices. But where Bach abandons the syncopation after variation 2, Reger is more systematic in continuing and developing it across the first five variations. A feature of Bach's C-Minor Passacaglia that Reger may be said to have adopted via Brahms is moving the ostinato in a middle group of variations into the upper voices, then staging a kind of "return" in the bass. Reger's procedure in the passacaglia is again a kind of sophisticated synthesis of Bach and Brahms: the ostinato begins in the bass and remains there until variation 12, where, at the first dynamic climax *(fff)*, it moves into the top voice. Then it retreats into the bass again for the transition to the major variations and remains there during

Example 20. Reger, Organ Suite, op. 16, II, Passion chorale

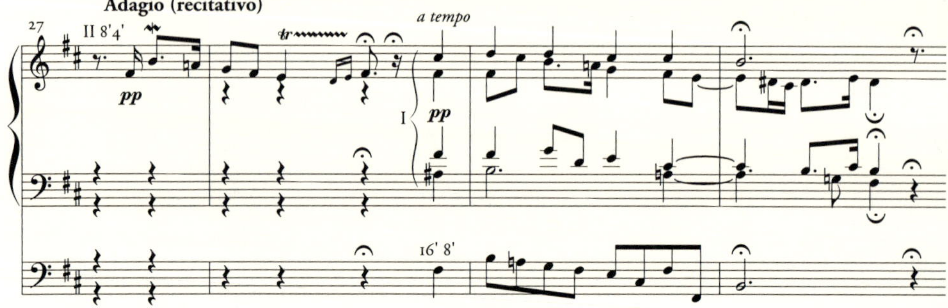

Example 21. Reger, Organ Suite, op. 16, II, superimposition of "Aus tiefer Not" and Passion chorale

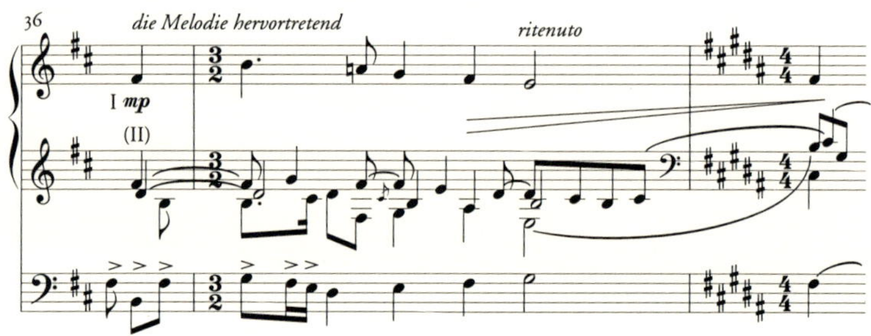

the major variations. For the return to minor in variation 22—a major articulation point in Reger's movement—the theme goes back to the melody, the exact inverse of what Bach and Brahms do at their "returns." At variation 25 Reger returns the theme to the bass for the final, culminating group of variations.

Another model lies behind Reger's passacaglia (as it does behind Brahms's), Bach's Chaconne in D Minor for Solo Violin (BWV 1004), which turns to the major mode for a series of variations almost exactly halfway through the movement (a feature shared by neither Bach's C-Minor Passacaglia nor Rheinberger's). As in Bach's chaconne and Brahms's finale, the turn to the major mode is associated with softer dynamics and a slowing of the rhythm. In all three works—Bach's chaconne and Brahms's and Reger's passacaglias—these changes make for a kind of internal slow movement.

From Brahms Reger also takes the concept of creating countermelodies

Example 22. Passacaglia themes

a. Bach, Passacaglia, BWV 582

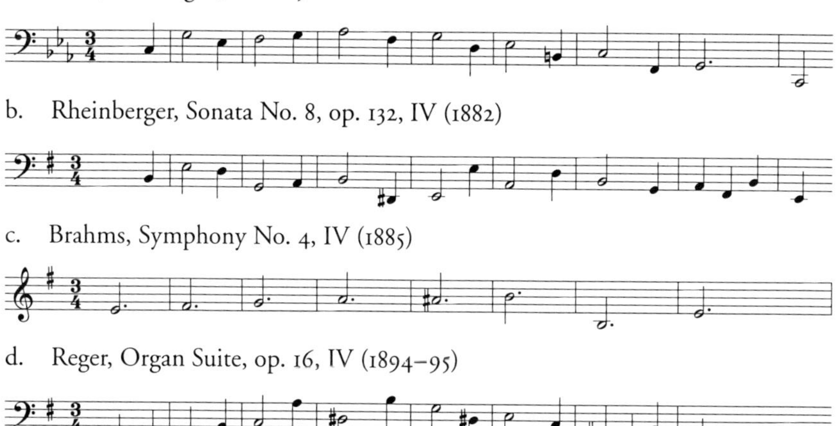

that at times overshadow the passacaglia theme. Brahms begins that process already with the second variation, and in the fourth a broad violin melody emerges, to which the passacaglia theme is now subordinated. In his first variation Reger introduces an idea that is, as already noted, treated imitatively. This idea becomes augmented and transformed into a more genuinely melodic gesture, marked *hervortretend* by Reger. Other important countermelodies are introduced in variations 9 and in the slower major variations (16 and 18).

REGER'S *BACH VARIATIONS,* OP. 81

The self-critical Reger recognized the Organ Suite as a milestone in his development as a composer. Yet we sense a young composer of enormous technical ability flexing historicist muscles that also seem to get in his way. (As the German saying goes, "Er kann vor Kraft nicht gehen"—He is so powerful that he cannot move.) For all his prowess and imagination, Reger cannot be said in the Organ Suite, except perhaps in the Adagio, to transcend any of his models. By the time he composed the *Variations and Fugue on a Theme of Bach* for piano, op. 81, a decade later in 1904, and on the other side of the Weiden organ works, Reger was in his full maturity as a composer. Reger acknowledged the Variations, like the Organ Suite, as a special work in his compositional development. To Karl Straube he wrote that op. 81 was "the *best* that I have written up to now."[56] As in the case of the Suite, such a comment should be taken seriously.

Outside of the theme itself and the final fugue there is no hint of neo-Baroquism in op. 81, which falls clearly into the tradition of monumental piano variations of the nineteenth century. Reger's models were the *"Eroica"* and *Diabelli Variations* of Beethoven and the *Handel Variations* of Brahms, along with the ultimate source of all those works, Bach's *Goldberg Variations.* (In the generic background as well are two other large variation sets for keyboard, Schumann's *Symphonic Etudes,* op. 13 [1834], and Mendelssohn's *Variations sérieuses,* op. 54 [1841].) What immediately distinguishes Reger's op. 81 from any other variation set in the literature, however, is the nature of the theme. He uses the entire opening instrumental ritornello of the duet "Sein' Allmacht zu ergründen" from Bach's Cantata 128, *Auf Christi Himmelfahrt allein.*[57] Bach's ritornello, scored for oboe d'amore and continuo, lacks the rounded and clearly segmented phrase structure of traditional variation subjects. Its fourteen measures may be said to divide, as with most Baroque ritornellos, into units that contain no large-scale returns or repetition, only small internal ones.

The theme has three larger units (example 23): A (mm. 1–6), B (7–10), and C (11–14). The A unit subdivides into three smaller phrases: A1 (mm. 1–2), which closes on the tonic; A2 (mm. 3–5), which is a parallel or answering phrase that also moves to the tonic; and a concluding gesture, A3 (mm. 5–6), which cadences on the dominant minor. The B unit has two parallel phrases, treated as a sequence, of two and a half measures each: B1 (mm. 7–8), which moves to the subdominant minor, and B2 (mm. 9–10), which moves to III, or D major. The final unit, C, has two broader phrases: the first, C1 (11–12), builds upward to the climax of the ritornello; the second, C2 (13–14), leads downward to the final cadence and echoes aspects of the melody of B (a downward curve).

The ritornello selected by Reger is an entirely different creature from the rounded and/or binary themes used by Bach, Beethoven, and Brahms in their variation sets. As Elmar Budde puts it, Reger's op. 81 presents a "remarkable paradox: Reger writes variations on a theme on which no variations, in the sense of a traditional horizon of expectations, can be written."[58] One might supplement Budde's paradox in the following way: Reger creates his finest homage to Bach not by allusion to Bach's compositional techniques or structures, as in the Organ Suite, but by challenging himself to write variations on an unvariable theme. The text of Bach's duet, which reads "Sein Allmacht zu ergründen, wird kein Mensche finden" (No

Example 23. Reger, *Bach Variations,* op. 81, theme

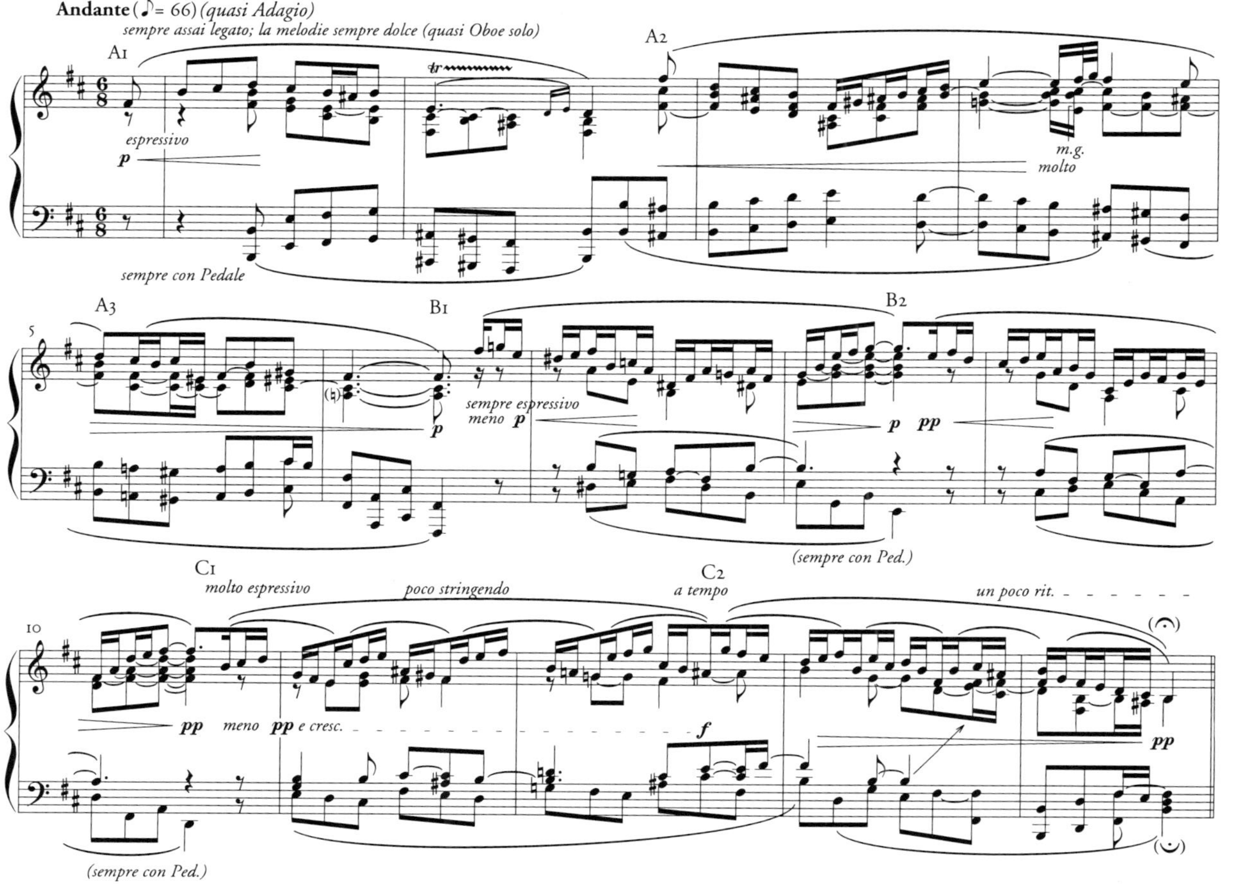

man can fathom His omnipotence), may be significant in this regard. By selecting the melody associated with these words, Reger expresses awe of Bach's own compositional *Allmacht,* which no one can possibly comprehend or equal.

The fourteen variations of op. 81 are not numbered; they are separated from one another only by double bar lines. (See table 1 for a formal synopsis.) This practice, exceptional among Reger's variations, suggests that the work is to be understood as a more continuous, organic composition. One can agree with the Munich critic Alexander Berrsche, who suggested that the *Bach Variations* were *gedichtet,* as compared with Reger's other great solo piano set, the *Telemann Variations,* op. 134, which were *komponiert.*[59]

Harmonically, Reger divides his variations into two large groups of seven. The first group remains in the tonic, B minor; the second begins to modulate, first in an abrupt shift to the remote key of the Neapolitan, C major (var. 8), then to B major (var. 9), G♯ minor (var. 10, ending on G♯ major, or V of C♯), C♯ minor (var. 11, moving to V of B), B major (var. 12), and back to the tonic B minor (vars. 13–14). The fugue concludes in B major.

Crosscutting this harmonic scheme is an approach to treating the theme that is as unique as the theme itself in the variation literature up to that time. The risk of writing variations on a theme as long, complex, and irregular as the Bach ritornello (which lasts close to two minutes in performance) is that complete variations would seem too independent and self-contained, and would sap the overall flow of the work. Reger steps up to the challenge by constantly changing the kind of variation he writes, from stricter ones that retain the original melodic and harmonic structure, to freer fantasy-like variations based on a motivic fragment or two from the ritornello. Such variety is, to be sure, not unusual in the literature. Beethoven's *Diabelli Variations* and Brahms's *Handel Variations* also progress from stricter to freer, although the overall number (or proportion) of measures and essential harmonic framework of the original theme remain intact. But in op. 81 Reger avoids any simple trajectory.

In table 1 the terms "strict" and "free" must be taken as relative, where the former indicates a variation that follows the original ritornello closely at least as to sequence of thematic ideas (and often actual number or proportion of measures), while the latter abandons the ABC formal-thematic structure in significant ways. In the freer variations one has the impression that fragments of the original theme are being cited, recollected, or meditated upon, rather than "varied." Any attempt on the part of the listener to follow the standard narrative of a variation set is thus thwarted.

TABLE I

Reger, *Variations and Fugue on a Theme of Bach,* Op. 81

Formal Unit	*Measure No.*	*Tempo*	*Key*	*Comments*
Theme	1–14	Andante	B minor	
Variation 1	15–28	L'istesso tempo	B minor	Strict; "past"
Variation 2	29–42	[slightly faster]	B minor	Strict; "past"
Variation 3	43–56	Grave assai	ambiguous → B minor	Free; "present"
Variation 4	57–70	Vivace	B minor	Strict; "past"
Variation 5	71–92	Vivace	B minor	Free; "past"
Variation 6	93–115	Allegro moderato	B minor	Strict; "past"
Variation 7	116–27	Adagio	B minor	Strict; "past"
Variation 8	128–45	Vivace	C major	Free; "present"
Variation 9	146–55	Grave e sempre molto espressivo	B major	Free; "present"
Variation 10	156–78	Poco vivace	G♯ minor	Free; "present"
Variation 11	179–201	Allegro agitato	C♯ minor	Free; "present"
Variation 12	202–16	Andante sostenuto	B major	Free; "present"
Variation 13	217–40	Vivace	B minor	Free; "present"
Variation 14	241–54	Con moto	B minor	Strict; "past"
Fugue	255–384	Sostenuto	B minor → major	"Past" and "present"

The first two variations, which form a pair, remain very close to the theme and to traditional variation technique. The fourteen-measure structure remains intact, as do the melody, harmony, and bass; variation consists principally in the rhythmic animation of the inner parts. Variation 3, however, brings a sudden change (example 24). Reger slows the tempo to Grave assai, and instead of the theme in the tonic, we get a two-measure sequence of highly ambiguous harmony, based on a fragment of the descending figure of C2, which has just been heard at the end of the previous variation. Gradually there emerges in the bass a rising three-note figure based on A1 (B♮–C♮–D♮, m. 45), whose first phrase then appears complete in its original form in the melody of m. 48.

We might now interpret the preceding measures (43–47) as having been an introduction to a standard variation, but after only one measure A1 is

Example 24. Reger, *Bach Variations*, op. 81, var. 3

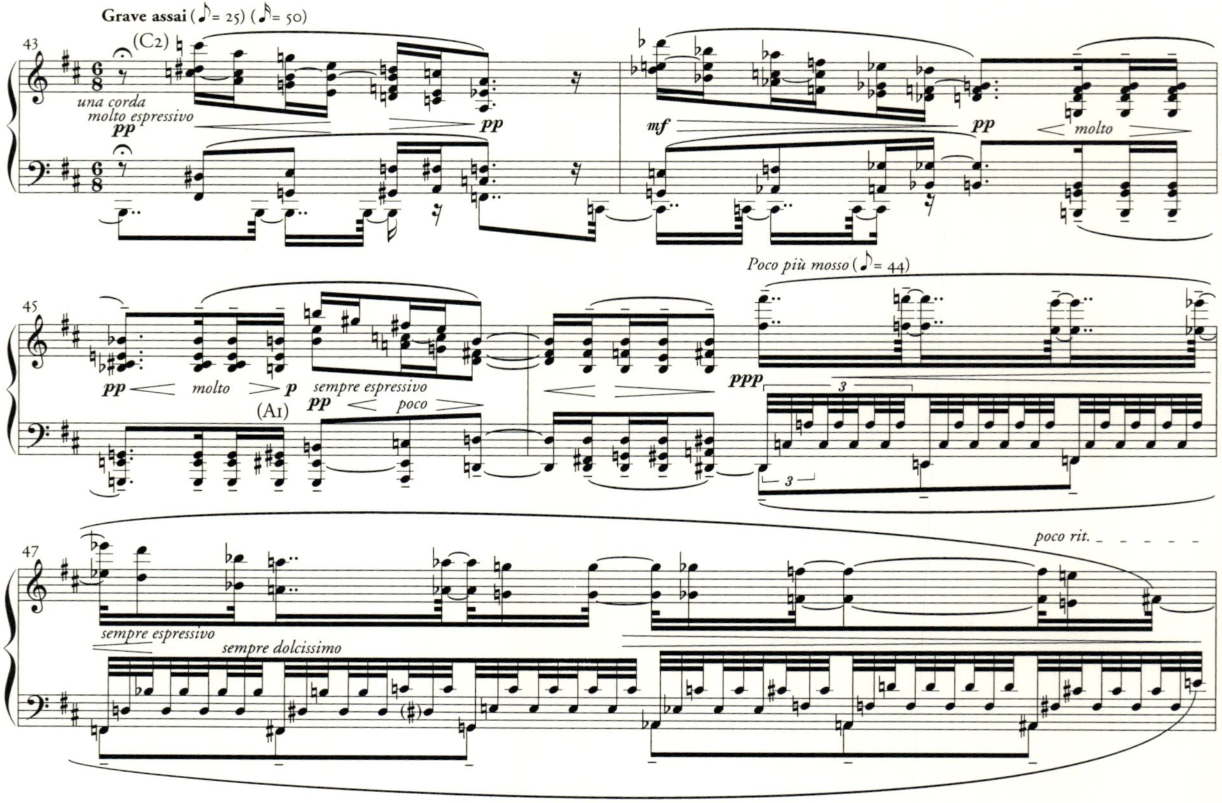

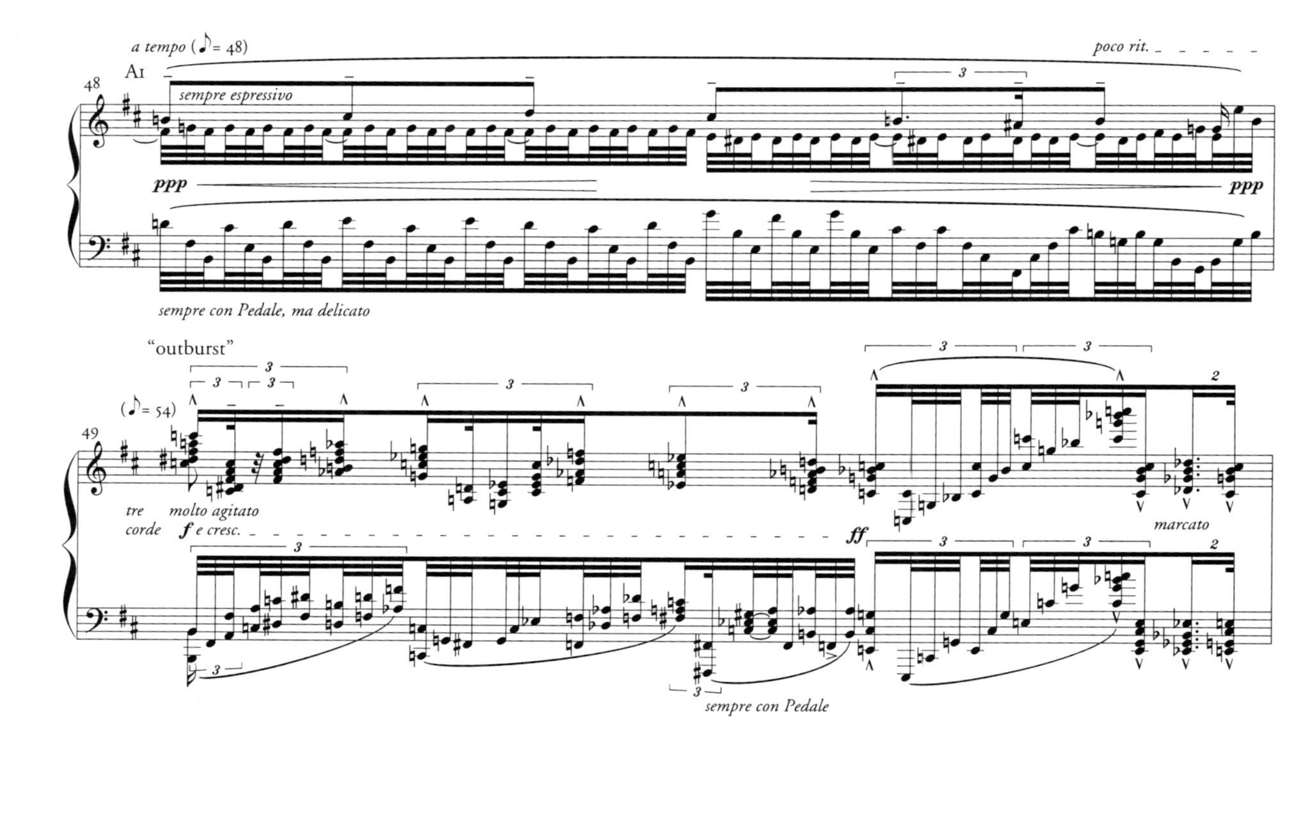
48
A1
a tempo (♪= 48)
poco rit.
sempre espressivo
ppp
ppp
sempre con Pedale, ma delicato
"outburst"
49
(♪= 54)
tre
corde
molto agitato
f e cresc.
ff
marcato
sempre con Pedale

interrupted by a furious, crashingly dissonant outburst that seems unrelated to any aspect of the original ritornello (m. 49). The whole process begins again (not shown in the example): we return first to the introductory measures of this variation, based on the fragments of C2 and A1, then once again to the start of an apparently "real" variation on A1, in the tonic (m. 53). But as before, only a first phrase is allowed to be heard before the fantasy-like C2 interrupts again. Now C2 miraculously metamorphoses into its original cadential form and ends the variation on B minor.

An extraordinary aspect of variation 3 is that despite the freely unfolding fantasy style, its fourteen measures correspond exactly to the dimensions of the ritornello. But the main point to be made is that this variation interrupts the traditional flow of a variation set quite early in its course and dramatizes that very action. The variation twice tries and fails to "begin" when A1 appears in B minor; the second time, it seems to give up and moves immediately to the final cadential phrase, C2, thus collapsing the entire variation process.

Variation 4 returns to the structure of the theme and first two variations, but variation 5 dissolves it anew, and in a different way. The first ten measures are based almost exclusively on sequential treatment of a figure derived from A1. The "real" A1, in its original form, emerges in m. 81, and we might think that a conventional variation is about to begin. But, as in variation 3, the process is interrupted, and this form of A1 becomes treated sequentially, as at the beginning of the variation. Reger exploits a distinction in op. 81—and this is perhaps its most original contribution to the variation literature up to that time—between "real-time," complete variations and freer, more fragmentary ones, which seem generated by memory.

Reger's strategy in the second half of the piece is, at first, to round off the individual variations with a return to the initial motive of that variation (var. 8, m. 140; var. 9, mm. 152–53; var. 10, m. 170; var. 11, m. 193). In doing so, Reger omits the C portion of the ritornello and creates an actual thematic return where one was not present in the original. He may thus be said to "Classicize" or "Romanticize" what was a more open-ended Baroque aspect of the theme. In variation 12, the C section returns (m. 211) after a long absence, and the effect is quite striking. But this variation, like the immediately preceding ones, is also rounded off by a return of its initial motive (in m. 215); aspects of Classical-Romantic and Baroque thus commingle.

A different but related way of thinking of op. 81 is that there is an implied past and present (as indicated in table 1). The past is represented by the theme and the stricter variations, which together embody for Reger the Baroque, Classical, and Romantic traditions, extending from Bach, the author of the theme, through to Beethoven and Brahms, who wrote monumental keyboard variations to which Reger pays homage. The freer variations in op. 81, in which the standard structure is disrupted by motivic fragmentation or motion to distant harmonic regions, may represent the present—the present of 1904. Here contemporary music has undergone a kind of language crisis analogous to what Hofmannsthal described in the contemporaneous *Lord Chandos Letter* cited earlier in this study: "Everything fell into fragments . . . the fragments into further fragments, until it seemed impossible to contain anything at all within a single concept."[60] Reger acknowledged in the musical culture of his time a similar crisis or malady, which he felt Bach could help to heal.

In portions of Reger's op. 81, perhaps especially in variations 3 and 5, the variation structure tends to break down and thus capitulate to the contingency of musical language and syntax. But the work also resists dissolution. In variations 8–13, the rounded returns represent an assertion of order, which becomes still more explicit in variation 14, the only "strict" variation in the second half. The fugue, which lasts almost eight minutes, might be heard as a heroic effort both to accept fragmentation (in the form of the fugue subject) and to reestablish coherence through powerful formal and harmonic closure.

However we choose to explain the complex temporal-structural framework, it is clear that Reger writes directly into the *Bach Variations,* in a way that he could not have done in the Organ Suite, an awareness of historical time that is the essence of historicism. He composes out the distance between himself and Bach, and between himself and Beethoven and Brahms as well.

REGER'S PIANO CONCERTO, OP. 114

Reger composed his only Piano Concerto, op. 114, in 1910. Here, as in so many other works, Brahms was his most immediate model. Reger described his concerto as a "pendant" to the Brahms D-Minor Concerto, and also as the D-Minor "translated into modern terms."[61] But even here in a standard Classic-Romantic form, the remote past is not far from the surface. Reger builds into his slow movement citations from three different chorale melodies, first "O Welt, ich muss dich lassen" and the Passion chorale "O Haupt voll Blut und Wunden," both in the first part of the movement, and then "Vom Himmel hoch" in the coda (example 25). Only the first few notes of each chorale appear, just enough for the listener to make the association. Then the melodies dissolve or continue freely. The fragmentary quality of the chorales, and their untraditional harmonizations, contribute to what Susanne Popp has called their "homeless" quality, as well as to the broader "destabilizing" technique of this movement.[62]

There seems little question that the Bach references were intentional. In a letter to Duke George II of Meiningen, one of his patrons, Reger wrote, "It's very comical how the German critics are once again at a loss over my piano concerto. In the Largo, the chorale 'Wenn ich einmal soll scheiden' [he referred to the Passion chorale by that title] is there, note for note as a principal melody. But none of the asses have noticed that *[das merkt keiner von den Eseln].*"[63] (Even Reger's insults are modeled on those of Brahms.) Reger, ever the chip on the shoulder, writes as if recognition of the chorale melodies should have redeemed him in the eyes of the critics (and presumably the public). Yet it is clear that he did not insert the well-known melodies merely as life rafts for those who might otherwise drown in the churning sea of his harmony and counterpoint. The chorale fragments are complex manifestations of Reger's historicist modernism. Unlike in the Organ Suite, they are distant, ephemeral memories of the actual melodies.

The closest analogy that comes to mind is the way Charles Ives, composing at around the same time, presents fragments of American tunes in dissonant orchestral textures. But Reger's treatment of the foreign materials is different from Ives's. For one thing, the chorales play a central structural role in the slow movement; there is little sense of an Ivesian collage. The chorales seem clearly chosen by Reger for their thematic interrelationships, which are demonstrated in example 26. "O Haupt" and "O Welt" exist in a free but recognizable inversional relationship. The link with "Vom Himmel hoch" is less obvious, but still suggestive. The fourth and fifth notes of "Vom Himmel hoch," a descending third, echo the opening of "O Welt." And the expected continuation of "Vom Himmel hoch," with the rising stepwise scale, as shown in parentheses, would make the association still clearer. Reger avoids that continuation; in fact, he inverts it. We might say that he is avoiding the obvious; he knows (or hopes) his listeners will recognize the melodies.

Moreover, the chorales are clearly part of a larger plan in that they shape themes from the first movement. The descending third of the main mo-

Example 25. Reger, Piano Concerto, op. 114, II, comparison with Bach chorales

a.

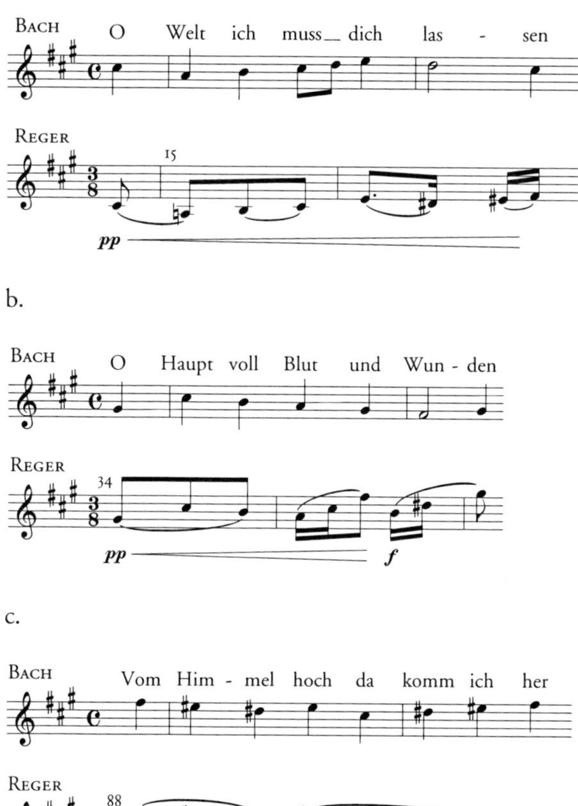

tive of the first movement, A♭–G–F, can be plausibly derived from the opening of "Vom Himmel hoch." That association is strengthened in the coda of the first movement (mm. 252–53), where the chorale melody emerges more distinctly and occupies the formal position analogous to that in the slow movement. The second theme of the first movement (m. 71) is built from a pair of ascending perfect fourths (A♭–D♭, E♭–A♭), thus replicating the opening interval of the Passion chorale "O Haupt voll Blut."

Example 26. Chorale-based thematic relationships in Reger, Piano Concerto, op. 114, II

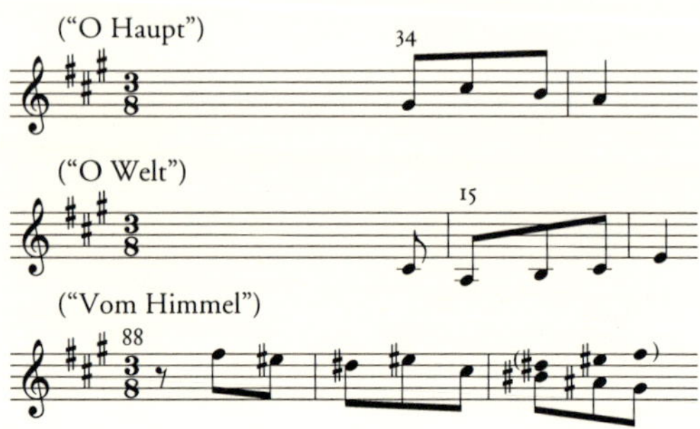

Of course, all these allusions in the first movement may be recognized only after the fact, as it were, from the perspective of the Largo. The first movement thus gives premonitions, or what Alan Walker referred to as "pre-hearings," of the chorale melodies.[64] However we analyze the relationships, there is a subtle kinship—what Hans Mersmann would have called a *Substanzgemeinschaft*—among the chorale melodies. It is as though they well up from one Ur-chorale somewhere in the depths of the music's psyche—or the music's past.

Reger commented to the critic Arthur Seidl in 1913: "Haven't you noticed yet how the chorale 'Wenn ich einmal soll scheiden' sounds through all my works?"[65] Taking Reger more or less at his word, Popp has sought to demonstrate that the all eight phrases of the Passion chorale—and not just the head motive—form an "unnamed common fund of material" for Reger's slow movement.[66] Whether or not we agree that this chorale serves as a quarry for the slow movement of Reger's concerto (I think Popp stretches her argument too far), it is nonetheless clear that Reger's treatment of chorale melodies is almost painfully "sentimental" in Schiller's sense and "relativistic" in Dahlhaus's. We are aware of the presence of the past, and at the same time of an unbridgeable distance.

Reger was proud of his Piano Concerto, claiming that in it he had "found a path that is more likely to lead to a goal than all the other new paths."[67] The other *neuen Wege* to which Reger refers include the recent works of Schoenberg, especially the op. 11 Piano Pieces, which fascinated but repelled him. Reger does not specify what his own "new path" is, but surely it lies in part in the powerful assimilation of historicism into modernism manifested by the slow movement of the Piano Concerto.

BUSONI'S BACH

Although he did not share Reger's neurotic obsession, Ferruccio Busoni was the other Austro-German modernist most intensely engaged with Bach. Though Italian by birth, Busoni made most of his professional career—as pianist, composer, conductor, editor, and teacher—within the German-speaking world, and as such must be considered in that context. If Bach and Brahms, or Bach-via-Brahms, may be said to have been the guiding model for Reger's historicist modernism, the magic combination for Busoni was Bach and Liszt.

Liszt's relationship with Bach had been no less powerful than Brahms's; it was reflected above all in Liszt's self-image as an interpreter-promoter of great masterworks. Among Liszt's virtuoso transcriptions and arrangements are many of Bach works, including vocal and choral pieces. Liszt also wrote original compositions based on Bach, such as the *Prelude and Fugue on BACH* for organ and the *Variations on "Weinen, Klagen"* for piano.[68] Liszt was not interested in producing Urtexts or historically faithful editions.[69] For him, Bach was the *fons et origo* of modern piano playing, an idea that was imparted to his students and followers, including Busoni. In the preface to his first major Bach publication, an 1894 Schirmer edition of the first book of the *Well-Tempered Clavier,* Busoni showed his Lisztian inheritance by depicting Bach as the foundation of both modern compositional styles and piano technique.[70]

Like Liszt and Reger, Busoni produced both arrangements and original compositions based on Bach. In Busoni's case, sorting out the categories becomes especially difficult. Albrecht Riethmüller and Larry Sitsky have proposed similar typologies of Busoni's Bach-related works, ranging from the most neutral, so to speak, or faithful to the original, to the most interventionist or creative.[71] First, there is Busoni serving principally as editor, as preparer of *instruktiven* and *revidierten* editions of the Bach keyboard works, in particular the *Well-Tempered Clavier* and the *Two-* and *Three-Part Inventions.* These editions span a good part of Busoni's career, from 1894 to 1922.[72] Here Busoni's tinkering with the actual notes is relatively minimal, although the interpretive apparatus, including markings of dynamics, phrasing, as well as analytic commentary, can be enormous—and enormously important.

Second, there are Busoni's arrangements, called by him variously *Übertragung, Transkription, Bearbeitung, Freie Bearbeitung,* and *Konzertbearbeitung,* in which harpsichord or organ works are adapted to the modern piano, sometimes in a virtuoso manner.[73] It is at times impossible to draw a clear line between the first and second categories. Some of Busoni's "editions" are really records of his own performances. "Interpretiert von Ferruccio Busoni" is how he describes his edition of the *Chromatic Fantasy and Fugue* in 1902; in 1915, the same version is "herausgegeben von Ferruccio Busoni."[74]

The third category includes Busoni's original compositions based on Bach. The major works are the second movement of the Second Violin Sonata, op. 36a, from 1898, reworked as an Improvisation for two pianos in 1916; the *Fantasia nach Johann Sebastian Bach,* written in memory of Busoni's father in 1909; the *Fantasia Contrappuntistica* (1910; abbreviated in 1912; arranged for two pianos in 1922); and the *Sonatina Brevis in Signo Joannis Sebastiani Magni* of 1918. The *Fantastia Contrappuntistica,* which went through four different versions, combines elements of all types of Busoni's engagement with Bach, because it is at once a free composition and a completion of Bach's *Art of Fugue.*[75]

Busoni's relationship with Bach is closely bound up with his idea of the "unity of music." For Busoni, a piece of music remained the same—had the same essence—no matter what form it took. Arrangements or transcriptions never violate the basic quality of music because, as he put it in one of his most famous dicta, every act of notation is already one of transcription.[76] For Busoni, music was always "pure": no text, context, or extramusical additions could ever alter its basic condition. He held fast to the idea that "music remains, wherever and in whatever form it appears, exclusively music and nothing else."[77]

Busoni's aesthetic and his attempt to recapture a spirituality in music in the modern age bring him into line with Kandinsky, whose ideas we examined in the previous chapter. For Busoni as for Kandinsky (as also for Schoenberg), outward "form" was a relatively insignificant or transient aspect of a work of art. Only "spirit and emotion" give the artwork its "essence." Busoni turns the traditional definition of "absolute" music on its head. Absolute music is not about "form-play without poetic program." On the contrary, form is "the opposite pole of absolute music," which is attained only in the absence of any imposed structure.[78]

For Busoni, Bach (and secondarily, Mozart and Beethoven) represented the greatest example of music's unity or "oneness." He wrote: "The instinct of 'Oneness' made Bach use the same music as a work for choir or for an organ piece, and he continually carries his ideas from one instrument to another, from 'Church' music to 'chamber' music."[79] Busoni's attitude is clearly reflected in his own compositional work. Many of his compositions, including his magnum opus *Doktor Faust,* are reworkings of his own earlier compositions, often adapted or transcribed among different media. This applies as well to his original compositions based on Bach, which, as noted above, often migrated among media or *Klangträger,* as he put it.

At the heart of Busoni's Bach-related works is the use of chorales or chorale-like melodies, which held enormous symbolic significance for him, as they did for Reger. The third movement of the Second Violin Sonata consists of a theme and variations on the melody "Wie wohl ist mir, o Freund der Seelen" (BWV 517), from the second *Klavierbüchlein* for Anna Magdalena Bach of 1725.[80] The Third Elegy is also a set of variations, on the chorale "Meine Seele Bangt und Hofft zu Dir." For the *Fantasia nach Bach* of 1909 Busoni turned to Bach's chorale variations for organ on "Christ, der du bist der helle Tag" (BWV 766), from *Clavierübung* III. Busoni uses the chorale and two of Bach's variations (Partita II and VI). Other chorales based on Bach organ works appear in the *Fantasia* as well, including Bach's fughetta on "Gottes Sohn ist Kommen" (BWV 703) and "Lob sei dem allmächtigen Gott" (BWV 602) from the *Orgelbüchlein.* The *Fantasia Contrappuntistica* in its most definitive form, for solo piano (1910), opens with a "Preludio corale" that is lifted largely from the Third Elegy, as a set of variations on "Meine Seele Bangt."

Why would the chorale have been such an important symbol for Busoni? Riethmüller has considered this question in some detail. He suggests that for Busoni, Bach was the model of a musical arranger, and that it is with the chorale that Bach assumed this role "par excellence."[81] Chorale melodies are for Busoni like a sacred text that can—must—be continually reinterpreted; they become, says Riethmüller, "primal musical shapes." In this sense they are less religious symbols than musical "archetypes" in a Jungian sense.

The variations that form the third movement of Busoni's Second Violin Sonata represent one of his most powerful engagements with Bach; and they make a convenient point of comparison with the Reger works examined above. Busoni was especially proud of this work. He wrote in 1900 to his publisher Breitkopf & Härtel, "This piece remains my best and most characteristic, in spite of the two years that separate me from its completion. I venture to say that in recent times, hardly any piece of chamber music as good has been written."[82] Of course, there is a bit of puffery in such a statement to a publisher, but as in the case of Reger's similar statements about his opp. 16 and 81, we should take Busoni's assessment seriously.

Though they make up one movement—the finale—the variations on "Wie wohl ist mir" occupy ten minutes, almost half the entire temporal space of the sonata. The Bach melody itself lies, as Riethmüller points out, almost in the exact center of the work.

As in Reger's *Bach Variations,* op. 81, the theme itself is a gigantic entity, an *aa'bb'* form that extends forty measures (see example 27 for the beginning). What Budde observed about the Bach ritornello selected by Reger is to some extent true of Busoni's choice (although it has a more conventional form for a variation theme): Busoni is attempting to write variations on an unvariable theme. Like Reger, Busoni does not number the variations; and he departs far sooner than Reger from the original structure. Busoni's variations are similarly *gedichtet* rather than *komponiert* (one thinks of Busoni's category of *Nachdichtungen* for some of his Bach arrangements). Indeed, it is hard to say exactly how many "variations" there are—most likely seven plus a coda:

Mm. 1–39, Introduction

Mm. 40–79, Theme, E major, $\frac{3}{4}$, Andante con moto (Bach, "Wie wohl ist mir, o Freund der Seelen," BWV 517)

Mm. 80–114, Variation 1, E major, $\frac{6}{4}$, Poco più andante

Mm. 115–79, Variation 2, E major, $\frac{2}{4}$, Alla marcia, vivace

Mm. 180–218, Variation 3, E major, $\frac{3}{4}$, Lo stesso movimento (♩ = ♩)

Mm. 219–64, Variation 4, E minor, **C**, Andante (based on piano piece "Das Calvarium"; uses chorale "Christus der uns selig macht" together with "Wie wohl ist mir"; combined at m. 197ff.)

Mm. 265–307, Variation 5, E major, $\frac{9}{8}$, Tranquillo assai; fugue based on head motive of "Wie wohl ist mir"

Mm. 308–47, Variation 6, E major, **C**, Allegro deciso, un poco maestoso (big climax on Neapolitan F major at end)

Mm. 348–57, Variation 7 (= Coda, part 1?), E major, Più lento

Mm. 358–63, Coda, part 2, Più tranquillo, apoteotico

Mm. 364–73, Coda, part 3, $\frac{3}{4}$, Tempo del tema

Mm. 374–78, Coda, part 4, **C**, Adagio

Example 27. Busoni, Violin Sonata No. 2, op. 36a, III, beginning of theme

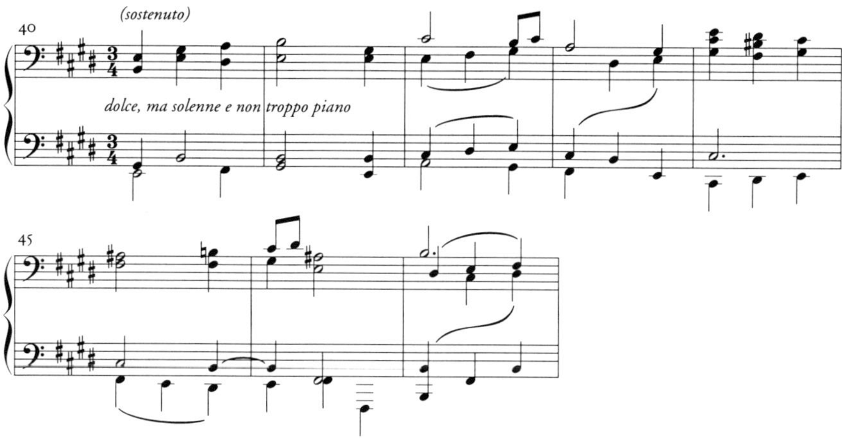

Antony Beaumont has suggested that Busoni modeled his movement "directly" on the finale of Beethoven's E-Major Piano Sonata, op. 109, whose "external framework" is "reproduced almost exactly."[83] To be sure, as Beaumont points out, the key is the same, and the bass of Beethoven's theme maps quite closely onto the first four notes of the melody of "Wie wohl ist mir." Yet Busoni's variations are far freer in structure than Beethoven's, which stay quite close to the form of the theme. If Beethoven's op. 109 is a model, it is far from "direct." For Busoni, Bach's theme was less an "entity" to be varied than a source for shapes and figures on which to base the variation-like segments.

Somewhat as in Reger, Busoni's first three variations are traditional in style—well within the "horizon of expectations" for a variation movement. They remain in the tonic major key, but are strongly varied in character. The first variation is distinctly Brahmsian; it has a 6/4 meter with triplet figuration and, in mm. 82–84, a chromatically inflected harmony strongly reminiscent of Brahms, especially the first movement of the G-Major Violin Sonata, op. 78, in the same meter. The second variation is a brisk *alla marcia,* and the third follows directly on it, in the tradition of the "paired" variations common in the Baroque era and in more recent works like Brahms's *Handel Variations.* The third variation ends suddenly and unexpectedly on a sustained dominant (B).

After this, the fourth variation breaks the mould, much as Reger's third variation did. The key changes to E minor, and the piano alone begins a variation that has the texture and feel of a chorale prelude (example 28). The right hand begins a repeating figuration, while the second and third measures of the piano's left hand present the head motive of the "Wie wohl ist mir" melody. In m. 223, the head motive, played in parallel chords in the left hand, is joined in the violin by another melody, which Riethmüller has plausibly identified as the Passion chorale "Christus der uns selig macht."[84] Elements of the two melodies continue to be juxtaposed in the rest of this long variation (example 29).

Riethmüller has established that Busoni drew for this variation on a fragmentary piano piece called "Das Calvarium," whose beginning is identical to that of variation 4 and breaks off just when beginning to incorporate the Passion chorale. For the Violin Sonata, Busoni modified the piano part to include the head motive of "Wie wohl ist mir." The fourth variation breaks from the traditional variation scheme not only by its texture and thematic content, but also by its scope. At forty-five measures, it is almost like a composition within a composition. It is followed in variation 5 by a fugue based on the initial profile of "Wie wohl ist mir" (example 30). Here again the bounds of conventional variation are superseded: the fugue extends forty-three measures, building to a large climax and flowing directly into the sixth variation. The fugue is unusual for its placement not as the final, culminatory variation (as in Reger and Reger's models), but as part of the variation set.

With the seventh variation begins what might be considered the coda of the movement, which includes an "apotheosis" (marked *apoteotico* by Busoni) in a radiant E major and a five-measure Adagio conclusion that returns to the opening motto of the sonata, marked *quasi sacro.* Riethmüller has sensitively assessed the significance of this marking. With the *sacro* and its qualifier *quasi,* Busoni seems to suggest that "a sacred music is possible only in quotation marks." Riethmüller continues: "Busoni's Violin Sonata occupies the horizon of art religion of the nineteenth century—the replacement of the sacred by art and the concomitant penetration of art by sacred elements. Within this horizon is also the name of Bach as used by Busoni. It does not stand for a composer of Protestant church music, but acts as a cipher for a music that is to be understood purely as music, that is, as pure music."[85]

Busoni may thus be said to universalize Bach—in a sense to de-Germanize him. He may have done so in part in reaction to figures like Reger for whom Bach was quintessentially German. Busoni was resentful of this aspect of Reger's reputation. In 1910, at the time of a large Reger festival in Dortmund,

Example 28. Busoni, Violin Sonata No. 2, op. 36a, III, var. 4

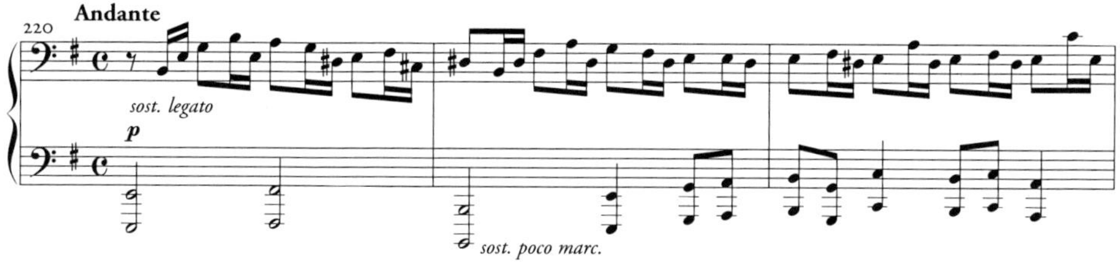

Example 29. Busoni, Violin Sonata No. 2, op. 36a, III, var. 4, juxtaposition of chorales

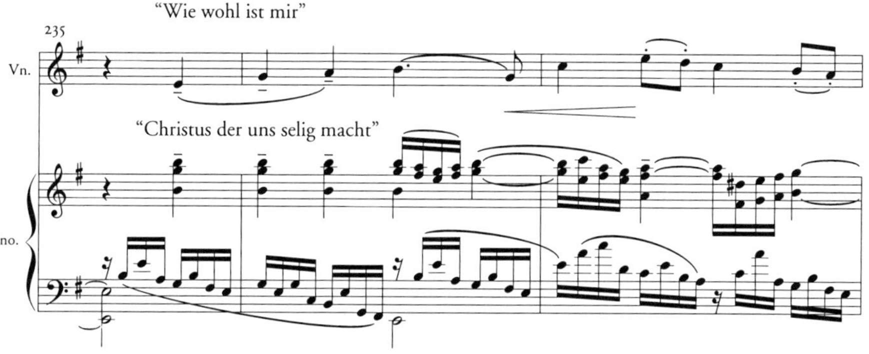

Example 30. Busoni, Violin Sonata, No. 2, op. 36a, III, var. 5

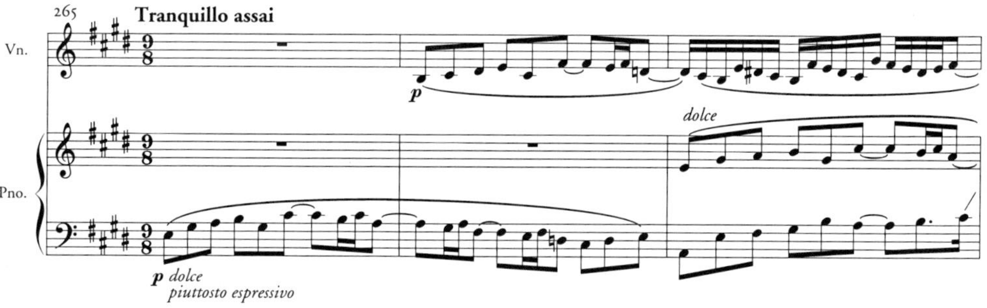

Busoni expressed bemusement that critics failed to find "German profundity" *(deutsche Tiefe)* in his own "Italian" works. He wrote to the composer Hans Huber, "I wish I knew what German profundity in music were. . . . German is: *Lohengrin, Freischütz,* men's choruses, and our celebrated contemporary Max Reger. Schumann, too. But where do these works have profundity that Dante and Michelangelo don't have?"[86]

Reger problematizes and historically contextualizes the chorales in a way very different from Busoni. In the slow movement of Reger's Organ Suite, as we have seen, each of the three chorales is given a different treatment, which in at least two of the cases—the six-part imitative setting of "Aus tiefer Not" and the recitative-style setting of the Passion chorale—reflects but utterly transforms their original contexts in Bach. In the *Fantasia nach Bach* for piano of 1909, written in memory of his father, Busoni takes a different approach to Bach's chorales. The work takes over parts of three of Bach's organ works: the chorale variations on "Christ, der du bist der helle Tag" (BWV 766); the fughetta on "Gottes Sohn ist kommen" (BWV 703), a melody more familiar as "In dulce jubilo"; and the chorale prelude from the *Orgelbüchlein* "Lob sei dem allmächtigen Gott" (BWV 602). Busoni weaves more literal transcription (of Bach's Partita II and part of Partita VII from BWV 766) with freer chorale-based fantasy. These chorales are selected largely for their melodic similarity to each other and to "Wie wohl ist mir," the melody used in the Second Violin Sonata. All tend to begin with an ascent from the tonic to the dominant. In the Organ Suite, Reger selected his chorales more for their *dis*similarity, such that their contrapuntal combination at the end of the middle part of the slow movement is all the more striking and disturbing.

Beside the chorale, the fugue is the main Bachian topos in Busoni's works, especially in the *Sonatina brevis* (based on the Fantasy and Fugue in D Minor [BWV 905], now considered spurious), and in the *Fantasia Contrappuntistica.* The *Fantasia* exists in what Larry Sitsky has called a "vast landscape" of versions and variants, written for one or two pianos. The work first published under the name *Fantasia Contrappuntistica* in 1910 was itself a version of a composition based largely on Bach's *Art of the Fugue*—including a completion of the final, fragmentary Contrapunctus 19—and written earlier that year during a concert tour of the United States, where Busoni encountered and was inspired by two émigré German teachers of counterpoint in Chicago, Bernhard Ziehn and Wilhelm Middelschulte.[87]

The *Fantasia* in its "edizione definitiva" of 1910 lasts close to forty minutes and is Busoni's summary statement of his relationship to Bach. It contains virtually every Bachian topos, including chorale prelude, fugue, fantasy, stretto, and variation:

Chorale Prelude (mm. 1–201): based on "Allein Gott in der Höh' sei Ehr'"; Moderato, un po' maestoso, **c**

Fugue I (mm. 202–311): transcription of Contrapunctus 19 from Bach's *Art of Fugue* (BWV 1080, 19), mm. 1–115

Fugue II (mm. 312–84): transcription of Contrapunctus 19 from Bach's *Art of Fugue* (BWV 1080, 19), mm. 115–93

Fugue III (mm. 385–432): transcription of Contrapunctus 19 from Bach's *Art of Fugue* (BWV 1080, 19), mm. 193–239; mm. 432–565: completion of Bach's fragmentary fugue

Intermezzo (mm. 565–85): based on BACH motive in transposition

Variation I (mm. 586–622): based on the three fugue themes

Variation II (mm. 623–50): based primarily on BACH

Variation III (mm. 651–83)

Cadenza (mm. 684–716)

Fugue IV (mm. 717–74): uses material from Contrapunctus 2 of Bach's *Art of Fugue* (BWV 1080, 2)

Chorale (mm. 775–95): based on "Allein Gott in der Höh' sei Ehr'"

Stretta (mm. 796–864)

Some parts of the *Fantasia* are transcribed quite faithfully from the different Contrapuncti of Bach's *Art of Fugue* (especially the last, No. 19); others are more freely adapted or modified from Bach; some, including the variations and the completion of Bach's Contrapunctus 19 by bringing in the main theme of *Art of Fugue* as the fourth subject, are pure Busoni. In places Busoni applies the principle of "symmetrical inversion" he had picked up from Ziehn, whereby in contrapuntal combinations motives or themes retain their original intervallic structure, rather than being adjusted to generate traditional harmonic patterns.[88] (Ziehn's ideas would seem to anticipate Kurth's notion of linear counterpoint as discussed above, in which vertical/harmonic considerations take second place to horizontal/linear ones.)

Busoni's musical language is far more eclectic than Reger's. Reger may be said to subsume or absorb Bach's techniques within his own style. Busoni, especially in the *Fantasia Contrappuntistica,* moves in and out of "real" Bach and "fantasy" Bach, which sound very different from one another. The juxtaposition was, to be sure, intentional—for Busoni the music does not lose its "oneness"—but creates a listening experience very different from Reger. Beaumont reasonably asks whether "the spirits of Bach and Busoni harmonize" in the *Fantasia,* or whether "they lock in perpetual combat." He answers the question by suggesting that Busoni essentially erects a new structure beside Bach's fragment, which is used as "the starting point for a musical voyage of discovery."[89]

TOWARD IRONY: MAHLER AND BACHIAN COUNTERPOINT

Reger, Busoni, and Schoenberg all took their Bach—and their musical history—very seriously. Gustav Mahler also developed a reverential attitude toward Bach in the years around 1900. He acquired all forty-seven volumes of the Bach edition, which had just reached its completion in 1899 after fifty years of work. Mahler's companion in the pre-Alma years, Nathalie Bauer-Lechner, reported that she always found him busy with the Bach edition when she went to his room. Alma Mahler notes that in his summer composing hut in Maiernigg, where Mahler worked from 1902 to 1908, the only music he had on his shelves was Bach.[90] Two aspects of Bach that Mahler seemed to admire most were the polyphony, which he called "miraculous" and "unparalleled . . . for all time," and the imaginative, varied treatment of chorale melodies.[91]

Mahler's intense involvement with the music of Bach coincided with the composition of his Fifth Symphony, in 1901–3. The Fifth is often admired for the richness of its counterpoint, which marks a new stage in Mahler's development as a composer and the beginning of his "middle" period of symphonies, comprising the Fifth, Sixth, and Seventh. The contrapuntal aspect of the symphony may well be indebted to Bach's influence more generally, but Bachian polyphony makes a specific appearance in the rondo finale, where the effect is, to say the least, very different from other early German modernists.

After the folklike main theme cadences in m. 56, Mahler initiates a bustling neo-Baroque fugato that is unique in his oeuvre up to this point (example 31). The subject (marked S) is a perpetuum mobile in eighth notes, and it is accompanied as it progresses by two countersubjects (CS^1, CS^2),

Example 31. Mahler, Symphony No. 5, V

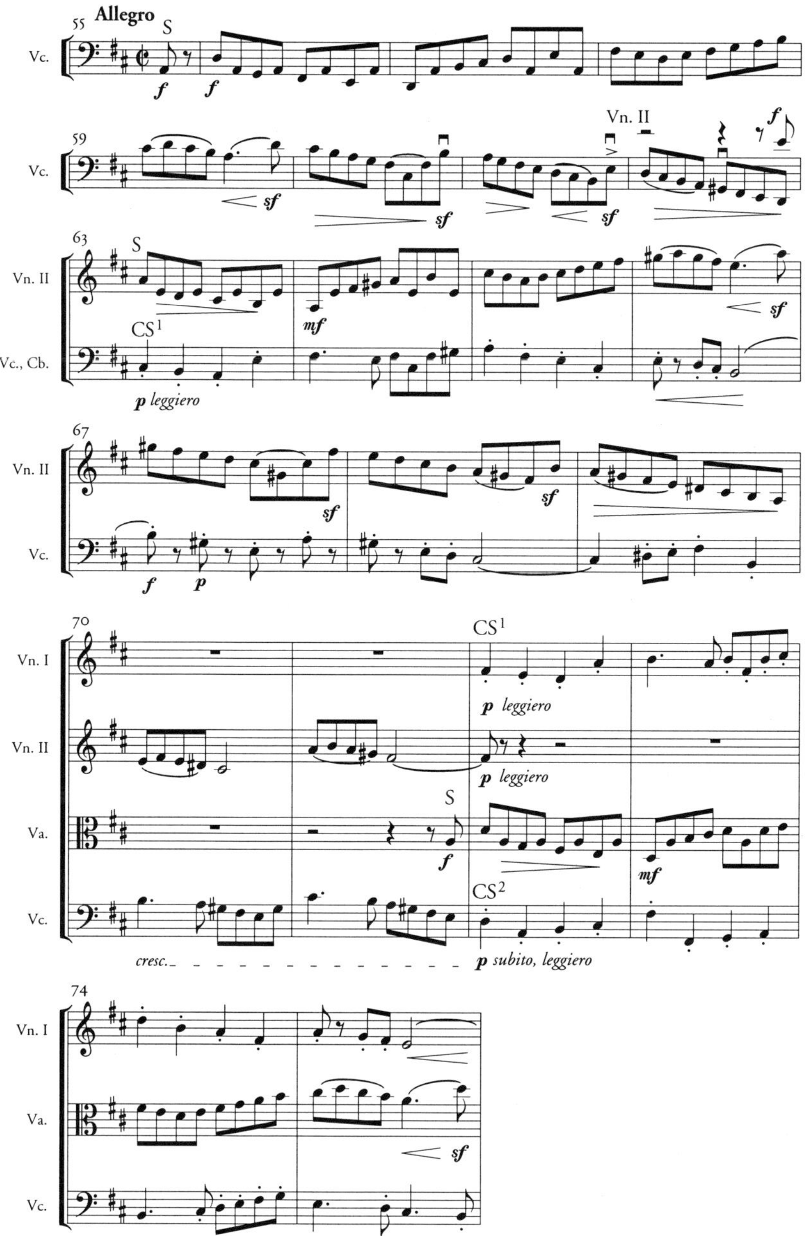

Example 32. Goldmark, *Rustic Wedding* Symphony, V

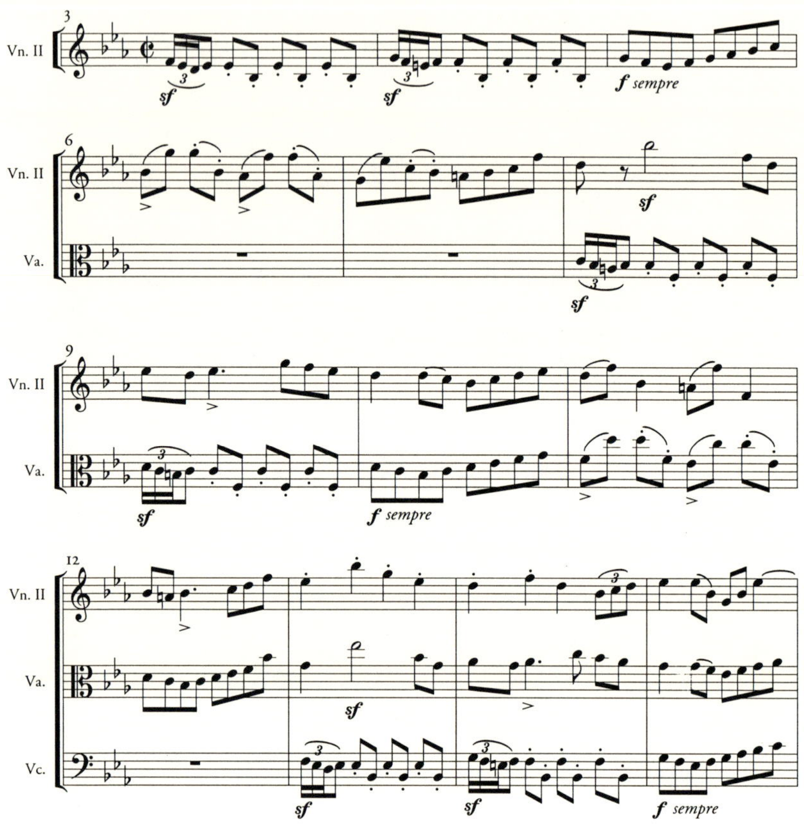

both derived from the main theme of the movement. This fugato partakes of what might be called irony, in that there is a tension between the actual material (complex counterpoint) and the almost comic manner in which it is unfolded.

Fugatos of this *giocoso* type are certainly not unknown in the Austro-German symphonic tradition. The Overture of Mozart's *Magic Flute* has one, as does the beginning of the Trio in the Scherzo of Beethoven's Fifth Symphony. The finale of Goldmark's *Rustic Wedding* Symphony (1876) breaks into a lively fugato that closely resembles Mahler's, and may well have served as a model. Like Mahler, Goldmark's subject tends to alternate rapidly between the tonic and dominant notes, and then breaks into a scalar passage that first descends, then ascends (example 32). Another model for Mahler was the fast-paced fugal counterpoint in Wagner's *Die Meistersinger*

Prelude, based on the theme later associated with the mocking of Beckmesser ("Scheint mir nicht der Rechte"). But when we view Mahler's fugato against the practices of his fellow early modernists, this passage from the Fifth strikes a new tone and reflects a new, more detached attitude toward the music of the past. Mahler is writing, to paraphrase Gérard Genette, a fugue in the second degree.[92]

Something similar can be said of Mahler's treatment of the D-major chorale in the Fifth Symphony. Unlike Reger or Busoni, he does not select any actual chorale tune used by Bach. The chorale is of his own making, and it is related motivically to the main themes of the finale.[93] The chorale is also treated cyclically by Mahler across the symphony. It first emerges, in its ultimate key of D major, near the end of the second movement (m. 464), as a ray of hope amid raging anguish. But it does not achieve real "breakthrough" here, instead collapsing back (at m. 520) into the main material and key (A minor) of the movement. The chorale reappears in the finale at m. 511 in D major; but once again it and its associated tonality are pulled away at the deviation to B♭ major and return of the fugato at m. 526. At m. 711, the chorale finally comes into its own: it is made to grow from the other themes of the movement, including the fugato. In this sense it is fully integrated into—indeed indispensable to—the overall plan of the symphony.

In neither his chorale nor fugue, two aspects of Bach's art he most admired, can Mahler be said to participate in the historicist modernism of Reger or Busoni. For Mahler in the Fifth Symphony, Bach is only a starting point, or a touchstone, for what becomes a fully symphonic—and quintessentially Mahlerian—process. Irony is a fundamental part of this process, in the sense not of poking fun at Bach, but of viewing the past self-consciously, and in this case with some humor, from the vantage point of the present. It is to an investigation of irony in the context of early modernist culture that we should now turn.

FIVE

Ironic Germans

THOMAS MANN, WAGNER, AND IRONY

At the end of chapter 4, I introduced the term "irony" to characterize, at least in part, Mahler's distanced but affectionately humorous relationship to Bach in the finale of the Fifth Symphony. Irony becomes a key strategy for a number of Austro-German modernists in the years around 1900, especially in their attitude to music of the remote or immediate past. I shall return to Mahler at the end of this chapter, but to explore and clarify the concept of irony shall first confront the premier ironist of the era, Thomas Mann. In a well-known study of 1958 called *The Ironic German,* Erich Heller explores Mann's narrative strategies, which he calls ironic because of "a calculated and artistically mastered incongruity between the meaning of the story told and the manner of telling it."[1] This is probably as good a basic definition of literary or linguistic irony as one could find. As has long been recognized, this style gave Mann a distinctive voice in twentieth-century fiction.

In the same period as Mahler's Fourth and Fifth Symphonies, this ironic vision dominates Mann's first novel *Buddenbrooks* (written 1897–1901), the novella *Tristan* (1901–3), and the story *Blood of the Wälsungs* (1905–6). In each of these works the ironic stance involves a distinctly detached attitude to Wagner, who represents for Mann the music of the immediate past that continues to haunt the present. Mann's strategy at once celebrates and exorcises Wagner. We have already seen something of this distancing in Mahler's treatment of Bachian fugal techniques in the finale of the Fifth Symphony. But Mann's strategies of irony, as well as of parody, mark a key moment in German modernism. They are also are harbingers of—not necessarily direct influences upon—two operas by Hugo von Hofmannsthal and Richard Strauss, *Der Rosenkavalier* (1910) and *Ariadne auf Naxos* (1912/1916). An investigation of those works will occupy the next chapter.

It needs just brief restating here that Mann's involvement with Wagner's music was lifelong and profound, yet, like Nietzsche's, ambivalent. In his most famous and extended statement on Wagner, the essay "The Sorrows and Grandeur of Richard Wagner," which would precipitate his departure from Germany in 1933, Mann wrote:

> A passion for Wagner's enchanted *oeuvre* has been a part of my life ever since I first became aware of it and set out to make it my own, to invest it with understanding. . . . I never tire of listening to it, admiring it, following it—not without certain misgivings, I confess; but all the doubts, reservations and objections have in no way detracted from its appeal, any more than Nietzsche's immortal critique of Wagner, which I have always taken to be a panegyric in reverse, another form of eulogy. It was an expression of love-hate, an act of self-mortification.[2]

For Mann, the "love-hate" took in part the form of incorporating Wagner into his fiction, at the same time keeping it at an expressive distance from the narrator and reader.

Wagner also inspired in Mann some of the finest examples of what Steven Scher has called "verbal music," prose that captures musical processes or structures.[3] Many commentators over the last century have observed the musicality of Mann's prose. His works have undergone analysis as "scores" or as operas in words; they have been examined as symphonic or operatic compositions, with structural divisions analogous to movements or acts. Critics have noted the use of "motives," deemed to be analogous to Wagner's leitmotives. Mann himself referred to his works as "compositions" and wrote of "spiritual thematic webs."[4] What concerns me here is less this aspect of Mann, which has been well treated, than the ironic tone of his verbal music. To understand this, we must first define more closely Mann's brand of irony.

Mann's irony may be said to grow from several nineteenth-century trends in Germany, beginning with those ironic strategies identified more specifically as Romantic and associated with Friedrich Schlegel and the Jena circle.[5] In Schlegel's irony, as set out in his literary fragments, and as practiced in fiction, drama, and poetry by other early Romantics like Novalis, Tieck, Brentano, Jean Paul, and (slightly later) Heine, the author distances himself from his own creation. A key tactic is what Schlegel referred to as *Illusionsstörung,* the destruction of illusion. (Some ironists, like Fielding and Swift, had developed these narrative devices well before the actual "Romantic" period.) For Schlegel, irony was the "duty" *(Pflicht)* of an author, a way of acknowledging the contradictory, unresolvable qualities of the relationship between an individual and the world. Schlegel described the ironic method for an author as a "continual alternation between self-creation and self-denial."[6]

The gap between Romantic irony and that of Mann is bridged in part by the ironic visions of Hegel and Nietzsche. Hegel had little use for Romantic irony, which he dubbed "trifling with everything," which "can transform all things into show" and in which "all noble or divine truth vanishes away or becomes mere triviality."[7] More important for Hegel was tragic irony, as understood by Socrates and practiced by the ancient Greek playwrights. Tragic irony presented individuals as being in the grip of larger forces beyond their control and knowledge. Here was the foundation of what Hegel called the "universal irony of the world," or what Heine would label *Weltironie* (world irony), which was fundamental to dialectical processes of history, in which the events characteristic of tragic drama are projected onto the world stage.[8]

Nietzsche, who took a few jabs at Hegel in his essay "On the Utility and Liability of History for Life" (1873–74), nonetheless seems to subscribe to the basic notion of world irony. Nietzsche saw as one of the negative consequences of his history-obsessed age a "dangerous attitude of self-irony," or what he also called "ironic self-consciousness." The ironic attitude comes from modern man's "awareness that he must live in a historicizing and, as it were, twilight atmosphere, his fear that he will not be able to salvage for the future anything whatsoever of his youthful hopes and energies."[9]

But Nietzsche, especially in *Thus Spoke Zarathustra* (1885), also puts a humorous spin on world irony. In commenting on the death of the "old Gods," Zarathustra reports that "they had a good gay *[fröhliches]* godlike end. They did not end in a 'twilight,' though this lie is told. Instead: one day they *laughed* themselves to death." Later, in his paean to eternity and eternal recurrence, Zarathustra observes that "in laughter all that is evil comes together, but is pronounced holy and absolved by its own bliss." Zarathustra also says, "This crown of him who laughs, this rose-wreath crown: I myself have put on this crown, I myself have pronounced my laughter holy."[10] As Ernst Behler suggests, the laughter is ironic in that the crown of laughter is really a crown of thorns. In an aphorism on "German pessimism" written in 1885, shortly after the completion of *Thus Spoke Zarathustra,* Nietzsche captures the tragi-comic paradox: "Perhaps I know best why man alone laughs: he alone suffers so deeply that he *had* to invent laughter. The unhappy and melancholy creature is, as it should be, the most cheerful."[11]

This Nietzschean-Zarathustrian affirmation of life had a powerful influence on Mann's notion of irony. In a key passage in *Reflections of a Nonpolitical Man* (Betrachtungen eines Unpolitischen) from 1918, Mann praises Nietzsche's "self-denial of intellect *[Geist]* in favor of life, of 'strong' and especially 'beautiful' life." He elaborates: "With me, the experience of the self-denial of intellect in favor of life became irony—a moral attitude for which I know no other description and designation than precisely this one: that it is the self-denial, the self-betrayal of the intellect in favor of life—and here I define 'life' just as the Renaissance estheticism did, but with a different, lighter, and more reserved nuance of feeling that signifies lovableness, happiness, power, grace, the pleasant normality of lack of intellect, and of nonintellectuality." Mann explains that the intellect can never be completely suppressed, and that irony serves to "woo" on its behalf. But in that "it does not believe in the possibility of winning life for the intellect," this irony or ironic attitude is, says Mann, a "form of play."[12] Here then is the inheritance of the Nietzschean *Spiel* and *Heiterkeit.*

Romantic and Nietzschean irony come together for Mann in something that he called "ironic objectivism" and saw as particularly characteristic of epic narrative. In his essay "The Art of the Novel," originally given as a lecture to Princeton students in 1939, Mann suggested that objectivity and irony are not, as one might think, antithetical, but together constitute the spirit of epic poetry and its successor, the prose novel of the nineteenth century. This irony is different and broader in its implications, he says, than "Romantic subjectivism." Irony in this epic sense is "the meaning of *art* itself, at once all-confirming and all-denying; an all-encompassing perspective that is sunnily clear and cheerful. This is precisely the perspective of art, the perspective of the greatest freedom, repose, and an objectivity that remains untarnished by moralism."[13] In his essay Mann points to Goethe, Tolstoy, Fontane, Dickens, and other nineteenth-century novelists. He does not mention his own work, and yet what he describes seems fully characteristic of it.

It is worth mentioning that in a radio discussion late in his life, in 1953, Mann sought to downplay the ironic aspects of his own work, or to recast them in terms of "humor." He suggests here that irony "is the artistic spirit that elicits from the reader or listener a smile, an intellectual smile, so to speak. Humor, however, engenders the laughter that wells up from the heart, which I personally value more highly as the effect of art—and that I welcome with more joy as the effect of my own works—than the erasmic smile that is elicited through irony." Mann adds that in *Buddenbrooks,* which (he says) laid the basis for all that followed in his work, "I believe irony is not, for the most part, to be found. It is really much more a book of pessimistic humor, if you will excuse the paradoxical formulation." As "sources and ingredients" he points to not only Schopenhauer, Wagner, and the French, English, and Russian novelists, but also "low German humor" as found in the works of the German dialect writer Fritz Reuter.[14]

The kind of irony that is clearest in Mann's fiction and in some of his critical writings is that manifested by the relationship (and often tension) between art and life, or more specifically between the values of an artist and those of the middle class. This irony is Mann's own special variant of the Nietzschean irony of intellect-versus-life. In *Reflections of a Nonpolitical Man,* Mann devoted an entire chapter to "Burgherly Nature."[15] There he explores what he calls a "paradox come true," the existence of "burgherly artistic genius" (p. 76). "An artist is burgherly," he explains, "when he transfers the ethical characteristics of the burgherly way of life: order, sequence, rest, 'diligence'—not in the sense of industriousness, but of faithful workmanship—to the exercise of art" (p. 73). Mann specifically relates the notion of the burgherly artist to a concept of Nietzsche, the "double optic" *(zweifache Optik),* which involves "seeing artistic *and* burgherly nature side by side" (p. 76).

Mann describes the burgherly artist as an essentially German phenomenon of the nineteenth century and posits Schopenhauer and Wagner as prime examples. Schopenhauer led a restricted, orderly middle-class existence, all the while writing his profound philosophy; Wagner needed to surround himself with luxury and "burgherly pomp" in order to create his masterpieces. We might add into this mix Brahms and Max Klinger, discussed in chapter 3. They were persuasively interpreted by Jan Brachmann as two burgherly artists who transcended some of the restrictions and expectations of German middle-class existence to create an "artistic dialogue." The pianist in Klinger's engravings *Accorde* and *Evocation* seems to be just such a figure, summoning elaborate visions from his burgherly parlor.

Mann distinguishes between "burgherly" *(bürgerlich)* and the French word *bourgeois* from which it derives as a "mechanical-literary translation" (p. 96). For Mann the burgher is a particularly German, nonpolitical, and "spiritual" type; he is a "Romantic individualist." The bourgeois is a more "internationalized" figure; he is capitalistic and imperialistic, characterized by "dehumanization" and "loss of soul" (p. 98). Mann sees the German burgher as having developed, largely involuntarily, across the later nineteenth century in two directions. One is the more modern capitalistic bourgeois. The other direction is captured, as Mann himself noted in *Reflections,* by the figures of Thomas and Hanno in the novel *Buddenbrooks.* It is the "decay" *(Entartung)* of "the old and genuine burgherly nature into something subjective-artistic" (p. 99).

BUDDENBROOKS

Thomas Buddenbrook, the last director of the family business, has many traces of the newer expedient capitalist—against his own better judgment, he makes some risky investments—but he is also, as Mann describes him in *Reflections,* an "overburdened, overdisciplined *moralist of accomplishment.*" Thomas is a symbol of the "heroism" of a "modern, neoburgherly character" (p. 103). As the novel progresses, he becomes a man of increasing subjectivity, self-doubt, and reflection. In chapter 5 of part 10 of *Buddenbrooks,* Thomas takes one of his ever more frequent afternoon breaks from managing the firm to meditate deeply on life and death; he reads what is generally recognized as Schopenhauer's *World as Will and Representation.* Thomas's only child Hanno represents the continuation, or further "decay" of this trend toward the "subjective-artistic." The music-making that Thomas's wife Gerda brings into the Buddenbrook family creates discord between her and her husband, and then defines the identity of Hanno. Hanno is no German burgher—indeed, never has the chance to be, because of his early death and his full rejection of his father's world in favor of music. Hanno's unsuitability to continue the family business and his inclination toward music—both of which cause his father distress—spell the end of the Buddenbrook dynasty.

For all Mann's disclaimers cited above, we can still understand *Buddenbrooks* as one of the great modernist efforts at epic irony. Mann never injects himself directly into the narrative; nor do the characters step out of it. But he makes his authorial presence felt throughout the three-generation chronicle of the Buddenbrook family. Among his strategies are frequent shifts between past and present tense. The former takes on a more "neutral," reportorial tone; the latter, as in the lengthy description of Hanno's christening in part 7, chapter 1, can be laced with irony, as though the corners of Mann's mouth are curled upward in the detached amusement of an "intellectual smile."[16] The account of Hanno's death from typhoid in the penultimate chapter is powerfully ironic. Mann writes the entire chapter as if quoting from a medical manual, without any reference to the actual patient: "Typhoid runs the following course: In the incubation period, a person feels depressed and moody . . ." (p. 642).

Music begins to loom large about two thirds of the way through the novel. The organist of the local church, Edmund Pfühl, comes to play duets with Gerda, while Hanno watches and listens silently, absorbing it all. Pfühl is a musical conservative and a champion of Bach; he warns against harmonic experimentation and has "little use for music that pleases" (p. 435). Gerda tries to convert Pfühl to the music of Wagner she so admires. Gradually he is won over, though "he would not admit his growing irresistible attachment, and it almost frightened him—he would grumble and deny it" (p. 437). One day, after Pfühl has played Haydn, Mozart, and Beethoven with Gerda, Wagner's music comes to him almost involuntarily at the keyboard:

> [Pfühl] gradually drifted into a very strange style, while a kind of embarrassed joy lit his faraway gaze. And from under his fingers came a swelling, blossoming, interweaving melody, from which arose in elegant counterpoint—at first only sporadic, but then ever more clear and vigorous—a march motive that was great, old-fashioned, wonderful, and grandiose. . . . An intensification, an intertwining, a transition . . . and with the resolution the violin entered *fortissimo.* The Prelude to *Meistersinger* marched past. (adapted from p. 436)

This passage, the first extended musical description in *Buddenbrooks,* is characteristic on a small scale of Mann's verbal music, his ability to re-create deftly in prose the processes of an actual musical work. There is a mixture of more purely formal or neutral terms, like "march motive," "transition," "resolution," and more interpretive expressions, like "vigorous," "old-fashioned," and "grandiose." Mann does not describe every individual musical gesture, but gives a sense of the larger whole. If the reader has not already guessed what music is being described, Mann gives the answer in the punch line, which not only provides the culmination of the prose passage, but in naming the work creates an ironic distance.

A still larger example of verbal music comes later in the same chapter when Hanno plays with his mother a fantasy of his own composition. Though Mann does not identify the musical source, the fantasy is clearly modeled on the *Liebestod* (Wagner's own title was *Verklärung,* Transfiguration) from *Tristan und Isolde.* Mann's account of the fantasy unfolds on three levels simultaneously. On one level, it is a description of the actual performance, with particular emphasis on Hanno's physical gestures and appearance; on another, it is a detailed technical account of the music; and finally, it is a metaphorical-expressive paraphrase of Wagner's libretto. What gives the passage its ironical aspect is not only the multilevel approach, but also the way that it is further embedded into the novel's epic narrative structure.

Mann's description of the performance by Hanno and Gerda goes in part as follows: "Hanno stressed each modulatory note with a tilt and bob of his head, and shifting forward to the edge of the seat, he used the soft and damper pedals to give each new chord an emotional value" (adapted from p. 442). As Hanno approaches his "beloved ending," Mann describes the music itself in detail. He writes of an E-minor chord played *pianissimo* and with tremolo:

> It grew, broadened, swelled slowly, very slowly. With a forte Hanno added the dissonant C-sharp, which would lead back to the original key. . . . He delayed the resolution, withheld it from himself and his listeners. What would it be like, this resolution, this ravishing and liberating submersion in B major? Incomparable joy, the delight of sweet rapture. Peace, bliss, heaven itself. . . . And while he depressed the soft and damper pedals, the violin whispered, wove, surged, and dashed around his tremolo, which, now accompanied by a bass line, slid into B major, abruptly swelled to fortissimo and then, with one brief burst, broke off without a trace of echo. (adapted from p. 443)

This passage is unmistakably a prose account of Wagner's *Liebestod.* Twelve bars before the end of the *Tristan,* Wagner also moves to an E-minor chord, played as a tremolo (example 33). This chord functions as the subdominant of the final tonic, B major. Precisely as in Hanno's fantasy, Wagner adds a "dissonant" C♯ to the E-minor triad (m. 1689 in example). The result is a transposition of the "Tristan" chord that has been heard throughout the opera. That chord, in its original inversion and at its original pitch (from the bottom, F♮–B–D♯–G♯), then gives way to the E-minor chord, in which

Example 33. Wagner, *Tristan und Isolde,* ending

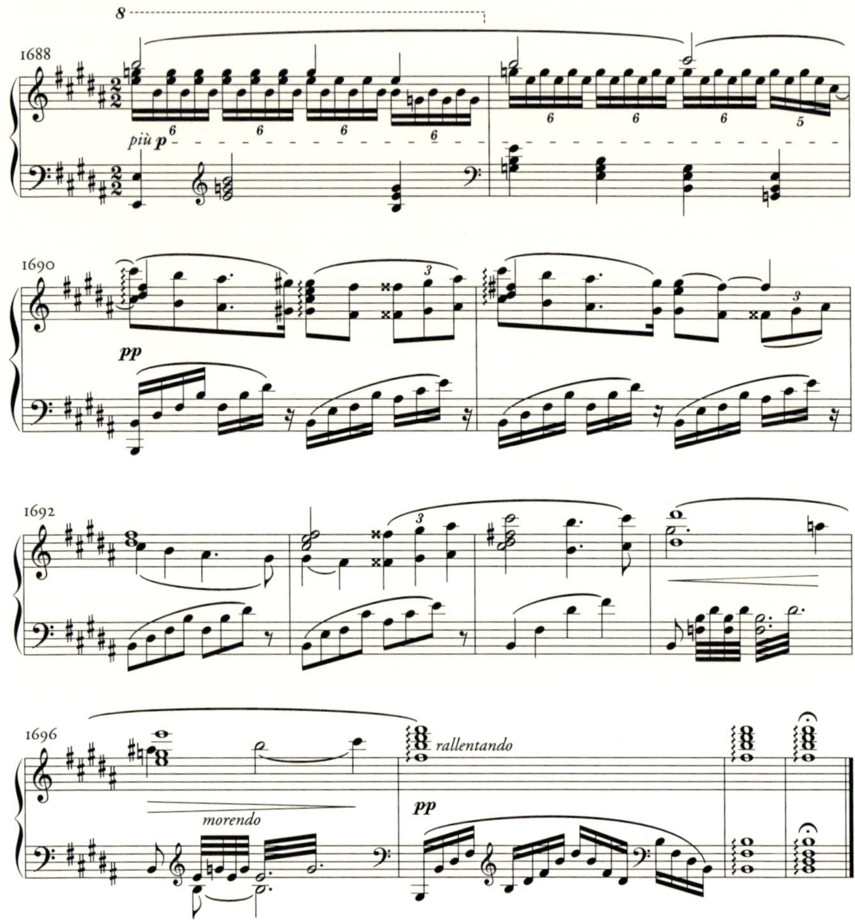

again the B rises to C♯ (m. 1696), before the final resolution to B major. Wagner approaches the final B major in the manner implied by Mann's account of Hanno's fantasy. Wagner "slides" into the tonic plagally, via the E-minor chord, avoiding a more forceful, direct cadence from the dominant, F♯.

Mann's description of Hanno's fantasy not only includes the musical-technical aspects of Wagner's *Liebestod,* but also paraphrases the libretto. Phrases like "sweet rapture" *(überschwengliche Süßigkeit)* render ironically certain images in Isolde's final monologue, where she sings of "Süßer Atem" and "Süß in Düften" and finally achieves peace and "höchste Lust." Mann may also have been influenced here by Wagner's own program notes for the *Tristan* Prelude, written in 1859 (and later republished in his collected writings), which in themselves constitute verbal music: "He [the composer] let that insatiable longing swell up from the timidest avowal of the most delicate attraction, through anxious sighs, hopes and fears, laments and wishes, raptures and torments, to the mightiest onset and to the most powerful effort to find the breach that will reveal to the infinitely craving heart the path into the sea of love's endless rapture."[17]

Hanno's fantasy is recapitulated near the end of *Buddenbrooks,* when, alone in the salon, he plays a much longer and more elaborate improvisation. Again, the model seems to be Wagner's *Tristan.* Hanno's piece begins, like Wagner's Prelude, with "a very simple theme, nothing really, a fragment of a nonexistent melody, a figure of a bar and a half" (though unlike Wagner's, Hanno's theme appears in the bass, "like a chorus of trombones") (p. 639). It ends, like the *Liebestod,* with "a long, soft arpeggio in the minor, which rose up one note, and resolved itself in the major, hesitated, and died a wistful death" (adapted from p. 641).

The fact that the description of Hanno's improvisation is followed immediately by the chapter describing his death from typhoid reinforces the association between music and death that is evident in Mann's works. The very act of creating and performing the improvisation seems literally to consume Hanno, who, after he finishes playing, "was very pale, his knees had gone weak, his eyes burned. He went into the adjoining room, stretched out on the chaise longue, and lay there for a long time without stirring a muscle" (p. 641).

MANN'S *TRISTAN*

The connection between Wagner's *Tristan* and death, and the contrast between art and bourgeois life, are developed with gentle but persistent irony in *Buddenbrooks.* In the novella *Tristan,* which Mann wrote in 1901 even as he was awaiting news about the publication of *Buddenbrooks,* these juxtapositions move into the realm of actual parody. *Tristan,* which appeared in 1903 at the head of a collection of stories, has received a considerable amount of attention from literary scholars, especially for the ways in which Wagner's music is integrated into the text on many structural and thematic levels.[18] "Rarely has there been as perfect a coalescence of music with literature," remarks Sophia Schnitman in her study of the novella.[19] It is not hard to agree with her. We might even speak of convergence.

In *Tristan,* the figure of the artist embodied by Hanno in *Buddenbrooks* may be said to be split into two characters, Detlev Spinell and Gabriele Klöterjahn. Spinell is an aesthete rather than a genuinely creative figure; Gabriele displays a truly artistic temperament and, like Hanno Buddenbrook, is marked for death. Both Gabriele and Spinell are patients at a sanatorium called Einfried. ("Hier ist 'Einfried,' das Sanatorium!" Mann begins, immediately injecting both Wagner and an ironic tone into the novella.) Spinell's most prominent mannerism is blurting out "Wie schön!" (How beautiful!) at a pleasing sight or thought. He is a writer of great pretension but little achievement. Mann refers to a novel Spinell has published, which he keeps in his room and is described (in obvious reference to Jugendstil design) as being "printed on the kind of paper one might use for filtering coffee, in elaborate typography with every letter looking like a Gothic cathedral."[20] Gabriele is deposited at the sanatorium by her husband, Anton, the ultimate bourgeois (not burgherly) figure, who immediately dashes off to deal with his business affairs. Gabriele, a fine amateur musician, is at Einfried ostensibly because of a non-life-threatening illness of the trachea, though as we learn across the story her real problem is lung-related and fatal.

The climax of the novella comes when some of the patients at Einfried go out on a sleigh ride one winter day. Gabriele and Spinell stay behind at the sanatorium, where he persuades her to play the piano, even though she has been forbidden to do so by her doctors because of her weak condition. She first plays through the Chopin E♭-Major Nocturne, op. 9, no. 2, for which Mann provides some elegant verbal music. Spinell then discovers *Tristan und Isolde* among the scores lying on the piano bench, and Gabriele plays through three different sections of the opera: the Prelude, the act 2 love duet, and the final *Liebestod.* A day later, her condition worsens, and, like Hanno after the exertions of his improvisation in *Buddenbrooks,* she dies.

It is in the lengthy description of the "performance" of *Tristan und Isolde* in the drawing room of Einfried, in chapter 8 of *Tristan,* where Mann's story and Wagner's opera come together in such a remarkable manner. As in the descriptions of Hanno's fantasies in *Buddenbrooks*—but now on a much larger scale—Mann manages a multilevel integration of music and narrative that only can be called virtuosic. We are aware of the physical motions and reactions of the participants, Gabriele and Spinell; we follow the music itself by means of detailed technical description; and as in *Buddenbrooks* there is paraphrase of—and, in this case, literal quotation from—the libretto of Wagner's *Tristan.*

With his precise account of the Prelude, Mann begins to compose his verbal music: "The *Sehnsucht* motif, a lonely wandering voice in the night, softly uttered its tremulous question. Silence followed, a silence of waiting. And then the answer: the same hesitant, lonely strain, but higher in pitch, more radiant and tender. Silence again" (p. 116). The Prelude is disturbing to the one listener in the drawing room, Rätin Spatz, who at its conclusion excuses herself and departs. This little interruption is dramatically analogous to the warnings of Brangäne in act 2 of Wagner's *Tristan.* Indeed, the Rätin Spatz functions in Mann's novella somewhat like Brangäne in the opera; she is described by Mann as Gabriele's frequent companion at Einfried.[21]

After Frau Spatz's departure, Gabriele begins to play through the act 2 meeting and love duet between Tristan and Isolde. Mann's verbal music still follows Wagner closely but now unfolds at greater length, and its layers become more complex. Mann first describes the sounds of the hunting horns retreating into the distance, the extinguishing of the torch, and the waving of the white cloth as a signal to Tristan, "who approached with outspread arms through the darkness" (p. 117).

With the arrival of Tristan, Mann switches from description of actions in Einfried into the actual "present" of the opera. In a new paragraph he begins to paraphrase the passionate exchanges between the lovers from Wagner's libretto: "Oh boundless, oh unending exultation of this meeting in an eternal place beyond all visible things! Delivered from the tormenting illusion, set free from the bondage of space and time, self and not-self blissfully mingling, 'thine' and 'mine' mystically made one!" (p. 117). The source material here is obviously the word play between Wagner's Tristan and Isolde on "Du" and "Ich":

ISOLDE: Bin ich 's? Bist du 's?
TRISTAN: Bin ich 's? Bist du 's?
BEIDE: Mein Tristan / Isolde mein!
  Mein und dein

Mann reverts briefly to narrative: "The mocking falsehoods of day could divide them, but its pomp and show no longer had power to deceive them, for the magic potion had opened their eyes" (p. 117). Then he presents a still more extended and complex paraphrase that begins with a direct quotation of the core of Wagner's love duet. The relevant passages should be given here in German:

> O sink hernieder, Nacht der Liebe, gib ihnen jenes Vergessen, das sie ersehnen, umschließe sie ganz mit deiner Wonne und löse sie los von der Welt des Truges und der Trennung. Siehe, die letzte Leuchte verlosch! Denken und Dünken versank in heiliger Dämmerung.
>
> *Mann*

> BEIDE: O sink hernieder, / Nacht der Liebe, / gib Vergessen, / daß ich lebe; / nimm mich auf / in deinen Schoß, / löse von / der Welt mich lost! / TRISTAN: Verloschen nun / die letzte Leuchte; / ISOLDE: was wir dachten, / was uns deuchte; / TRISTAN: all Gedenken / ISOLDE: all Gemahnen / BEIDE: heil'ger Dämm'rung / hehres Ahnen / löscht des Wähnens Graus / weiterlösend aus.
>
> *Wagner*

Even where Mann does not follow the words exactly, he adopts the Wagnerian *Stabreim,* or root rhyme.[22] Perhaps even more significantly, Mann retains his authorial, epic voice. He alters the imprecation to night such that it seems to come from him, not directly from the lovers. Thus he has "gib ihnen jenes Vergessen" (give *them* that oblivion) where Wagner's lovers sing "gib Vergessen." Only later in the paragraph does Mann enter the persona of the lovers—or perhaps more specifically Tristan—when he writes of being excluded from "the falsehood of day," and of "my" torment and desire. As it began with "sink hernieder," this paragraph culminates with another direct citation from the libretto: "selbst dann bin ich die Welt."

At this point Mann follows Wagner in breaking the dramatic continuity, and does so on two different levels. First, he steps back even further into his authorial voice to register Brangäne's interruption of the lovers: "And there followed Brangäne's warning call, with those rising violin phrases that pass all understanding" (p. 118). Mann engineers a break on still another level when Gabriele, puzzled by the words of Wagner's libretto, stops playing and asks, naively, "I am not always sure what it means, Herr Spinell; I can only guess at some of it. What is 'then I myself am the world'?" Spinell "explains it to her, softly and briefly," but the reader is not privy to the explanation. Gabriele seems satisfied, though she asks Spinell why it is that he "can understand it all so well, and yet not be able to play it." Spinell, agitated by the question, says, "The two," by which he means appreciation and execution, "seldom go together."

There are several things to remark about this moment. First, as suggested above, is Mann's "double" interruption of the love duet. On the level of the opera's plot, Brangäne breaks into the lovers' reverie. On the level of the novella, Mann may be said to re-create the interruption by having Gabriele stop playing and ask about the meaning of the text. Second, one should note the masterful irony of Gabriele's reaction to Spinell's clarification of the densely Schopenhauerian phrase "selbst bin ich die Welt." Mann reinforces or adapts here something of the intellect-versus-life irony that he was to identify in *Reflections.* Spinell has the intellectual ability to explain the phrase, but he cannot play it. Gabriele can play it—and feel it—but cannot intellectualize it.

After this two-level interruption, Gabriele plays through the rest of the love scene. Mann presents as before a mix of paraphrase, direct quotation, and description. Then, after citing "Du Isolde, Tristan ich, nicht mehr Tristan, nicht mehr Isolde," Mann stages another interruption, this one corresponding to Kurwenal's sudden entry in the love scene, alerting Tristan of the arrival of King Mark. This time Mann does not return to the plot of the opera, as he did with the mention of Brangäne's call, but moves directly to the level of the novella's action: "At this point there was a startling interruption. The pianist suddenly stopped playing . . . and Herr Spinell swung round on his chair." Mann goes on to recount the entry into the room of one of the other Einfried patients, the Pastorin Höhlenrauch, who is always described in the novella as having had nineteen children and being "no longer capable of thought." (These phrases make up her identifying leitmotive.) When she enters the drawing room where Gabriele and Spinell are playing, she is merely passing through on the arm of her attendant, "dumb and staring and conscious of nothing." This is another superb ironic touch. Mann could easily have had the sleigh party return and discover Gabriele and Spinell at the piano, an event that would have been more precisely analogous to Mark's arrival in the opera. Instead, Gabriele and Spinell are interrupted by someone with no awareness, no involvement in their situation.

After this break, Gabriele plays through Isolde's *Liebestod,* and Mann revisits the piece he had described as Gerda's and Hanno's duet in *Buddenbrooks.* The description, briefer than that of the love duet, is now more in the nature of a coda to the scene. After Gabriele has finished playing, she and Spinell hear the sound of the sleigh bells, announcing the return of the other Einfried patients.

Very much as in *Buddenbrooks,* the musical scene is followed quickly in Mann's *Tristan* by the illness and death of the protagonist. Two days after her afternoon of Wagner, Gabriele begins to cough up blood; she weakens and takes to her bed. Within a few days she is dead. At the moment of death she is described as sitting quietly in her bed "humming a little snatch of music to herself" (p. 130). That music is not identified by Mann, but one could well imagine it as the *Liebestod* of Gabriele's alter-ego Isolde.

PARODY

The quality of irony and humor in *Tristan* differs from that in *Buddenbrooks.* With Wagner's opera as a direct model, both structural and thematic, *Tristan* approaches genuine parody. In a letter to his brother Heinrich of 1901, Mann referred to the story as "*a burlesque* that I'm working on, and which will probably be called 'Tristan.' (That's right! A burlesque that's called 'Tristan'!)."[23] Karsten Witte has suggested we take Mann at his word, arguing that the boundaries between burlesque, parody, farce, caricature, and travesty are fluid, at least in Mann, whose narrative style often incorporates several of these elements. The literary tradition of burlesque, he says, has as its goal a *moquerie d'esprit* and aims for "a comic *Imitatio* of a serious literary work. Its typical characteristic is a tension-filled opposition of subject and treatment, of elevated claim and baser effect. Incongruence shapes the form." Witte understands *Tristan* as "poking fun at Wagner," especially in the long scene in the drawing room.[24] And yet as we have seen, any element of burlesque is embedded in the larger ironic framework. The main characters of Mann's *Tristan* are in themselves parodic: Spinell as the decadent aesthete; Klöterjahn as the boor without real culture; Gabriele as the consumptive, delicate artist.

Although Mann used the term burlesque, parody might be more useful to describe the range of techniques in *Tristan.* In more recent literary criticism, especially since the work of Bakhtin, parody has come to be a universal term for what Simon Dentith has called "a range of cultural practices which are all more or less parodic." Dentith offers a broad definition of parody as "any cultural practice which provides a relatively polemical allusive imitation of another cultural production or practice."[25] Margaret Rose's narrower but denser definition comes closer to our present concerns. Parody is, for her: "at first imitating and then changing either, and sometimes both, the 'form' and 'content,' or style and subject-matter, or syntax and meaning of another work, or, most simply its vocabulary. In addition to, and at the same time as the preceding, most successful parodies may be said to produce from the comic incongruity between the original and its parody some comic, amusing, or humorous effect."[26]

There is disagreement among literary historians as to whether parody need always be comic or even polemical. But what seems essential is that a relationship be set up between what Gérard Genette calls the "hypertext," the text that makes the parody, and the "hypotext," the text that is being parodied.[27] (We will return to Genette's categories in the next chapter.) Rose proposes a more complex model based on the theories of Siegfried J. Schmidt, who posits a text-world (TW) that is received within a reader's world (RW) at X time and place. In the case of parody, we are dealing with at least two text-worlds, that created by the parodist and that of the "target" as reproduced by the parodist (thus TW1 and TW2, respectively). Both of these texts are received by the reader (RW), but the parodied text (TW2) is also received by the parodist within TW1. Thus TW2 has at least two, perhaps multiple, readers. As Rose says, this model of parody "as containing at least two texts and their 'worlds' can be applied to most parodies, from the basic to the complex."[28]

In the case of Mann's *Tristan,* we have a parody across genres: a novella parodies an opera. This makes the "incongruity" (of which both Witte and Rose write) especially obvious. But there is also a further complexity to the parody in that the characters in the novella are not only themselves "parodies" of Tristan and Isolde, but also "perform" the opera and thus might be said to create a parody within a parody. Or, in the Schmidt-Rose terms, Mann's *Tristan* may be said to have two text-worlds, that of Mann's story (TW1) and of Wagner's opera (TW2), but three reader's worlds, our own as external readers, Mann's as a reader/receiver of Wagner's opera, and also that of Gabriele and Spinell, who receive and perform the opera.[29]

In at least one important respect, the Schmidt-Rose model must be modified for Mann's novella, as for much modern parody. As Linda Hutcheon has shown, the "target" is often shifted in parodic art of the twentieth century. That is, the work on which the parody is based (TW2, Wagner's *Tristan* in Mann's novella), traditionally considered the target, is not really being mocked, but has become a "weapon." It is being used to reflect an ironic light on the main text or text-world (TW1).[30] What is parodied in Mann's novella is not TW2, the world of Wagner's characters, but TW1, the world of Gabriele and Spinell.

It is clear from these examples that parody makes use of, but is not identical to, irony. Irony is more of a strategy or "trope," as Hutcheon says, and need not involve two or more text-worlds. Parody requires intertextuality, and often creates an ironic—but not necessarily comic—relationship between the texts. "The pleasure of parody's irony," Hutcheon observes, "comes not from humor in particular but from the degree of engagement of the reader in the intertextual 'bouncing' (to use E. M. Forster's famous term) between complicity and distance."[31] Certainly the success and sophistication of Mann's *Tristan* derive at least in part from the pleasure the reader takes in "bouncing" among the different text-worlds and reader's worlds.

BLOOD OF THE WÄLSUNGS

Mann never surpassed the verbal music or the parody of *Tristan.* But he uses Wagner again very effectively as a weapon of irony and parody in the story *Blood of the Wälsungs (Wälsungenblut),* which first appeared in 1906 but was then withdrawn by Mann and published in a revised version in 1921. In *Tristan,* Mann seemed to be parodying aestheticism (in Spinell) and middle-class bourgeois values (Anton Klöterjahn). Gabriele is caught in the middle of this art-versus-life struggle so characteristic of Mann. In *Blood of the Wälsungs,* Mann's target is an upper-middle-class assimilated Jewish family in Berlin, named Aarenhold, which contains a pair of inseparable nineteen-year-old twins, Siegmund and Sieglinde. (As with the title and the name Einfried in *Tristan,* Mann does not hide his parodic intentions.) Sieglinde's upwardly mobile father has arranged her engagement to a gentile businessman named Beckerath. After a lunch at the Aarenhold mansion, at which Beckerath is present, the twins ask and receive permission to go off to a performance of *Die Walküre.*

The opera becomes the occasion for Mann's verbal music. All three acts of *Walküre* are rendered, the first more extensively than the other two, since this is the one that depicts the growing love and recognition between the Wälsung siblings who are the "weapons" and the parallels to Mann's characters. (Hunding clearly stands in for the hapless Beckerath.) The verbal music, similar in style to that of *Tristan,* requires no detailed discussion here.[32] As in the earlier novella and in *Buddenbrooks,* physical description of the characters is interwoven with paraphrase of the music and libretto on several levels. There are also the characteristic moments of *Illusionsstörung.* The brief exchanges between Mann's twins, and descriptions of the hall, the patrons, and the chocolate bonbons shared by the siblings, return us frequently to the "reality" of the story.

As the opera progresses, Mann's characters become ever more aware of their powerful attraction for each other. What had been sibling affection ripens into sexual desire. After the opera is over, they ride home in their carriage: "They sat as silent and remote as they had sat in their opera-box facing the stage—almost, one might say, in the same atmosphere. Nothing was there which could alienate them from that extravagant and stormily passionate world which worked upon them with its magic power to draw them to itself."[33]

The story culminates in an incestuous union that even more than in *Tristan* serves to parody both the opera and the twins. After having a light meal with his sister, Siegmund goes in his room. Mann's Siegmund is, like Spinell, a decadent who clearly takes pleasure in his perfumes and clothes: "The subtle, bitterish scent of the tobacco mingled with that of the cosmetics, soaps, and toilet waters; their combined perfume hung in the tepid air of the room and Siegmund breathed it in with conscious pleasure" (p. 313). He studies himself in the mirror. Then, like his counterpart in the opera, he throws himself onto a bearskin rug. Sieglinde comes in. Their similarity of appearance is stressed by Mann, just as is that of Wagner's characters: "You are just like me," Siegmund says to Sieglinde. "Everything about you is just like me" (p. 315). They consummate their love on the rug.

In *Buddenbrooks, Tristan,* and *Blood of the Wälsungs,* irony and parody become mechanisms to create distance from the Wagnerism that dominated much music and artistic thought in the last two decades of the nineteenth century. Mann's elaborate verbal and narrative music shows at once a profound knowledge of and respect for Wagner, as well as a skeptical detachment. Nietzsche, as we have seen, had a similarly two-edged relationship to Wagner, which served as a catalyst for much of his philosophical thought. It was Mann, however, who in the years around 1900 showed how such a relationship could generate artworks of great originality and integrity. From the purely literary point of view, Mann demonstrated (especially in *Buddenbrooks*) how the bourgeois realist novel of the later nineteenth century, such as those of Fontane, could be transformed and updated through the use of irony. But Mann's achievements reached well beyond literature and may be said to have opened up new paths for German modernism more generally.

MAHLER'S IRONY

For Gustav Mahler, as for Mann, irony provided both an escape hatch from German Romanticism and a lens through which to view it in sharp focus.

Irony and parody have been evoked by numerous commentators in relationship to Mahler's works. Indeed, an entire symposium was devoted to this topic in 1996.[34] For most of the authors, irony is a *Weltanschauung* or worldview that informs Mahler's oeuvre in one way or another from beginning to end. Stephen Hefling calls Mahler "the first composer for whom irony is a fundamental and restlessly recurring element of his works."[35]

The principal historical sources of Mahler's irony were essentially the same as Mann's: the early German Romantics and Nietzsche. Mahler was deeply attached to the writings and philosophy of Jean Paul (1763–1825). In his *Vorschule der Ästhetik* (School for Aesthetics) of 1804 Jean Paul had provided an account of irony in much the same vein as that of his fellow early Romantic Friedrich Schlegel. For Jean Paul, irony differs from other forms of humor (wit, whimsy) in being "serious" and "objective," and in involving "self-restraint." "Irony is more difficult in the enthusiasm of youth," Jean Paul suggests, "but becomes easier in age. . . . That is why men of understanding tend more to irony, those of imagination more to whimsy."[36] Jean Paul's novel *Titan* (1800–1803) was almost certainly an impetus for the work that eventually became Mahler's First Symphony and that in its early performances between 1889 and 1894 bore the title "Titan." Mahler himself appears never to have associated that title directly with Jean Paul, but several members of his circle, including Bruno Walter, reported the connection as authentic. Numerous authors have explored the parallels or analogies.[37]

The Nietzschean strain of irony is less obvious in early Mahler. The Third Symphony (1895–96) would be the obvious place to look. For a considerable period during its gestation, Mahler's programmatic outlines for the symphony bore the title "Die fröhliche Wissenschaft" (The Gay Science), after Nietzsche's book. That book, completed in 1882 in the mild winter climate of Genoa during a period of emotional and physical recuperation, is one of Nietzsche's more optimistic works. It is filled with images of nature and landscape; and it is the first work in which Nietzsche develops his doctrine of eternal recurrence, the idea that time and experience recycle within themselves. Some of these aspects—not specifically ironic in content or tone—pervade Mahler's Third, whose programs and sonic content are imbued with the processes of nature. The fourth movement strikes a darker Nietzschean tone. In it, Mahler sets a poem from Part Three of *Thus Spoke Zarathustra,* a poem of midnight that celebrates the notion of eternal recurrence in reminding us that "all joy wants eternity."

We should also note that during his student period in Vienna in the mid-

1870s, well before his maturity as a composer, Mahler formed part of a group of young men, the so-called Pernerstorfer Circle, who avidly read the early works of Nietzsche, especially *The Birth of Tragedy* and *Unfashionable Observations.*[38] As we saw above, in the essay on history from *Unfashionable Observations* Nietzsche identified an "ironic self-consciousness" characteristic of his era, an awareness of living in a "twilight" period. Surely that description could fit much of Mahler's work, especially his self-conscious treatment of the standard symphonic forms, as I will suggest further below.

Irony is readily apparent in Mahler's *Wunderhorn* works, comprising the first four symphonies and many of the songs written up to about 1900, for which he employed or evoked texts from the collection of early Romantic folk poetry *Des Knaben Wunderhorn* (The Youth's Magic Horn). In the *Wunderhorn* works, elements of a folklike musical style—including diatonic melodies, strophic or modified strophic forms, and simple accompaniment patterns—are sometimes offset by moments of harsh dissonance, sudden modulations, or a lean and sharply profiled orchestration. The effect is ironic in a classic sense in that there is a disjunction between what is (or seems to be) being communicated and the manner of communicating it; at the very least, there is a juxtaposition of expressive worlds.

The First Symphony (not strictly speaking a *Wunderhorn* work, since it draws upon Mahler's *Songs of a Wayfarer*) was frequently received as ironic, especially its third movement, a funeral march based on a canonic treatment of a minor-mode version of the "Bruder Martin" tune (better known as "Frère Jacques"). The first trio, which evokes the sounds and style of a Bohemian village band, is marked by Mahler to be played "with parody." A critic of the original Budapest performance of the First, August Beer, caught the "parodistic tone" and "ironic accents" of this movement.[39] In a commentary distributed to the audience for the Hamburg performance of the First in October 1893, Mahler himself described the funeral march as alternating between moods that are "ironically merry" *(ironisch lustig)* and "weirdly brooding" *(unheimlich brütend).*[40] In Vienna in 1900, the conservative critic Robert Hirschfeld thought the First Symphony a "satire" that Mahler did not intend to be taken seriously. Another Viennese critic, Max Kalbeck, who unlike Hirschfeld saw Mahler as earnest and sincere, nonetheless dubbed the First a "Sinfonia ironica" and attributed the structural discontinuities in the outer movements to the "solvent harshness of irony."[41]

A macabre, unsettling irony is built directly into some of the *Wunderhorn* poetry employed by Mahler during these years. In "Das irdische Leben" (Earthly Life), a starving child repeatedly begs his mother for bread. She dismisses his cries ("Warte nur," Just wait), explaining that the bread will be ready once the grain has been harvested and threshed. When the bread is at last baked, the child already lies dead.[42] The dramatic plan of "Earthly Life" is somewhat analogous to Goethe's "Erlkönig," with a narrator and "characters," including the parent and sick child. As in Schubert's setting of the Goethe, the child's cries become more insistent across Mahler's song: Mahler introduces alterations in the melody and orchestration that heighten the tension. The mother's implacable replies remain almost the same in each stanza. Of course, the major difference from "Erlkönig"—and this accounts for the irony that is not characteristic of Goethe and Schubert—is that in "Earthly Life" the child's death would seem easily preventable. A child should not be allowed by his own mother to starve amid plenty.

The Fourth Symphony, completed in 1899 and intimately bound up with the *Wunderhorn* poetry and music, is perhaps Mahler's most conspicuously and complexly ironic work. The final movement, "Das himmlische Leben" (Life in Heaven), based on a *Wunderhorn* poem that is in some ways the complement to "Earthly Life," was composed many years before the rest of the work, in 1892, as a song for voice and orchestra. It was projected to be the finale of the Third Symphony in 1896, but Mahler withheld it—the Third now ends with a slow instrumental movement—and used it instead for the Fourth. The composition of the first three movements of the Fourth can thus be said to have been "backshadowed" by a finale already in existence.

"Earthly Life" is characterized by a tragic or bitter irony. "Heavenly Life" is very different; Hefling has dubbed its ironic stance *ingenu* after a category used by D. C. Muecke.[43] The child seems to take her own view of heaven at face value despite evidence to the contrary. She assures us that heavenly life avoids all earthly things and is devoid of worldly clamor *(weltlich' Getümmel),* at the same time that she describes a very healthy celestial appetite, sated by the slaughter of animals for food. The image of heaven is very materialistic or hedonistic; the goal is to "cheer the senses" *(ermuntern die Sinnen).* Anything one wants in the way of food or wine—or music—is readily and abundantly available. Mahler sets this text as a modified strophic form. The soprano is directed by Mahler to perform "with childishly cheerful expression; without parody at any point!" *(mit kindlich heiterem Ausdruck; durchaus ohne Parodie!). Ingenu* irony is thus irony that is light-hearted but without parody.

The "worldly clamor" in "Heavenly Life" is represented most obviously by the percussive, rhythmically insistent outbursts (beginning at m. 40) that feature sleigh bells and sharp grace-note accents. When he wrote the Fourth

Symphony, Mahler imported these passages back into the first movement, where they serve to offset not images of heavenly life, but rather the poise and elegance of a classicizing instrumental style. Adorno makes the striking observation that the sleigh-bell passage at the very opening of the Fourth announces that "none of what you now hear is true."[44] He does not use the term "irony," but clearly suggests that the sleigh bells create an immediate distancing effect from what follows.

Adorno also commented that the Fourth was "composed within quotation marks."[45] More recently, Manfred Angerer has sought to elaborate on this claim, suggesting that the Fourth "consists only of conventions, of the linking together, in an artistically artificial way, of traditional clichés or . . . of familiar musical topoi." According to Angerer, "almost everything in this symphony is quotation, although Mahler borrows hardly at all from other works. The composer cites not themes but accents *[Tonfälle],* traditional manners of expression, movement types, and formal schemes." The form of the first movement of the Fourth is for Mahler "conceivable only as an aesthetically shattered and fragile-seeming As-If." In comparing Mahler with Beethoven, Angerer observes that Beethoven's symphonic music is "present-oriented through and through," while Mahler's is "ironic."[46]

Angerer surely exaggerates the degree to which "everything is quotation," but it is true that Mahler reverts, at least in his first movement, to the more traditional proportions and structures of the standard symphony. The form inside the "quotation marks" of the sleigh bells is readily recognizable as sonata form. The phrase structure, the accompaniment, the harmonic syntax, and the general *Stimmung* of the main theme lack what Angerer calls the "panic-stricken shock effects" of Mahler's earlier works.[47] The theme, which begins in m. 4, divides into two balanced statements of fifteen measures each (first statement shown in example 34). Each half divides further into 4 + 4 + 7 (where 7 = 6 + 1).[48] The slight asymmetry is thus compensated by a large-scale symmetry, which is also reflected tonally. The first fifteen-measure unit departs from and returns to the tonic, G, hinting at the dominant along the way (m. 11). The next unit or counterstatement (mm. 18–32) leads to a transition (mm. 30–37), which moves to the dominant key for the second group (arriving at m. 38).

The quotation-mark sleigh bells reappear to introduce the development section at m. 72. The opening of the development is distinctive for returning to and remaining for so long in the tonic key and in a genial (hence undevelopmental) mood. It is as if—how naturally one falls into that telltale "as if" in discussing this music!—the form has somehow forgotten itself and

Example 34. Mahler, Symphony No. 4, I, main theme

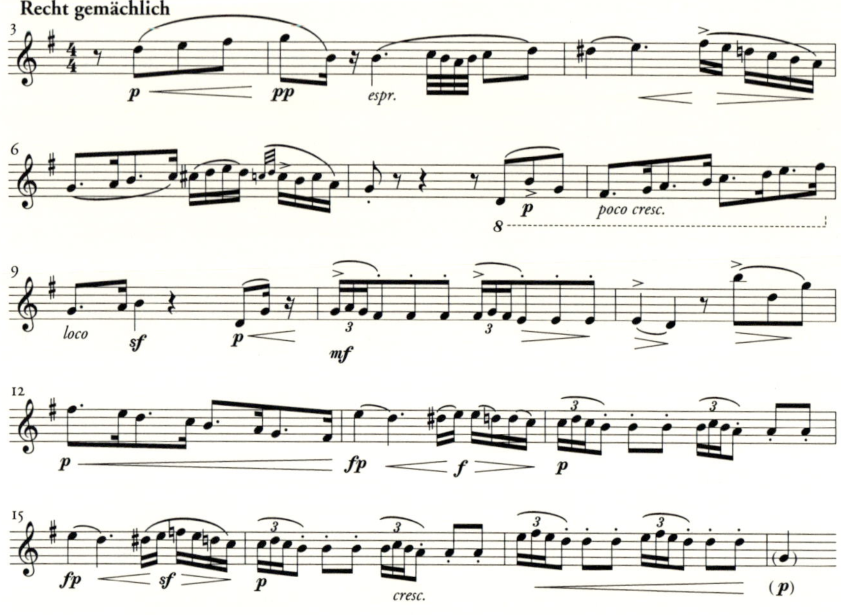

seeks to repeat the exposition. But the false return dies away to *ppp* over a tonic triad (m. 101), and the sleigh bells come forward once again to lead us into the "real" development—how naturally one also introduces quotation marks when discussing the movement—which now continues in earnest ("earnest"?) in E minor (m. 109).

Near the end of the long development the sleigh bells reappear yet again (m. 225) to announce a change. They are now accompanied by an ominous new trumpet fanfare in minor (anticipatory of the opening of the Fifth Symphony). But the music seems to disregard any message of doom. At m. 238, the development winds down—really unravels—to *ppp* over an ambiguous harmony that is distinctly *not* a dominant preparation for the tonic G major. And after a perplexed fermata—"What happens next?" it seems to ask—the recapitulation begins in midphrase, almost insouciantly, with what was the third measure of the original theme (cf. m. 6). "Once again as at the beginning," Mahler instructs, "comfortably and pleasingly."

The sleigh bells appear one last time in this movement, to usher in the coda (m. 297). Mahler's final action is to restore the beginning of the theme—the languid upbeat figure—that was missing from the start of the recapitulation. It enters *ppp* and very hesitantly (m. 340), held back by two fermatas, then plunges ahead into a stringendo and crescendo that bring the movement to a conclusion that is at once sudden and satisfying.

The adoption of convention in an "as-if," ironic mode, in the "second degree," or in a "none-of-this-is-true" manner—all are different ways of naming essentially the same phenomenon—is a fundamental aspect of the first movement of Mahler's Fourth. It makes Mahler's relation to the musical past very different from that of Reger or Busoni, with whom there was no trace of irony, but rather a strong identification with Bach.

In the scherzo of Mahler's Fourth, the two recurring trios offer up sound worlds that contrast sharply with the unsettling main section in C minor, characterized by the scordatura solo violin. In the first trio (m. 34), the tonality slips into a radiant, even celestial C major, in which gentle, sustained chords in the horns support arabesques in the strings, each one capped by a high "ping" from the harp. The second trio, in F major (m. 69), is much earthier; its stolid woodwind melodies are marked *lustig* (merry). The irony of the second movement consists in the juxtaposition of expressive worlds—a juxtaposition more extreme than one would find in most scherzos of the nineteenth century. The closest analogy would be with the mature Schubert, where a trio will often transport us to a remoter and happier world, as in the G-Major Piano Sonata (D. 894) and the G-Major String Quartet (D. 887).[49] In Schubert we sense a nostalgia for that lost, innocent world. In Mahler, who is so indebted to Schubert in many respects, that nostalgia takes on an ironic cast in that the contrast between the scherzo and the trios is still more extreme, more difficult to contain within a single movement.

The expressive trajectory of the Fourth Symphony moves from the most obviously ironic or "as-if" (first two movements) toward the "straightest" or "this-*is*-real" mode (last two movements). The third movement, by far the longest of the four, occupies the still center of the symphony. It is in the form of a double variation, modeled to some extent on the Andante of Beethoven's Ninth Symphony. Like the finale, this movement seems comfortable within its universe, until near the end, when the gates of heaven open suddenly at the enormous climax that passes from G major into E major (m. 315). This passage represents one of Mahler's greatest "breakthrough" moments, in which we seem to move cataclysmically into another realm.[50]

The *ingenu* irony of the finale is the perfect conclusion to this symphony in that it can capture the various stances of the previous movements—the "as-if" mode of the first, the caustic irony of the second, and the sobriety of the third. The final forty measures, which (as prefigured at the end of the slow movement) turn from G to E major, and which celebrate specifically the music of heaven, seem to exist in a world beyond irony. Mahler marks them to be played "very sweetly and full of mystery."

It should not surprise us that the tone and the content of Mahler's Fourth, like the First, confused listeners at its premiere with the Kaim Orchestra in Munich in November 1901, and on the subsequent tour. The public, expecting something in the tragic-and-sublime mode along the lines of the Second Symphony, did not know what to make of the Fourth. (The Third had not yet been performed.) De la Grange, who documents the early reception extensively, demonstrates that critics were mostly "unanimous in condemning the Fourth Symphony on grounds of style, form, and content." One commentator reported that the public did "not know whether it should take the composer seriously or whether he just wants to dazzle it with the fireworks of his irony and his skill as a sensation-monger."[51] The reviews of, and reported reactions to, the Fourth are in fact filled with puzzled (or angry) references to the work's apparent irony, parody, sarcasm, satire, burlesque, pasticcio, and the like. One rare critic who seemed more attuned to the genuine complexity of tone and technique in the symphony was Arthur Seidl: "I thus disagree entirely with the widespread opinion that, as a musician, he [Mahler] is content to exercise his biting irony and his misplaced scepticism at the expense of celestial joys. . . . The truth is quite different: it is the critics who consider him with an ironic eye and find only affectation in his music; it is they who are stubborn and who cannot find the key to his naïve and childlike fairy-tale world!"[52] That "key" is, as our consideration of the Fourth Symphony has shown, not an easy one to find. For the world is both ironic and sincere, sophisticated and naive.

The finale of Mahler's Seventh Symphony, composed in 1905, is the true problem child among Mahler's movements—and may well be the most ironic. Is the movement genuinely jubilant and affirmative? Or are the high jinks merely an "as if" phenomenon, a triumph in the "second degree"? Mahler designated the last movement of the Seventh a "rondo-finale," like that of the Fifth. As in the Fifth, an initial theme or ritornello alternates with contrasting episodes, but the treatment of the form is far less straightforward than in the earlier work. The returns are constantly undermined or called into question by metric, thematic, and harmonic surprises. Thus, for example, as Jonathan Kramer has suggested, the return of the main theme at m. 120 appears to be a major articulation point. Yet the C-major tonality does not have the force of a return since the music has not wandered far from that key for almost fifty measures. Earlier in the movement, at m. 79, a more significant return to C has not been supported by a real cadence; Mahler leaps back to the tonic from A♭.[53]

Despite these and similar anomalies, the Seventh was greeted enthusiastically at its premiere. Unlike the Fourth Symphony—where listeners could not read the tone—no mention was made of possible irony. The critic Felix Adler heard the finale of the Seventh as "cheerful, joyous, and life-affirming." He added, "The sun has risen; it has become *day*."[54] Elsa Bienenfeld wrote that if the finale was not entirely successful as a movement, it was not because of any ironic detachment but because of overexuberance. Mahler "cannot do enough to depict joy: as he places climax after climax, the piece founders in its sheer breadth."[55] Only for later commentators did the finale of the Seventh become a problem. The most renowned disparagement of the movement comes from Adorno, for whom it "embarrasses even those who concede everything to Mahler." For Adorno, Mahler is a "poor yea-sayer." His "voice cracks . . . when he makes music as if joy were already in the world."[56]

Kramer casts the finale of Mahler's Seventh in terms not of irony, but of postmodernity. "The movement's title leads us to expect certain kinds of structures," he comments. "They are not absent, but they are radically redefined, losing much of their traditional meaning and gaining new meanings in the process."[57] The formal and harmonic procedures Kramer considers postmodern have been characterized by Martin Scherzinger as deconstructive in the Derridean sense. For Scherzinger, the ambiguities in the movement are so fundamental that "the act of interpretation itself is foregrounded; the listener is drawn into the text."[58]

The postmodern and deconstructive interpretations of Mahler's finale are plausible. But since the goal of the present study is to historicize the work's qualities, we should ask to what extent can the finale of Mahler's Seventh be understood in light of turn-of-the-century German irony. Mahler's Fourth Symphony revisits Classical forms and idioms, but not specific musical works. Its irony is thus, as we have seen, more general. The Seventh appears to make allusion to actual pieces, specifically the cymbal-crashing, triangle-beating Janissary Music from act 3 of Mozart's *Abduction from the Seraglio* (also in C major); Franz Lehar's operetta *The Merry Widow;* and the main theme of Wagner's Prelude to *Die Meistersinger.*[59] We thus enter the realm of ironic parody.

The *Meistersinger* references provide the most direct point of contact with the issues and the literary works discussed in this chapter. The radiant—or "as if" radiant—tonality of C major in which Mahler's finale begins is

Example 35.

a. Mahler, Symphony No. 7, V

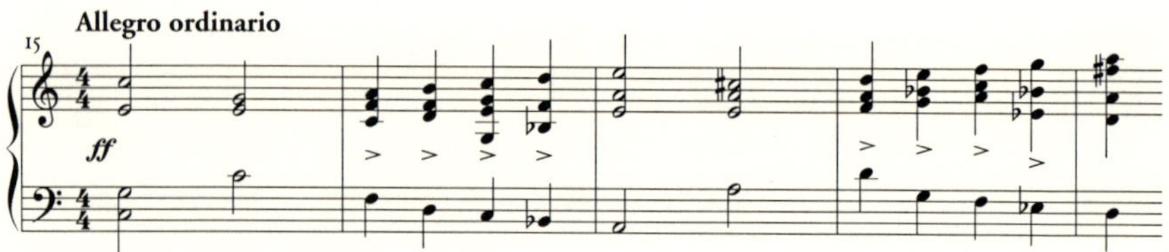

b. Wagner, *Die Meistersinger,* Prelude

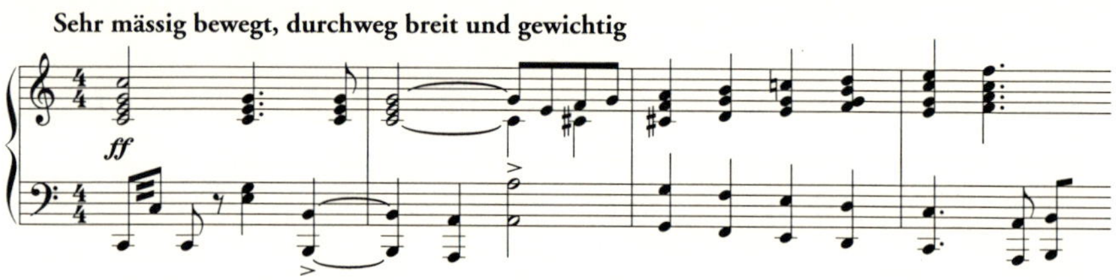

already a hint of what Bernd Sponheuer has called the "*Meistersinger*-like cheerfulness" that pervades the movement.[60] The theme at m. 15 is an unmistakable allusion to Wagner's overture (example 35). The melodic line leaps down a fourth from the tonic to the dominant, then ascends by step; it is underpinned, as in Wagner, by a contrapuntally conceived bass line moving in contrary motion. The quotation is, however, exaggerated or distorted. Where Wagner's theme and accompaniment remain at least initially diatonic, Mahler's is quickly derailed from C major by the introduction of foreign triads on B♭ major and A major. Though arrived at in a deliberately shocking way, the A proves to be V/V/V; it leads to D, then G, and Mahler eventually cadences back into the tonic at m. 23.

What is the effect of this Wagner-on-steroids process? How are we to understand the Wagner reference and Mahler's own treatment of C-major diatonicism? Dahlhaus refers to Wagner's sophisticated diatonicism in *Die Meistersinger* as "second" in nature. The term, which he draws from Hegel, is similar in meaning to Genette's "in the second degree."[61] In the terms of our present discussion, it suggests that the tonal language of Wagner's opera exists in an "as if" zone. By extension, we can understand Mahler's C-major diatonicism in the finale of the Seventh as "tertiary," as operating in an "as-if as-if" sphere. As Hermann Danuser suggests, Mahler appropriates the *Meistersinger* idiom not to imitate it, but to create distance from it. The distorted quotation of *Meistersinger* is meant to signal to us that we should hear Mahler's treatment of tonality in the movement as multiply filtered. Thus the C major of Mozart's Janissary music, or of the "Jupiter" Symphony (to choose a still more archetypical and largely jubilant work in that key), is already mediated by Wagner's opera, which in turn is mediated by Mahler. This temporal layering is fully characteristic of ironic discourse among German artists working around 1900.

As with the references to Wagner in Mann's fiction, we cannot speak of traditional parody here. The "target" is surely not Wagner or Wagner's music. In Mann, the targets are the characters—Detlev Spinnell, Gabriele Klöterjahn, the Aarenhold twins—and their bourgeois milieu. What would be the target for Mahler? It might in fact be something analogous to Mann: the late bourgeois concert audience that is listening to the symphony. Mahler is not mocking his audience; in accusing him of that, the early critics of the Fourth Symphony were mistaken. Rather, he is acknowledging for the listeners and critics (and for himself, like Mann a part of the bourgeoisie) an unbridgeable distance between them and the musical past. The consciousness of that distance is the condition of modernity, and it must be reflected in music that is to be true to its age.

SIX

"Dancing in Chains"

Strauss, Hofmannsthal, Pfitzner, and Their Musical Pasts

WE RECALL THAT IN *Human, All Too Human* Nietzsche called for a new classicism in which creative artists would, like the ancient Greeks, impose fetters upon themselves—"make things look difficult"—at the same time as giving the illusion of spontaneity and lack of effort. He called this practice "dancing in chains." Composers around 1900, as we have seen, readily put themselves in historical fetters. Reger, Busoni, and Mahler took on Bachian chains, for different reasons, in different ways, and to very different effects. In each case, however, the relationship to the musical past forms a strong part of their modernist identity. For Mahler, as we saw in the last chapter, irony became a key strategy for working with and within older structures. In this chapter I shall examine two strongly contrasting cases of operatic configurations of the past in the early modern period: the team of Richard Strauss and Hugo von Hofmannsthal, and Hans Pfitzner. All three men were profoundly aware of their historical positions as post-Wagnerian artists; their operas reflect complicated attitudes toward, and assimilation of, the past.

STRAUSS AND HOFMANNSTHAL

In chapter 2 we examined Strauss's *Salome* and *Elektra* in the context of German naturalism. Through thematic, metrical, declamatory, and orchestral aspects, the music for Herod in the former and for Clytemnestra in the latter conveys a neurasthenic, hypersensory state that represents a heightened naturalism bordering on expressionism. Though *Elektra* represented the first time the names of Strauss and Hofmannsthal appeared together on an operatic score, it was less a joint effort than a literature opera based on a preexisting play text (with a few emendations). The first actual collaborations between composer and poet made for a significant shift in Strauss's operatic trajectory, as has often been observed. In *Der Rosenkavalier* (1910) and *Ariadne auf Naxos* (1912, rev. 1916), Strauss and Hofmannsthal manifest an extraordinary ability to "dance in chains," to work with élan within the limits of strongly retrospective forms and styles. They do so with a profound sense of irony and, to some extent, parody that may have been stimulated at least in part by Mann's achievements in the first decade of the twentieth century, as discussed in the last chapter. Certainly their treatment of Wagner's music bears fruitful juxtaposition with Mann's fiction.

Mann had good if not close personal relations with Hofmannsthal. The two writers had become acquainted in 1908 when Mann visited Vienna. Hofmannsthal invited Mann to his home in Rodaun, an event that greatly impressed Mann, who wrote about it in several letters. From then on, they had frequent encounters; the correspondence between them extends up to Hofmannsthal's death in 1929 and comprises some twenty-eight items.[1] Yet Mann and Hofmannsthal were of very different artistic temperaments. Hans Wysling has suggested that Mann found Hofmannsthal's work "too soft, too lascivious in its erotic compliance." For his part, Hofmannsthal may have found Mann "too 'Prussian,' too conscious, too disciplined, too virtuous, too efficient."[2]

The text of *Der Rosenkavalier* delighted Mann, as he wrote Hofmannsthal, with its "charm" and "lightness."[3] Mann's response to Strauss's music, however, was profoundly negative, as he reported to the librettist a few days after attending the Munich premiere of the opera in February 1911. Mann's comments are worth reproducing at some length here:

> But how, for God's sake, do you really feel about the way in which Richard Strauss has weighed down and stretched out your delicate creation?! Four hours of loud noise laid over a charming trifle! And if this incongruity were the only contradiction of style! Where is Vienna, where is the eighteenth century in this music? Certainly not in the waltzes? They are anachronistic and thus mark the whole thing as an operetta. If only it were one. But it is a music drama of the highest caliber. Moreover, Strauss under-

stands absolutely nothing of Wagner's art of *not* covering up the declamation with his giant orchestra; not a single word is understandable. All the thousand linguistic delicacies and curiosities of the text are crushed to death and swallowed up. In the end that's good, for they stand in a blatant stylistic contradiction to the refined noise in which they perish, and which should have been twice as refined, but had much less noise.[4]

It is a pity that Mann could not appreciate what Strauss achieved musically in *Der Rosenkavalier,* because in many ways its "refined noise" is close in spirit to the techniques of irony and parody used by Mann himself.

TRISTAN IN *DER ROSENKAVALIER*

The polyvalent qualities of the music of *Der Rosenkavalier,* which Bryan Gilliam has identified as a "critical layering of musical styles" involving Mozart, Wagner, and Johann Strauss, are today recognized as the source of its modernity (or even postmodernity).[5] This layering reflects musically the multiplicity of linguistic styles that Hofmannsthal wrote into his libretto and described in a late commentary as "a language through which each person depicts simultaneously himself and his social rank; a language which in the mouths of all these figures is the same—it is the imaginary language of the period—and yet in each mouth is also different."[6]

Hofmannsthal proposed to characterize *Der Rosenkavalier* on the title page of both libretto and score as a "burlesque," the very term Mann had used to describe *Tristan* to his brother Heinrich. Strauss objected that such a generic designation would make people think of "Offenbach, *Mikado,* etc." and that "there's nothing burlesque about it."[7] He may have missed the point: Hofmannsthal was probably thinking, like Mann, of "burlesque" in a literary, theatrical tradition, rather than as music-hall farce. Burlesque may not have been a conscious part of Strauss's creative arsenal, but parody certainly was.

In none of the surviving correspondence between Hofmannsthal and Strauss about *Der Rosenkavalier,* nor in any of the correspondence that either man had with other people about the project, is there any mention that the opening scene is a parody of the love duet from act 2 of Wagner's *Tristan und Isolde,* one that is fully the equal of chapter 8 of Mann's *Tristan.* The collaborators acknowledge other models from Mozart and Wagner. These include the analogies between characters in *The Marriage of Figaro* (the

Countess, Cherubino, and Susanna) and their counterparts in *Der Rosenkavalier* (the Marschallin, Octavian, and Sophie); and the contemplative trio near the end of act 3 that evokes the Quintet from *Die Meistersinger.*[8] Commentators on the opera have often remarked how the melody of the final duet between Octavian and Sophie closely resembles the Pamina-Pageno duet from act 1 of *The Magic Flute.*[9] Whatever elements of parody these characters or moments display, the parody of Wagner's *Tristan,* which has gone largely uninvestigated, is far more extensive.[10]

In the first draft of the libretto that Hofmannsthal prepared early in 1909, the materials of acts 1 and 2 of *Der Rosenkavalier* as we now know it are essentially reversed: the Octavian-Marschallin scene is placed in act 2, precisely the point where the love duet occurs in Wagner's *Tristan.* Hofmannsthal's prose sketch for the act begins: "Bedroom of the Marquise [as the Marschallin was called at this point]. Night of love. Morning. Thanks."[11] When Hofmannsthal decided to move the love scene to the beginning of the opera—where it is now more a *Liebesmorgen* than a *Liebesnacht*—the Wagnerian aspects were further developed. Portions of the exchange between Octavian and the Marschallin are taken directly from the *Tristan* love scene, but freely reshuffled or paraphrased, as the following excerpts indicate:

Der Rosenkavalier	*Tristan und Isolde*
OCTAVIAN:	
Wie du warst! Wie du bist!	
Das weiß niemand, das ahnt keiner!	Ungeahnte, nie gekannte!
. . . .	. . . .
Du, du—was heißt das "du"? Was "du und ich"?	Mein und dein!
Hat denn das einen Sinn?	. . . .
Das sind Wörter, bloße Wörter, nicht? Du sag!	Dies süße Wörtlein: und,
Aber dennoch: Es ist etwas in ihnen:	was es bindet,
	. . . .
ein Schwindeln, ein Ziehen, ein Sehnen, ein Drängen!	Tagessonne,
	. . . .
	drang mir ein
	. . . .

Wie jetzt meine Hand zu deiner
  Hand kommt,
das Zudirwollen, das Dichum-
  klammern,
das bin ich, das will zu dir,
aber das Ich vergeht in dem Du.
. . . .
Warum ist Tag? Ich will nicht den
  Tag!

Du Isolde,
Tristan ich,
. . . .
Dem Tage! Dem Tage!
Dem tückischen Tage.[12]

Among the elements Hofmannsthal takes over from Wagner's libretto are the play on "Du" and "Ich"; the hatred-of-day theme; the rapid parallel questions or word repetitions; and other verbal cues ("Hand," the verbs "ahnen," "drängen," and "sehnen"). Much as in Mann's *Tristan,* however, the real "target" in *Der Rosenkavalier* is the modern bourgeois world into which the Wagnerian vocabulary is ironically placed, in this case the bedroom of an eighteenth-century noblewoman. For Hofmannsthal as for Mann, Wagner becomes the weapon to poke fun at the lovers.

Wagner's love duet suffuses not only the language of Hofmannsthal's libretto, but also its structure and other dramatic details. The Field Marshal is out on a hunt, like King Mark in *Tristan.* In Wagner's opera, the world of the hunt—the "real" or external world—is represented by the horns, which Isolde actually hears in the opera at the beginning of act 2 ("Hörst du sie noch?" she asks Brangäne). Those horns were transformed by Mann into sleigh bells—a step closer toward middle-class domesticity. Hofmannsthal may be said to move even further in this direction by introducing a hand bell that rings in the background a few minutes into the scene and then gets closer ("ein feines Klingeln" . . . "das Klingeln näher"). The bell is diegetic; it is "inside" the plot, heard and remarked upon by the operatic characters, like the sleigh bells in Mann's story and the horns in Wagner's opera.

Brangäne's warning in act 2 of Wagner's *Tristan,* which was represented by the interruption of Rätin Spatz in Mann's novella, may be said in *Der Rosenkavalier* to be conveyed by the little servant who comes into the room bringing the breakfast chocolate, at which point the dialogue between the Marschallin and Octavian settles into everyday practicality. "Stop philosophizing, my dear, and come over here," the Marschallin says to Octavian. "Let's have breakfast. Everything has its time." The final or climactic interruption of the love duet, which in act 2 of Wagner's opera occurs with the arrival of Mark's retinue and in Mann's *Tristan* with the surprise entrance of the Pastorin Höllenrauch, is captured in *Rosenkavalier* by the arrival of Baron Ochs. His appearance is especially ironic because the Marschallin is convinced that it is her husband (the true stand-in for King Mark) who has arrived.

Strauss responded masterfully to the nuances of Hofmannsthal's libretto by making the orchestral Introduction to act 1 of *Der Rosenkavalier* in part a parody of the music that signals the meeting of the lovers in act 2, scene 2, of Wagner's *Tristan.* As Isolde perceives Tristan arriving in the distance, Wagner's orchestral music is characterized by a short figure with dotted rhythm (underpinned by the motive that represents "impatient expectation" in some leitmotive tables) that is repeated and intensified by means of sequences (example 36a). This music, which culminates in the meeting of the lovers and is repeated and transformed elsewhere in the scene, is a prime example of Wagnerian *Steigerung* or intensification, of which *Tristan* is the locus classicus. In his Introduction to *Rosenkavalier,* Strauss appropriates Wagner's dotted rhythmic figure, which first appears just before reh. 1, and then gives it a broad, *Tristan*-derived sequential treatment from two measures before reh. 3 (example 36b). Strauss writes in the score at this point "die ganze Steigerung von hier ab durchaus parodistisch!" (the entire intensification from here on in a thoroughly parodistic manner!).

A brief excursus: Strauss's indication of *durchaus parodistisch* raises intriguing questions about performance style. How can the conductor and orchestra perform the passage of intensification in the *Rosenkavalier* Introduction in a parodic manner that is fundamentally different from the "weapon," Wagner's original? Would not the same build-up, the same increase in energy and tension, be necessary as in act 2 of *Tristan?* What adjustments in tempo or articulation might be made in the Strauss to bring out the parody? (In principle we cannot see the musicians, so any physical gestures would be irrelevant.) Perhaps parody emerges less from the performers than from the ear of the listener, who must be clued into the Wagner reference. In considering such issues, one might examine Strauss's marking in light of the contrary marking by Mahler cited in chapter 5, where the last movement of the Fourth Symphony is to be played "without any parody."

In act 2 of *Tristan* the first climax is reached with the embrace of the lovers. In *Der Rosenkavalier,* as has often been pointed out, the climax just before reh. 5, with the whooping horns and the *fff* E-major $^6_4$ chord, seems to represent an orgasm, the sexual highpoint to which the first scene of

Example 36.

a. Wagner, *Tristan und Isolde,* act 2, scene 2

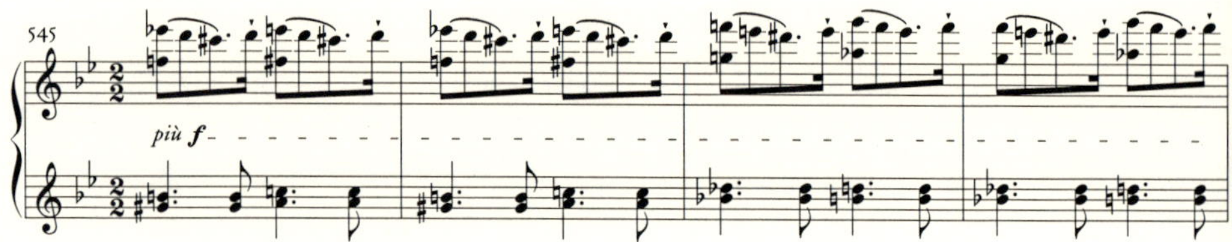

b. Strauss, *Der Rosenkavalier,* Introduction

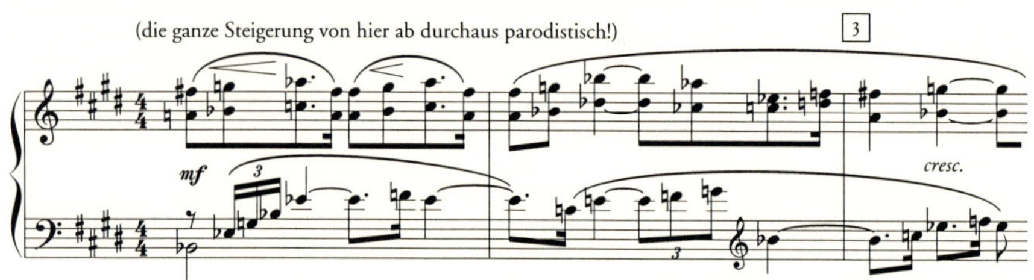

the opera is a lovers' postlude. Just as Hofmannsthal's libretto for the first scene freely reorders a number of ideas, gestures, and locutions from Wagner's love duet, so too does Strauss's music. The pulsating, syncopated accompaniment that begins underneath the arching violin melody at reh. 11 and continues after the curtain goes up, underneath Octavian's first sung notes at reh. 14, seems a parody—one can comfortably use this word since Strauss has authenticated it himself in the Introduction—of the accompaniment in the central part of Wagner's love duet in A♭ major ("O sink' hernieder") (see m. 2 of example 37 for a later return of these syncopated chords).

Octavian's initial motive on "Wie du warst," a rising minor third (F♯–G♯–A), derives from the *Sehnsucht* (Longing) motive of *Tristan,* which, though it contains four notes, also rises through a minor third (G♯–A–A♯–B). A little later on, at reh. 23, at Octavian's Wagner-inspired words "das Ich vergeht in dem Du," Strauss directly quotes the "Tristan" chord, after which the orchestra alternates hesitantly between C and D♭—as if reluctant to take the final step—and then plays what is now clearly to be heard as a version of Wagner's *Sehnsucht* motive (example 37; see bracket).

Example 37. Strauss, *Der Rosenkavalier,* act 1

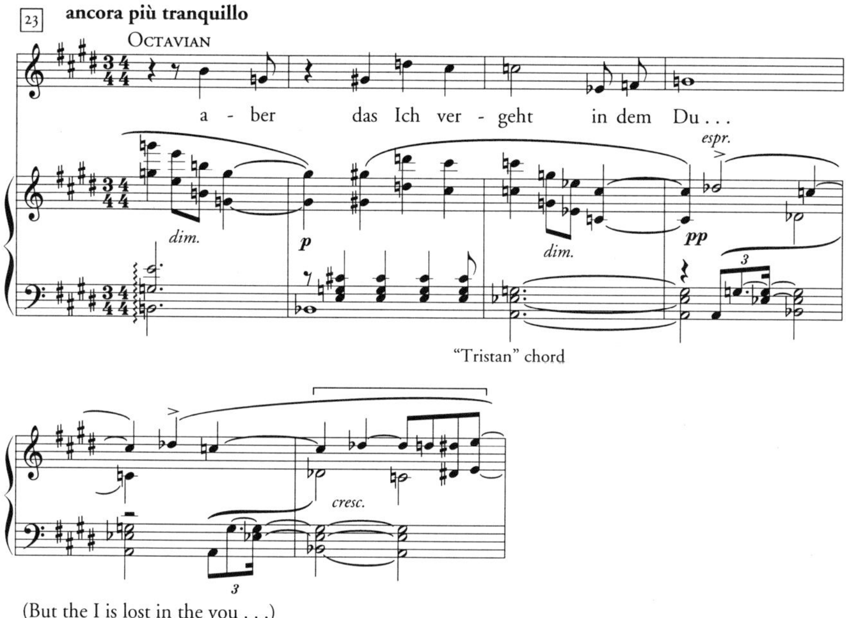

(But the I is lost in the you . . .)

This moment completes the transformation of Strauss's motive from its original form as announced by the horns at the beginning of the Introduction: a bold three-note diatonic ascent up the first three notes of the E-major scale (E–F♯–G♯). From there it becomes slightly more chromatic at Octavian's first words, filling out scale degrees 2–3–4 in the dominant seventh harmony (B^7). The three-note chromatic motive A–A♯–B that Octavian then sings at reh. 21 ("Wie jetzt meine Hand") seems a further step in the Tristanization of the figure, which just before reh. 24 makes its ultimate metamorphosis into an actual citation of Wagner's *Sehnsucht* motive.

Like Mann in *Tristan* and like his librettist Hofmannsthal, Strauss is able to break the Wagnerian spell, to produce the ironic *Illusionsstörung,* almost instantaneously. The musical change occurs first with the ringing of the bell and continues when the servant brings in the breakfast tray to a dance-like theme in $\frac{2}{4}$ (at reh. 37). At precisely the moment that the Marschallin announces "Jetzt wird gefrühstückt" and "Jedes Ding hat seine Zeit" (reh. 48), Strauss moves even further from the world of Wagner, and into that of Johann Strauss, Jr., introducing the first waltz of the opera to accompany the pantomime of the lovers' breakfast.

Following the Schmidt-Rose model of parody discussed in chapter 5, we might posit at least three text-worlds (TW) in the opening scene of *Der Rosenkavalier:* that of Hofmannsthal's libretto (TW1), that of Strauss's music (TW2), and that of Wagner's opera (TW3). (I am not taking into account here the possibility of more text-worlds based on other operas, such as Mozart's *Marriage of Figaro,* which are also alluded to—if not directly parodied—in this scene of *Rosenkavalier.*) We also have multiple reader's worlds. Hofmannsthal and Strauss, individually, are readers of Wagner's opera. As the composer, Strauss is also reader of Hofmannsthal's libretto, which he is setting to music. The audience are at once listeners to the opera (and readers of the libretto) and listeners to (rememberers of) Wagner's *Tristan.* It is this perspectival richness that makes *Rosenkavalier,* as the creators themselves realized, such a successful opera—and a thoroughly "modern" one in the context of early-twentieth-century German culture.

Parody is, of course, only a part of what happens in *Der Rosenkavalier* and is much less apparent in act 1 after the opening scene. Indeed, one of the remarkable features of this act is the way comic elements recede before more serious ones in the Marschallin's monologue, her final exchanges with Octavian, and her actions and gestures before the curtain comes down. Having consciously set aside "philosophizing" earlier in the act ("Everything has its time"), the Marschallin now takes it up most magnificently with her thoughts about the passing of time, growing older, the evolution of intimate relationships, and the importance of being "leicht" in the face of it all.

At this moment parody yields to, or is folded back into, irony. Within the world of the opera, Marschallin is the one character who achieves an ironic distance from the action even as she partakes in it. The Marschallin in effect engineers the union between Octavian and Sophie, acknowledges its rightness, and renounces her own claim to the young count. On the authorial-compositorial level Hofmannsthal and Strauss realize in operatic terms the very kind of epic irony that Mann articulated as being "objectivity untarnished by moralism." They create characters both noble and ignoble, self-aware and self-oblivious. But none of them is judged too harshly. As Ochs and the Marschallin both acknowledge when they face each other in the final scene and acknowledge their respective indiscretions, life is really a "quid pro quo"; it has elements of a "Viennese masquerade," and no one should be a "spoil sport."[13] The quality of "lightness" that the Marschallin advocates is realized with almost miraculous success in the ironic authorial stances of Hofmannsthal and Strauss.

The Marschallin has rightly been compared, even by Hofmannsthal himself, with Hans Sachs, who in *Die Meistersinger* likewise manages at the same time to observe, manipulate, and participate in the action. He senses the affection between Eva and Walther, works to bring about its fulfillment, and gives up his own claim to Eva.[14] The Marschallin is not a parody of Sachs in the sense that the opening scene is a parody of the love duet from *Tristan.* But Sachs is an obvious model for the ironic stance taken by the Marschallin. Both Sachs and the Marschallin embody the kind of "world irony" addressed in the last chapter, an acknowledgment of the fragility, futility, and irrationality of much human endeavor *(Wahn,* or illusion, as Sachs calls it). At the same time both show a willingness to act, to intervene to bring about desired and positive results.

The Marschallin's operatic pedigree also includes, as already noted, the Countess from Mozart's and da Ponte's *Marriage of Figaro,* another figure who achieves distance from the action, intervenes in it by plotting the complicated rendezvous in the garden, and generally manifests a stance of world irony as she comes to accept the foibles of her husband and the other characters around her. The Marschallin thus exists in the "third" degree, much like the finale of Mahler's Seventh Symphony examined in the last chapter, where Mozart is mediated by Wagner, who in turn is mediated by Mahler. Indeed, the same earlier composers are implicated in the operatic world of Strauss and Hofmannsthal, and in a similar way. We understand the Marschallin in part through our awareness of her two previous incarnations, Mozart's Countess and Wagner's Hans Sachs.

ARIADNE AUF NAXOS

The collaborators carried over many of the techniques and principles of *Der Rosenkavalier* into their next major effort, *Ariadne auf Naxos,* in which the historical layers and the "chains" of older forms and conventions are far more self-conscious and apparent. The impetus came again from Hofmannsthal, who proposed the project to Strauss in March 1911, less than two months after the triumphant premiere of *Rosenkavalier,* as "a combination of heroic mythological figures in eighteenth-century costumes with hooped skirts and ostrich feathers and, interwoven in it, characters from the commedia dell'arte."[15] The opera was to function as a divertissement after an adaptation by Hofmannsthal of Molière's *Le bourgeois Gentilhomme* (in German, *Der Bürger als Edelmann).* A short spoken linking scene or *Zwischenszene,* written by Hofmannsthal, was to make the transition between the two works and create a dramatic justification for the opera. The whole was to be a tribute and a sign of gratitude to Max Reinhardt, the renowned director of the Deutsches Theater in Berlin, who had helped with (indeed, according to Strauss and Hofmannsthal, had rescued) the premiere of *Rosenkavalier* in Dresden.

Though initially cool to Hofmannsthal's new idea, Strauss had by May 1911 mapped out what he called "set musical numbers" *(Musikstücke geschlossen)* for *Ariadne,* including recitatives, arias, and ensembles.[16] He completed the score, including incidental music for the Molière play, by late July 1912. Reinhardt's theater in Berlin had been the original destination of the hybrid play-plus-opera. But various difficulties led to the premiere taking place in Stuttgart, where it was a decidedly mixed success. Some of the singers originally desired by Strauss could not be available, and a long reception after the play delayed the starting time of the opera and necessitated omitting the linking scene. Ultimately, though, as Strauss later said, the reason for the lukewarm reception may have been that "the playgoing public had no wish to listen to opera and vice versa. The proper cultural soil for this pretty hybrid was lacking."[17]

Within a few weeks of the premiere, Strauss hatched the idea of a radical reworking that would jettison Molière and set the linking scene to music in secco recitative as a Prelude to the *Ariadne* opera. Hofmannsthal was enthusiastic, but Strauss changed his mind and argued against any reworking. Not until 1916 was the librettist able to persuade his composer to proceed, at which point Strauss took up the project with enthusiasm. The premiere of the revision took place on November 4, 1916, in Vienna.[18]

Strauss and Hofmannsthal felt that the musico-dramatic language of the new Prelude was the most progressive and innovative aspect of the revised opera. The whole text of the Prelude is written by Hofmannsthal as prose, in the style of his adaptation of Molière (and the original linking scene), and is set to music in what Strauss called "secco recitative in strict rhythm."[19] Strauss wrote to his collaborator in July 1916, when the revised opera was ready, "I entirely share your opinion that the Vorspiel to *Ariadne* marks the peculiar new road which we must follow, and my own inclination is for realistic comedy with really interesting people—either like *Rosenkavalier* with its splendid Marschallin, or with a burlesque, satirical content, something in the manner of Offenbach's parodies."[20] It is of interest that while Strauss had sought to distance himself from an Offenbachian mode when discussing the generic title of *Rosenkavalier*—he wanted to avoid "burlesque"—he now seems willing to embrace it.

There is some truth to Strauss's claim about the "new" style of the Prelude, which is a sparkling, fast-paced mixture of spoken words (for the dour Haushofmeister), rapid dialogue in recitative, and lyrical interludes (especially the duet for Zerbinetta and the Composer, and the latter's famous paean to music). Yet the most profound originality of *Ariadne* was already present in the 1912 version. The 1912 version presented the opera within a "frame": that is, characters from the Molière play, Jourdain and his guests, are on stage at times during the opera and comment on the action. Hofmannsthal frequently refers to the Molière play as the *Rahmenwerk,* or framing structure, for the opera.[21] In the 1912 version, after Ariadne and Bacchus have been completely hidden by the baldaquin and sung their final notes, the frame reasserts itself. Zerbinetta reprises a large portion of her rondo; she dances with her commedia colleagues; and Jourdain has the last (spoken) word, commenting wistfully on how he wishes he were a nobleman.[22]

These features were changed in the 1916 version in three significant ways: (1) the Molière characters (Jourdain and his guests Dorantes and Dorimenes) appear in neither the new Prelude nor the "opera"; (2) Zerbinetta's reprise of her rondo at the end of the opera is greatly abbreviated and is recast so as to mute its originally sarcastic tone of "mocking triumph" (*mit spöttischem Triumph* was Hofmannsthal's stage direction, changed by Strauss in the 1916 score to *leise und diskret* [softly and discretely]); and (3) the opera ends with the Ariadne-Bacchus duet and an orchestral postlude, and thus lacks the final, framing commentary of Jourdain.[23]

The original bracketing of the opera within the world of the Molière drama provided a level of irony beyond that already present within the opera. In the 1912 version, we view Jourdain and his guests as they observe an opera that in itself, through its juxtaposition of buffa and serious elements, has its own built-in ironic dimension. At the opening of the opera the commedia players (and the nymphs) are "viewers" as well; they observe Ariadne and comment on her situation. From the viewpoint of the Schmidt-Rose model discussed above, we thus have multiple reader's worlds in or around *Ariadne auf Naxos.*

It is clear that in 1916, even in the absence of the Molière play, Hofmannsthal still sought to preserve some quality of framing by means of the stage sets. In his instructions that appear in the printed version of the revised libretto, he writes about the "opera": "Some indication that we intend a play within a play, a stage upon a stage, is indispensable." Hofmannsthal goes on to suggest that this effect can be achieved by building an onstage proscenium surrounded by theater boxes occupied by few supernumeraries.[24] It is of interest that Hofmannsthal also wanted the stage sets and costumes to be "straight." In his instructions in the 1916 libretto, he specified, "The decoration (and costumes) of the opera 'Ariadne' should be handled not parodistically but seriously in the heroic opera style of the older period (Louis XIV or XV)."[25]

Even without the extra frame of the Molière characters or the supernumeraries, irony remains paramount in the "opera," as Hofmannsthal acknowledged in his famous "*Ariadne* Letter" *(Ariadne-Brief)* of 1911, written to Strauss as a clarification of the opera's meaning and then, at Strauss's urging, published in an adapted form in 1913. In it, Hofmannsthal stresses the ironic tension between the two "spiritual worlds" (*Seelenwelten)* of Ariadne and Zerbinetta and their respective entourages. Ariadne is faithful to one man, Theseus; Zerbinetta moves happily from lover to lover. Zerbinetta understands Bacchus's arrival only as Ariadne's exchanging one man for another. But, says Hofmannsthal in the *Ariadne* Letter, Ariadne is not simply entering into another relationship; rather, she experiences transformation, or *Verwandlung,* which the librettist saw as the key element of existence. Only through either death (which Ariadne awaits) or transformation can her faithfulness be fulfilled. Hofmannsthal argues that the two spiritual worlds of Ariadne and Zerbinetta "are in the end ironically brought together in the only way in which they can be brought together: in non-comprehension."[26]

Karen Forsyth has suggested that *Ariadne auf Naxos* may manifest "formal irony," an irony that is created at a high structural level by the mixture or juxtaposition of different styles, in this case buffa and seria, Wagnerian and Mozartian, and so forth. For Forsyth, the authors make no "active intervention in the irony of these juxtapositions" and thus avoid any direct authorial statement, creating in effect "a passive synthesis of these heterogeneous elements."[27] What Forsyth describes is quite close to what Mann characterized as "epic irony."

Other critics have argued for this kind of formal irony in *Ariadne.* Barbara Könneker claims that the libretto is less important for any message or meaning than for the mixture of styles that relativize our values (another Nietzschean echo). What is essential, according to Könneker, is "the exchangeability of the spheres and levels created by the linking of opposed formal and stylistic elements, the evaporation of absolute values, and the destruction of unequivocally fixed referential frames."[28] Such a view clearly puts *Ariadne* into a postmodern framework.

Recent writers on Strauss, including Gilliam and Leon Botstein, have voiced similar ideas, and have given them a more social or sociological spin. For Gilliam, the Strauss of *Der Rosenkavalier* (and then *Ariadne*) "recognized the disunities of modern life and believed that such incongruities should not be masked by a unified musical style."[29] For Botstein, the original *Ariadne* was "an attempt to elevate the comic and parodistic to a polemic about modernity itself" and to attack the idea of an autonomous, stylistically unified artwork. In *Ariadne* Hofmannsthal and Strauss also sought to affirm a "remarkably affectionate conception of the relations between the audience and the composer and the playwright."[30]

THE ARIADNE YEAR 1911

The year 1911, in which Hofmannsthal began drafting his libretto, seems to have been something of an *Ariadne-Jahr* in the German-speaking world. In 1911 the prominent dramatist and literary theorist Paul Ernst (1866–1933) wrote a serious three-act play, *Ariadne auf Naxos*. Ernst was one of the most prominent spokesmen for the German literary movement of neoclassicism *(neue Klassik)* in the first decade of the twentieth century. This movement arose in part as a reaction to naturalism and its successors symbolism and impressionism. There was a call for a return to tragedy and purer forms, away from impressionistic and symbolic ones, toward what one of the leading theorists of neoclassicism, Samuel Lublinski, called "dramatic style, a closed form, a logical construction, a clear plot and a thought-out and carried-out conflict of wills."[31] There was also a demand for the observance of Aristotelian unities. The neoclassicists looked back to Schiller and Hebbel as well as the dramas of antiquity.

Ernst produced several tragedies and dramas based on Nordic or Greek myths, including the *Ariadne auf Naxos* of 1911. The plot of Ernst's play has little to do with Hofmannsthal and deviates considerably from the traditional Ariadne myths. In Ernst's drama, Ariadne becomes a secondary player and Theseus a tragic hero who tries to form a larger community out of people living on the island of Naxos, but is killed by a mob when they discover that Ariadne had poisoned her father to escape with him.[32]

Although Hofmannsthal took no active part in the German neoclassical movement, he had a profound and lifelong involvement in Greek drama and myth, of which his *Elektra* (1903) is the most famous manifestation. He began using Greek sources and preparing translations and adaptations of Greek plays as early as 1893, a practice that continued to his death in

1929.[33] It is not clear whether Hofmannsthal knew Ernst's play when he conceived his own Ariadne scenario in the same year. But if he did, he may have found its burnished neoclassicism very ripe for parody.

Another German Ariadne drama of 1911, brought to light by the editor of Hofmannsthal's libretto for the *Sämtliche Werke,* Manfred Hoppe, brings us a bit closer to the opera, for it is a parody mixing commedia and serious elements in ways that strikingly resemble Hofmannsthal. This is an opera libretto, *Scaramuccia auf Naxos: eine heitere Oper,* by the Viennese writer Franz Blei (1871–1942), created in 1909 and published in 1911 (but probably never set to music).[34] In it, Scaramuccia, a director of a theater troupe, has come to Naxos to fetch Ariadne, with whom he has signed a contract because she has become "ein Star" since her abandonment by Theseus. Scaramuccia learns that Ariadne is now partnered with Dionysus, whom he also thinks to sign for his troupe. ("A god is surely less trouble nowadays than an actor," he remarks.)[35] When they appear on stage, Ariadne and Dionysus both speak in the same elevated tone, and even in some of the same images, that Hofmannsthal gives these characters in his libretto. The moment of their arrival is announced by a solemn march, to which Scaramuccia comments: "Ariadne? With music? Richard Strauss does that better than I do."[36] Blei seems to have written this line before Strauss and Hofmannsthal had completed their *Ariadne;* perhaps he knew about their work in progress.

Another, earlier Ariadne parody of which Hofmannsthal may have been aware, though it appeared outside the Viennese orbit, was a carnival farce *Ariadne auf Naxos: ein tragikomisches Drama,* published in Berlin in 1893.[37] There is no admixture of commedia characters here, but the Ariadne tale is presented as a comedy in three short scenes, with four actors who speak in rhymed couplets. The cast is not dissimilar from Hofmannsthal's: Ariadne, Theseus, an Oread (a nymph, analogous to Hofmannsthal's Naiade and Dryade), and Bacchus. The play begins, like many Ariadne dramas, with Ariadne sleeping on her rock. Theseus arrives and says, in a style typical for this parody: "Beloved Ariadne mine! You're sleeping there like a sack. Don't you see Theseus in his travel cloak? Are you dreaming of me?—You're snoring?—O, tones that move me!"[38] As Ariadne dreams, her first utterance—the same that she is given by Hofmannsthal—is "Ach!" After Ariadne learns she has been abandoned by Theseus and delivers her lament (rolling around on the ground), the Oreade announces the arrival of Bacchus in a way not dissimilar from Hofmannsthal: "He comes, a hero, from head to toe; he hurries here, in thunder and lightning!"[39] When Bacchus appears on the scene, he tells Ariadne—and I will leave this couplet in German—"Wirst Du in meinem Haus als Königin regieren; / Denn eh' es Abend wird, soll man uns kopulieren."[40]

MOZART, WAGNER, AND *ARIADNE*

By 1911, when Hofmannsthal and Strauss embarked on the little "trifle" that was to occupy them between the larger projects of *Der Rosenkavalier* and *Die Frau ohne Schatten,* the idea of parodic and ironic approaches to the Ariadne story were clearly in the air. Of course, Hofmannsthal's and Strauss's heroine comes from a long line of operatic Ariadnes stretching back at least to Monteverdi in 1608, and extending through the seventeenth and eighteenth centuries, when there were no fewer than forty operas based on the Ariadne myth.[41] What concerns me here is principally the aspects of the opera that involve the two opera composers with whom Strauss and Hofmannsthal had already engaged so creatively in *Rosenkavalier,* Mozart and Wagner. These parodic allusions, which are built into the libretto by Hofmannsthal and realized in music by Strauss—and yet, as with *Rosenkavalier,* never mentioned in their correspondence—are no less important than the more obvious evocations to which the collaborators openly confessed: the use of Greek myth, opera seria, commedia dell'arte, and set numbers.

The allusions have been little addressed in writing on the opera, with the notable exception of an article by Stefan Kunze, "The Aesthetic Reconstruction of Opera," which discusses the "character of quotation," or *Zitatcharakter,* that pervades the opera. As Kunze points out, the character of quotation in *Ariadne* can be less specific, evoking earlier styles or forms without direct citation. Zerbinetta's big aria might be an instance of this kind of allusion. Coloratura numbers from Mozart through Bellini, Donizetti, and Verdi serve (as Strauss himself implied in a letter to his collaborator) as a generalized background for Zerbinetta's rondo.[42] Kunze's principal example is the overture to the opera, whose structure "has the character of quotation without being a quotation." The overture adopts the form of the French overture, slow–fast, but the formal framework is "transformed by odd-sounding notes and sonorities."[43]

As we can see in example 38, the first part of the overture is built from conventional two-measure units that are grouped on a higher level into traditional structures like paired phrases (*aa',* mm. 1–2) and antecedent-consequent (mm. 1–4; 5–8). The small- and large-scale harmonic goals are also traditional, such as the dominants in mm. 2, 5, and 8. Yet, as Kunze points out, the local voice-leading and resultant harmonies clash with the outward form. The melody begins very unconventionally for the eighteenth century by leaping down a major seventh, such that the G-minor harmony on the downbeat supports a dissonant E♭. In m. 2, the melody manages to be both lyrical and awkward, outlining a diminished triad, which contains within it a prominent upward tritone leap (C–F♯). This triad is, of course, part of the dominant chord of G minor, which would be a normal harmonic goal for this measure, but which is distorted or diffused by the voice-leading. The melodic phrase of mm. 3–4 consists of a chromatic rise followed by a dissonant leap, again a seventh (A–G), and as such is like a compressed, transformed version of mm. 1–2 (hence *aa'*).

One could continue this kind of analysis of the overture, which is one of Strauss's greatest instrumental efforts. But suffice it to say that its character of quotation comprises, in the terms of the present chapter, a perfect example of irony, in which the larger structure is at odds with the details. The phrases and gestures are "right," but the melodic style and voice-leading are "wrong." As Kunze observes, Strauss is by no means seeking to copy or parody historical forms. Rather, Strauss composes out the distance between himself and the earlier models. "The overture is thus no overture," Kunze concludes, "but rather its infinitely sublimated reflection."[44]

Strauss's overture sets the ironic tone that is to be developed in the opera through direct, or more directly traceable, parodies involving both Mozart and Wagner. These parodies range from rather brief allusions, especially in the case of Ariadne's opening monologue, to more extended and complex kinds of references. Even more than in *Der Rosenkavalier,* the collaborators manage to incorporate Mozart and Wagner simultaneously. For example, the three nymphs who serve Ariadne, named Najade, Dryade, and Echo, have ancestors in both the Three Ladies of Mozart's *The Magic Flute* and the Rhinemaidens of Wagner's *Ring,* especially in act 3 of *Götterdämmerung.* Strauss's gently rocking $\frac{6}{8}$ meter, triadic melody, and flowing sixteenth-note accompaniment in the strings make clear reference to Wagner, as do the florid vocalises on "gleitet's."[45] The similarity of the three nymphs to Mozart's Three Ladies is admittedly less obvious and not, as far as I can tell, made through musical allusion at the opening. The relationship is clearer at the beginning of the third scene of *Ariadne,* when the nymphs announce the arrival of Bacchus. Their excited descriptions of his appearance are not too different from those by the Three Ladies of the handsome young Tamino at the very beginning of *The Magic Flute.*

Example 38. Strauss, *Ariadne auf Naxos,* Overture

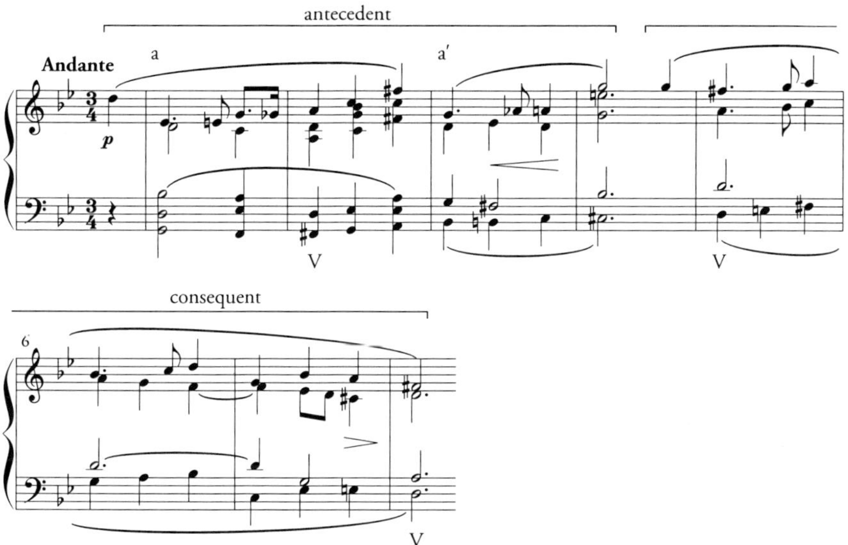

Other aspects of the opera's third scene make clear reference to *Tristan und Isolde.* One can be especially struck by the similarity of Bacchus's apparent confusion about where he is and what has happened to him to Tristan's delirium in act 3 of Wagner's opera. Tristan's three-phase awakening to consciousness is here compressed to two, in which Bacchus twice addresses Circe and celebrates the freedom he has won.

The connection with *Tristan* is made explicit by both Hofmannsthal and Strauss in the reference, during the nymphs' passage at the opening of scene 3, to the magic potion, the *Zaubertrank,* that Circe gave Bacchus. Strauss manages to engineer things such that not only is there an allusion to Wagner's chromatically rising *Sehnsucht* or *Liebestrank* motive (they are essentially the same motive in *Tristan*), but the "Tristan" chord is cited at its original pitch (example 39). The irony seems quite strong, and it is heightened by Strauss's orchestration: he gives the passionately Wagnerian top line to a solo violin.[46] As in the opening scene of *Der Rosenkavalier,* so in the *Zaubertrank* episode of *Ariadne,* in Zerbinetta's outsized rondo, and perhaps in the nymphs' Rhinemaiden-like music, one might speak of parody, in the sense of an obvious allusion that is characterized by exaggeration and humor.

One other sly Wagnerian reference might be noted. At the end, as Ariadne and Bacchus depart, they are enveloped by the baldaquin to the ac-

Example 39. Strauss, *Ariadne auf Naxos*

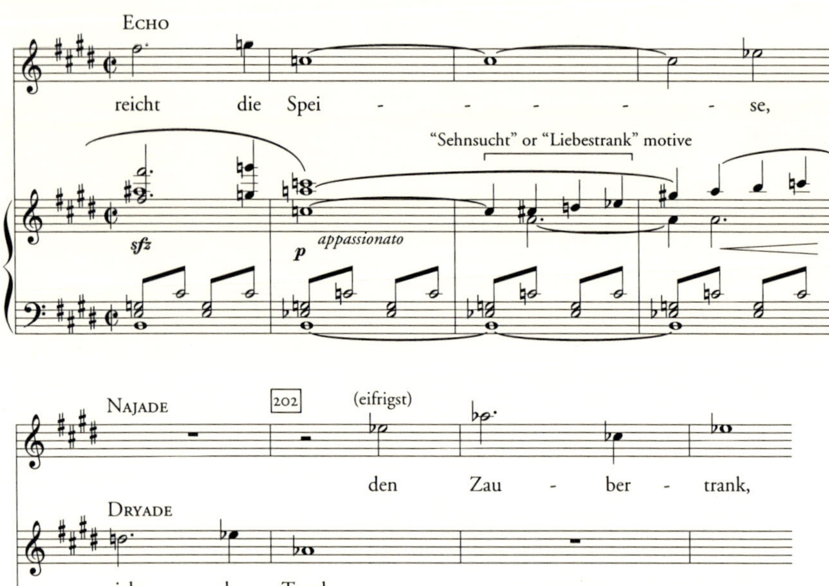

(She gives him food, the magic potion.)

companiment of a radiant orchestral wash of D♭ major (considerably beefed up in the 1916 revision, where it is the last thing we hear). The key and mood recall the Immolation Scene in the same key in Wagner's *Götterdämmerung*, where Brünnhilde makes her exit enveloped by a rather different phenomenon.

THE CHARACTER OF ARIADNE

In the title character of *Ariadne auf Naxos* the Mozartian and Wagnerian parodies converge most completely. For some commentators Ariadne remains opaque, less fully humanized or rounded than other Strauss heroines. Del Mar remarks that Strauss "was unable to bring Ariadne to life in the same way he had succeeded with Elektra and the Marschallin."[47] Because she is an as-if figure who is ironically conceived from the beginning—as a seria "type" within an opera within a play—the librettist and composer set themselves a stiffer challenge than with any of their previous heroines. Strauss had less operatic time to develop her; she has fewer lines than Salome, Elektra, or the Marschallin.

Yet Ariadne is one of Hofmannsthal's and Strauss's most subtly fashioned figures, one who, however, is formed by parody and the character of quotation, like so much else in this opera. In constructing the musico-dramatic personality of their heroine, Hofmannsthal and Strauss were interested making references not to her previous operatic incarnations as Ariadne, but to Mozart and Wagner characters who find themselves in similar situations. Ariadne is a palimpsest, a figure in whom one can read traces of earlier figures. In this sense she is very much like the Marschallin, who as we saw was a kind of palimpsest of the Countess and Hans Sachs.

In his original plan as outlined in a letter to Hofmannsthal, Strauss had designated Ariadne's Monologue simply as "recitative and aria."[48] In fact, as the opera advanced, the Monologue grew into a larger structure that Daviau and Buelow have plausibly analyzed as a *pair* of recitative-aria combinations.[49] There may also be more than a hint of the nineteenth-century Italian opera convention of the two-part aria with a slower first part ("cantabile"), an interruption of some kind ("tempo di mezzo"), and a faster conclusion ("cabaletta"). In that Italian model, the tempo di mezzo often brings in another character or characters, and something happens to change the mind or mood of the singer.

The scheme is as follows:

Recitative I: "Wo war ich?"

(*Commedia interruption:* "Wie jung und schön")

Aria I: "Ein Schönes war"

(*Longer commedia interruption:* "Ich fürchte, großer Schmerz")

Recitative II: "Es gibt ein Reich"

Aria II: "Bald aber naht ein Bote"

Ariadne's longing for death because of abandonment brings her into line with Pamina, who in act 2 of *The Magic Flute* decides to commit suicide when she thinks Tamino has rejected her. She sings her G-minor aria "Ach, ich fühl's" and a little later, in the act 2 finale, is about to kill herself when the Three Boys intervene. Pamina's innocent and steadfast faithfulness, temporarily derailed by her despair over Tamino's silence, is clearly echoed in Hofmannsthal's conception of Ariadne's plight, and in Strauss's realization of it. The first section of Ariadne's Monologue is in the key of E♭, then shifts between the tonic and the third-related key G♭. We see such a shift in example 40a. At the words "mit einem Tuch bedecken" Strauss is back in, or really on, G♭. At the words "und eine Tote sein" there is a sudden, chilling change of texture—the orchestra drops out, leaving only the bare harmonium as accompaniment—and Strauss moves from a $^6_4$ chord on G♭ to a $^6_4$ a half step higher, on G minor, where he cadences.

The effect of "und eine Tote sein" is shocking, and seems designed to bring to the surface the virtual quotation from Pamina's aria, "Ach, ich fühl's" (example 40b).[50] Hofmannsthal takes the words almost verbatim from the end of the aria, "im Tode sein." Strauss in turn picks up on the allusion, shifts abruptly into Pamina's key, G minor, and provides a melodic phrase that is quite close to Mozart's. The stripped-down accompaniment reinforces the allusion. The harmonium serves to reveal the Mozartian layer beneath the Straussian one, as in a palimpsest, where one can detect traces of the earlier writing.[51]

Although there is no reference to this moment in the published correspondence, Strauss seems to have caught the allusion early on. When reading through the handwritten libretto sent him in June 1911 by Hofmannsthal and making on it his preliminary annotations and sketches, Strauss wrote the phrase "G moll $^6_4$ nach Ges dur," or "G minor $^6_4$ after G♭ major," in between the lines "Und darf da drinnen liegen" and "Und eine Tote sein." Strauss also underlined the word "Tote."[52] At about the same time, thinking on a broader level, Strauss associated Pamina's key of G minor with Ariadne's melancholy and planned the overture, which is her musical image, in that key.[53]

Ariadne is fashioned in part in the image of Pamina. But we might also see in her a more distant allusion to another Mozart heroine, the Countess from *The Marriage of Figaro,* who, while not exactly abandoned, is dejected and even contemplates suicide because of her husband's infidelity. In her two great arias, as Hofmannsthal surely knew, the Countess is preoccupied with thoughts similar to Ariadne's. In "Porgi amor" she says that unless her husband once again shows her his love, she wants to die ("O mi lascia almen morir"). In "Dove sono" she recalls the beautiful moments

Example 40.

a. Strauss, *Ariadne auf Naxos*

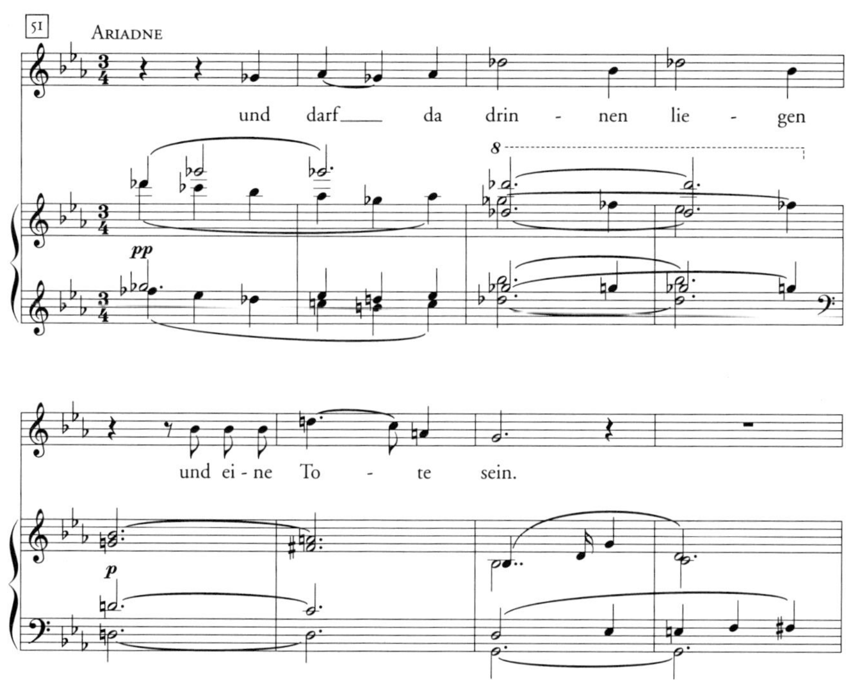

(And may lie [in her shroud] and be dead.)

b. Mozart, *The Magic Flute*

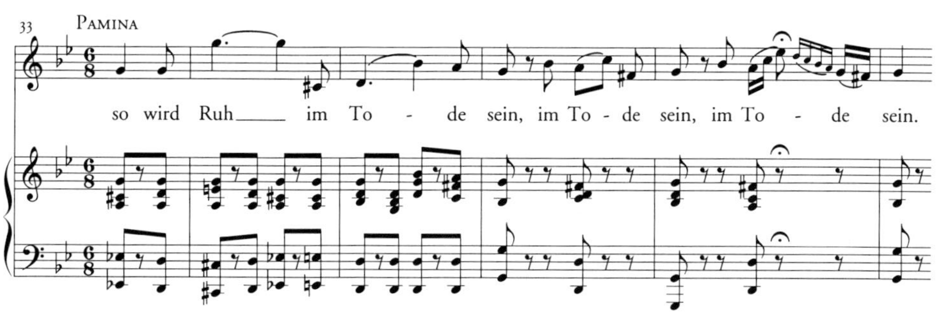

(I will find peace in death.)

("i bei momenti") they have shared; her words and sentiments are not far from Ariadne's glowing memories in "Ein schönes war."

Ariadne then is two parts Mozart: Pamina and the Countess who long for death in the face of abandonment or infidelity. But she is also two parts Wagner, in this case Isolde and Elsa. Isolde also longs for death, seeks (but fails) to drink a death potion, and in the end succeeds in a "love death." Strauss signals the Isolde connection with Ariadne's very first utterance, her mournful "Ach!," which is accompanied by a half-diminished seventh chord that a listener already sensitized to the Wagner references would immediately recognize as a version of the "Tristan" chord. Strauss elegantly ironizes the moment by alternating the "Tristan" chord with a very un-Wagnerian E♭ major seventh chord (example 41). This wonderful sonority, played by the harmonium and strings, hangs in the air, unconnected to the surrounding sonorities by timbre, voice-leading, or harmonic logic. A seventeenth-century composer would likely have set Ariadne's "Ach!" with the conventional musical gesture for a lament, a descending chromatic bass line. Strauss has updated the older "trope" with a newer Wagnerian one, which had become almost as conventional for the later nineteenth century as the lament bass had been for earlier periods.

The Isolde-derived characteristics of Ariadne become still more apparent and audible at the beginning of the last large segment of Ariadne's Monologue, "Es gibt ein Reich" (There Is a Realm). Ariadne's mood is now at its darkest as she imagines the realm of death, the "Totenreich." The melody descends by half-steps from B♭ to A over third-related harmonic shifts. Both melody and bass eventually settle on A♭ (example 42a). The gaping octave drop on "Totenreich" echoes directly the moment from act 1, scene 4, of *Tristan und Isolde* when Isolde invokes the *Todestrank* (death potion; see example 42b).

In *Ariadne auf Naxos* the Isolde-style pessimism is soon replaced by Ariadne's joyous anticipation of the arrival of Hermes as messenger of death. This change of mood is reflected by a modulation to B♭ major (the relative major of G minor) and a transformation of the fanfare motive that had appeared in somber form at "Es gibt ein Reich" (example 43). When she sings "Bald aber naht ein Bote," Ariadne takes on the attributes of another Wagnerian heroine, Elsa, who in act 1 of *Lohengrin,* in the large number known as Elsa's Dream, confidently awaits rescue by a knight-hero. Both Elsa and Ariadne take the advent of their rescuers on faith: neither Lohengrin nor Hermes have given their heroines (or the audience) any visible indication of their presence.

Example 41. Strauss, *Ariadne auf Naxos*

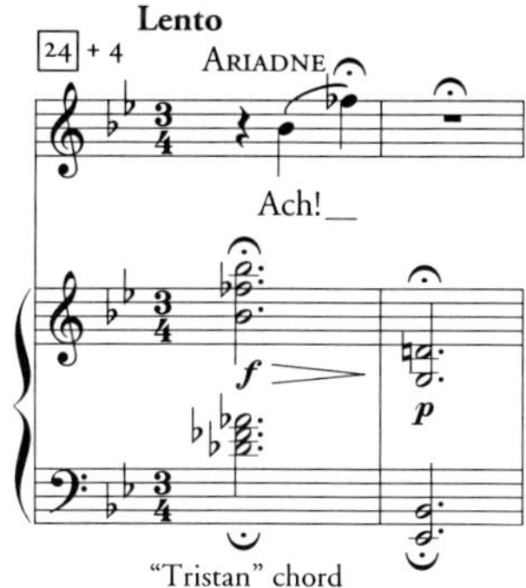

Example 42.

a. Strauss, *Ariadne auf Naxos*

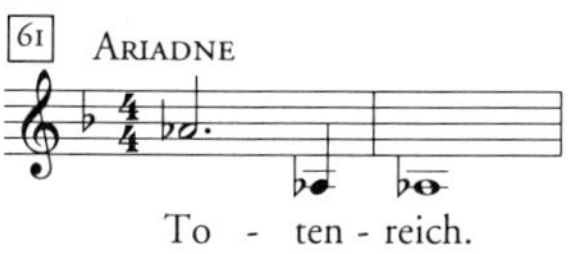

b. Wagner, *Tristan und Isolde*

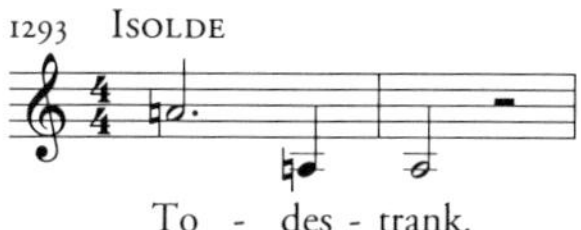

Elsa and Ariadne become transformed in similar ways. From inward contemplation or self-pity, they turn outward in radiant anticipation. Elsa's mood changes, as we read in Wagner's stage directions, from *träumerische Entrücktsein* (dreamlike trance) to *schwärmerische Verklärung* (rapturous transfiguration). Ariadne's analogous change of mood is captured by Strauss as *sanfte extatische Bewegung* (gentle, ecstatic emotion). Both women have distinct visions of the appearance and qualities of their respective heroes. Hermes is a "handsome, still god." He "rules souls with his staff. They rush before him like birds in flight." Lohengrin appears in Elsa's Dream in "splendid shining armor." He has a golden horn at his hip and leans on his sword.

Harmonic motion by thirds is a fingerprint in *Lohengrin.* Elsa's Dream has one especially rich example, at the words "mit züchtigem Gebahren," where Wagner cycles rapidly by minor third through the octave from the tonic A♭, to C♭, to D, to F, and back to A♭ (example 44). In the "Bald aber

Example 43. Strauss, *Ariadne auf Naxos*

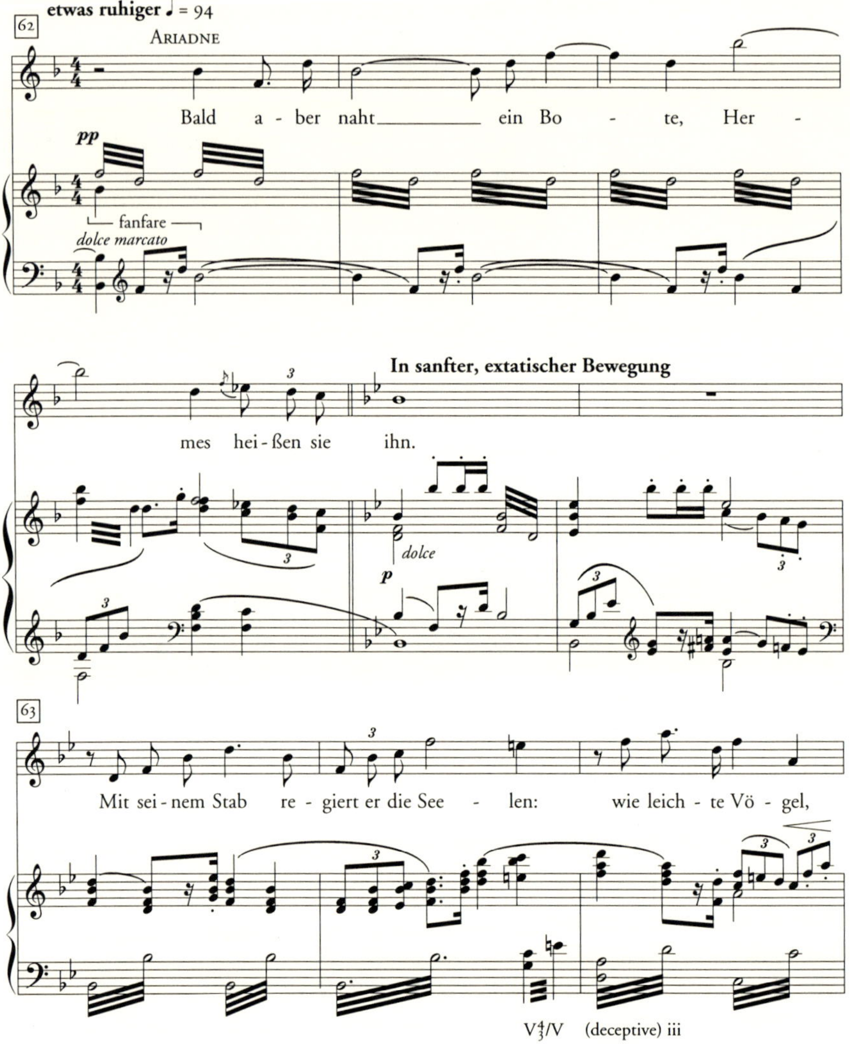

(But soon a herald will come, they call him Hermes. With his staff he rules souls; [before him they rush] like birds in flight.)

Example 44. Wagner, *Lohengrin,* act 1

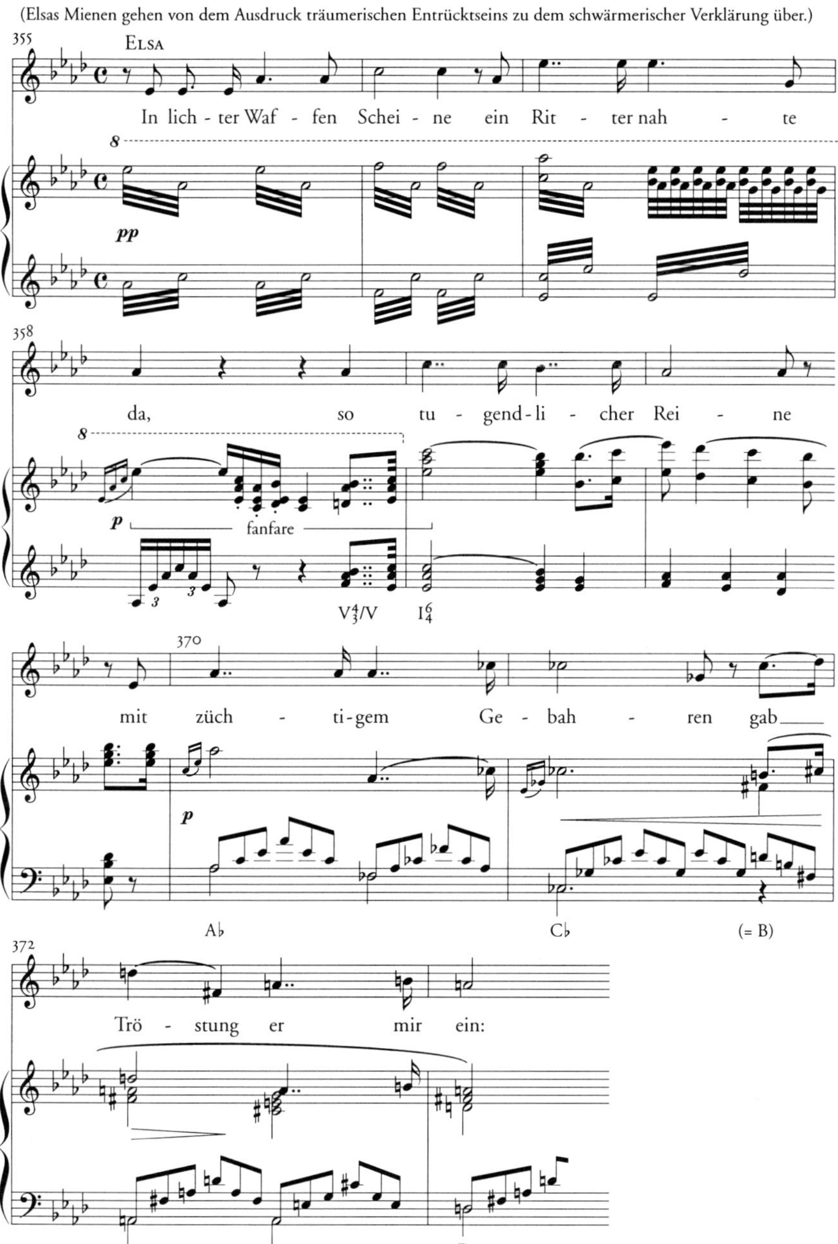

(In splendid, shining armor, a knight approached, a man of such pure virtue. . . .
With kindly gestures he gave me comfort.)

naht" section of Ariadne's Monologue Strauss makes frequent and highly profiled third-related shifts of harmony, including the move from B♭ to D♭ at four measures after reh. 64, to F major at reh. 65, and C♭ major at two measures before reh. 66 (not shown in example 43).[54]

But Ariadne's scene contains still more specific musical allusions. The fanfare-like motive that is introduced at first at "Es gibt ein Reich," then taken up again at "Bald aber naht," becomes associated with the expectation of Hermes, and, later, the arrival of Bacchus. This motive bears a distinct resemblance to the one in Elsa's aria that represents Lohengrin's arrival and is in fact a transformation of the slow dotted rhythm in the Prelude. There is also a similarity in the orchestration, which cannot be seen on the piano reduction in example 43. Strauss adopts Wagner's shimmering string tremolos (though not the mutes) and like Wagner gives the fanfare figures primarily to the woodwind choir.

Perhaps even more striking than these allusions is the similarity of harmonic progression at certain moments in the two arias. On the words "so tugendlicher" Wagner moves from a V^4_3 of V directly to a I^6_4 in his tonic key of A♭ (marked on example 44). At the end of Ariadne's phrase "Mit seinem Stab regiert er die Seelen" (as shown in example 43), Strauss begins exactly the same progression. The C^4_3 chord on the "-len" of "Seelen" is V^4_3 of V in the key of B♭ and would lead by analogy to Wagner to a $B\flat^6_4$ chord. But Strauss resolves the chord deceptively, to D minor in root position. Strauss provides just enough material to make the allusion, but then cheekily sidesteps an exact imitation.

The treatment of the musical past in *Der Rosenkavalier* and *Ariadne* has little to do with the many Wagner- and especially *Tristan*-inspired parodies that cropped up in the later nineteenth century, such as Chabrier's *"Tristan" Quadrille,* or Debussy's *Golliwog's Cake-walk.* Nor does it fundamentally resemble the neoclassicism of the following two decades as exemplified in the work of Stravinsky and Hindemith. Works like Stravinsky's Octet (1923) or Hindemith's *Kammermusik* series (1921) tend to exaggerate or magnify the distance from their models in brash, provocative ways. Mann, Strauss, and Hofmannsthal manifest a greater sense of continuity with the past. Their irony is always tempered, or perhaps even motivated, by the basic affection they feel for the earlier music. Distance and epic irony become their strategies for creating a modern art without resorting to either epigonism or iconoclasm, that is, resolute conservatism or radical avant-gardism.

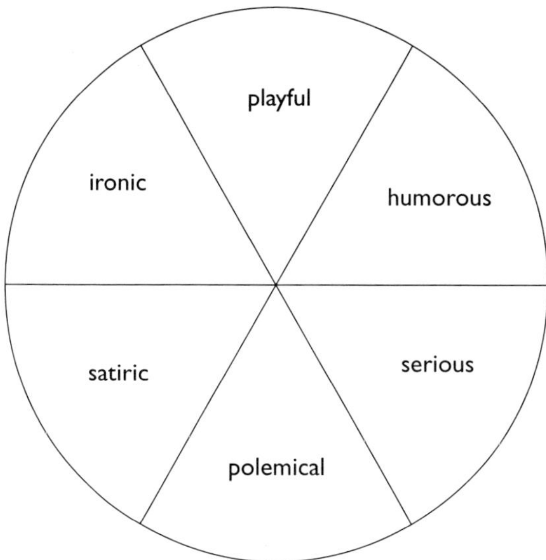

Figure 13. Gérard Genette, "Rose window" of intertextual relationships. From Genette, *Palimpsests: Literature in the Second Degree,* trans. Channa Newman and Claude Doubinsky; used by permission of the University of Nebraska Press. © 1997 by the University of Nebraska Press. © Éditions du Seuil 1982.

ARIADNE AS HYPERTEXT

I have suggested above that the character Ariadne is a palimpsest revealing traces of earlier operatic figures. In Genette's terms, Strauss's and Hofmannsthal's opera is also a "hypertext" that has complex relationships with numerous "hypotexts" from Mozart, Wagner, and other composers. These relations fall under Genette's broader category of "transformation," not "imitation." But what is the nature of the transformation? Figure 13 reproduces the range of possible transformational "moods" given by Genette as a "rose window." I would tend to place *Ariadne* in the upper half of the circle, perhaps closest to irony for the reasons we have discussed in the previous chapter. Ariadne and Zerbinetta are two opposite poles in the opera. Ariadne is faithful and steadfast; as Hofmannsthal said in his *Ariadne* Letter, “Ariadne could be the wife or mistress of *one* man only,” whereas Zerbinetta is “frivolous” and “is in her element drifting out of the arms of one man into the arms of another.” The two are juxtaposed—in the sense of Forsyth’s formal irony—but neither one is really favored or harshly judged.

My impression of the opera is that Ariadne and her retinue remain in entirely separate worlds from Zerbinetta and hers. A careful reading of the libretto suggests that Ariadne may not even be aware of them. After Brighella and Truffaldin suggest (from the wings) that Ariadne is mad (“sie ist toll”), she responds “to herself, without turning her head, as if she heard the last words in a dream” (at reh. 53). This implies that she has not heard the commedia characters. Later on, when Zerbinetta addresses Ariadne directly and delivers her famous aria, “Grossmächtige Prinzessin,” Ariadne pays no attention to her and goes off to her cave, so that Zerbinetta sings to an empty stage.

Strauss and Hofmannsthal achieve *Illusionsstörung* not only through what one might think of as the horizontal juxtaposition of elements in formal irony, through the separate worlds of Ariadne and Zerbinetta, but also in a more vertical layering of dramatic levels. Since that vertical layering is hard to capture with Genette’s categories, I might return here to those proposed by Siegfried Schmidt (as discussed in the previous chapter). Schmidt suggests that a text has its own world (TW), which is received by a reader in his or her own world (RW). That is a fairly straightforward model, and mutatis mutandis, we might say that the text is in this case the opera *Ariadne auf Naxos,* and we as viewers or listeners are the readers.

Yet embedded within the opera are the other text-worlds to which reference or allusion is made, as I have already suggested—that of Mozart’s *The Magic Flute,* of Wagner’s *Lohengrin* and *Tristan,* and undoubtedly many other works, or characters from works, that are even further sublimated. In figure 14, I have limited these to TW2–5, because those are the most obvious. All these text-worlds are also received by the listener as part of his or her experience of the opera. This situation is, of course, not unusual for most artworks, which are almost always intertextual to some degree. But in *Ariadne* the model is complicated by multiple reader’s worlds, some of which overlap with the text-worlds. In the case of the original 1912 *Ariadne,* there is the reader’s world of the Molière characters whom we observe as they watch and comment upon the opera. Jourdain, in fact, has the very last word in this version, after all the operatic characters have left the stage. These Molière characters form their own reader’s world, but they are also part of the text-world of the entire theatrical piece.

The Molière characters were omitted when the opera was revised in 1916

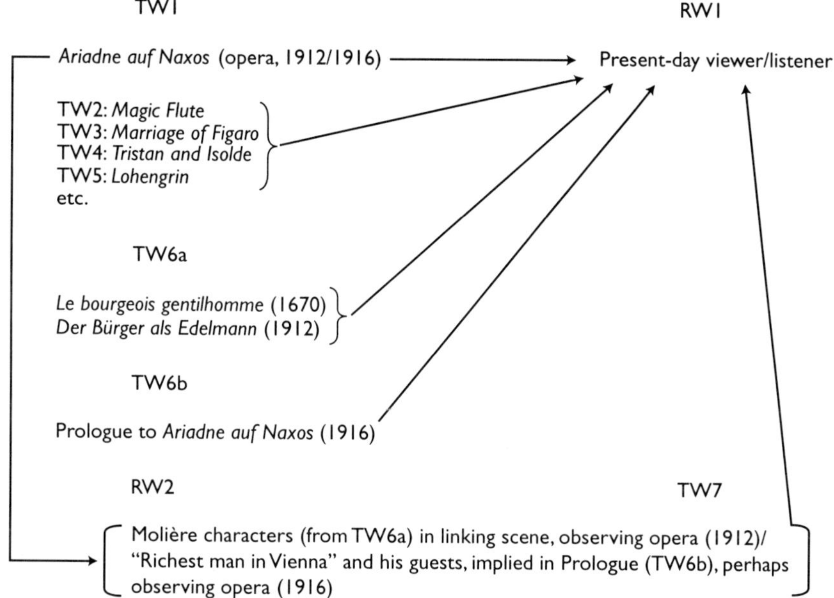

Figure 14. Text-worlds and reader's worlds in *Ariadne auf Naxos*

and the Prologue added. However, they survived as a strange ghost in the orchestral score of the 1916 version, published by Fürstner. At reh. 29, the spaces in the harmonium part are filled with a fragment of a conversation in which Jourdain and Dorantes comment on the musical style of Ariadne's aria. (In the full text of this amusing passage from the 1912 version, Jourdain asks Dorantes, "Don't you find what she's singing a bit monotonous?" Dorantes replies: "Hush! That is the simplicity of the Grand Style [*großen Stils,* the same term used by Nietzsche, as discussed in chapter 1], which connoisseurs value above everything.") In the most recent collected works of Strauss, these lines have been airbrushed out.[55]

Even without the Molière frame, some kind of hybrid text-reader's world outside the opera is established by the Prologue added by Strauss and Hofmannsthal in 1916. Here the operatic characters have their "real world" roles as singers and players within the house of the "richest man in Vienna," who has commissioned the opera. Unlike the Molière characters, this rich man and his guests never make an actual appearance onstage. Presumably neither the Molière characters nor the rich Viennese man and his guests are aware of, or receive, the text-worlds of Mozart and Wagner; those are exclusively for our reader's world.

One other layer of reader's and text-world might be mentioned, though it is not represented in figure 14. As I suggested above when discussing formal irony, Ariadne and the commedia players seem to occupy different spheres. Ariadne is unaware of the commedia players, but they are very much aware of her. They observe her, they try to interact with her. Thus we might say that Ariadne herself represents a further text-world within the opera that is received by the commedia players in their reader's world.

Although packed with irony, parody, stylistic juxtapositions, complex superposition of Mozart and Wagner, the play of hypo- and hypertexts and of text-worlds and reader's worlds, *Ariadne auf Naxos* is ultimately more than the sum of its techniques. Hofmannsthal and Strauss were able to make the character of Ariadne well rounded, coherent, and moving. In their hands, the multiple perspectives yield a kind of aesthetic coherence—a modernist coherence. The subtlety of *Ariadne auf Naxos* can never be captured by any of the models explored above. *Ariadne* remains one of the most extraordinary achievements of the operatic repertory. It was also, as Hofmannsthal admitted, an "unrepeatable" experiment, one that, however, would have much to teach the twentieth century about how to be modern while still holding on to, or being held by, the past.

PFITZNER'S REGRESSIVE MODERNISM

In Hans Pfitzner's opera *Palestrina,* written between 1909 and 1915, the musical past plays a more prominent and far more self-conscious role than in the roughly contemporary *Der Rosenkavalier* and *Ariadne auf Naxos.* Lighter irony—whether of the Marschallin's bittersweet kind, Mahler's "as-if" mode, or Mann's epic variety—is not part of Pfitzner's worldview. Nor is Reger's severe historicist modernism. For Pfitzner, the great music of the Austro-German tradition was under attack and in danger of extinction in the years around 1900. His was an ideological and compositional crusade to preserve it, but also to acknowledge the passing of an era.

Pfitzner made his concerns clear in numerous writings, including his two most famous polemics, "Futuristengefahr" (Dangerous Futurists, 1917) and "Die neue Aesthetik der musikalischen Impotenz" (The New Aesthetic of Musical Impotence, 1919). In the first he locked horns with Busoni. In the *Sketch for a New Aesthetic of Music,* Busoni had espoused a view of music in which Bach, Beethoven, and other German masters were not the apogees of a great tradition now in decline, but rather were part of a progressive, transnational trajectory that included such figures as Berlioz and Liszt and could lead to a bold and bright future in the twentieth century. For Pfitzner, the German tradition was the only meaningful one, and it could not progress or advance, at least not past the heights reached in Richard Wagner. Pfitzner wrote:

> Busoni hopes *the future* will provide everything for occidental music, and he interprets the present as a stammering beginning, as preparation. But what if it were otherwise? What if we found ourselves on the pinnacle or had already past the pinnacle? What if the last century or the last century-and-a-half constituted the blossoming of occidental music, the height, the true shining period that will never come again and upon which follows a decay, a decadence, like that after the blossoming of Greek tragedy? My feeling tends far more toward this interpretation.[56]

Palestrina, for which Pfitzner wrote his own libretto, is often regarded as his opus summum, and it certainly represents his worldview better than any other work. He put his concerns directly into the figure of Palestrina, who is depicted (in the character's own words) as an "old, dead-tired man at the end of a great era," which is exactly how Pfitzner saw himself. Palestrina is out of sympathy with newer musical trends, but at the same time is unwilling, and feels unable, to compose the mass that will help save the tradition of sacred music. (Pfitzner based his libretto on the long-standing myth, fostered by the music historian Ambros, that with his *Pope Marcellus Mass* Palestrina rescued church music, whose fate was being debated at the Council of Trent.)[57] After his friend Cardinal Borromeo has commanded him to compose the work, Palestrina is visited in the night by the spirits of past masters and of his dead wife. They encourage him, and subsequently a choir of angels inspires him to create the mass. The second act of *Palestrina* is taken up entirely with the political and personal debates at the Council of Trent, at which the role of church music is discussed. At the end of the opera, in the brief third act, Palestrina's mass has been performed, and the composer is widely acclaimed in the streets of Rome. But Palestrina shuns the public and remains quietly in his house, playing his organ and praying gently to be granted his role as the "last stone" in the "ring" ("edifice" is another metaphor used by Pfitzner in the libretto) of great composers.

In this study I have proposed different "modernisms" to characterize musical culture in the decades surrounding 1900, including ambivalent modernism and historicist modernism. Pfitzner's brand has traces of both, but might more properly be considered "regressive." In introducing that term, I adapt the one articulated by Carl Dahlhaus, as discussed in chapter 4. Dahlhaus proposed "retrospective" historicism to describe a naive traditionalism based on a "belief in the timeless, unchanging substance and validity of an old style."[58] One example of retrospective historicism adduced by Dahlhaus is nineteenth-century masses written in the Palestrina style. Pfitzner's *Palestrina,* and the aesthetic philosophy implicated there and in his writings, are anything but naive. Pfitzner certainly believes in the timeless validity of the Austro-German tradition. But his stance is militant, his view of the present very bleak. Hence we might speak of a kind of *regression,* in the more psychological or Freudian sense of returning emotionally to a former state. Pfitzner wishes for—but also realizes the impossibility of—a return to premodern music, a music that ends with Wagner. Hence his regressive modernism.

In writing about *Palestrina* the historian Michael P. Steinberg has advanced several other terms that could be put in dialogue with regressive modernism. Steinberg suggests that Pfitzner and his protagonist are characterized by "modernist ambivalence" or "modernist conservatism," "wherein reaction is tempered by a certain critical self-questioning, but ultimately not with any functional result, aesthetically or politically."[59] The actual character of Palestrina in the opera is less extreme, less regressive, than Pfitzner himself appears to have been. Palestrina admits that his pupil Silla might be justified in being attracted to a new florid, monodic style emerging from Florence, a style that Silla has enthusiastically tried out at the opening of the opera. "Who can know whether the world now follows unimagined paths," Palestrina asks the more doctrinaire Cardinal Borromeo, "and whether what seemed eternal to us is not going with the wind?" About Silla, Palestrina says, "I feel no right to hinder him."

In his discussion of Pfitzner's *Palestrina* in *Reflections of a Nonpolitical Man* of 1917, Thomas Mann picked up this aspect of Palestrina's attitude, which he described as not a rigid traditionalism, like that of Borromeo, but a "conservatism that is free, knowing, tender, intellectual, in a word: *ironical.*"[60] Mann's formulation of ironical conservatism seems close to the mark. He is clearly impressed by Palestrina's irony—a kind to which, as we know from the previous chapter, he would relate strongly. Mann also describes Pfitzner's Palestrina admiringly as an "ambivalent master."

The most fruitful analogue to the dramatic scenario of *Palestrina*—it was noted as early as 1917 by Mann—is found in Wagner's *Die Meistersinger,* another *Künstleroper,* an opera about the creative artist, the self-conscious fashioning of a masterwork, and the relation between art and society. Mann reports that he discussed these analogies with Pfitzner shortly after the premiere of *Palestrina* in 1917, when "we compared Ighino with David, Palestrina with Stolzing and Sachs, the mass with the prize song; [and] we talked of Bach and of Italian church music as stylizing forces."[61]

Mann and Pfitzner seem to have hit most of the points of contact between *Die Meistersinger* and *Palestrina.* The master and would-be master of Wagner's opera, Hans Sachs and Walther von Stolzing, respectively, are fused into the single figure of Palestrina. The rule-bound David is close in spirit to Palestrina's son Ighino. But Walther might also be said to be embodied in Palestrina's apprentice Silla, who rejects his master's polyphonic art and is seduced by the new monodic style. Unlike Walther, who comes to appreciate the Masters' art at the same time that he reforms it, Silla abandons his training and his master for the progressive world of Florence.

The music of Bach does indeed constitute a "stylizing force" in *Die Meistersinger.* Much of the orchestral polyphony in the opera, with busily moving inner parts, represents Wagner's attempt to create what he called "applied Bach." (His comment referred specifically to the instrumental accompaniment to the entry of the Masters in act 1, scene 4.) The Bach "style" in *Meistersinger* is not, of course, historically accurate. There is no pastiche; and no one would mistake a bar of the opera for actual Bach. It is rather Bach in the second degree, Bach "as if." Moreover, Bach is, as Wagner obviously knew, a sonic anachronism within the historical world of the opera, which is that of the Renaissance Germany. When the members of the congregation of St. Catherine's lift their voices in the first scene of the opera, they sing neither in the polyphonic style of Isaac or Lassus, nor in the simpler homophonic idiom of the chorale settings of Johann Walter. They harmonize an "as-if" Protestant chorale in a full Bachian manner. The *Meisterlied* that Walther creates in act 3 is in the style of neither the Renaissance nor Bach; it follows only the formal structure—the all-powerful *Barform*— of the actual songs of the period.

Although it plays a less prominent sonic role than does Bach in *Die Meistersinger,* the high Renaissance Italian style of church music is significant in *Palestrina.* John Williamson has observed that Pfitzner aims for "a general sense of the archaic" and "an impression of antiquity captured within his own idiom."[62] Kunze's description of Strauss's *Ariadne* seems appropriate here as well. Parts of Palestrina have the character of quotation without actually quoting anything. Mann articulated forcefully and colorfully Pfitzner's ability to capture the old within a post-Wagnerian modern idiom: "What great artistry, in combination with the most nervous agility, penetrating harmonic audacity with a pious ancestral style! . . . The psychologically modern element, all the refinement of this insertion of harmonic retardations, how purely organically it joins itself to what is musical milieu, what, therefore, is humble-primitive, Middle Ages, frugality, the breath of the grave, crypt and skeleton, in this Romantic musical score!"[63]

Mann rightly identifies the "nervous agility" as a "psychologically modern" element that informs—and largely destabilizes—the ancient and Romantic ones in *Palestrina.* The orchestral Prelude to the opera conveys this modern aspect in a fashion at once beautiful and searing (example 45). Pfitzner's white-note treatment of D minor is analogous to Wagner's adaptation of C major in *Die Meistersinger:* it is "second," or "as-if," diatonicism. The only two chromatic notes in the first ten measures are the leading tone, C♯ (not at all a surprise in D minor, of course), and the B♮ that forms the third of the major subdominant chord played by the oboes. Pfitzner's is not the chromatically and contrapuntally charged D minor of a contemporaneous work like Schoenberg's First Quartet, op. 7 (examined in chapter 3), or even the D minor of Beethoven's Ninth Symphony. Pfitzner's is a key that, so to speak, has regressed anxiously and "modernly" to modal antiquity.

At the beginning of the Prelude to *Palestrina,* the divisi strings, doubled by flutes, rise upward in a series of broad intervals—a fifth, a seventh, and an octave. If we are expecting a thematic language commensurate with the implied neomodal harmony, the seventh between E and D is surprising much in the way the downward leap of a seventh between D and E♭ was in the Overture to Strauss's *Ariadne* examined above: it seems outside the style implied for the work at hand. The superimposition of fourths on the downbeat of m. 2 (from the bottom, E–A–D) is both modern and neomedieval at the same time. The means are similar to a work like Debussy's piano prelude *La Cathédrale engloutie,* but the effect is entirely different. With Debussy the quasi organum has a touch of the exotic, the pictorial, the impressionist. In Pfitzner, who also uses his share of organum style (at eight measures before reh. F; and see below, example 47), we have a regressive modernism—modernism with an attitude.

This charged juxtaposition of old and new is also clear in scenes 5 and 6 of act 1 of *Palestrina,* where Palestrina is visited by the spirits of the dead masters and then creates his mass with the assistance of an angel choir. The

Example 45. Pfitzner, *Palestrina,* Prelude

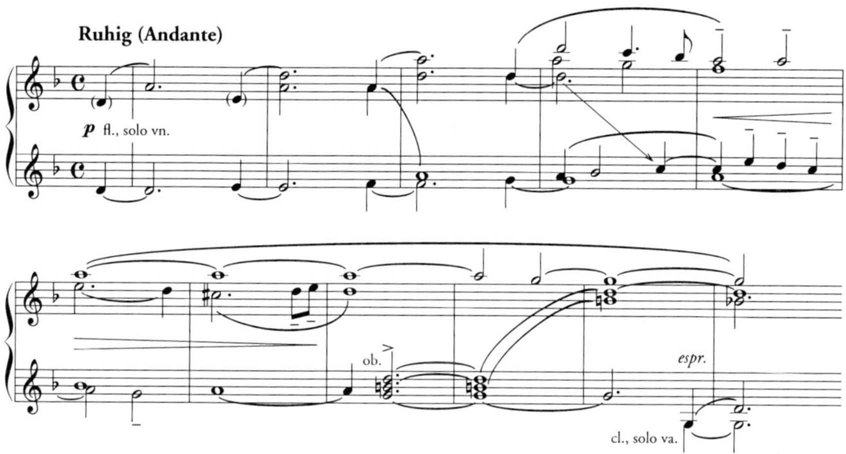

appearance of the Masters at the beginning of scene 5 is analogous to the entry of the Masters in act 1, scene 4, of *Die Meistersinger,* the moment where Wagner "applies" Bach. In Pfitzner, we may speak of gestures of applied neo-Medieval and neo-Renaissance music. Like Wagner, Pfitzner makes no attempt at this point to produce historically authentic sounds. Rather, he seeks, as he himself said, "a somewhat archaic, i.e., stylistically antique, character."[64] Thus when the spirit of Josquin greets Palestrina, his musical accompaniment contains a chain of 6–5 and 4–3 suspensions that clearly evoke Renaissance polyphonic practice (example 46). When the masters take up Josquin's melody as a group, they perform it in parallel organum over a B♭ pedal point (example 47). Organum of this type is obviously anachronistic for the sixteenth century, but the device serves its archaizing function.

These stylistic features contrast with Palestrina's own interjections, which remain very much in an expressive post-Wagnerian style, as in the dissonant orchestral outburst of brass and woodwinds that follows the Masters' organum (shown in example 47). Here Pfitzner recomposes the descending parallel fourths and the suspensions within a more chromatic context. The chord on the downbeat of 130 is an augmented triad (E–G♯–C♮), with an F♮. The F♮–C♮ fourth resolves down in the second half of the measure as a $^{9-6}_{8-5}$ suspension to E–B. This gesture brings us directly from the sonic world of the Masters back to the present-day anguish of Palestrina. As if to underline the contrast, Pfitzner employs the "Tristan" chord, in its original Wagnerian transposition and with its original upward half-step resolution

Example 46. Pfitzner, *Palestrina,* act I

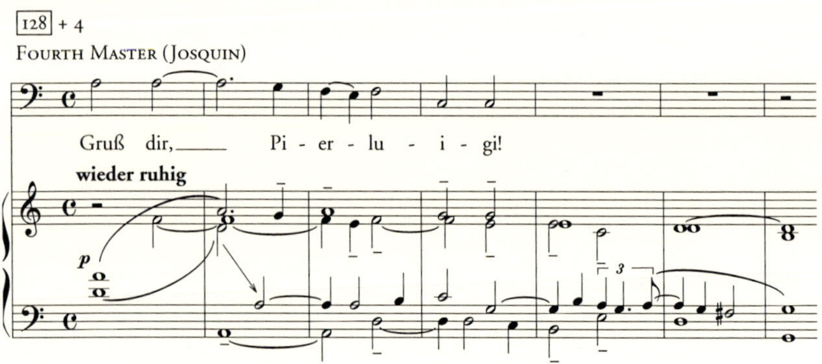

(Greetings, Pierluigi!)

Example 47. Pfitzner, *Palestrina,* act I

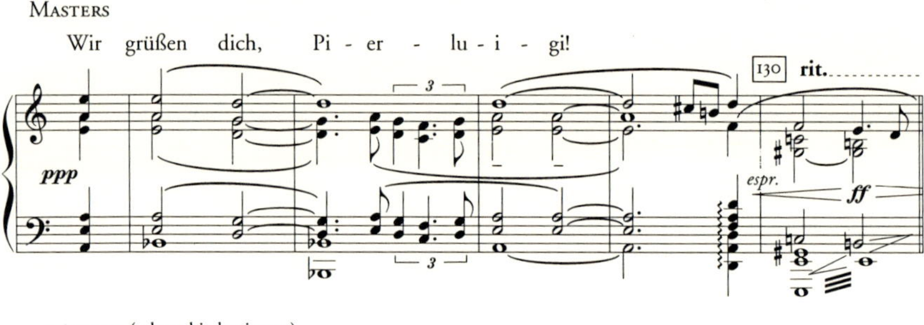

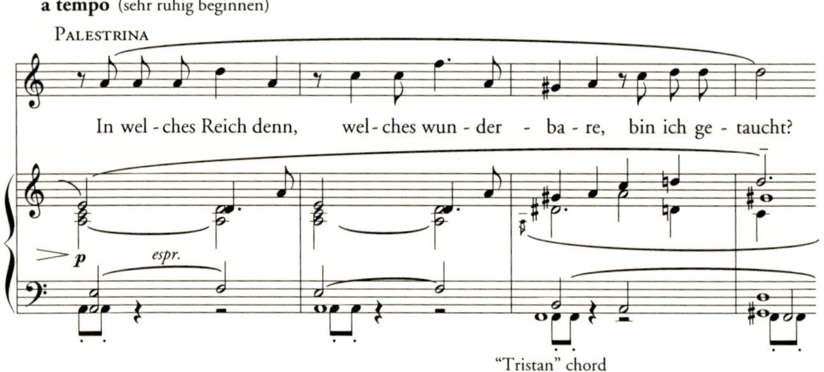

(We greet you, Pierluigi! To what realm, what wonderful realm have I been transported?)

(G♯–A), on the downbeat of three measures after reh. 130, on the "ba-re" of "wunderbare." The sharp contrast in this scene between the Masters' music and Palestrina's recalls acts 1 and 3 of Wagner's *Parsifal,* where the more hieratic, ascetic music of the Grail knights is juxtaposed with the chromatically tormented utterances of Amfortas. Like Amfortas in *Parsifal,* Palestrina is reluctant to perform what the masters deem to be his duty.

In scene 6, Palestrina composes his mass with the help of an angel choir that sings motives he repeats and notates, with the encouragement of the spirit of his dead wife, Lucrezia. Pfitzner weaves in actual musical motives from Palestrina's *Pope Marcellus Mass,* as well as from his *Missa Aspice Domine,* which Pfitzner is likely to have found in the same volume of Palestrina's Collected Works as the *Pope Marcellus.*[65] We first hear the "Kyrie eleison," made up of the upward leap of a fourth, followed by a descending scale, a figure taken directly from the *Pope Marcellus.* A subsequent phrase of Palestrina, sung in German as part of his "character" ("Ach, wo ergießt er," at reh. 163) is adapted from a tenor line in the Kyrie of the mass.

In this scene, Pfitzner follows the order of the Latin mass text, proceeding selectively from textual fragments of the Kyrie to the last lines of the Agnus Dei, "Dona nobis pacem." The whole scene, which lasts about ten minutes, is one of the most effective and best proportioned in *Palestrina,* where *longueurs* are not uncommon. It has a clear musical and spiritual trajectory, starting in the dark of night and in anguish ("Allein in dunkler Tiefe voll Angst ich armer Mensch" is Palestrina's description of himself) and ending, after the creation of the mass, with the pealing of bells in a Rome awakening at dawn. The scene begins in a chromatically inflected A major and moves through a wide tonal range before concluding in a radiant C major.

As has often been pointed out, Pfitzner does not attempt to reproduce Palestrina's actual *Pope Marcellus Mass,* or any other integral Renaissance work. He creates, as Williamson notes, a "fantasy."[66] What we hear is the act of inspiration and creation, rather than a finished work. Indeed, we never do hear the mass itself in *Palestrina.* In this sense the opera also deviates significantly from *Die Meistersinger,* where the Prize Song evolves conspicuously across act 3 and in its finished form dominates the final scene. In the last moments of *Palestrina,* in contrast, Palestrina sits alone in his house, ignoring the cries of adulation from the street. Where the Prize Song "makes" Walther—gives him the girl and his place in the community, and solidifies his artistic skills—the mass has essentially finished off Palestrina. One senses that this Palestrina (not the historic one) will write no more music.

In his conversation with Mann, Pfitzner acknowledged the sharp differences with *Die Meistersinger* at the end of *Palestrina.* Mann reported that Pfitzner told him: "At the end of the *Meistersinger* there is a stage full of light, rejoicing of the people, engagement, brilliance and glory; in my work there is, to be sure, Palestrina, who is also celebrated, but in the half-darkness of his room under the picture of the deceased one, dreaming at the organ. The *Meistersinger* is the apotheosis of the new, a praise of the future and of life; in *Palestrina* everything tends toward the past, it is dominated by *sympathy with death.*" Mann italicizes the final phrase and points out how he himself had used the very same words in an early unfinished novel. Mann describes "sympathy with death" as "the formula and basic definition of all Romanticism" and posits Pfitzner's *Palestrina* as "the grave song of Romantic opera."[67]

If we reflect back on the role that Wagner's *Die Meistersinger* has played in the works examined in the past three chapters, revealing differences emerge. For Mahler in his Seventh Symphony, and for Strauss and Hofmannsthal in *Der Rosenkavalier,* Wagner served as a "weapon" for irony, and often outright parody. The "targets" were Classical instrumental forms (for Mahler), world-wise operatic heroes and heroines (for Strauss and Hofmannsthal), and their modern listeners (for all three). For Pfitzner, however, Wagner's *Meistersinger* constitutes a negative or opposite universe to that of his protagonist Palestrina. Palestrina may, as Mann suggested, have an ironic worldview; but for Pfitzner, Wagner is not wielded as an ironic weapon, at least not as in Mahler and Strauss. Pfitzner saw himself, like his Palestrina, at the end of a great era. By 1909, when he began active work on the opera, Pfitzner felt out of sympathy with contemporary trends in Austro-German music. He became a true cultural conservative in the mold of Frantz and Lagarde. With Pfitzner we have come almost full circle to a strain of the ambivalent modernism examined in chapter 1.

EPILOGUE: "OUR PLAY HAS LONG AGO FINISHED ITS RUN"

By the middle of the 1920s, very divergent strands of musical modernism were in play in the Austro-German sphere. Reger and Mahler were dead. Strauss and Hofmannsthal, after the monumental detour of *Die Frau ohne Schatten,* continued in the general stylistic vein of *Ariadne,* but never again quite captured its magic formula of irony, parody, and transfiguration. Busoni, whose Bach-related activities had turned away from composition and more toward preparing the definitive Bach-Busoni edition of 1920, worked on his magnum opus *Doktor Faust* until his death in 1924.

In the early 1920s Schoenberg determined to dance in chains with a remarkable group of works, including the Serenade, op. 24, and the Suite for Piano, op. 25, in which he revisited Baroque and Classical forms at the same time as developing the twelve-tone method. One set of chains, the earlier formal models, helped reinforce the other, the new restrictions of pitch organization. At almost exactly the same time, the young Paul Hindemith began to produce his *Kammermusik* series—the first set was op. 24, in 1921—with shorter movements in traditional forms. Self-imposition of generic, formal, harmonic, and contrapuntal fetters had become an integral part of the ideology of *neue Sachlichkeit* and of Stravinskian neoclassicism, of which the initial icons were the Octet (1923) and the Concerto for Piano and Winds (1924).

The first generation of Austro-German modernists examined in this book felt overall a greater sense of continuity with the musical past, a continuity that, as has often been pointed out, was broken to a large extent by World War I. That is why I have chosen to end this book essentially at 1915–16, with the composition of *Palestrina* and the revised version of *Ariadne auf Naxos.* The way of revisiting and drawing materials from the past in these operas differs fundamentally from the tactics of Hindemith and Stravinsky.

By the mid-1920s Thomas Mann realized that Austro-German culture was occupying a very different world from before the war, as became clear in *The Magic Mountain,* which he had begun in 1913, but completed only in 1924. Hans Castorp becomes even more isolated from society and everyday life than Hanno Buddenbrooks, and he grapples with the fundamental Mannian issue of life versus art, or in this case more specifically life and engagement-in-the-world versus intellectual-spiritual detachment. Mann assumes in this novel something of the same epic irony he had displayed in *Buddenbrooks.* He views Castorp and the cast of characters at the sanatorium with an amused detachment. The advent of World War I at the end of the novel ruptures the tranquil world of the sanatorium. After seven years—he originally had intended to stay three weeks—Castorp leaves the sanatorium to enlist in the army; we never learn his fate. Mann ends with the following ironic statement: "Farewell, Hans Castorp, life's faithful problem child. Your story is over. We have told it to its end; it was neither short on diversion nor long on boredom—it was a hermetic story. We told it for its own sake, not yours, for you were a simple fellow."[68]

In the 1920s Mann, who as the "nonpolitical" man had been a strong supporter of Imperial Germany and its values during the war, now endorsed the democratic framework of the Weimar Republic. His widely noted speech "On the German Republic" of 1922 represented his new outlook. At the same time, it served to distance Mann from some of his former allies in cultural conservatism. Hans Pfitzner strongly disagreed with Mann's new stance, and told him so in a letter sent just after the celebrations of the writer's fiftieth birthday in June 1925. "I would like tell you what you probably have long since sensed," Pfitzner wrote on June 18, after offering his belated congratulations, "that your most recent 'political' (to use a word that is not entirely appropriate) statements have created a painful distance between us."[69]

A week later, Mann wrote a warm but pointed response. He knew his most recent positions would be repellent to Pfitzner. But, he observed, a musician might not feel the same "sense of responsibility" as a writer, nor be subject to the same "conscious and by no means painless self-disciplining which earn a man the name of Judas." Then Mann commented, in a passage that could in some senses sum up the concerns of the present study, on how his own relationship to Pfitzner had changed and had taken on aspects of the Nietzsche-Wagner one:

> Our play, dear Maestro, speaking in the grand and representational sense of intellectual history, has long ago finished its run; we are only a latter-day, journalistic acting out of the case of Nietzsche versus Wagner. Nietzsche's conscience made him free himself from Wagner, but he loved him unto death. And Nietzsche, like Wagner, was a late-born son of Romanticism. But Wagner was a great and greatly fortunate self-glorifier and self-consummator, whereas Nietzsche was a revolutionary self-conqueror and "became a Judas." With the result that Wagner remained only the last glorifier and supremely effective consummator of an epoch, whereas Nietzsche became a seer and the leader for mankind toward a new future.[70]

Mann is saying that Wagnerian Romanticism, the "sympathy with death," has played itself out: *hat sich abgespielt* is his actual phrase. He observes that the Mann-Pfitzner relationship—in which one figure chooses life, engagement, and the future, the other death, detachment, and the past—stands in a journalistic, superficial relationship to the original Nietzsche-Wagner one we examined in chapter 1. In other words, in the terms we have used in preceding chapters, Mann-Pfitzner is Nietzsche-Wagner in an "as if" mode; it is Nietzsche-Wagner in the second degree. The Mann-Pfitzner relationship thus replicates to a large extent the way in which Mann, Mahler, Pfitzner, Reger, and Strauss treat the music of the past.

Mann's comments bring us directly back to the issues raised in the first chapter. There we saw how in Nietzsche's intellectual break with Wagner around 1880, he called for a newer classicism and for a renunciation of the Grand Style. Subsequent chapters have developed a view of early German modernism as responding in various ways to Nietzsche's mandate, whether or not all the creative artists discussed were in fact specifically aware of it. As we have seen, Wagnerism and Wagner held sway in important ways for most of the period of early German modernism, at the same time that efforts were made to achieve distance from them. The Wagnerian legacy took a long time to play itself down, *sich abzuspielen.* For all the differences among the creative artists examined in this study, including Nietzsche and Wagner, we can thus recognize certain principles in common. Mann acknowledged this touchingly in his letter to Pfitzner, where he said that beneath their own disagreements lay nonetheless a "curious kinship" and that the two should "recognize a fraternity which posterity is likely to insist on."[71]

NOTES

INTRODUCTION

1. See, for example, *The Weimar Republic Sourcebook,* ed. Anton Kaes, Martin Jay, and Edward Dimendberg (Berkeley: University of California Press, 1994); Detlev Peukert, *Weimar Republic: The Crisis of Classical Modernity,* trans. Richard Deveson (New York: Hill and Wang, 1992); Peter Gay, *Weimar Republic: The Outsider as Insider* (New York: Harper and Row, 1968).

2. Carl Dahlhaus, *Nineteenth-Century Music,* trans. J. Bradford Robinson (Berkeley: University of California Press, 1989), p. 334.

3. Dahlhaus, *Nineteenth-Century Music,* p. 335.

4. See the valuable article by Hans Ulrich Gumbrecht, "Modern, Modernität, Moderne," in *Geschichtliche Grundbegriffe,* ed. Otto Brunner, Werner Conze, and Reinhard Koselleck (Stuttgart: Klett-Cotta, 1978), vol. 4, pp. 93–131.

5. Cited in Gumbrecht, "Modern," p. 110. A useful recent anthology of documents of and about modernism, from a European-wide perspective and from the midnineteenth to the midtwentieth century, is *Modernism: An Anthology of Sources and Documents,* ed. Vassiliki Kolocotroni, Jane Goldman, and Olga Taxidou (Edinburgh: Edinburgh University Press, 1998).

CHAPTER 1

1. An excellent survey of German history during this period is David Blackbourn, *The Long Nineteenth Century: A History of Germany, 1790–1914* (New

York: Oxford University Press, 1998). See also Volker Berghahn, *Imperial Germany, 1871–1914: Economy, Society, Culture, and Politics* (Providence: Berghahn Books, 1994); and James Sheehan, *Imperial Germany* (New York: New Viewpoints, 1976).

2. Peter Gay, *Freud, Jews and Other Germans* (New York: Oxford University Press, 1978), p. 12.

3. On Vienna, see Allan Janik and Stephen Toulmin, *Wittgenstein's Vienna* (New York: Touchstone Books, 1973); and Carl Schorske, *Fin-de-Siècle Vienna: Politics and Culture* (New York: Alfred Knopf, 1980). On Munich, see Peter Jelavich, *Munich and Theatrical Modernism: Politics, Playwriting, and Performance, 1890–1914* (Cambridge, Mass.: Harvard University Press, 1985) and Maria Makela, *The Munich Secession: Art and Artists in Turn-of-the-Century Munich* (Princeton: Princeton University Press, 1990). On Berlin, see Peter Fritzsche, *Reading Berlin 1900* (Cambridge, Mass.: Harvard University Press, 1996); Peter Jelavich, *Berlin Cabaret* (Cambridge, Mass.: Harvard University Press, 1993); and Peter Paret, *The Berlin Secession: Modernism and Its Enemies in Imperial Germany* (Cambridge, Mass.: Harvard University Press, 1980). See also the collection of Paret's essays, *German Encounters with Modernism, 1840–1945* (Cambridge: Cambridge University Press, 2001).

4. Gay, *Freud, Jews and Other Germans,* p. 12.

5. Hinrich Seeba, "'So weit die deutsche Zunge klingt': The Role of German Language in German Identity Formation," in *Searching for Common Ground: Diskurse zur deutschen Identität 1750–1871,* ed. Nicholas Vazsonyi (Cologne: Böhlau, 2000), p. 53.

6. Françoise Forster-Hahn, "Introduction: Modernity and the Building of Nation," in *Imagining Modern German Culture: 1889–1910,* ed. Françoise Forster-Hahn (Washington, D.C.: National Gallery of Art, 1996), p. 10.

7. Marion F. Deshmukh, "'Politics Is an Art': The Cultural Politics of Max Liebermann in Wilhelmine Germany," in Forster-Hahn, *Imagining Modern German Culture,* p. 167.

8. The essays are in Richard Wagner, *Sämtliche Schriften und Dichtungen*, 5th ed., ed. Richard Sternfeld and Hans von Wolzogen (Leipzig: Breitkopf & Härtel, 1911), vol. 8, pp. 30–124 ("Deutsche Kunst und deutsche Politik"); and vol. 10, pp. 36–53 ("Was ist deutsch?") and pp. 54–60 ("Modern"). They appear in English in Richard Wagner, *Prose Works*, trans. W. Ashton Ellis, vol. 4 (London: Kegan Paul, Trench, Trübner, 1895; repr. as *Art and Politics* [Lincoln: University of Nebraska Press, 1995]), pp. 34–148 ("German Art and Policy") and pp. 149–69 ("What Is German?"); and vol. 6 (London: Kegan Paul, Trench, Trübner, 1897; repr. as *Religion and Art* [Lincoln: University of Nebraska Press, 1994]), pp. 41–49 ("Modern"). Further references will be to the English edition (PW) and will be given in the text. The translations borrow but are adapted from Ashton Ellis's.

9. See Jakob and Wilhelm Grimm, *Deutsches Wörterbuch* (Leipzig: Hirzl, 1860; repr. Munich, 1984), vol. 2, cols. 1046–47. Seeba, " 'So weit die deutsche Zunge klingt,' " in Vazsonyi, *Searching for Common Ground,* p. 51.

10. See Hannu Salmi, *Imagined Germany: Richard Wagner's National Utopia* (New York: Peter Lang, 1999), p. 13. There is by now a large literature on the role of Wagner's *Meistersinger* in national identity formation, and vice versa. See Lydia Goehr, *The Quest for Voice: Music, Politics, and the Limits of Philosophy* (Berkeley: University of California Press, 1998), chap. 2; Thomas Grey, "Wagner's *Die Meistersinger* as National Opera," in *Music and German National Identity,* ed. Celia Applegate and Pamela Potter (Chicago: University of Chicago Press, 2002), pp. 78–104 (with further bibliography listed on pp. 102–4); Arthur Groos, "Constructing Nuremberg: Typological and Proleptic Communities in *Die Meistersinger,*" *19th-Century Music* 16 (1992): 18–34; and Hans Vaget, "The 'Metapolitics' of *Die Meistersinger:* Wagner's Nuremberg as Imagined Community," in Vazsonyi, *Searching for Common Ground,* pp. 269–82.

11. Salmi, *Imagined Germany,* p. 6; Benedict Anderson, *Imagined Communities,* rev. ed. (London: Verso, 1991), p. 6.

12. Salmi, *Imagined Germany,* p. 195.

13. Blackbourn, *Long Nineteenth Century,* p. 395.

14. Fritz Stern, *The Politics of Cultural Despair* (Berkeley: University of California Press, 1961), pp. 27–34. The first six chapters of Stern's classic study are concerned with Lagarde.

15. Constantin Frantz, "Offener Brief an Richard Wagner," *Bayreuther Blätter* 2 (1878): 149–50.

16. Frantz, "Offener Brief," pp. 168–69.

17. Stern, *Politics of Cultural Despair,* pp. 62–63, 64.

18. Stern, *Politics of Cultural Despair,* p. 89; Cosima Wagner is quoted here. Stern also discusses the close relationship between Lagarde and Bayreuth after Wagner's death.

19. Ferdinand Tönnies, *Community and Society,* trans. and ed. Charles P. Loomis (East Lansing: Michigan State University, 1957), p. 76.

20. Kevin Repp, *Reformers, Critics, and the Paths of German Modernity: Antipolitics and the Search for Alternatives, 1890–1914* (Cambridge, Mass.: Harvard University Press, 2000), p. 16. See pp. 67–103 for a discussion of Damaschke.

21. The title of this collection, *Unzeitgemäße Betrachtungen,* has been translated numerous different ways, including as *Thoughts Out of Season, Untimely Meditations, Unmodern Observations,* and most recently *Unfashionable Observations* (the title I will adopt here).

22. Three of the more recent studies that have been very valuable in helping me toward an understanding of Nietzsche's aesthetics are Rüdiger Safranski, *Nietzsche: A Philosophical Biography,* trans. Shelley Frisch (New York: W. W. Nor-

ton, 2002); Julian Young, *Nietzsche's Philosophy of Art* (Cambridge: Cambridge University Press, 1992); and Christopher Cox, *Nietzsche: Naturalism and Interpretation* (Berkeley: University of California Press, 1999).

23. Friedrich Nietzsche, *The Birth of Tragedy and The Case of Wagner,* trans. Walter Kaufmann (New York: Vintage, 1967), p. 31. Further citations will be given in the text.

24. Nietzsche, "David Strauss the Confessor and the Writer," in *Unfashionable Observations,* trans. Richard Gray (Stanford: Stanford University Press, 1995), p. 5. Further references will be given in the text.

25. The concern about art as epigonic, or weak, second-rate imitation is common in German culture of the nineteenth century. Hegelians tended to see art in terms of historical development (Hegel himself spoke of the "end of art"). Creative artists from about the 1820s on were thus often said to be following a golden period, after which no real originality was possible. In the case of music, that golden period included Bach, Haydn, Mozart, and Beethoven. This strong historical awareness, and fear of being an epigone, is already present among Mendelssohn, Schumann, and others of their generation.

26. See Wagner's letter to Nietzsche of September 21, 1873, in *The Nietzsche-Wagner Correspondence,* ed. Elizabeth Foerster-Nietzsche, trans. Caroline V. Kerr (New York: Liveright, 1949), p. 179.

27. Nietzsche, "On the Utility and Liability of History for Life," in *Unfashionable Observations,* pp. 131, 163.

28. Gary Brown, introduction to "Richard Wagner in Bayreuth," in Nietzsche, *Unmodern Observations,* ed. William Arrowsmith (New Haven: Yale University Press, 1990), p. 239. Hayman quoted by Brown.

29. Nietzsche, "Richard Wagner in Bayreuth," in *Unfashionable Observations,* p. 316.

30. Nietszche, *The Case of Wagner,* pp. 170, 171.

31. Friedrich Nietzsche, *Kritische Studienausgabe,* ed. Giorgio Colli and Mazzino Montinari (Munich and Berlin: Deutscher Taschenbuch Verlag and de Gruyter, 1988), vol. 8 *(Nachgelassene Fragmente 1875–1879),* p. 463.

32. Friedrich Nietzsche, *Human, All Too Human,* trans. R. J. Hollingdale (Cambridge: Cambridge University Press, 1996), p. 86. Further references to this edition will be given in the text.

33. *Ein Skizzenbuch von Beethoven* (Leipzig: Breitkopf & Härtel, 1865) and *Beethoveniana* (Leipzig: Breitkopf & Härtel, 1872).

34. See, for example, the review of the First Symphony by Brahms's own champion, Eduard Hanslick, in Hanslick, *Hanslick's Music Criticisms,* trans. and ed. Henry Pleasants (New York: Dover, 1988), pp. 125–28.

35. Colli, "Nachwort," in Nietzsche, *Menschliches, Allzumenschliches I und II, Kritische Studienausgabe,* vol. 2, pp. 708, 709.

36. Cox, *Nietzsche,* p. 5.

37. Nietzsche, *On the Genealogy of Morals,* section 25; cited in Cox, *Nietzsche,* p. 65; Cox, *Nietzsche,* p. 66.

38. Safranski, *Nietzsche,* p. 199.

39. Colli, "Nachwort," p. 707.

40. Frederick R. Love, "Nietzsche's Quest for a New Aesthetic of Music: 'Die Allergrösste Symphonie,' 'Grosser Stil,' 'Musik des Südens,'" *Nietzsche-Studien* 6 (1977): 190.

41. Bernd Sponheuer, "Reconstructing Ideal Types of the 'German' in Music," in Applegate and Potter, *Music and German National Identity,* p. 40.

42. Friedrich Nietzsche, *Beyond Good and Evil,* trans. Marion Faber (Oxford: Oxford University Press, 1998), pp. 136–37.

43. Nietzsche, *Beyond Good and Evil,* p. 138.

44. Friedrich Nietzsche, *Selected Letters of Friedrich Nietzsche,* ed. and trans. Christopher Middleton (Chicago: University of Chicago Press, 1969), p. 251.

45. Love, "Nietzsche's Quest," pp. 180, 175, 185.

46. See the excellent discussion of the Nietzsche-Gast relationship as related to musical aesthetics in Love, "Nietzsche's Quest," esp. pp. 157–64. Love's is the clearest and best-informed exposition of Nietzsche's musical aesthetics that I have found.

47. Letter to Peter Gast, in Nietzsche, *Selected Letters* p. 333.

48. Gast, cited in David S. Thatcher, "Nietzsche and Brahms: A Forgotten Relationship," *Music & Letters* 54 (1973): 278–79; translation amended.

49. Hugo von Hofmannsthal, *The Lord Chandos Letter,* trans. Russell Stockman (Marlboro, Vt.: Marlboro Press, 1986), pp. 19, 21.

50. Cited in Love, "Nietzsche's Quest," pp. 175, 173.

51. Love, "Nietzsche's Quest," p. 171.

52. See the letter to Carl Fuchs of winter 1884–85 in Nietzsche, *Selected Letters,* p. 233.

53. "Musik—und der große Stil," cited in Love, "Nietzsche's Quest," p. 178; translation mine.

54. Wagner, "Public and Popularity," PW 6:77. Cited in Paul Lawrence Rose, *Wagner: Race and Revolution* (New Haven: Yale University Press, 1992), p. 142.

55. Rose, *Wagner,* pp. 163, 166. Klingsor and Kundry are interpreted as manifesting many Jewish physical stereotypes by Marc Weiner, *Richard Wagner and the Anti-Semitic Imagination* (Lincoln: University of Nebraska Press, 1995), for example, at pp. 241–50. Before Rose (and with greater moderation), Robert Gutman also interpreted the opera in the framework of Wagner's ideas on Aryan Christianity, in *Richard Wagner: The Man, His Mind, and His Music* (New York: Harcourt, Brace & World, 1968), pp. 421–32.

56. A reception history of *Parsifal* is sketched in Lucy Beckett, *Richard Wagner: Parsifal* (Cambridge: Cambridge University Press, 1981), chap. 5.

57. Nietzsche, *Selected Letters,* pp. 259–60.

58. Nietzsche, *Nietzsche contra Wagner,* in *The Portable Nietzsche,* ed. and trans. Walter Kaufmann (New York: Penguin, 1959), p. 675.

59. Margaret Notley, "Late Nineteenth-Century Chamber Music and the Cult of the Classical Adagio," *19th-Century Music* 23 (1999): 33, 37.

60. Theodor W. Adorno, "On the Score of 'Parsifal,'" trans. with commentary by Anthony Barone, *Music & Letters* 76 (1995): 384–85. Further references will be given in the text. (The original German essay is "Zur Partitur des 'Parsifal,'" in Adorno, *Gesammelte Schriften,* vol. 17, ed. Rolf Tiedemann [Frankfurt: Suhrkamp, 1982], pp. 47–51.)

61. See *Cosima Wagner's Diaries,* vol. II, ed. Martin Gregor-Dellin and Dietrich Mack, trans. Geoffrey Skelton (New York: Harcourt Brace Jovanovich, 1980), p. 666. This passage is cited and discussed in Rose, *Wagner,* pp. 140–41.

62. Arthur de Gobineau, *Essai sur l'inégalité des races humaines,* ed. Hubert Juin (Paris: Éditions Pierre Belfond, 1967), p. 502.

CHAPTER 2

1. Fritz Schlawe, *Literarische Zeitschriften 1885–1910* (Stuttgart: Metzler, 1961), p. 18.

2. Among the best introductions to naturalist thought, on which I draw here, are Roy Pascal, *From Naturalism to Expressionism* (New York: Basic Books, 1973); Theo Meyer, "Einleitung," in *Theorie des Naturalismus,* ed. Theo Meyer (Stuttgart: Reclam, 1973), pp. 3–49; and Erich Ruprecht, "Einleitung," in *Literarische Manifeste des Naturalismus, 1880–1892,* ed. Erich Ruprecht (Stuttgart: Metzler, 1962), pp. 1–19. The latter two volumes are anthologies of naturalist theoretical writings and give a fine overview of the issues and polemics of German naturalism.

3. Cited in Meyer, "Einleitung," p. 6.

4. Karl Bleibtreu, "Realismus und Naturwissenschaft," in *Literarisch-kritische Rundschau* 1 (1888), repr. in Meyer, *Theorie des Naturalismus,* p. 121; Bleibtreu, *Der Kampf ums Dasein der Literatur* (1888), repr. in *Theorie des Naturalismus,* p. 123.

5. Gerald Needham, "Naturalism," in *groveart.com* (2001), www.groveart.com (May 24, 2002).

6. Émile Zola, "Aussprüche über die bildende Kunst," *Die Gesellschaft* 1 (1885); repr. in Meyer, *Theorie des Naturalismus,* p. 110; Zola's credo is cited by Ruprecht, "Einleitung," p. 3.

7. Jens Christian Jensen, "Menzel, Adolph," in *groveart.com* (2001), www.groveart.com (May 30, 2003).

8. See Blackbourn, *Long Nineteenth Century,* p. 200.

9. *Die Berliner Moderne, 1885–1910,* ed. Jürgen Schutte and Peter Sprengel (Stuttgart: Reclam, 1987), p. 24.

10. Arno Holz, *Werke,* ed. Wilhelm Emrich and Anita Holz (Neuwied am Rhein: Luchterhand, 1962), vol. 5, p. 42.

11. Arno Holz, *Die Kunst: Ihr Wesen und ihre Gesetze* (1891), repr. in Meyer, *Theorie des Naturalismus,* pp. 173, 174.

12. The term *konsequenter Naturalismus* was coined by Adolf Bartels in 1902. See Heinz-Georg Brands, *Theorie und Stil des sogennanten "Konsequenten Naturalismus" von Arno Holz und Johannes Schlaf* (Bonn: Bouvier, 1978), p. 9.

13. See Brands, *Theorie und Stil,* p. 121–22. I am indebted to Suzanne Lodato for her illuminating and informative account of Holz's theories of naturalism in "Richard Strauss and the Modernists: A Contextual Study of Strauss's Fin-de-Siècle Song Style" (Ph.D. diss., Columbia University, 1999), chap. 4.

14. Cited from Annemarie und Wolfgang van Rinsum, *Deutsche Literaturgeschichte,* vol. 7: *Realismus und Naturalismus* (Munich: Deutscher Taschenbuch Verlag, 1999), pp. 319–20.

15. Rinsum, *Deutsche Literaturgeschichte,* p. 320.

16. Arno Holz, *Revolution in der Lyrik* (1899), excerpted in *Literarische Manifeste der Jahrhundertwende, 1890–1910,* ed. Erich Ruprecht and Dieter Bänsch (Stuttgart: Metzler, 1970), pp. 26, 52.

17. See Klaus M. Rarisch, "Über die typographische Mittelachse des 'Phantasus' von Arno Holz," *fulgura frango,* www.fulgura.de/autor/holz/ueber/achse.htm (May 28, 2003).

18. Arno Holz, *Phantasus: Verkleinerter Faksimiledruck der Erstfassung,* ed. Gerhard Schulz (Stuttgart: Reclam, 1968), p. 5.

19. Pascal, *From Naturalism to Expressionism,* pp. 59–60.

20. Cited in the introduction to Gerhart Hauptmann, *Plays: Before Daybreak, The Weavers, The Beaver Coat,* ed. Reinhold Grimm and Caroline Molina y Vedia (New York: Continuum, 1994), p. xviii.

21. Pascal, *From Naturalism to Expressionism,* p. 19.

22. Christian von Ehrenfels, "Wahrheit und Irrtum im Naturalismus," *Freie Bühne* 2 (1891); repr. in Ehrenfels, *Ästhetik,* in *Philosophische Schriften,* vol. 2, ed. Reinhard Fabian (Munich: Philosophia Verlag, 1986), p. 34. Further references will be given in the text.

23. Hermann Bahr, *Zur Überwindung des Naturalismus: Theoretische Schriften 1887–1904,* ed. Gotthart Wunberg (Stuttgart: Kohlhammer, 1968), p. 47. Further references will be given in the text.

24. See especially Michael Worbs, *Nervenkunst: Literatur und Psychoanalyse in Wien der Jahrhundertwende* (Frankfurt: Europäische Verlagsanstalt, 1983).

25. A valuable discussion of these and other literary-oriented journals of the time is Schlawe, *Literarische Zeitschriften 1885–1910.* Schlawe has entries on each of the journals, with a bibliographic summary, a discussion of the journal's philosophy, a listing of the principal authors, and further references. On *Die*

Gesellschaft, see pp. 17–19; on *Freie Bühne* (which changed its name to *Neue deutsche Rundschau* in 1894, and to *Neue Rundschau* in 1904), see pp. 23–28.

26. Hans Frank, "Der Bayreuther Meister und die deutsche Weltstellung," *Die Gesellschaft* 1 (1885): 11.

27. Oskar Bie, "Der Naturalismus in der Musik," *Die Gesellschaft* 1 (1885): 400.

28. Carl Dahlhaus, *Realism in Nineteenth-Century Music,* trans. Mary Whittall (Cambridge: Cambridge University Press, 1985), pp. 18–21.

29. Dahlhaus, *Realism,* p. 55.

30. See *Die Gesellschaft* 1 (1885): 790–71, 805–7, 838–39; 2 (1886): 318–20; 2 (1886): 244–49; prefatory comments to *Wagneriana* in *Die Gesellschaft* 2 (1886): 318.

31. See Erich Stahl, "Viktor E. Neßler und die Wagnerianer," *Die Gesellschaft* 1 (1885): 117–19, about the composer of the popular operetta *Der Trompeter von Säkkingen;* Stahl, "Die Operette: eine unzeitgemäße Betrachtung," *Die Gesellschaft* 1 (1885): 448–50; and Stahl, "Hanswurst in der Operette," *Die Gesellschaft* 1 (1885): 917–18.

32. Christian von Ehrenfels, "Richard Wagner und der Naturalismus," *Freie Bühne* 2 (1891); repr. in Ehrenfels, *Ästhetik,* p. 12. Further references will be given in the text.

33. For a discussion of the origins and early history of the term "leitmotive," see Thomas Grey, " . . . *wie ein rother Faden:* On the Origins of 'Leitmotif,'" in *Music Theory in the Age of Romanticism,* ed. Ian Bent (Cambridge: Cambridge University Press, 1996), pp. 187–210. Grey does not address the issue of when a more psychological interpretation of leitmotivic technique like Ehrenfels's became current.

34. See Gerhart Hauptmann, *Einsame Menschen,* 22nd ed. (Berlin: Fischer, 1908), pp. 26–27.

35. Ernst Otto Nodnagel, "Das naturalistische Melodrama," in his *Jenseits von Wagner und Liszt* (Königsberg: Ostpreussischen Druckerei und Verlagsanstalt, 1902), p. 152.

36. Nodnagel, "Das naturalistische Melodrama," pp. 152–53.

37. Edward Kravitt, *The Lied: Mirror of Late Romanticism* (New Haven: Yale University Press, 1996), chap. 4, from which I draw for the following discussion.

38. See, e.g., Wagner, "Actors and Singers," in *Prose Works,* trans. W. Ashton Ellis, vol. 5 (London: Kegan Paul, Trench, Trübner, 1895; repr. in *Actors and Singers* [Lincoln: University of Nebraska Press, 1995]), esp. pp. 202–7.

39. Kravitt, *The Lied,* pp. 54, 302.

40. Nodnagel, "Das naturalistische Melodrama," p. 154. This work of Geisler's (1856–1919) appears not to have been published (as Nodnagel himself implies). Melodrama in this context refers specifically to the tradition or genre of using spoken dialogue over instrumental accompaniment, which flourished in France

and Germany in the late eighteenth century and was still employed in the early nineteenth century in operatic works by Beethoven (the Dungeon Scene in *Fidelio*) and Weber (the Wolf's Glen scene in *Der Freischütz*).

41. Nodnagel, "Das naturalistische Melodrama," p. 155.

42. Nodnagel, "Richard Strauss," in *Jenseits von Wagner und Liszt,* p. 95.

43. See his essay "Der Symbolismus in der Musik," in *Jenseits von Wagner und Liszt,* pp. 169–75, esp. p. 174. For a recent analysis of *Enoch Arden,* see Kravitt, *The Lied,* pp. 100–103.

44. See Kravitt, *The Lied,* p. 90.

45. Arnold Schoenberg, Preface to *Pierrot lunaire*, in *A Schoenberg Reader*, ed. Joseph Auner (New Haven: Yale University Press, 2003), p. 118.

46. Kravitt, *The Lied,* p. 64.

47. See Amanda Glauert, *Hugo Wolf and the Wagnerian Inheritance* (Cambridge: Cambridge University Press, 1999).

48. Lodato, "Richard Strauss and the Modernists," p. 160.

49. On French naturalist opera, see Steven Huebner, *French Opera at the Fin de Siècle : Wagnerism, Nationalism, and Style* (New York: Oxford University Press, 1999); and Jane Fulcher, *French Cultural Politics & Music: From the Dreyfus Affair to the First World War* (New York: Oxford University Press, 1999).

50. In his small book *Das Musikdrama der Gegenwart* of 1909, Paul Bekker identified Strauss, Pfitzner, and Schillings as the three finest post-Wagnerian composers of music drama. See Bekker, *Das Musikdrama der Gegenwart* (Stuttgart: Schreker & Schröder, 1909), p. 69. This book was written before Bekker's discovery of Schreker. Bekker's is one of a number of valuable contemporary studies on opera between the death of Wagner and the First World War. Others, some of which consist of collected criticism, include Rudolf Louis, *Die deutsche Musik der Gegenwart,* 3rd ed. (Munich: George Müller, 1912), pp. 47–133; Edgar Istel, *Die moderne Oper vom Tode Wagners bis zum Weltkrieg* (Leipzig: Teubner, 1915); and Julius Korngold, *Deutsches Opernschaffen der Gegenwart* (Leipzig: Leonhardt, 1921). For a revisionist view of Strauss's *Guntram,* see Charles Youmans, "Richard Strauss's *Guntram* and the Dismantling of Wagnerian Musical Metaphysics" (Ph.D. diss., Duke University, 1996). Youmans suggests that *Guntram* in fact is not epigonic, but is a critique of the Wagnerian *Erlösungsoper* and uses the Wagnerian style against itself.

51. For a helpful survey of German reception of *Cavalleria* and *Pagliacci,* see Ulla Zierau, *Die veristische Oper in Deutschland* (Frankfurt: Peter Lang, 1994), pp. 79–94. See also Josef-Horst Lederer, *Verismo auf der deutschsprachigen Opernbühne, 1891–1926* (Vienna: Bohlau, 1992). Zierau and Lederer, who both focus on professional music criticism, fail to discuss the writers in the main naturalist journals.

52. Hans Merian, "'Cavalleria rusticana,'" *Die Gesellschaft* 7 (1891): 1451–52.

53. Merian, "'Cavalleria,'" p. 1452.

54. Merian, "'Cavalleria,'" p. 1451.

55. Dahlhaus, *Realism,* p. 69.

56. Hans Merian, "Leoncavallo's 'Pagliacci' und die modern-realistische Oper," *Die Gesellschaft* 9 (1893): 734. Further references to this article will be given in the text.

57. Max Marschalk, "Nachträgliches zum Mascagni-Cultus," *Freie Bühne* 2 (1891): 1109–10.

58. Max Marschalk, "Mascagni und sein *Freund Fritz,*" *Freie Bühne* 3 (1892): 423.

59. Marschalk, "Mascagni," pp. 423–24.

60. Josef-Horst Lederer, "*Cavalleria Rusticana* auf Deutsch: Zu den Anfängen des deutschen realistischen Einakters im ausgehenden 19. Jahrhundert," in *Geschichte und Dramaturgie des Operneinakters,* ed. Winfried Kirsch and Sieghart Döhring (Laaber: Laaber Verlag, 1991), pp. 127–62.

61. Zierau, *Die veristische Oper,* pp. 138–39.

62. Zierau, *Die veristische Oper,* pp. 156–57, 192–93; see also Erik Levi, *Music in the Third Reich* (London: Macmillan, 1994), p. 193.

63. *Tosca* received its German premiere in Berlin on October 21, 1902. See Lederer, *Verismo auf der deutschsprachigen Opernbühne,* p. 161. (Lederer's facsimile of the original program seems to contradict his assertion elsewhere [p. 159] that *Tosca* had its premiere in Dresden.)

64. See Ingo Leiß and Hermann Stadler, *Deutsche Literaturgeschichte:* vol. 8, *Wege in die Moderne, 1890–1918* (Munich: Deutscher Taschenbuch Verlag, 1997), pp. 67–69.

65. See Sabine Hake, *German National Cinema* (London: Routledge, 2002), pp. 42–43.

66. See Robert von Dassanowsky, "'Wherever you may run, you cannot escape him': Leni Riefenstahl's Self-reflection and Romantic Transcendence of Nazism in *Tiefland,*" originally published in *Camera Obscura* 35 (1995–96); repr. at www.powernet.net/~hflippo/cinema/tiefland.html (August 16, 2003).

67. See Dassanowsky, "'Wherever you may run"; and Helma Sanders-Brahms, "Tyrannenmord: *Tiefland* von Leni Riefenstahl," in Sanders-Brahms, *Das Dunkle zwischen den Bildern,* ed. Norbert Grob (Frankfurt: Verlag der Autoren, 1992), pp. 245–50.

68. One of the few discussions in English of this aspect of d'Albert's operas is John Williamson, "Eugen d'Albert: Wagner and Verismo," *Music Review* 45 (1984): 26–46.

69. Zierau, *Die veristische Oper,* p. 182.

70. See *Richard Strauss–Max von Schillings: Ein Briefwechsel,* ed. Roswitha Schlötterer (Pfaffenhofen: W. Ludwig Verlag, 1987).

71. Karl Mennicke, *Über Max Schillings Mona Lisa* (Berlin: Drei Masken-Verlag, 1915), p. 3.

72. Mennicke, *Über Max Schillings Mona Lisa,* p. 35.

73. Zierau suggests that Francesco's behavior is "excusable or at least understandable" (*Die veristische Oper,* p. 201).

74. Mennicke, *Über Max Schillings Mona Lisa,* p. 41.

75. See the extensive correspondence with Strauss about the *Ariadne* premiere in *Richard Strauss–Max von Schillings,* pp. 151–72.

76. In June 1911, while at work on *Ariadne,* Strauss drew Hofmannsthal's attention to this very poem of Lorenzo's: see *A Working Friendship: The Correspondence between Richard Strauss and Hugo von Hofmannsthal,* trans. Hanns Hammelmann and Ewald Osers (New York: Vienna House, 1974), p. 89. Strauss may have been suggesting it as a model for some of the verses in the *Ariadne* libretto. It is certainly possible that Strauss mentioned Lorenzo's poem to Schillings as well.

77. See Christopher Hailey, *Franz Schreker, 1878–1934: A Cultural Biography* (Cambridge: Cambridge University Press, 1993), p. 21.

78. Franz Schreker, "Entstehungsfragen der Oper" (1930), cited in Ulrike Kienzle, *Das Trauma hinter dem Traum: Franz Schrekers Oper "Der ferne Klang" und die Wiener Moderne* (Schliengen: Argus, 1998), p. 104.

79. Hailey, *Franz Schreker,* p. 38.

80. See Kienzle, *Das Trauma hinter dem Traum,* p. 102. See also Carl Dahlhaus, "Schreker und die Moderne: Zur Dramaturgie des *Fernen Klangs,*" in Dahlhaus, *Vom Musikdrama zur Literaturoper* (Munich: Katzbichler, 1983), pp. 158–64.

81. See Franz Schreker, *Der ferne Klang: Oper in drei Aufzügen,* Studienpartitur (Schliengen: Argus, 1998), p. 11.

82. Hauptmann, *Einsame Menschen,* p. 1.

83. Kienzle, *Das Trauma hinter dem Traum,* p. 106.

84. Kienzle, *Das Trauma hinter dem Traum,* p. 128.

85. Kienzle, *Das Trauma hinter dem Traum,* pp. 151–52.

86. Kienzle, *Das Trauma hinter dem Traum,* p. 157.

87. Kienzle, *Das Trauma hinter dem Traum,* p. 27.

88. Theodor Adorno, "Schreker," in *Gesammelte Schriften,* vol. 16, ed. Rolf Tiedemann (Frankfurt: Suhrkamp, 1978), p. 370. This passage is badly garbled in the translation by Rodney Livingstone in Adorno, *Quasi una fantasia: Essays on Modern Music* (London: Verso, 1992), p. 132. Wagner's "note" *(Notiz)* probably refers to the discreet comments made by Gurnemanz and Parsifal about the appearance of nature on Good Friday; these contrast with the elaborate and (for Adorno) overdetermined stage directions provided by Schreker. I am grateful to John Deathridge for his assistance with interpreting Adorno's remark.

89. Walter Niemann, *Die Musik der Gegenwart,* 5th ed. (Berlin: Schuster & Loeffler, 1913), p. 121. See also Niemann's discussion of the "painterly" as an aspect of modern music (including Strauss's) on pp. 175–86. Niemann also writes here of "musical landscape painting" in works by Strauss and other composers.

90. For such aspects of the dramaturgy of *Salome,* see Wolfgang Krebs, "Zur musikalischen Dramaturgie von Richard Strauss' *Salome,*" in Kirsch and Döhring, *Geschichte und Dramaturgie des Operneinakters,* pp. 251–75.

91. Carolyn Abbate, "Opera; or, the Envoicing of Women," in *Musicology and Difference: Gender and Sexuality in Musical Scholarship,* ed. Ruth Solie (Berkeley: University of California Press, 1993), pp. 246–52.

92. Bekker, *Das Musikdrama der Gegenwart,* p. 45.

93. See John and Dorothy Crawford, *Expressionism in Twentieth-Century Music* (Bloomington: Indiana University Press, 1993), which also includes an extensive bibliography. See also *Expressionism Reassessed,* ed. Shulamith Behr, David Fanning, and Douglas Jarman (Manchester: Manchester University Press, 1993).

CHAPTER 3

1. Carl Dahlhaus, *Between Romanticism and Modernism: Four Studies in the Music of the Later Nineteenth Century,* trans. Mary Whittall (Berkeley: University of California Press, 1980), pp. 1–18; Dahlhaus, *Nineteenth-Century Music,* p. 362.

2. Theodor W. Adorno, "On Some Relationships between Music and Painting," trans. Susan Gillespie, in *Musical Quarterly* 79 (1995): 67. Further references will be given in the text. (The original German essay is "Über einige Relationen zwischen Musik und Malerei," in Adorno, *Gesammelte Schriften,* vol. 16, ed. Rolf Tiedemann [Frankfurt: Suhrkamp, 1978], pp. 628–42.)

3. The concept of "convergence" is proposed, apparently independently of Adorno and with a somewhat different meaning, by Philippe Junod in "The New *Paragone:* Paradoxes and Contradictions of Pictorial Musicalism," in *The Arts Entwined: Music and Painting in the Nineteenth Century,* ed. Marsha L. Morton and Peter L. Schmunk (New York: Garland, 2000), pp. 26–27. For Junod, convergence is one of four possible "rubrics" under which music and painting could interact in the nineteenth century: the others are parallelism, divergence, and succession. Another recent collection of essays that explore relationships between music and the visual arts is *Töne–Farben–Formen: Über Musik und die bildenden Künste,* ed. Elisabeth Schmierer, Susanne Fontaine, Werner Grünzweig, and Matthias Brzoska (Laaber: Laaber Verlag, 1995). See also Simon Shaw-Miller, *Visible Deeds of Music: Art and Music from Wagner to Cage* (New Haven: Yale University Press, 2002).

4. Wassily Kandinsky, *Complete Writings on Art,* ed. Kenneth C. Lindsay and Peter Vergo (New York: Da Capo Press, 1994), p. 153. Further references will be given in the text.

5. See the comprehensive bilingual catalogue and discussion of Schoenberg's paintings in *Arnold Schoenberg: Paintings and Drawings,* ed. Thomas Zaunschirm (Klagenfurt: Ritter Verlag, 1991). See also *Schoenberg, Kandinsky, and the Blue Rider,* ed. Esther da Costa Meyer and Fred Wasserman (London: Scala, 2003).

6. See the transcription of Schoenberg's interview with Halsey Stevens about the paintings, in *Arnold Schoenberg: Paintings and Drawings,* pp. 446–51.

7. In *Dialectic of Enlightenment,* Adorno and Horkheimer similarly write of "Wagner's dream" of the Gesamtkunstwerk. See Theodor Adorno and Max Horkheimer, *Dialectic of Enlightenment,* ed. Gunzelin Schmid Noerr, trans. Edmund Jephcott (Stanford: Stanford University Press, 2002), p. 97.

8. See Richard Wagner, "The Art-Work of the Future," in Wagner, *Prose Works,* trans. W. Ashton Ellis, vol. 1 (London: Kegan Paul, Trench, Trübner, 1895; repr. as *The Art-Work of the Future and Other Works* [Lincoln: University of Nebraska Press, 1993]), p. 190.

9. The massive catalog is *Der Hang zum Gesamtkunstwerk: Europäische Utopien seit 1800,* ed. Harald Szeemann (Aarau: Sauerländer, 1983).

10. *Gesamtkunstwerk: Zwischen Synästhesie und Mythos,* ed. Hans Günther (Bielefeld: Aisthesis, 1994).

11. Philipp Otto Runge, excerpts from a letter to his brother of 1802, included in Szeemann, *Der Hang zum Gesamtkunstwerk,* pp. 132, 137.

12. See Michael Lingner, "Die Musikalisierung der Malerei bei P. O. Runge," in Szeemann, *Der Hang zum Gesamtkunstwerk,* p. 150. Reproductions of the cycle are viewable at http://runge.de.ki (January 1, 2005).

13. The painting can be seen at www.onlinekunst.de/januar/21_01_3_Schwind.htm (January 1, 2005).

14. Schwind's description of *Eine Symphonie,* from a letter to Franz Schober, is given in *Neue Pinakothek: Erläuterung zu den Ausgestellten Werken* (Munich: Bayerische Staatsgemäldesammlungen, 1982), p. 304.

15. Peg Weiss, *Kandinsky in Munich: The Formative Jugendstil Years* (Princeton: Princeton University Press, 1979), pp. 7–8.

16. "Bei beiden [piano music and poetry] macht sich der Geber von den Interpretation Vieler, von den strengen Forderungen von Szene und Orchester frei, und darf in zwangloser Folge und Form, nur von ihrer Stärke geleitet, seine eigensten Freuden und Schmerzen, flüchtigsten und tiefsten Gefühle freikünsterlisch geben." Max Klinger, *Malerei und Zeichnung,* 6th ed. (Leipzig: Thieme, 1913), pp. 33, 21.

17. J. Kirk T. Varnedoe and Elizabeth Streicher, "Introduction," in *Graphic Works of Max Klinger* (New York: Dover, 1977), p. xix.

18. Varnedoe and Streicher, "Introduction," p. xv. One of the few recent art-historical considerations of Klinger is Jonathan Crary's sensitive analysis of *Der Handschuh* in his *Suspensions of Perception: Attention, Spectacle, and Modern Culture* (Cambridge, Mass.: MIT Press, 1999), pp. 128–34. See also Streicher, "Max Klinger's *Malerei und Zeichnung:* The Critical Reception of the Prints and Their Text," in Forster-Hahn, *Imagining Modern German Culture,* pp. 229–49.

19. See Ursula Kersten, *Max Klinger und die Musik* (Frankfurt: Peter Lang, 1993), vol. 2, pp. 17–46.

20. The history of the personal relationship between Brahms and Klinger is handsomely treated and documented in Jan Brachmann, *"Ins Ungewisse hinauf": Johannes Brahms und Max Klinger im Zwiespalt von Kunst und Kommunikation* (Kassel: Bärenreiter, 1999), pp. 23–53. Facsimiles of Klinger's unrealized sketches for title pages are in Kersten, *Max Klinger und die Musik,* vol. 2, pp. 30–32.

21. "reiche phantastische Erfindung, die zugleich von so schönem Ernst, von so bedeutender Tiefe ist und die dann so schön immer weiter denken und ahnen läßt." Cited in Brachmann, *"Ins Ungewisse hinauf,"* p. 38.

22. "gar zu rätselhaft und unverständlich." Cited in Brachmann, *"Ins Ungewisse hinauf,"* p. 38. The lithograph cover of op. 96 is reproduced in Kersten, *Max Klinger und die Musik,* vol. 2, p. 26; Kersten also reproduces (p. 30) Klinger's sketch for this lithograph, originally intended for an edition of op. 86.

23. See Varnedoe and Streicher, *Graphic Works of Max Klinger,* pp. 89 and 96–98. On the *Brahms Fantasy,* see also Karin Mayer-Pasinski, *Max Klingers Brahmsphantasie* (Frankfurt: Rita G. Fischer, 1982); and Thomas K. Nelson, "Klinger's *Brahmsphantasie* and the Cultural Politics of Absolute Music," *Art History* 19 (1996): 26–43, quotation from p. 28.

24. "Vor allem war es mir bei diesen Sachen nicht um 'Illustrations' zu thun, sondern darum, von den Entscheidungen aus, in die uns Dichtung und vor allem Musik zieht, uns blind zieht, Blicke über den Gefühlskreis zu werfen, und von da aus mitzusehen[,] weiterzuführen, zu verbinden oder zu ergänzen." Letter transcribed in Kersten, *Max Klinger und die Musik,* vol. 1, p. 166. According to Brachmann, the word *Entscheidungen* in this sentence has, up until Kersten's publication, also been transcribed or interpreted as *Empfindungen* (Brachmann, *"Ins Ungewisse hinauf,"* p. 41). In fact, *Empfindungen,* or feelings, might make more sense in this context.

25. "da mir für das Gesamte eine Idee zu Grunde lag, die wohl im Stimmungsgehalte Ihrer Werke vorhanden war, aber für diesen Fall unausgesprochen blieb." Brachmann, *"Ins Ungewisse hinauf,"* p. 41.

26. *Johannes Brahms an Max Klinger* (Leipzig: Klinger-Haus, 1924), p. 7. In the penultimate sentence, Brahms says, "manchmal, mich freuen, daß ich es nicht zu sein brauche," literally, "at other times I am glad I don't need to be it." By this he means, I take it, "to be an artist like you who can achieve such clarity by visual means." I have taken the liberty of translating *sein* as "do," which gives a similar sense more compactly.

27. This view of a two-part structure has semiofficial corroboration, in that it is given in the commentary to the *Brahms Fantasy* in Hans Wolfgang Singer, *Max Klinger: Radierungen, Stiche, und Steindrucke 1873–1903* (Berlin: Amsler und Ruthardt, 1909; trans. as *Etchings, Engravings and Lithographs, 1878–1903* [San Francisco: Alan Wofsy, 1991]), p. 243 (in the translation). Klinger worked closely

with Singer, and it is assumed by art historians that he either provided or approved of the designations (see Mayer-Pasinski, *Max Klingers Brahmsphantasie,* p. 11b).

28. See the discussion of various possible articulations of the *Brahms Fantasy* in Brachmann, *"Ins Ungewisse hinauf,"* pp. 121–35.

29. Nelson, "Klinger's *Brahmsphantasie.*"

30. Brachmann, *"Ins Ungewisse hinauf,"* p. 51.

31. Another recent study of Klinger's *Brahms Fantasy* is Beate Reifenscheid, "Kosmologiegedanken im Werk Max Klingers und Gustav Klimts," in *1900: Musik zur Jahrhundertwende,* ed. Werner Keil (Hildesheim: Olms, 1995), pp. 123–48.

32. Böcklin painted numerous versions of *Isle of the Dead;* they can be viewed at a Web site devoted entirely to this painting, www.die-toteninsel.de.vu (January 7, 2005).

33. *Im Spiel der Wellen* can be viewed at the Web site for the Neue Pinakothek: www.pinakothek.de/neue-pinakothek/ (January 7, 2005).

34. "Dieses weiche, zu weiche, zurückdenken an Vergangenes[-]Verlorenes durch kräftiges energisches Selbstaufraffen—wie es Ihr Lied 'Kein Haus keine Heimath', welches ich eben desswegen für mich allein stehen ließ, ausdrückt—in eine grössere energische und im Grunde doch verwandte Gefühlssphäre zu versetzen—das war mein Grundgedanke." Cited in Kersten, *Max Klinger und die Musik,* vol. 1, p. 166. Klinger's statement "allein stehen ließ" suggests that he never intended to provide illustrations for the song; thus, Varnedoe and Streicher may mislead readers when they write that "the prints to accompany the poem of Friedrich Halm ['Kein Haus, keine Heimath'] were never completed" (*Graphic Works of Max Klinger,* pp. 88–89).

35. Brachmann, *"Ins Ungewisse hinauf,"* p. 158.

36. A facsimile edition is Richard Strauss, *"Wir beide wollen springen": Ein Meisterlied aus der Zeit des Jugendstils,* ed. with an intro. by Alfons Ott (Tutzing: Hans Schneider 1968). See also Ludwig Finscher, "Richard Strauss and Jugendstil—The Munich Years," in *Art Nouveau and Jugendstil and the Music of the Early 20th Century, Adelaide Studies in Musicology* 13 (1984): 169–80 (facsimile on p. 179).

37. See *Mozarts Opern im Werk von Max Slevogt und Hans Meid* (Bad Honnef: Bock, 1996), pp. 77–123.

38. John Daverio, "The *Wechsel der Töne* in Brahms's *Schicksalslied,*" *Journal of the American Musicological Society* 46 (1993): 107.

39. Descriptive titles for each of the forty-one illustrations of the *Brahms Fantasy* appear in Singer, *Max Klingers Radierungen, Stiche und Steindrucke.*

40. Max Lehrs, "Max Klinger's 'Brahms-Phantasie,'" *Zeitschrift für Bildende Kunst* 6 (1895): 117. Lehrs notes that he consulted with Hans Singer (see p. 117, fn. 2), who was already planning a catalog of Klinger's graphic works, although

it was not to appear until 1909. These circumstances suggest that Lehrs's analysis of the iconography and meaning of the images in the *Brahms Fantasy* has some important connection with the artist's intentions.

41. See Jack Tresidder, *Dictionary of Symbols* (San Francisco: Chronicle Books, 1997), pp. 209–10.

42. Lehrs, "'Brahms-Phantasie,'" p. 117.

43. See Brachmann, *"Ins Ungewisse hinauf,"* p. 206, n. 37.

44. Daverio, "The *Wechsel der Töne,*" p. 107.

45. Brachmann, *"Ins Ungewisse hinauf,"* p. 208.

46. Brachmann, *"Ins Ungewisse hinauf,"* p. 211.

47. Max Schneider, *Arnold Böcklin: Ein Maler aus dem Geiste der Musik* (Basel: Holbein-Verlag, 1943).

48. See a thorough discussion in Schneider, *Arnold Böcklin.* For reproductions of several of these paintings, and an extensive account of Böcklin and his contemporaries, see *Kingdom of the Soul: Symbolist Art in Germany 1870–1920,* ed. Ingrid Ehrhardt and Simon Reynolds (Munich: Prestel, 2000).

49. Schneider, *Arnold Böcklin,* p. 67.

50. Klaus Schneider has compiled a helpful list of musical works based on paintings, including those of Böcklin, in *Vom Klang der Bilder: Die Musik in der Kunst des 20. Jahrhunderts,* ed. Karin von Maur (Munich: Prestel, 1985), pp. 452–60. Only Paul Klee rivals Böcklin among German modernists in the number of compositions created from his paintings.

51. Cited in Hans H. Hofstätter, "Symbolism in Germany and Europe," in Ehrhardt and Reynolds, *Kingdom of the Soul,* p. 9.

52. Cited in Ingrid Ehrhardt, "Kingdom of the Soul—An Introduction," in Ehrhardt and Reynolds, *Kingdom of the Soul,* p. 9.

53. For a helpful survey and discussion of the influence of Wagner on French symbolism, see David Michael Hertz, *The Tuning of the Word: The Musico-Literary Poetics of the Symbolist Movement* (Carbondale: University of Southern Illinois Press, 1987), esp. pp. 32–55. See also Gerald Turbow, "Art and Politics: Wagnerism in France," in *Wagnerism in European Culture and Politics,* ed. David C. Large and William Weber (Ithaca: Cornell University Press, 1984), pp. 134–66.

54. Ehrhardt, "Kingdom of the Soul," p. 9.

55. David Morgan, "The Idea of Abstraction in German Theories of Ornament from Kant to Kandinsky," *Journal of Aesthetics and Art Criticism* 50 (1992): 232.

56. Lipps, cited in Morgan, "The Idea of Abstraction," p. 234.

57. See Alois Riegl, *Late Roman Art Industry,* trans. Rolf Winkes (Rome: Giorgio Bretschneider, 1985), pp. xix–xx, 9–10.

58. Wilhelm Worringer, *Abstraction and Empathy,* trans. Michael Bullock (Chicago: Ivan R. Dee, 1997), p. 44.

59. Weiss, *Kandinsky in Munich;* Werner Hofmann, *Turning Points in*

Twentieth-Century Art: 1890–1917, trans. Charles Kessler (New York: Braziller, 1969).

60. There is by now a vast literature on the theory and practice of Jugendstil. The critical history of Jugendstil as a whole is traced in a comprehensive narrative bibliography by Jost Hermand, *Jugendstil: Ein Forschungsbericht, 1918–1964* (Stuttgart: Metzler, 1965). See also the useful anthology of criticism in *Jugendstil,* ed. Hermand, *Wege der Forschung 110* (Darmstadt: Wissenschaftliche Buchgesellschaft, 1971). More general surveys are Richard Hamann and Jost Hermand, *Stilkunst um 1900* (Berlin: Akademie Verlag, 1967), pp. 243–87; and Robert Schmutzler, *Art Nouveau* (New York: Abrams, 1962).

61. The painting and relief are reproduced in Weiss, *Kandinsky in Munich,* plates 48–49.

62. The *Cyclamen* tapestry can be viewed at http://mattis.kfki.hu/english/tanulman/4/31.html (October 20, 2003).

63. Schmutzler, *Art Nouveau,* p. 193.

64. Georg Fuchs, quoted in Weiss, *Kandinsky in Munich,* p. 33.

65. See Weiss, *Kandinsky in Munich,* p. 43 and figs. 32a–c.

66. Hölzel, from an article in *Kunst für Alle* (1904), cited in Weiss, *Kandinsky in Munich,* p. 43.

67. The Stuck painting can be viewed at www.gemaelde-kunstdrucke.de/Symbolismus/Franz_Stuck/Fruehling/Fruehling.htm (October 20, 2003).

68. *Riding Couple* and *Colorful Life,* as well as images of numerous other Kandinsky paintings, can be viewed at www.abcgallery.com/K/kandinsky/kandinsky.html (October 20, 2003).

69. Hans Hollander, *Music und Jugendstil* (Zurich: Atlantis-Verlag, 1975).

70. Hamann and Hermand, *Stilkunst um 1900,* p. 264.

71. Dahlhaus, *Nineteenth-Century Music,* p. 332.

72. Reinhold Brinkmann, "On the Problem of Establishing 'Jugendstil' as a Category in the History of Music—With a Negative Plea," in *Art Nouveau and Jugendstil and the Music of the Early 20th Century, Adelaide Studies in Musicology* 13 (1984): 31–35. Brinkmann also expresses skepticism (as well as curiosity) about the possibility of a musical Jugendstil in "Schönberg und George: Interpretation eines Liedes," in *Archiv für Musikwissenschaft* 26 (1969): 26–28.

73. Walter Frisch, "Music and Jugendstil," *Critical Inquiry* 17 (1990): 138–61.

74. August Endell, "Um die Schönheit," in Endell, *Vom Sehen,* ed. Helge David (Basel: Birkhäuser, 1995), p. 31. Further references will be given in the text.

75. For an account of the origins and development of the Munich Secession, see Makela, *The Munich Secession.*

76. Endell, "Formenschönheit und Dekorative Kunst," in *Vom Sehen,* p. 147. Further references will be given in the text.

77. Cited in Weiss, *Kandinsky in Munich,* p. 25.

78. See Gustav Vriessen, *August Macke* (Stuttgart: Kohlhammer, 1953), p. 83.

79. *August Macke, Franz Marc: Briefwechsel* (Cologne: M. Dumont Schauberg, 1964), p. 26. Further references will be given in the text.

80. The full concert, performed by the Rosé Quartet, Marie Gutheil-Schoder (soprano), and Etta Werndorff (piano), included the Second String Quartet, op. 10; Three Piano Pieces, op. 11; Five Lieder (*Erwartung,* op. 2, no. 1; *Verlassen,* op. 6, no. 4; *Am Wegrand,* op. 6, no. 6; *Mädchenlied,* op. 6, no. 3; and *Der Wanderer,* op. 6, no. 8); and the First String Quartet, op. 7. A facsimile of the program is in *Farben–Klänge: Wassily Kandinsky, Bilder 1908 bis 1914* (Riehen/Basel: Fondation Beyeler, 1998), p. 8; and in *Schönberg, Kandinsky, Blaue Reiter und die Russische Avantgarde* (Vienna: Arnold Schönberg Center, 2000 = *Journal of the Arnold Schönberg Center* 1 [2000]), p. 88. In some modern accounts (for example, *Arnold Schoenberg, Wassily Kandinsky: Letters, Pictures and Documents,* ed. Jelena Hahl-Koch, trans. John C. Crawford [London: Faber & Faber, 1984], p. 135), the date of the concert is mistakenly given as January 1. The printed program unambiguously states January 2.

81. *Schoenberg-Kandinsky Letters,* p. 21.

82. *Schoenberg-Kandinsky Letters,* p. 24. The sentences come from the segment on parallel octaves and fifths in Schoenberg, *Harmonielehre* (Leipzig: Universal, 1911), pp. 76, 81. The excerpt appeared as Schoenberg, "Über Oktaven- und Quinten-Parallelen: aus meiner Harmonielehre," *Die Musik* 10, no. 1 (1910): 96–105.

83. *Schoenberg-Kandinsky Letters,* p. 21.

84. My translation follows in part the excerpt in *Schoenberg-Kandinsky Letters,* p. 136. It is possible that "Kern-Seite" is a misprint for (or mistranscription of) "Kehr-Seite," which would mean the back or reverse side. "Kern-Seite," literally core side, does not make much obvious sense.

85. Sketches and surviving fragments of *Composition II* are reproduced in Jelena Hahl-Koch, *Kandinsky* (New York: Rizzoli, 1993), pp. 162–64.

86. See, for example, Klaus Kropfinger, "Latent Structural Power versus the Dissolution of Artistic Material in the Works of Kandinsky and Schönberg," in *Schönberg and Kandinsky: An Historic Encounter,* ed. Konrad Boehmer (Amsterdam: Harwood, 1997), p. 21.

87. On the Quartet, op. 7, see my *The Early Works of Arnold Schoenberg, 1893–1908* (Berkeley: University of California Press, 1993), pp. 181–219, and the literature cited there. See also Michael Cherlin, "Motive and Memory in Schoenberg's First Quartet," in *"Music of My Future": The Schoenberg Quartets and Trio,* ed. Reinhold Brinkmann and Christoph Wolff (Cambridge, Mass: Harvard University Department of Music, 2000), pp. 61–80.

88. Volker Klotz, "Jugendstil in der Lyrik," in Hermand, *Jugendstil,* pp. 362–65.

89. Richard Dehmel, *Bekenntnisse* (Berlin: Fischer, 1926), p. 21.

90. See Frisch, *Early Works,* p. 96.

91. See Weiss, *Kandinsky in Munich,* pp. 82–85.

92. For further analysis of Schoenberg's op. 15, no. 2, see Frisch, "Music and Jugendstil," pp. 154–59.

93. This painting has been often reproduced. The best color reproduction I have found is in von Maur, *Vom Klang der Bilder,* opposite p. 152. Other, lower-quality color reproductions are in Boehmer, *Schönberg and Kandinsky,* p. 22; and Hahl-Koch, *Schoenberg-Kandinsky Letters,* plate 15. The image is available online at numerous Web sites, including www.schoenberg.at/4_exhibits/asc/Kandinsky/Konzert.htm (October 20, 2003).

94. The sketch is located at the Musée National d'Art Moderne at the Centre Georges Pompidou, Paris (inventory number AM 81–65–196). The painting *Improvisation mit Pferden,* in which one can recognize especially the vertical figures of the "Andante," is repertoried and reproduced (in black and white) in Hans K. Roethel and Jean K. Benjamin, *Kandinsky: A Catalogue Raisonné of the Oil-Paintings* (Ithaca: Cornell University Press, 1982–), vol. 1, p. 378.

95. The sketches are inventoried as AM 81–65–198 and -199 at the Centre Pompidou. They have been reproduced in Hahl-Koch, *Kandinsky,* p. 152; and in *Schönberg, Kandinsky, Blaue Reiter und die Russische Avantgarde,* p. 108.

96. Hahl-Koch, *Kandinsky,* p. 153.

97. For the text of *Der gelbe Klang,* see *Schoenberg-Kandinsky Letters,* pp. 117–24.

98. See Sixten Ringbom, *The Sounding Cosmos: A Study of the Spiritualism of Kandinsky and the Genesis of Abstract Painting* (Åbo: Åbo Akademi, 1970); and Ringbom, "Transcending the Visible: the Generation of Abstract Pioneers," in *The Spiritual in Art: Abstract Painting, 1890–1950,* ed. Maurice Tuchman et al. (New York: Abbeville Press, 1986), pp. 131–53. The 1986 book was based on an exhibition at the Los Angeles County Museum of Art that took Ringbom's ideas as an organizing principle for a view of twentieth-century abstract art.

99. See Hahl-Koch, *Kandinsky,* pp. 177, 386–87.

100. Rose-Carol Washton Long, *Kandinsky: The Development of an Abstract Style* (New York: Oxford University Press, 1980); Hahl-Koch, *Kandinsky,* pp. 386–87. See also Washton Long's article "Expressionism, Abstraction, and the Search for Utopia in Germany," in Tuchman et al., *The Spiritual in Art,* pp. 201–17.

101. Hahl-Koch, *Kandinsky,* pp. 386–87.

CHAPTER 4

1. Nietzsche, *The Birth of Tragedy and The Case of Wagner,* pp. 166, 170.

2. Max Nordau, *Degeneration,* intro. by George L. Mosse (Lincoln: University of Nebraska Press, 1993). See the useful anthology of essays about degeneration, *Degeneration: The Dark Side of Progress,* ed. J. Edward Chamberlin and Sander L. Gilman (New York: Columbia University Press, 1985).

3. In an earlier article of mine, from which portions of this chapter are adapted

("Reger's Bach and Historicist Modernism," *19th-Century Music* 25 [2001–2002]: 296–312), I believed I had coined the term "historicist modernism," but I have recently learned that the term was used, in a much more general way, in a German article from 1996 of which I was unaware: Dirk Niefanger, "Historische und historistische Verfahren: Skizzenhaftes zu Paul Ernst und Hugo von Hofmannsthal im Kontext einer 'historistischen' Moderne," in *Historismus und Moderne*, ed. Harald Tausch (Würzburg: Ergon, 1996), pp. 181–90. I am grateful to Antonius Bittmann for drawing my attention to that article and collection.

4. "Praeludium," in *Die Musik* 1, no. 1 (1901): 1–2.

5. Ludwig Finscher, "Bach's Posthumous Role in Music History," in *Bach Perspectives,* vol. 3, ed. Michael Marissen (Lincoln: University of Nebraska Press, 1998), p. 5. Finscher points out that until recently, most studies of Bach reception have focused on verbal rather than musical aspects, that is, on theoretical or critical responses.

6. Wilibald Nagel, "Johann Sebastian Bach und die Deutsche Musik der Gegenwart," *Die Musik* 1, no. 3 (1901): 207.

7. "Was ist mir Johann Sebastian Bach und was bedeutet er für unsere Zeit?" *Die Musik* 5, no. 1 (1905): 3.

8. Albert Schweitzer, *J. S. Bach,* trans. [from the German ed.] Ernest Newman (Boston: Humphries, 1911), vol. 2, p. 468.

9. See Peter Ostwald, *Schumann: The Inner Voices of a Musical Genius* (Boston: Northeastern University Press, 1985), p. 200. At about this time Schumann composed several fugues based on the name BACH (op. 60), as well as the studies and sketches for pedal piano (opp. 56 and 58).

10. Cited in Siegmund Helms, "Johannes Brahms und Johann Sebastian Bach," *Bach-Jahrbuch* 57 (1971): 13.

11. For a brief history of the critical reception of *Salome,* see the essay by John Williamson in *Richard Strauss: Salome,* ed. Derrick Puffett (Cambridge: Cambridge University Press, 1989), pp. 131–44. See also the sampling of reviews from Vienna translated in *Richard Strauss and His World,* ed. Bryan Gilliam (Princeton: Princeton University Press, 1992), pp. 333–49.

12. Draeseke's article and the subsequent responses are collected and placed in historical context in the valuable volume *"Die Konfusion in der Musik": Felix Draeseke's Kampfschrift von 1906 und ihre Folgen,* ed. Susanne Shigihara (Bonn: Gudrun Schröder Verlag, 1990).

13. "Satzungen der Neuen Bachgesellschaft," in Arnold Schering, *Die neue Bachgesellschaft, 1900–1910* (Leipzig: Breitkopf & Härtel, 1911), p. 21.

14. Arnold Schering, ed., "Mitgliedversammlung der Neuen Bach-Gesellschaft," in *Bach-Jahrbuch* 5 (1908): 149.

15. "Mitgliedversammlung der Neuen Bach-Gesellschaft," pp. 151–52.

16. Schering, *Die neue Bachgesellschaft,* pp. 17–18.

17. Rudolf Stephan, "Max Regers Kunst im 20. Jahrhundert," in Stephan,

Musiker der Moderne: Porträts und Skizzen, ed. Albrecht Riethmüller (Laaber: Laaber Verlag, 1996), p. 37; Stephan, "Schoenberg and Bach," in *Schoenberg and His World,* ed. Walter Frisch (Princeton: Princeton University Press, 1999), p. 126.

18. August Halm, *Von zwei Kulturen der Musik,* 3rd ed. (Stuttgart: Klett, 1947), p. 33.

19. Halm, *Von zwei Kulturen,* pp. 148, 206, 218.

20. Rudolf Stephan, "Johann Sebastian Bach und die Anfänge der Neuen Musik," in Stephan, *Vom musikalischen Denken: Gesammelte Vorträge,* ed. Rainer Damm and Andreas Traub (Mainz: Schott, 1985), p. 22.

21. Cited in Ernst Kurth, *Selected Writings,* ed. and trans. Lee A. Rothfarb (Cambridge: Cambridge University Press, 1991), p. 21. For an assessment of Kurth's thought, see, in addition to Rothfarb's illuminating comments in this volume, his *Ernst Kurth as Theorist and Analyst* (Philadelphia: University of Pennsylvania Press, 1988).

22. Kurth, *Selected Writings,* p. 20.

23. Kurth, *Selected Writings,* pp. 27, 49.

24. Rudolf Stephan, "Schoenberg and Bach," p. 127. On the subject of Schoenberg's (and Webern's) relationship to Bach, see also Elmar Budde, "Bach-Aneignung: Zur Bach-Rezeption Schönbergs und Weberns," in *Bach und die Moderne,* ed. Dieter Schnebel (Wiesbaden: Harrassowitz, 1995), pp. 83–97.

25. Arnold Schoenberg, *Theory of Harmony,* trans. Roy E. Carter (Berkeley: University of California Press, 1978), pp. 318, 329.

26. Schoenberg, *Theory of Harmony,* p. 328.

27. Arnold Schoenberg, "Linear Counterpoint: Linear Polyphony," in Schoenberg, *Style and Idea: Selected Writings of Arnold Schoenberg,* ed. Leonard Stein (New York: St. Martin's Press, 1975), pp. 295–97. As Lee Rothfarb points out, Kurth was heavily criticized for his emphasis on linearity, and he defended himself by saying that he had not sought to ignore the harmonic aspects of Bach but to provide a corrective to a contemporary view weighted too much toward harmony (Kurth, *Selected Writings,* p. 26).

28. Schoenberg, "New Music, Outmoded Music, Style and Idea," in Schoenberg, *Style and Idea,* p. 118. See also Schoenberg's essay of 1950, "Bach," in *Style and Idea,* pp. 393–97, esp. p. 397, where he also mentions developing variation. Schoenberg's view of Bach's thematic art is perhaps best documented not in his prose writing, where he never lavished on Bach the kind of detailed analysis he did on Brahms or Mozart, but in his later orchestral arrangements of Bach organ works. In 1922 he orchestrated two chorale preludes, *Komm, Gott, Schöpfer, heiliger Geist* (BWV 631) and *Schmücke dich, o liebe Seele* (BWV 654); six years later, in 1928, he arranged the "St. Anne" Prelude and Fugue (BWV 552). As Klaus Velten and Rudolf Stephan have shown, Schoenberg uses the full resources of the modern orchestra to illuminate and to analyze Bach's melodic processes. In all these works Schoenberg frequently divides up Bach's continuous lines into

individual motives and then assigns those motives to different tone colors. (See Klaus Velten, *Schönbergs Instrumentationen Bachscher und Brahmsscher Werke als Dokumente seines Traditionsverständnisses* [Regensburg: Bosse, 1976]; and Stephan, "Schoenberg and Bach.") The effect, as in Webern's famous orchestration of Bach's six-part ricercar of 1934–35, is the transformation of Bach's thematic shapes into a *Klangfarbenmelodie.*

29. Paul Bekker, "Neue Musik," in Bekker, *Gesammelte Schriften,* Vol. 3: *Neue Musik* (Stuttgart: Deutsche Verlags-Anstalt, 1923), pp. 100–101.

30. Bekker, "Neue Musik," pp. 102, 100.

31. Carl Dahlhaus and Friedhelm Krummacher, "Historismus," in *Die Musik in Geschichte und Gegenwart,* ed. Ludwig Finscher (Kassel: Bärenreiter, 1994–), vol. 4, col. 335. Further references will be given in the text. For further discussion of musical historicism, see Dahlhaus, *Foundations of Music History,* trans. J. Bradford Robinson (Cambridge: Cambridge University Press, 1983); *Die Ausbreitung des Historismus über die Musik,* ed. Walter Wiora (Regensburg: Bosse, 1969); and Leo Treitler, *Music and the Historical Imagination* (Cambridge, Mass.: Harvard University Press, 1989). On historicism more generally within German thought, see Georg Iggers, *The German Conception of History: The National Tradition of Historical Thought from Herder to the Present,* rev. ed. (Wesleyan: Wesleyan University Press, 1983); and Reinhart Koselleck, *Futures Past: On the Semantics of Historical Time,* trans. Keith Tribe (Cambridge, Mass.: MIT Press, 1985).

32. Schoenberg, *Nacht,* from *Pierrot lunaire* (1912), and Passacaglia for Orchestra (fragment from 1926); Berg, *Altenberg* Lieder, op. 4, no. 5 (1912); Webern, Passacaglia for Orchestra, op. 1 (1908); Reger, finale of First Organ Suite, op. 16 (1895); Zemlinsky, finale of Symphony in B♭ (1897).

33. Cited in Johannes Lorenzen, *Max Reger als Bearbeiter Bachs* (Wiesbaden: Breitkopf & Härtel, 1982), p. 86.

34. "Seb. Bach ist für mich Anfang und Ende aller Musik; auf ihm ruht und fusst *jeder* **wahre** Fortschritt! Was Seb. Bach für unsere Zeit bedeutet—pardon—bedeuten **sollte**? Ein gar kräftiges, nie versiegendes Heilmittel nicht nur für alle jene Komponisten und Musiker, die an 'missverstandenem Wagner' erkrankt sind, sondern für alle jene 'Zeitgenossen,' die an Rückenmarkschwindsucht jeder Art leiden. 'Bachisch' sein heisst: *urgermanisch, unbeugsam* sein. Dass Bach *so* lange verkannt sein konnte, ist die *grösste Blamage* für die 'kritische Weisheit' des 18. und 19. Jahrhunderts." *Die Musik* 5, no. 1 (1905): 74.

35. Lorenzen, *Max Reger als Bearbeiter Bachs,* p. 55.

36. Lorenzen, *Max Reger als Bearbeiter Bachs,* p. 52.

37. Antonius Bittmann, *Max Reger and Historicist Modernisms* (Baden-Baden: Koerner, 2004), chap. 5 (revision of Ph.D. diss., Eastman School of Music, 2000). On Reger's Bach reception, see also Helmut Wirth, "Der Einfluss von Johann Sebastian Bach auf Max Regers Schaffen," in *Max Reger 1873–1973: Ein Sympo-*

sion, ed. Klaus Röhring (Wiesbaden: Breitkopf & Härtel, 1974), pp. 3–20; and Friedhelm Krummacher, "Auseinander im Abstand: Über Regers Verhältnis zu Bach," in *Reger-Studien 5,* ed. Susanne Shigihara (Wiesbaden: Breitkopf & Härtel, 1993), pp. 11–39.

38. For more details, see Lorenzen, *Max Reger als Bearbeiter Bachs,* pp. 18–25.

39. See Lorenzen, *Max Reger als Bearbeiter Bachs,* pp. 59–60.

40. Lorenzen, *Max Reger als Bearbeiter Bachs,* p. 30.

41. Hugo Riemann, "Degeneration und Regeneration in der Musik," in *Max Hesses Deutscher Musikerkalender für das Jahr 1908,* repr. in Shigihara, *"Die Konfusion in der Musik,"* p. 249.

42. Max Reger, "Degeneration und Regeneration in der Musik," *Neue Musik-Zeitung* 29 (1907): 49–51; repr. in Shigihara, *"Die Konfusion in der Musik,"* pp. 250–58.

43. Cited in Hermann Wilske, *Max Reger—Zur Rezeption in seiner Zeit* (Wiesbaden: Breitkopf & Härtel, 1995), p. 104.

44. The titling of multimovement organ works was fairly fluid in the nineteenth century. Reger even quipped that "our organ sonatas are really closer to suites" (cited in Martin Weyer, *Die Orgelwerke Max Regers* [Wilhelmshaven: Florian Noetzel, 1989], p. 31).

45. Anonymous review of 1 July 1896, repr. in Reger, *Der junge Reger: Briefe und Dokumente vor 1900,* ed. Susanne Popp (Wiesbaden: Breitkopf & Härtel, 2000), p. 275.

46. Max Reger, *Briefe eines deutschen Meisters: ein Lebensbild,* ed. Else von Hase-Koehler (Leipzig: Koehler & Amelang, 1928), p. 54. Despite Reger's strong advocacy, the four-hand arrangement was not published. See Reger, *Der junge Reger,* pp. 280–82.

47. Reger, *Der junge Reger,* p. 246. Reger refers, of course, to Bach's Passacaglia and Fugue in C Minor (BWV 582), a work he arranged for four-hand piano at this time (see Lorenzen, *Max Reger als Bearbeiter Bachs,* p. 18). By counting twenty-one variations in Bach, Reger seems to consider the initial thematic statement as a variation. In the Bach there are twenty-one total statements of the theme, and twenty actual "variations." Reger seems to reckon his own passacaglia in a similar way; yet he is nonetheless in error, unless he is referring to an earlier version of the passacaglia that no longer survives. Reger's movement, as it appears in the original manuscript and in printed editions, has twenty-nine variations, or thirty total statements of the theme. It is hard to see how he comes up with the number thirty-two.

48. Reger, *Der junge Reger,* p. 265. The letter is misdated as March 1897 in Reger, *Briefe eines deutschen Meisters,* pp. 54–55.

49. The photographs exchanged by Brahms and Reger are reproduced in Reger, *Der junge Reger,* p. 274.

50. Weyer, *Orgelwerke,* p. 17.

51. See Russell Stinson, *Bach: The Orgelbüchlein* (New York: Schirmer, 1996), pp. 70–73.

52. See Lorenzen, *Max Reger als Bearbeiter Bachs,* pp. 19–20. The arrangement for string orchestra has been given a ravishing (if slow) recording by Dennis Russell Davies and the Stuttgart Chamber Orchestra (Dabringhaus and Grimm, MDG 321 0940–2). The similarity of Reger's Adagio to Bach's "O Mensch" is noted by Rudolf Huesgen ("Der junge Reger und seine Orgelwerke" [Ph.D. diss., Freiburg, 1935], p. 72), who, however, does not comment on either the identity of tempo indication or Reger's later arrangements of the chorale prelude.

53. Huesgen, "Der junge Reger," p. 72.

54. To avoid confusion, I refer to this chorale tune by the more general designation, as the Passion chorale, following *J. S. Bach,* ed. Malcolm Boyd with John Butt (Oxford: Oxford University Press, 1999), p. 361, because it is associated in Bach's work with several different texts (including, in the *St. Matthew Passion,* "O Haupt voll Blut," "Herzlich tut mich verlangen," and "Wenn ich einmal soll scheiden").

55. In all the literature on Brahms's passacaglia, I have not seen the Rheinberger movement mentioned as a possible source, although it appeared two years before Brahms began to work on his finale. (For an assessment of the likely inspirations for Brahms, see Raymond Knapp, "The Finale of Brahms's Fourth Symphony: The Tale of the Subject," *19th-Century Music* 13 [1988]: 3–17.) It is certainly possible that Brahms knew the Rheinberger Sonata. Weyer (*Die Orgelwerke,* p. 26) adduces another possible source for Reger, a passacaglia theme in B minor from an organ work by Gustav Merkel, composed in 1885, which seems to borrow from both Bach and Brahms.

56. Max Reger, *Briefe an Karl Straube,* ed. Susanne Popp (Bonn: Dümmler, 1986), pp. 61, 63.

57. Reger did not actually seek out this theme himself; it was suggested (and sent) to him by his friend, the pianist August Schmid-Lindner, who was also the dedicatee and first performer of the work.

58. Elmar Budde, "Zeit und Form in Max Regers *Variationen und Fuge über ein Thema von Johann Sebastian Bach* op. 81," in *Reger-Studien 3: Analysen und Quellenstudien,* ed. Susanne Popp and Susanne Shigihara (Wiesbaden: Breitkopf & Härtel, 1988), p. 129. Budde's phrase "horizon of expectations" refers to Hans Robert Jauss's reception theory.

59. Cited in Budde, "Zeit und Form," p. 134.

60. Hofmannsthal, *Lord Chandos Letter,* p. 21.

61. Letters cited in Susanne Popp, "Preface" to Max Reger, *Concerto for Piano and Orchestra, F minor, Op. 114* (London: Eulenberg, 1990), p. VII.

62. Susanne Popp, "Destabilisierung als Kompositionsidee: zum langsamen Satz von Regers *Klavierkonzert,*" in Susanne Shigihara, ed., *Reger-Studien 5* (Wiesbaden: Breitkopf & Härtel, 1993), p. 231.

63. Cited in Popp, "Destabilisierung," p. 236.

64. Alan Walker, *A Study in Musical Analysis* (London: Barrie and Rockliff, 1962), pp. 76–77.

65. Cited in Popp, "Destabiliserung," p. 236.

66. Popp, "Destabiliserung," p. 232.

67. Cited in Popp, "Preface" to Reger, *Concerto,* p. x.

68. On Liszt's relationship to the music of Bach, see Michael Heinemann, "Bach : Liszt," in *Bach und die Nachwelt,* ed. Michael Heinemann and Hans-Joachim Hinrichsen, 4 vols. (Laaber: Laaber Verlag, 1997–), vol. 2, pp. 127–62.

69. See Hans-Joachim Hinrichsen, "Zwischen Bearbeitung und Interpretation: Zum Praktischen Umgang mit Bachs Instrumentalwerk," in Heinemann and Hinrichsen, *Bach und die Nachwelt,* vol. 2, pp. 374–83.

70. Hinrichsen, "Zwischen Bearbeitung und Interpretation," pp. 375–76.

71. Larry Sitsky, *Busoni and the Piano* (New York: Greenwood Press, 1986), p. 181; Albrecht Riethmüller, *Ferruccio Busonis Poetik* (Mainz: Schott, 1988), pp. 13–30.

72. For complete bibliographic details on Busoni's editions of Bach, see Sitsky, *Busoni and the Piano,* pp. 177–206.

73. All Busoni's arrangements of Bach are listed and discussed by Sitsky, *Busoni and the Piano,* chaps. 11 and 16.

74. See Sitsky, *Busoni and the Piano,* p. 188.

75. Complete bibliographic information on the versions of the *Fantasia Contrappuntistica* is given in Sitsky, *Busoni and the Piano,* pp. 139–62.

76. Ferruccio Busoni, *Sketch for a New Aesthetic of Music,* trans. Theodore Baker, in *Three Classics in the Aesthetics of Music* (New York: Dover, 1962), p. 17.

77. Ferruccio Busoni, *The Essence of Music and Other Papers,* trans. Rosamond Ley (New York: Dover, 1965), p. 1.

78. Busoni, *Sketch,* pp. 75–76, 78.

79. Busoni, *Essence of Music,* p. 3.

80. This melody, which appears in the *Klavierbüchlein* with an unfigured bass line, is not strictly speaking a chorale; it was referred to variously in the eighteenth and nineteenth centuries as a "sacred song," an "aria," a "sacred aria," and a chorale. See Riethmüller, *Busonis Poetik,* p. 141.

81. Riethmüller, *Busonis Poetik,* p. 156.

82. Letter cited in Albrecht Riethmüller, "Bach in Busonis 2. Violinsonate," in *Jahrbuch des Staatlichen Instituts für Musikforschung Preußischer Kulturbesitz 1995,* ed. Günther Wagner (Stuttgart: Metzler, 1995), p. 65.

83. Antony Beaumont, *Busoni the Composer* (London: Faber & Faber, 1985), p. 54.

84. Riethmüller, *Busonis Poetik,* p. 132.

85. Riethmüller, *Busonis Poetik,* p. 153.

86. Cited in Riethmüller, "Zu den Transkriptionen Bachscher Orgelwerke

durch Busoni und Reger," in *Reger-Studien 3: Analysen und Quellenstudien,* ed. Susanne Popp and Susanne Shigihara (Wiesbaden: Breitkopf & Härtel, 1988), p. 138.

87. The most widely available version of the *Fantasia Contrappuntistica* is in Busoni, *The Complete Elegies, the Six Sonatinas, and Other Original Works for Solo Piano* (New York: Dover, 1996). Confusingly, the editors identify this as the "3rd final version, 1912," while it seems in fact to correspond to the version published by Breitkopf & Härtel in 1910 and normally considered the definitive one (as described by Sitsky, *Busoni and the Piano,* pp. 147–50). See Sitsky, *Busoni and the Piano,* pp. 158–59, for a tabular comparison of the different versions of the *Fantasia.* The 1910 definitive edition is dedicated to Middelschulte as "master of counterpoint."

88. See Beaumont, *Busoni,* pp. 161–63.

89. Beaumont, *Busoni,* p. 170.

90. Alma Mahler, *Gustav Mahler: Memories and Letters,* ed. Donald Mitchell, trans. Basil Creighton (Seattle: University of Washington Press, 1975), p. 45.

91. See Henry-Louis de la Grange, *Gustav Mahler,* vol. 2, *Vienna: The Years of Challenge, 1897–1904* (New York: Oxford University Press, 1995), pp. 359–60. On Mahler and Bach, see also Donald Mitchell, *Gustav Mahler: The Wunderhorn Years* (Boulder: Westview Press, 1976), pp. 345–62; and Philipp Otto Naegele, *Gustav Mahler & Johann Sebastian Bach* (Northampton, Mass.: Smith College, 1983).

92. Gérard Genette, *Palimpsests: Literature in the Second Degree* (Lincoln: University of Nebraska Press, 1997).

93. These thematic relationships are traced and demonstrated in Bernd Sponheuer, *Logik des Zerfalls: Untersuchungen zum Finaleproblem in den Symphonien Gustav Mahlers* (Tutzing: Hans Schneider, 1978), pp. 237–67. See also Carolyn Baxendale, "The Finale of Mahler's Fifth: Long Range Musical Thought," *Journal of the Royal Musical Association* 112 (1987–88): 257–79.

CHAPTER 5

1. Erich Heller, *The Ironic German: A Study of Thomas Mann* (London: Secker & Warburg, 1958), p. 23.

2. Thomas Mann, "The Sorrows and Grandeur of Richard Wagner," in Mann, *Pro and Contra Wagner,* trans. Allan Blunden (Chicago: University of Chicago Press, 1985), pp. 100–101.

3. Steven P. Scher, *Verbal Music in German Literature* (New Haven: Yale University Press, 1968), p. 8. Scher devotes one chapter (chap. 6) to an account of Wagner's act 3 Prelude to *Meistersinger,* as described in verbal music by Adrian Leverkühn in *Doktor Faustus.*

4. See, for example, Hermann Fähnrich, *Thomas Manns episches Musizieren*

im Sinne Richard Wagners (Frankfurt: Herchen, 1986). See also Frank W. Young, *Montage and Motif in Thomas Mann's "Tristan"* (Bonn: Bouvier, 1975). In his chapter "The Musical Quality in Mann's Prose" (pp. 59–69), Young discusses some of the literature that has treated musical structures in Mann's works. He himself provides as an appendix a "thematic-motivic register" for *Tristan* (pp. 124–42). Mann quoted in Young, *Montage and Motif*, p. 59.

5. Mann's irony has been the subject of a number of studies. In addition to Heller, see Reinhard Baumgart, *Das Ironische und die Ironie in den Werken Thomas Manns* (Munich: Carl Hanser, 1964); Helmut Koopmann, "Thomas Mann: Theorie und Praxis der epischen Ironie," in *Deutsche Romantheorien,* ed. Reinhold Grimm, 2nd ed. (Frankfurt: Athenäum Fischer, 1974), vol. 2, pp. 318–40; and Käte Hamburger, *Der Humor bei Thomas Mann* (Munich: Nymphenburger Verlag, 1965). For general accounts of the concept and practice of irony, two of the most helpful in English are D. C. Muecke, *The Compass of Irony* (London: Methuen, 1969), and Wayne C. Booth, *A Rhetoric of Irony* (Chicago: University of Chicago Press, 1974).

6. Cited in Ernst Behler, *Ironie und literarische Moderne* (Paderborn: Schöningh, 1997), p. 98. Behler's is the most comprehensive historically oriented study of modern irony, including Schlegel's irony, that I have found. See also Behler's briefer study in English, *Irony and the Discourse of Modernity* (Seattle: University of Washington Press, 1990). An excellent anthology of writings by Schlegel and other German Romantic ironists translated into English is *German Aesthetic and Literary Criticism: The Romantic Ironists and Goethe,* ed. Kathleen Wheeler (Cambridge: Cambridge University Press, 1984).

7. Georg Wilhelm Friedrich Hegel, *Lectures on the History of Philosophy,* trans. E. S. Haldane (Lincoln: University of Nebraska Press, 1995), vol. 1, p. 401.

8. See Behler, *Ironie,* pp. 232–34. The term "world irony" had already been used in a similar sense by Jean Paul in his *School for Aesthetics* of 1804. See Jean Paul, *Horn of Oberon: Jean Paul Richter's School for Aesthetics,* trans. Margaret Hale (Detroit: Wayne State University Press, 1973), p. 113.

9. Nietzsche, "On the Utility and Liability of History for Life," in his *Unfashionable Observations,* pp. 115, 138, 146.

10. Nietzsche, *Thus Spoke Zarathustra,* in *The Portable Nietzsche,* pp. 294, 342, 406.

11. Nietzsche, *Nachgelassene Fragmente 1884–1885, Kritische Studienausgabe,* vol. 11, p. 571. Behler makes some errors in his citation of this passage in *Ironie,* p. 272.

12. Mann, *Reflections of a Nonpolitical Man,* trans. Walter D. Morris (New York: Ungar, 1983), p. 13.

13. Thomas Mann, "Die Kunst des Romans," in Mann, *Gesammelte Werke* (Frankfurt: S. Fischer, 1960), vol. 10, p. 353.

14. Mann, "Humor und Ironie," in Mann, *Gesammelte Werke,* vol. 11, pp. 802, 803.

15. Mann, *Reflections,* pp. 71–106. Further references will be given in the text.

16. Thomas Mann, *Buddenbrooks,* trans. John E. Woods (New York: Alfred Knopf, 1993), p. 347ff. Woods's translation, though the best currently available, is defective in some respects, especially in its rendering of Mann's passages of detailed musical description. Further references to this translation will be given in the text, which will be amended where necessary in light of the original German, cited from Mann, *Gesammelte Werke,* vol. 1.

17. Richard Wagner, *Prelude and Transfiguration from Tristan und Isolde,* ed. and trans. Robert Bailey (New York: Norton, 1985), p. 47. The original German is in Wagner, *Sämtliche Schriften,* vol. 12, pp. 344–45.

18. On the genesis of *Tristan,* see the helpful volume of documentary and commentary, Thomas Mann, *Tristan: Erläuterungen und Dokumente,* ed. Ulrich Dittmann (Stuttgart: Reclam, 1971). This is a companion to the text volume, *Tristan* (Stuttgart: Reclam, 1950). Comprehensive bibliographies of writings on Mann's *Tristan* can be found in *Tristan: Erläuterungen und Dokumente,* p. 95; and Young, *Montage and Motif.*

19. Sophia Schnitman, "Musical Motives in Thomas Mann's *Tristan,*" in *Modern Language Notes* 86 (1971): 399.

20. Thomas Mann, *Death in Venice and Other Stories,* trans. David Luke (New York: Bantam Books, 1988), p. 100. Further references to this edition will be given in the text.

21. Schnitman, "Musical Motives," p. 407.

22. E. Th. Scheltinga Koopman, "Die Funktion der Musik in Thomas Manns 'Tristan' und 'Zauberberg,'" *Duitse Kroniek* 17 (1965): 96.

23. Cited in Karsten Witte, "'Das ist echt! Eine Burleske!' Zur *Tristan*-Novelle von Thomas Mann," *German Quarterly* 41 (1968): 661.

24. Witte, "'Das ist echt!'" pp. 661, 662. For a theoretical and historical account of burlesque, see John D. Jump, *Burlesque* (London: Methuen, 1972).

25. Simon Dentith, *Parody* (London: Routledge, 2000), pp. 19, 9.

26. Margaret A. Rose, *Parody: Ancient, Modern, and Post-modern* (Cambridge: Cambridge University Press, 1993), p. 45.

27. These distinctions were formulated in Genette, *Palimpsests,* and are summarized in Dentith, *Parody,* p. 11.

28. Rose, *Parody,* pp. 40–41.

29. Rose acknowledges the possibility of three (or more) text-worlds (*Parody,* p. 41).

30. See Linda Hutcheon, *A Theory of Parody: The Teachings of Twentieth-Century Art Forms* (New York: Methuen, 1985), pp. 5, 51–52.

31. Hutcheon, *A Theory of Parody,* pp. 52, 32.

32. For an imaginative discussion of the how Mann's story can be mapped

quite precisely onto Wagner's first act, see Laurence Dreyfus, "Music and Motive in Thomas Mann's *Wälsungenblut,*" in *London German Studies* 8 (2003): 86–113.

33. Thomas Mann, "Blood of the Wälsungs," in *Death in Venice and Seven Other Stories,* trans. H. T. Lowe-Porter (New York: Vintage, 1989), pp. 311–12. Further references will be given in the text.

34. *Gustav Mahler et l'ironie dans la culture viennoise au tournant du siècle: Actes du Colloque Gustav Mahler Montpellier 1996,* ed. André Castagné, Michel Chalon, and Patrick Florençon (Castelnau-le-Lez: Éditions Climats, 2001).

35. Stephen Hefling, "Techniques of Irony in Mahler's Oeuvre," in Castagné et al., *Gustav Mahler et l'ironie,* p. 99.

36. Jean Paul, *Horn of Oberon,* p. 111

37. See the account in Ute Jung-Kaiser's comprehensive study, "Die wahren Bilder und Chiffren 'tragischer Ironie' in Mahlers 'Erster,'" in *Neue Mahleriana,* ed. Günther Weiß (Berne: Peter Lang, 1997), pp. 109–13. See also Herta Blaukopf, "Jean Paul, die erste Symphonie und Dostojewski," in *Gustav Mahler: Werk und Wirken,* ed. Erich Wolfgang Partsch (Vienna: Vom Pasqualatihaus, 1996), pp. 35–42; Henry Louis de La Grange, *Gustav Mahler: Chronique d'une Vie,* vol. 1, rev. ed. (Paris: Fayard, 1979), pp. 969–72; and Mitchell, *Gustav Mahler,* pp. 225–35.

38. William J. McGrath, *Dionysian Art and Populist Politics in Austria* (New Haven: Yale University Press, 1974). See esp. chap. 2, "Nietzsche as Educator," and chap. 5, "The Metamusical Cosmos of Gustav Mahler."

39. Mitchell, *Gustav Mahler,* p. 154.

40. Henri-Louis de La Grange, *Mahler* (Garden City, N.Y.: Doubleday, 1973), plate 47 (before p. 545).

41. De La Grange, *Mahler,* pp. 601–2. On ironic aspects of the First Symphony, see also Alain Leduc, "L'esprit de l'ironie dans la Première Symphonie de Gustav Mahler," in Castagné et al., *Gustav Mahler et l'ironie,* pp. 143–57.

42. See Stuart Feder, "Gustav Mahler: The Mind of the Ironist," in Castagné et al., *Gustav Mahler et l'ironie,* pp. 63–65.

43. Hefling, "Techniques of Irony," p. 114.

44. Theodor Adorno, *Mahler: A Musical Physiognomy,* trans. Edmund Jephcott (Chicago: University of Chicago Press, 1992), p. 56.

45. Adorno, *Mahler,* p. 96.

46. Manfred Angerer, "Ironisierung der Konvention und Humoristische Totalität: Über den Ersten Takte von Gustav Mahlers IV. Symphonie," in *Vergleichend-systematische Musikwissenschaft: Beiträge zu Methode und Problematik der systematischen, ethnologischen und historischen Musikwissenschaft,* ed. Elisabeth Hilscher and Theophil Antonicek (Tutzing: Hans Schneider, 1994), pp. 567, 577–78.

47. Angerer, "Ironisierung," p. 569.

48. Here Angerer ("Ironisierung," p. 570) surely errs in interpreting the structure as 4 + 4 + 6. The final six-measure phrase is extended a measure through rhythmic repetition (thus to 7), bringing the tonic in on the downbeat of the fifteenth measure of the theme (or m. 18 of the movement), as indicated in example 34.

49. See my article, " 'You Must Remember This': Memory and Structure in Schubert's String Quartet in G Major, D. 887," *Musical Quarterly* 84 (2000): 582–603.

50. The concept of "breakthrough" or *Durchbruch* seems first to have been articulated by Paul Bekker (*Gustav Mahler's Sinfonien* [Berlin: Schuster & Loeffler, 1921], pp. 44, 221) and then was taken up by Adorno (*Mahler,* pp. 5–6).

51. De La Grange, *The Years of Challenge,* pp. 402, 400. The quoted account of the Fourth, by a French-Swiss musician named William Ritter, is remarkable for its vivid prose and level of detail. Critical reactions to the Fourth are summarized and cited on pp. 395–416.

52. Cited in de La Grange, *Mahler,* p. 402.

53. Jonathan Kramer, "Postmodern Concepts of Musical Time," *Indiana Theory Review* 17 (1996): 34–45.

54. Felix Adler, "Mahler's 'Seventh Symphony'," in *Mahler and His World,* ed. Karen Painter (Princeton: Princeton University Press, 2002), pp. 319–20.

55. Elsa Bienenfeld, "Mahler's Seventh Symphony," in Painter, ed., *Mahler and His World,* p. 326.

56. Adorno, *Mahler,* pp. 136–37. A helpful critical survey of responses to the finale of the Seventh is Hermann Danuser, "Erkenntnis oder Verblendung? Zum Problem des Sachgehaltes polemischer und apologetischer Musikkritik—am Beispiel einiger früher Rezeptionszeugnisse zu Mahlers Siebenten Symphonie," in *The Seventh Symphony of Gustav Mahler: A Symposium,* ed. James L. Zychowicz (Cincinnati: College-Conservatory of Music, 1990), 107–23.

57. Kramer, "Postmodern Concepts of Musical Time," p. 47.

58. Martin Scherzinger, "The Finale of Mahler's Seventh Symphony: A Deconstructive Reading," *Music Analysis* 14 (1995): 85.

59. The Mozart allusion (which is also perhaps a more general reference to "Turkish" music as represented by the Classical composers) is at m. 87ff. of Mahler's finale. See Hefling, "Techniques of Irony," pp. 125–29. The Lehar allusion is shown (rather unpersuasively, to my mind) in Henry-Louis de La Grange, "Music about Music in Mahler: Reminiscences, Allusions, or Quotations?" in *Mahler Studies,* ed. Stephen Hefling (Cambridge: Cambridge University Press, 1997), p. 166.

60. Cited in Danuser, "Erkenntis oder Verblendung?" p. 121.

61. Carl Dahlhaus, *Richard Wagner's Music Dramas,* trans. Mary Whittall (Cambridge: Cambridge University Press, 1979), p. 75.

CHAPTER 6

1. See Peter de Mendelssohn, *Der Zauberer: Das Leben des Deutschen Schriftstellers Thomas Mann,* vol. 1 (Frankfurt: S. Fischer, 1975), pp. 754–57; Thomas Mann, *Briefwechsel mit Autoren,* ed. Hans Wysling (Frankfurt: Fischer 1988), pp. 195–226.

2. Wysling, in Mann, *Briefwechsel mit Autoren,* p. 197.

3. Mann, *Briefwechsel mit Autoren,* p. 202.

4. Mann, *Briefwechsel mit Autoren,* p. 202.

5. Bryan Gilliam, *The Life of Richard Strauss* (Cambridge: Cambridge University Press, 1999), p. 89.

6. Hugo von Hofmannsthal, "Der Rosenkavalier: Zum Geleit" (1927), in Hofmannsthal, *Sämtliche Werke,* vol. 23 (*Operndichtungen,* vol. 1), ed. Dirk O. Hoffmann and Willi Schuh (Frankfurt: S. Fischer, 1986), p. 549.

7. *A Working Friendship: The Correspondence between Richard Strauss and Hugo von Hofmannsthal,* trans. Hanns Hammelmann and Ewald Osers (New York: Vienna House, 1974), pp. 67, 68; *Richard Strauss–Hugo von Hofmannsthal Briefwechsel: Gesamtausgabe,* ed. Franz and Alice Strauss, with Willi Schuh (Zurich: Atlantis, 1955), pp. 86, 88.

8. Mention of the *Meistersinger* quintet is made in the Strauss-Hofmannsthal correspondence early in the collaboration, when Strauss asks Hofmannsthal to create if possible a "contemplative ensemble passage" at the end of act 2 and suggests Wagner's quintet as a possible model (*A Working Friendship,* p. 33; *Briefwechsel,* p. 51). No such ensemble was written for act 2, but the idea seems to have made its way to the end of the opera.

9. Willi Schuh, *Der Rosenkavalier: Vier Studien* (Olten: Vereinigung von Freunden der Oltner Liebhaberdrucke, 1968), p. 34; Lewis Lockwood, "The Element of Time in *Der Rosenkavalier,*" in *Richard Strauss: New Perspectives on the Composer and His Work,* ed. Bryan Gilliam (Durham: Duke University Press, 1992), pp. 252–55; and Norman del Mar, *Richard Strauss* (Ithaca: Cornell University Press, 1986), vol. 1, p. 411.

10. Willi Schuh is one of the few commentators to have observed and named as parody what occurs at the opening of *Rosenkavalier.* See his brief remarks in Schuh, *Der Rosenkavalier,* pp. 30–31.

11. "Schlafzimmer der Marquise. Liebesnacht. Morgen. Dank." Hofmannsthal, *Sämtliche Werke,* vol. 23, p. 156.

12. Hugo von Hofmannsthal, *Gesammelte Werke, Dramen V: Operndichtungen,* ed. Bernd Schoeller (Frankfurt: Fischer, 1979), pp. 11–12; Richard Wagner, *Tristan und Isolde: Texte, Materialen, Kommentare,* ed. Attila Csampai and Dietmar Holland (Reinbek: Rowohlt, 1983), pp. 61–73.

13. Hofmannsthal, *Sämtliche Werke,* vol. 23, pp. 93–94.

14. In a diary entry of November 4, 1910, well after the completion of the libretto, Hofmannsthal noted: "Similarity: the figure of the Marschallin in *Rosenkavalier* with that of Hans Sachs in *Meistersinger.* Renounces, and marries the young people to each other. Is the spiritual bond of the whole thing, is the main figure and yet not the hero." Hofmannsthal, *Sämtliche Werke,* vol. 23, p. 661. The extensive parallels with *Meistersinger* in the plot of *Rosenkavalier* (Marschallin = Sachs; Octavian = Walter; Sophie = Eva; Ochs = Beckmesser) have been noted by Roland Tenschert, whose arguments are summarized by Norman del Mar in *Richard Strauss,* vol. 1, pp. 349–50.

15. *Working Friendship,* p. 76; *Briefwechsel,* p. 95.

16. *Working Friendship,* p. 82; *Briefwechsel,* p. 102.

17. Richard Strauss, *Betrachtungen und Erinnerungen,* ed. Willi Schuh (Munich and Mainz: Piper and Schott, 1989), p. 241. Cited in English from del Mar, *Richard Strauss,* vol. 2, p. 9.

18. The long process of genesis and revision of *Ariadne* have been well covered in monographs, articles, and other sources. In English, see especially Donald G. Daviau and George J. Buelow, *The* Ariadne auf Naxos *of Hugo von Hofmannsthal and Richard Strauss* (Chapel Hill: University of North Carolina Press, 1975); and Karen Forsyth, Ariadne auf Naxos *by Hugo von Hofmannsthal and Richard Strauss* (Oxford: Oxford University Press, 1982). The best account, however, with much information about sources and origins not available elsewhere, is in the critical matter accompanying the libretto in Hugo von Hofmannsthal, *Sämtliche Werke,* vol. 24, ed. Manfred Hoppe (Frankfurt: S. Fischer, 1985), pp. 59–95.

19. "Secco recitative streng im Rytmus." Letter to Franz Schalk of June 7, 1916. Cited in Hofmannsthal, *Sämtliche Werke,* vol. 24, p. 223.

20. *Working Friendship,* p. 258; *Briefwechsel,* p. 353.

21. See, for example, his comments in an article in the *Neue Freie Presse* of Vienna in May 1912, reprinted in Hofmannsthal, *Sämtliche Werke,* vol. 24, p. 188.

22. The original 1912 ending of the libretto is given in *Sämtliche Werke,* vol. 24, pp. 149–50. A recording of the opera in its original form was made in 1997 by Kent Nagano and Opéra National de Lyon (Virgin 7243 5 45111 2 7).

23. The extent of Zerbinetta's final reprise—even its presence at all—was a source of friction between the collaborators. See *Working Friendship,* pp. 246–47; *Briefwechsel,* pp. 285–87.

24. Hofmannsthal, "Angaben für die Gestaltung des Dekorativen in 'Ariadne,'" in *Gesammelte Werke, Dramen V,* p. 294. The Metropolitan Opera production of 1962, with sets designed by Oliver Messel (available on video and DVD in a 1988 staging conducted by James Levine [DGG 440 073 028–9]), preserved the sense of a stage within the stage and actually included some boxes at the sides. These are not occupied by any independent spectators or supernumeraries (as Hofmannsthal proposes), but the commedia players appear in them to observe Ariadne during parts of the opera. The current Met production that replaced

the earlier one in the 1990s, produced by Elijah Moshinsky, with sets by Michael Yeargan, is visually stunning, but it considerably mutes or dissolves the stage-within-a-stage aspects of the opera.

25. Hofmannsthal, *Gesammelte Werke, Dramen V,* p. 294.

26. *Working Friendship,* p. 94; *Briefwechsel,* p. 116, italics added. The version of the *Ariadne* Letter as published in 1913 in the *Almanach für die Musikalische Welt* is given in Hofmannsthal, *Sämtliche Werke,* vol. 24, pp. 204–7. The passage cited is on p. 205.

27. Forsyth, *Ariadne auf Naxos,* p. 197.

28. Cited in Forsyth, *Ariadne auf Naxos,* p. 199. Translation amended.

29. Gilliam, *Life of Richard Strauss,* p. 89.

30. Leon Botstein, "The Enigmas of Strauss: A Revisionist View," in *Richard Strauss and His World,* ed. Bryan Gilliam (Princeton: Princeton University Press, 1992), p. 21.

31. Samuel Lublinski, *Ausgang der Moderne* (1909), cited in Ruprecht and Bänsch, *Literarische Manifeste der Jahrhundertwende, 1890–1910,* p. xxxiv.

32. Paul Ernst, *Ariadne auf Naxos,* in Ernst, *Dramen,* vol. 2 (Munich: Langen/Müller, 1932–33). See also Horst Thomé, "Ariadne bei Paul Ernst und Hugo von Hofmannsthal: Konzepte der Metatragik nach 1900," in *Paul Ernst: Außenseiter und Zeitgenosse,* ed. Horst Thomé (Würzburg: Königshausen & Neumann, 2001), pp. 37–60.

33. See especially Walter Jens, *Hofmannsthal und die Griechen* (Tübingen: Max Niemeyer, 1955); and Karl Esselborn, *Hofmannsthal und der Antike Mythos* (Munich: Fink, 1969).

34. Hoppe's discussion is in Hofmannsthal, *Sämtliche Werke,* vol. 24, pp. 94–95. Blei's text appeared in Blei, *Vermischte Schriften,* vol. 4: *Das schwere Herz: Zwiesprachen und Gedichte* (Munich: Georg Müller, 1911), pp. 323–54. Hoppe also points to an even earlier English work, *Scaramouch in Naxos* of 1888 by John Davidson, in which Scaramouch is also an impresario who arrives on Naxos to recruit Bacchus and Ariadne for his troupe.

35. "Ein Gott macht sicher weniger / Geschichten als heut ein Komödiant." Blei, *Vermischte Schriften,* vol. 4, p. 337.

36. "Ariadne? Zu der Musik? / Der macht der Richard Strauss mir besser." Blei, *Vermischte Schriften,* vol. 4, p. 345.

37. *Ariadne auf Naxos: ein tragikomisches Drama* (Berlin: Theater-Buchhandlung Eduard Bloch, [1893]). This was published as vol. 38 of a series called Fastnachts-Bühne, together with a "carnival revue" by Wilhelm Frerking (b. 1852), who does not, however, seem to be the author of the Ariadne parody in the same volume.

38. "Geliebt' Ariadne mein! Du schläfst ja wie ein Sack, / Du ahntest Theseus nicht in seinem Reise-Frack. / Träumst Du von mir?—Du schnarchst?—O, Töne die mich rühren!" *Ariadne auf Naxos,* p. 17.

39. "Er kommt, ein Held, vom Scheitel bis zur Spitz, / Er eilt herab, in Donner und Blitz!" *Ariadne auf Naxos,* p. 22.

40. *Ariadne auf Naxos,* p. 25.

41. Lilith Friedmann, "Die Gestaltungen des Ariadne-Stoffes von der Antike bis der Neuzeit" (Ph.D. diss., University of Vienna, 1933), cited in Forsyth, *Ariadne auf Naxos,* p. 25. See also the *New Grove Dictionary of Opera,* ed. Stanley Sadie (London: Macmillan, 1992), vol. 1, s.v. "Ariadne" (p. 178), and the various Ariadne operas with separate entries on pp. 178–86.

42. See Strauss's suggestions to Hofmannsthal, made early in the collaboration, about what numbers to study to get an idea of how to fashion the text for Zerbinetta's aria (*Working Friendship,* p. 82). A fine article that investigates how Zerbinetta's rondo imitates less specific pieces than it does vocal styles practiced around 1900 by singers like Selma Kurz and Frieda Hempel is Anne C. Shreffler, "The Coloratura's Voice: Another Look at Zerbinetta's Aria from *Ariadne auf Naxos,*" in *Richard Strauss und die Moderne: Bericht über das Internationale Symposium München, 21. bis 23. Juli 1999,* ed. Bernd Edelmann, Birgit Lodes, and Reinhold Schlötterer (Berlin: Henschel, 2001), pp. 361–90.

43. Stefan Kunze, "Die ästhetische Rekonstruktion der Oper: Anmerkungen zur 'Ariadne auf Naxos,'" in *Hofmannsthal und das Theater,* ed. Wolfram Mauser (Vienna: Halosar, 1981), p. 170.

44. Kunze, "Die ästhetische Rekonstruktion," pp. 170, 171.

45. The allusions to the Rhinemaidens were noticed by William Mann (*Richard Strauss: A Critical Study of the Operas* [New York: Oxford University Press, 1966], p. 160.) It is striking—and perhaps characteristic of the failure of many critics to recognize the character of quotation that lies at the core of this opera—that Daviau and Buelow (*Ariadne auf Naxos,* p. 172) take pains to deny this obvious relationship. For them, there is no resemblance in melodic shape, phrase pattern, tonality, or harmony between Strauss's nymphs and Wagner's Rhinemaidens: hence there can be no relationship.

46. Even the skeptical Daviau and Buelow are compelled to acknowledge this very obvious quotation. See Daviau and Buelow, *Ariadne auf Naxos,* p. 203. See also Günther von Noé, "Das Zitat bei Richard Strauss," *Neue Zeitschrift für Musik* 125 (1964): 236.

47. Del Mar, *Richard Strauss,* vol. 2, p. 31.

48. *Working Friendship,* p. 82; *Briefwechsel,* p. 102.

49. Daviau and Buelow, *Ariadne auf Naxos,* pp. 173–74. Karl Gräwe proposes a simpler three-part division of the Monologue: A ("Ach! Wo war ich?"), B ("Ein Schönes war"), C ("Es gibt ein Reich"). See Karl Gräwe, "Sprache, Musik und Szene in 'Ariadne auf Naxos' von Hugo von Hofmannsthal und Richard Strauss" (Ph.D. diss., Munich, 1969), p. 191.

50. It is surprising to me that no author has picked up on the references to Pamina. The only exception, to the best of my knowledge, is Gräwe, who, how-

ever, seems not to recognize the allusion, but only a "similar situation" between Ariadne and Pamina. Gräwe is interested in making a comparison but not in entertaining the possibility of quotation. See Gräwe, "Sprache, Musik und Szene," p. 208.

51. I am grateful to Giorgio Biancorosso for suggesting this compelling interpretation of the harmonium accompaniment at this moment. I am also grateful to John W. Hill for pointing out to me that "palimpsest" may not be the most appropriate metaphor for Strauss's score and other works that are historically layered in a self-conscious, intentional way. As Hill suggests, a palimpsest is a document in which the various layers of writing were not intended to be read, but survive essentially by accident. With that caveat duly noted, however, I will stay with Genette's attractive metaphor in this study.

52. See Charlotte E. Erwin, "Richard Strauss's Presketch Planning for *Ariadne auf Naxos,*" *Musical Quarterly* 67 (1981): 350, 357–59. Erwin, who discusses the G♭–G minor shift in some detail, does not mention the Mozartian allusion. Strauss makes a similar G♭ $^{6}_{4}$ to G-minor $^{6}_{4}$ shift, at the words "stille Höhle wird mein Grab," at three measures before reh. 67, where Ariadne's reference to the "grave" evokes a musical response similar to that for "eine Tote sein."

53. See Erwin, "Presketch Planning," p. 357. In the very first thoughts that Strauss sketched onto the scenario *(Szenarium)* sent him by Hofmannsthal in May 1911, the composer had written that the "Introduction" (presumably the Overture) was to begin in a "melancholy C minor." (See Willi Schuh, "Zu Hofmannsthals 'Ariadne'-Szenarium und -Notizen," *Die neue Rundschau* 71 [1960]: 92.) By the time of his annotations to the libretto in June-July 1911, Strauss had already settled on G minor (as shown in Erwin).

54. Kunze ("Die ästhetische Rekonstruktion," p. 174) is the only critic that seems to pick up on Strauss's *Lohengrin* references.

55. Compare the full score as reprinted by Dover in 1993, where the dialogue is still to be seen (p. 103), and the more recent Richard Strauss Edition printed from the same plates (Vienna: Verlag Dr. Richard Strauss, 1996), where it has disappeared.

56. Hans Pfitzner, "Futuristengefahr," cited in Marc A. Weiner, *Undertones of Insurrection: Music, Politics, and the Social Sphere* (Lincoln: University of Nebraska Press, 1993), p. 48.

57. For a helpful discussion of the relationship between Pfitzner's libretto and the facts—or at least better-known facts—about the historical Palestrina, see Gottfried Scholz, "The Image of Giovanni Pierluigi da Palestrina in Pfitzner's *Palestrina,*" *Musical Quarterly* 85 (2001): 76–83.

58. See chap. 4, at n. 31.

59. Michael P. Steinberg, "Opera and Cultural Analysis: The Case of Hans Pfitzner's *Palestrina,*" *Musical Quarterly* 85 (2001): 56, 58.

60. Mann, *Reflections,* p. 306.

61. Mann, *Reflections,* p. 311.

62. John Williamson, *The Music of Hans Pfitzner* (Oxford: Clarendon Press, 1992), pp. 186–87. On *Palestrina,* see also Owen Toller, *Pfitzner's Palestrina: The "Musical Legend" and Its Background* (London: Toccata Press, 1997).

63. Mann, *Reflections,* p. 298.

64. Cited in Williamson, *Hans Pfitzner,* p. 188.

65. See Williamson, *Hans Pfitzner,* p. 189.

66. Williamson, *Hans Pfitzner,* p. 189.

67. Mann, *Reflections,* pp. 311, 312–13.

68. Thomas Mann, *The Magic Mountain,* trans. John E. Woods (New York: Alfred Knopf, 1995), p. 706.

69. Hans Pfitzner, *Briefe,* ed. Bernhard Adamy (Tutzing: Hans Schneider, 1991), p. 405.

70. *Letters of Thomas Mann, 1889–1955,* ed. Richard and Clara Winston (New York: Alfred Knopf, 1971), p. 145. Original German in Thomas Mann, *Briefe, 1889–1936,* ed. Erika Mann (Berlin: Fischer, 1978), p. 241.

71. *Letters of Thomas Mann,* p. 146; original German in Mann, *Briefe,* p. 242.

BIBLIOGRAPHY

Abbate, Carolyn. *Unsung Voices: Opera and Musical Narrative in the Nineteenth Century.* Princeton: Princeton University Press, 1991.

Adorno, Theodor W. *Mahler: A Musical Physiognomy.* Translated by Edmund Jephcott. Chicago: University of Chicago Press, 1992.

———. "On Some Relationships between Music and Painting" [1965]. Translated by Susan Gillespie. *Musical Quarterly* 79 (1995): 66–79.

———. "On the Score of 'Parsifal'" [1956]. Translated, with commentary, by Anthony Barone. *Music & Letters* 76 (1995): 384–97.

———. *Quasi una fantasia: Essays on Modern Music.* Translated by Rodney Livingstone. London: Verso, 1992.

Adorno, Theodor, and Max Horkheimer. *Dialectic of Enlightenment.* Edited by Gunzelin Schmid Noerr. Translated by Edmund Jephcott. Stanford: Stanford University Press, 2002.

Anderson, Benedict. *Imagined Communities.* Revised edition. London: Verso, 1991.

Angermuller, Rudolph, Franz Hermann Franken, and Hars Jurgen Imiela. *Mozarts Opern im Werk von Max Slevogt und Hans Meid.* Bad Honnef: Bock, 1996.

Applegate, Celia, and Pamela Potter, eds. *Music and German National Identity.* Chicago: University of Chicago Press, 2002.

Ariadne auf Naxos: ein tragikomisches Drama. Berlin: Theater-Buchhandlung Eduard Bloch, 1893.

August Macke, Franz Marc: Briefwechsel. Cologne: M. Dumont Schauberg, 1964.

Auner, Joseph. *A Schoenberg Reader.* New Haven: Yale University Press, 2003.

Bahr, Hermann. *Zur Überwindung des Naturalismus: Theoretische Schriften 1887–1904.* Edited by Gotthart Wunberg. Stuttgart: Kohlhammer, 1968.

Baumgart, Reinhard. *Das Ironische und die Ironie in den Werken Thomas Manns.* Munich: Carl Hanser, 1964.

Baxendale, Carolyn. "The Finale of Mahler's Fifth: Long Range Musical Thought." *Journal of the Royal Musical Association* 112 (1987–88): 257–79.

Beaumont, Antony. *Busoni the Composer.* London: Faber & Faber, 1985.

Beckett, Lucy. *Richard Wagner: Parsifal.* Cambridge: Cambridge University Press, 1981.

Behler, Ernst. *Ironie und literarische Moderne.* Paderborn: Schöningh, 1997.

———. *Irony and the Discourse of Modernity.* Seattle: University of Washington Press, 1990.

Behr, Shulamith, David Fanning, and Douglas Jarman, eds. *Expressionism Reassessed.* Manchester: Manchester University Press, 1993.

Bekker, Paul. *Gesammelte Schriften.* Vol. 3, *Neue Musik.* Stuttgart: Deutsche Verlags-Anstalt, 1923.

———. *Gustav Mahler's Sinfonien.* Berlin: Schuster & Loeffler, 1921.

———. *Das Musikdrama der Gegenwart.* Stuttgart: Schreker & Schröder, 1909.

Bent, Ian, ed. *Music Theory in the Age of Romanticism.* Cambridge: Cambridge University Press, 1996.

Berghahn, Volker. *Imperial Germany, 1871–1914: Economy, Society, Culture, and Politics.* Providence: Berghahn Books, 1994.

Bie, Oskar. "Der Naturalismus in der Musik." *Die Gesellschaft* 1 (1885): 399–400.

Bittmann, Antonius. *Max Reger and Historicist Modernisms.* Baden-Baden: Koerner, 2004.

Blackbourn, David. *The Long Nineteenth Century: A History of Germany, 1790–1914.* New York: Oxford University Press, 1998.

Blei, Franz. *Vermischte Schriften.* Vol. 4, *Das schwere Herz: Zwiesprachen und Gedichte.* Munich: Georg Müller, 1911.

Bleibtreu, Karl. *Der Kampf ums Dasein der Literatur* (1888). Reprinted in *Theorie des Naturalismus,* edited by Theo Meyer, pp. 123–26. Stuttgart: Reclam, 1973.

———. "Realismus und Naturwissenschaft." In *Literarisch-kritische Rundschau* 1 (1888). Reprinted in *Theorie des Naturalismus,* edited by Theo Meyer, pp. 121–22. Stuttgart: Reclam, 1973.

Boehmer, Konrad, ed. *Schönberg and Kandinsky: An Historic Encounter.* Amsterdam: Harwood, 1997.

Bonds, Mark Evan. *After Beethoven: Imperatives of Originality in the Symphony.* Cambridge, Mass.: Harvard University Press, 1996.

Booth, Wayne C. *A Rhetoric of Irony.* Chicago: University of Chicago Press, 1974.

Boyd, Malcolm, ed., with John Butt. *J. S. Bach.* Oxford: Oxford University Press, 1999.

Brachmann, Jan. *"Ins Ungewisse hinauf": Johannes Brahms und Max Klinger im Zwiespalt von Kunst und Kommunikation.* Kassel: Bärenreiter, 1999.

Brahms, Johannes. *Johannes Brahms an Max Klinger.* Leipzig: Klinger-Haus, 1924.
Brands, Heinz-Georg. *Theorie und Stil des sogenannten "Konsequenten Naturalismus" von Arno Holz und Johannes Schlaf.* Bonn: Bouvier, 1978.
Brinkmann, Reinhold. "On the Problem of Establishing 'Jugendstil' as a Category in the History of Music—With a Negative Plea." *Art Nouveau and Jugendstil and the Music of the Early 20th Century. Adelaide Studies in Musicology* 13 (1984): 31–35.
———. "Schönberg und George: Interpretation eines Liedes." *Archiv für Musikwissenschaft* 26 (1969): 26–28.
Brinkmann, Reinhold, and Christoph Wolff, eds. *"Music of My Future": The Schoenberg Quartets and Trio.* Cambridge, Mass: Harvard University Department of Music, 2000.
Brunner, Otto, Werner Conze, and Reinhard Koselleck, eds. *Geschichtliche Grundbegriffe.* Stuttgart: Klett-Cotta, 1978.
Busoni, Ferruccio. *The Essence of Music and Other Papers.* Translated by Rosamond Ley. New York: Dover, 1965.
———. *Sketch for a New Aesthetic of Music.* Translated by Theodore Baker. In *Three Classics in the Aesthetics of Music.* New York: Dover, 1962.
Castagné, André, Michel Chalon, and Patrick Florençon, eds. *Gustav Mahler et l'ironie dans la culture viennoise au tournant du siècle. Actes du Colloque Gustav Mahler Montpellier 1996.* Castelnau-le-Lez: Éditions Climats, 2001.
Chamberlin, J. Edward, and Sander L. Gilman, eds. *Degeneration: The Dark Side of Progress.* New York: Columbia University Press, 1985.
Cox, Christopher. *Nietzsche: Naturalism and Interpretation.* Berkeley: University of California Press, 1999.
Crary, Jonathan. *Suspensions of Perception: Attention, Spectacle, and Modern Culture.* Cambridge, Mass.: MIT Press, 1999.
Crawford, John, and Dorothy Crawford. *Expressionism in Twentieth-Century Music.* Bloomington: Indiana University Press, 1993.
Da Costa Meyer, Esther, and Fred Wasserman, eds. *Schoenberg, Kandinsky, and the Blue Rider.* London: Scala, 2003.
Dahlhaus, Carl. *Between Romanticism and Modernism: Four Studies in the Music of the Later Nineteenth Century.* Translated by Mary Whittall. Berkeley: University of California Press, 1980.
———. *Foundations of Music History.* Translated by J. Bradford Robinson. Cambridge: Cambridge University Press, 1983.
———. *Nineteenth-Century Music.* Translated by J. Bradford Robinson. Berkeley: University of California Press, 1989.
———. *Realism in Nineteenth-Century Music.* Translated by Mary Whittall. Cambridge: Cambridge University Press, 1985.
———. *Richard Wagner's Music Dramas.* Translated by Mary Whittall. Cambridge: Cambridge University Press, 1979.

———. *Vom Musikdrama zur Literaturoper.* Munich: Katzbichler, 1983.

Dassanowsky, Robert von. "'Wherever you may run, you cannot escape him': Leni Riefenstahl's Self-reflection and Romantic Transcendence of Nazism in *Tiefland.*" Originally published in *Camera Obscura* 35 (1995–96); repr. at www.powernet.net/~hflippo/cinema/tiefland.html (August 16, 2003).

Daverio, John. "The *Wechsel der Töne* in Brahms's *Schicksalslied.*" *Journal of the American Musicological Society* 46 (1993): 85–113.

Daviau, Donald G., and George J. Buelow. *The* Ariadne auf Naxos *of Hugo von Hofmannsthal and Richard Strauss.* Chapel Hill: University of North Carolina Press, 1975.

Dehmel, Richard. *Bekenntnisse.* Berlin: Fischer, 1926.

Del Mar, Norman. *Richard Strauss.* 3 vols. Ithaca: Cornell University Press, 1986.

De Mendelssohn, Peter. *Der Zauberer: Das Leben des Deutschen Schriftstellers Thomas Mann.* Vol. 1. Frankfurt: S. Fischer, 1975.

Dentith, Simon. *Parody.* London: Routledge, 2000.

Dreyfus, Laurence. "Music and Motive in Thomas Mann's *Wälsungenblut.*" *London German Studies* 8 (2003): 86–113.

Edelmann, Bernd, Birgit Lodes, and Reinhold Schlötterer, eds. *Richard Strauss und die Moderne: Bericht über das Internationale Symposium München, 21. bis 23. Juli 1999.* Berlin: Henschel, 2001.

Ehrenfels, Christian von. *Philosophische Schriften.* 4 vols. Edited by Reinhard Fabian. Munich: Philosophia Verlag, 1982–90.

Ehrhardt, Ingrid, and Simon Reynolds, eds. *Kingdom of the Soul: Symbolist Art in Germany 1870–1920.* Munich: Prestel, 2000.

Endell, August. *Vom Sehen.* Edited by Helge David. Basel: Birkhäuser, 1995.

Ernst, Paul. *Dramen.* 3 vols. Munich: Langen/Müller, 1932–33.

Erwin, Charlotte E. "Richard Strauss's Presketch Planning for *Ariadne auf Naxos.*" *Musical Quarterly* 67 (1981): 348–65.

Esselborn, Karl. *Hofmannsthal und der Antike Mythos.* Munich: Fink, 1969.

Fähnrich, Herrmann. *Thomas Manns episches Musizieren im Sinne Richard Wagners.* Frankfurt: Herchen, 1986.

Farben–Klänge: Wassily Kandinsky, Bilder 1908 bis 1914. Riehen/Basel: Fondation Beyeler, 1998.

Finscher, Ludwig. "Richard Strauss and Jugendstil—The Munich Years." *Art Nouveau and Jugendstil and the Music of the Early 20th Century. Adelaide Studies in Musicology* 13 (1984): 169–80.

Foerster-Nietzsche, Elizabeth, ed. *The Nietzsche-Wagner Correspondence.* Translated by Caroline V. Kerr. New York: Liveright, 1949.

Forster-Hahn, Françoise, ed. *Imagining Modern German Culture: 1889–1910.* Washington, D.C.: National Gallery of Art, 1996.

Forsyth, Karen. Ariadne auf Naxos *by Hugo von Hofmannsthal and Richard Strauss.* Oxford: Oxford University Press, 1982.

Frank, Hans. "Der Bayreuther Meister und die deutsche Weltstellung." *Die Gesellschaft* 1 (1885): 10–12.
Frantz, Constantin. "Offener Brief an Richard Wagner." *Bayreuther Blätter* 2 (1878): 149–70.
Friedmann, Lilith. "Die Gestaltungen des Ariadne-Stoffes von der Antike bis der Neuzeit." Ph.D. dissertation, University of Vienna, 1933.
Frisch, Walter. *Brahms: The Four Symphonies.* New York: Schirmer, 1996.
———. *The Early Works of Arnold Schoenberg, 1893–1908.* Berkeley: University of California Press, 1993.
———. "Music and Jugendstil." *Critical Inquiry* 17 (1990): 138–61.
———. "'You Must Remember This': Memory and Structure in Schubert's String Quartet in G Major, D. 887." *Musical Quarterly* 84 (2000): 582–603.
———, ed. *Schoenberg and His World.* Princeton: Princeton University Press, 1999.
Fritzsche, Peter. *Reading Berlin 1900.* Cambridge, Mass.: Harvard University Press, 1996.
Fulcher, Jane. *French Cultural Politics & Music: From the Dreyfus Affair to the First World War.* New York: Oxford University Press, 1999.
Gay, Peter. *Freud, Jews and Other Germans.* New York: Oxford University Press, 1978.
———. *Weimar Culture: The Outsider as Insider.* New York: Harper and Row, 1968.
Genette, Gérard. *Palimpsests: Literature in the Second Degree.* Lincoln: University of Nebraska Press, 1997.
Gilliam, Bryan. *The Life of Richard Strauss.* Cambridge: Cambridge University Press, 1999.
———. *Richard Strauss: New Perspectives on the Composer and His Work.* Durham: Duke University Press, 1992.
———, ed. *Richard Strauss and His World.* Princeton: Princeton University Press, 1992.
Glauert, Amanda. *Hugo Wolf and the Wagnerian Inheritance.* Cambridge: Cambridge University Press, 1999.
Gobineau, Arthur de. *Essai sur l'inégalité des races humaines.* Edited by Hubert Juin. Paris: Éditions Pierre Belfond, 1967.
Goehr, Lydia. *The Quest for Voice: Music, Politics, and the Limits of Philosophy.* Berkeley: University of California Press, 1998.
Gräwe, Karl. "Sprache, Musik und Szene in 'Ariadne auf Naxos' von Hugo von Hofmannsthal und Richard Strauss." Ph.D. dissertation, University of Munich, 1969.
Grimm, Reinhold, ed. *Deutsche Romantheorien.* 2nd ed. Frankfurt: Athenäum Fischer, 1974.
Groos, Arthur. "Constructing Nuremberg: Typological and Proleptic Communities in *Die Meistersinger.*" *19th-Century Music* 16 (1992): 18–34.

Günther, Hans, ed. *Gesamtkunstwerk: Zwischen Synästhesie und Mythos.* Bielefeld: Aisthesis, 1994.

Gutman, Robert. *Richard Wagner: The Man, His Mind, and His Music.* New York: Harcourt, Brace & World, 1968.

Hahl-Koch, Jelena, ed. *Arnold Schoenberg, Wassily Kandinsky: Letters, Pictures and Documents.* Translated by John C. Crawford. London: Faber & Faber, 1984.

———. *Kandinsky.* New York: Rizzoli, 1993.

Hailey, Christopher. *Franz Schreker, 1878–1934: A Cultural Biography.* Cambridge: Cambridge University Press, 1993.

Hake, Sabine. *German National Cinema.* London: Routledge, 2002.

Halm, August. *Von zwei Kulturen der Musik.* 3rd ed. Stuttgart: Klett, 1947.

Hamann, Richard, and Jost Hermand. *Stilkunst um 1900.* Berlin: Akademie Verlag, 1967.

Hamburger, Käte. *Der Humor bei Thomas Mann.* Munich: Nymphenburger Verlag, 1965.

Hanslick, Eduard. *Hanslick's Music Criticisms.* Edited and translated by Henry Pleasants. New York: Dover, 1988.

Hauptmann, Gerhart. *Einsame Menschen.* 22nd ed. Berlin: Fischer, 1908.

———. *Plays: Before Daybreak, The Weavers, The Beaver Coat.* Edited by Reinhold Grimm and Caroline Molina y Vedia. New York: Continuum, 1994.

Hefling, Stephen, ed. *Mahler Studies.* Cambridge: Cambridge University Press, 1997.

Hegel, Georg Wilhelm Friedrich. *Lectures on the History of Philosophy.* Translated by E. S. Haldane. 3 vols. Lincoln: University of Nebraska Press, 1995.

Heinemann, Michael, and Hans-Joachim Hinrichsen, eds. *Bach und die Nachwelt.* 4 vols. Laaber: Laaber Verlag, 1997–.

Heller, Eric. *The Ironic German: A Study of Thomas Mann.* London: Secker & Warburg, 1958.

Helms, Siegmund. "Johannes Brahms und Johann Sebastian Bach." *Bach-Jahrbuch* 57 (1971): 13–81.

Hermand, Jost, ed. *Jugendstil. Wege der Forschung 110.* Darmstadt: Wissenschaftliche Buchgesellschaft, 1971.

———. *Jugendstil: Ein Forschungsbericht, 1918–1964.* Stuttgart: Metzler, 1965.

Hertz, David Michael. *The Tuning of the Word: The Musico-Literary Poetics of the Symbolist Movement.* Carbondale: University of Southern Illinois Press, 1987.

Hilscher, Elisabeth, and Theophil Antonicek, eds. *Vergleichend-systematische Musikwissenschaft: Beiträge zu Methode und Problematik der systematischen, ethnologischen und historischen Musikwissenschaft.* Tutzing: Hans Schneider, 1994.

Hofmann, Werner. *Turning Points in Twentieth-Century Art: 1890–1917.* Translated by Charles Kessler. New York: Braziller, 1969.

Hofmannsthal, Hugo von. *Gesammelte Werke in zehn Einzelbänden.* Frankfurt: Fischer Taschenbuch Verlag, 1979.

———. *The Lord Chandos Letter.* Translated by Russell Stockman. Marlboro, Vt.: Marlboro Press, 1986.

———. *Sämtliche Werke: Kritische Ausgabe.* 31 vols. Frankfurt: S. Fischer, 1975–.

Hollander, Hans. *Music und Jugendstil.* Zurich: Atlantis-Verlag, 1975.

Holz, Arno. *Die Kunst: Ihr Wesen und ihre Gesetze* (1891). Excerpted in *Theorie des Naturalismus,* edited by Theo Meyer, pp. 168–74. Stuttgart: Reclam, 1973.

———. *Phantasus: Verkleinerter Faksimiledruck der Erstfassung.* Edited by Gerhard Schulz. Stuttgart: Reclam, 1968.

———. *Revolution in der Lyrik* (1899). Excerpted in *Theorie des Naturalismus,* edited by Theo Meyer, pp. 214–24. Stuttgart: Reclam, 1973.

Huebner, Steven. *French Opera at the Fin de Siècle : Wagnerism, Nationalism, and Style.* New York: Oxford University Press, 1999.

Huesgen, Rudolf. "Der junge Reger und seine Orgelwerke." Ph.D. dissertation, University of Freiburg, 1935.

Hutcheon, Linda. *A Theory of Parody: The Teachings of Twentieth-Century Art Forms.* New York: Methuen, 1985.

Iggers, Georg. *The German Conception of History: The National Tradition of Historical Thought from Herder to the Present.* Revised edition. Middletown, Conn.: Wesleyan University Press, 1983.

Istel, Edgar. *Die moderne Oper vom Tode Wagners bis zum Weltkrieg.* Leipzig: Teubner, 1915.

Janik, Allan, and Stephen Toulmin. *Wittgenstein's Vienna.* New York: Touchstone Books, 1973.

Jean Paul. *Horn of Oberon: Jean Paul Richter's School for Aesthetics.* Translated by Margaret Hale. Detroit: Wayne State University Press, 1973.

Jelavich, Peter. *Berlin Cabaret.* Cambridge, Mass.: Harvard University Press, 1993.

———. *Munich and Theatrical Modernism: Politics, Playwriting, and Performance, 1890–1914.* Cambridge, Mass.: Harvard University Press, 1985.

Jens, Walter. *Hofmannsthal und die Griechen.* Tübingen: Max Niemeyer, 1955.

Jensen, Jens Christian. "Menzel, Adolph." In *groveart.com,* www.groveart.com (May 30, 2003).

Jump, John D. *Burlesque.* London: Methuen, 1972.

Kaes, Anton, Martin Jay, and Edward Dimendberg, eds. *The Weimar Republic Sourcebook.* Berkeley: University of California Press, 1994.

Kandinsky, Wassily. *Complete Writings on Art.* Edited by Kenneth C. Lindsay and Peter Vergo. New York: Da Capo Press, 1994.

Keil, Werner, ed. *1900: Musik zur Jahrhundertwende.* Hildesheim: Olms, 1995.

Kersten, Ursula. *Max Klinger und die Musik.* 2 vols. Frankfurt: Peter Lang, 1993.

Kienzle, Ulrike. *Das Trauma hinter dem Traum: Franz Schrekers Oper "Der ferne Klang" und die Wiener Moderne.* Schliengen: Argus, 1998.

Kirsch, Winfried, and Sieghart Döhring, eds. *Geschichte und Dramaturgie des Operneinakters.* Laaber: Laaber Verlag, 1991.

Klinger, Max. *Malerei und Zeichnung.* 6th ed. Leipzig: Thieme, 1913.

Knapp, Raymond. "The Finale of Brahms's Fourth Symphony: The Tale of the Subject." *19th-Century Music* 13 (1989): 3–17.

Kolocotroni, Vassiliki, Jane Goldman, and Olga Taxidou, eds. *Modernism: An Anthology of Sources and Documents.* Edinburgh: Edinburgh University Press, 1998.

Korngold, Julius. *Deutsches Opernschaffen der Gegenwart.* Leipzig: Leonhardt, 1921.

Koselleck, Reinhart. *Futures Past: On the Semantics of Historical Time.* Translated by Keith Tribe. Cambridge, Mass.: MIT Press, 1985.

Kramer, Jonathan. "Postmodern Concepts of Musical Time." *Indiana Theory Review* 17 (1996): 21–61.

Kravitt, Edward. *The Lied: Mirror of Late Romanticism.* New Haven: Yale University Press, 1996.

Kurth, Ernst. *Selected Writings.* Edited and translated by Lee A. Rothfarb. Cambridge: Cambridge University Press, 1991.

La Grange, Henry-Louis de. *Gustav Mahler.* Vol. 2, *Vienna: The Years of Challenge, 1897–1904.* New York: Oxford University Press, 1995.

———. *Gustav Mahler: Chronique d'une Vie.* Vol. 1. Revised ed. Paris: Fayard, 1979. First ed. translated as *Mahler.* Garden City, N.Y.: Doubleday, 1973.

Large, David C., and William Weber, eds. *Wagnerism in European Culture and Politics.* Ithaca: Cornell University Press, 1984.

Lederer, Josef-Horst. *Verismo auf der deutschsprachigen Opernbühne, 1891–1926.* Vienna: Bohlau, 1992.

Lehrs, Max. "Max Klinger's 'Brahms-Phantasie.'" *Zeitschrift für Bildende Kunst* 6 (1895): 113–18.

Leiß, Ingo, and Hermann Stadler. *Deutsche Literaturgeschichte.* Vol. 8, *Wege in die Moderne, 1890–1918.* Munich: Deutscher Taschenbuch Verlag, 1997.

Levi, Erik. *Music in the Third Reich.* London: Macmillan, 1994.

Lodato, Suzanne. "Richard Strauss and the Modernists: A Contextual Study of Strauss's Fin-de-Siècle Song Style." Ph.D. dissertation, Columbia University, 1999.

Long, Rose-Carol Washton. *Kandinsky: The Development of an Abstract Style.* New York: Oxford University Press, 1980.

Lorenzen, Johannes. *Max Reger als Bearbeiter Bachs.* Wiesbaden: Breitkopf & Härtel, 1982.

Louis, Rudolf. *Die deutsche Musik der Gegenwart.* 3rd ed. Munich: George Müller, 1912.

Love, Frederick R. "Nietzsche's Quest for a New Aesthetic of Music: 'Die Allergrösste Symphonie,' 'Grosser Stil,' 'Musik des Südens.'" *Nietzsche-Studien* 6 (1977): 154–94.

Mahler, Alma. *Gustav Mahler: Memories and Letters.* Edited by Donald Mitchell, translated by Basil Creighton. Seattle: University of Washington Press, 1975.

Makela, Maria. *The Munich Secession: Art and Artists in Turn-of-the-Century Munich.* Princeton: Princeton University Press, 1990.
Mann, Thomas. *Briefe, 1889–1936.* Edited by Erika Mann. Berlin: Fischer, 1978.
———. *Briefwechsel mit Autoren.* Edited by Hans Wysling. Frankfurt: Fischer 1988.
———. *Buddenbrooks.* Translated by John E. Woods. New York: Alfred Knopf, 1993.
———. *Death in Venice and Other Stories.* Translated by David Luke. New York: Bantam Books, 1988.
———. *Death in Venice and Seven Other Stories.* Translated by H. T. Lowe-Porter. New York: Vintage, 1989.
———. *Gesammelte Werke.* 13 vols. Frankfurt: S. Fischer, 1960.
———. *Letters of Thomas Mann, 1889–1955.* Edited by Richard and Clara Winston. New York: Alfred Knopf, 1971.
———. *The Magic Mountain.* Translated by John E. Woods. New York: Alfred Knopf, 1995.
———. *Pro and Contra Wagner.* Translated by Allan Blunden. Chicago: University of Chicago Press, 1985.
———. *Reflections of a Nonpolitical Man.* Translated by Walter D. Morris. New York: Ungar, 1987.
———. *Tristan.* Stuttgart: Reclam, 1950.
———. *Tristan: Erläuterungen und Dokumente.* Edited by Ulrich Dittmann. Stuttgart: Reclam, 1971.
Mann, William. *Richard Strauss: A Critical Study of the Operas.* New York: Oxford University Press, 1966.
Marissen, Michael, ed. *Bach Perspectives 3: Creative Responses to Bach from Mozart to Hindemith.* Lincoln: University of Nebraska Press, 1998.
Marschalk, Max. "Mascagni und sein *Freund Fritz.*" *Freie Bühne* 3 (1892): 423–27.
———. "Nachträgliches zum Mascagni-Cultus." *Freie Bühne* 2 (1891): 1108–10.
Maur, Karin von, ed. *Vom Klang der Bilder: Die Musik in der Kunst des 20. Jahrhunderts.* Munich: Prestel, 1985.
Mauser, Wolfram, ed. *Hofmannsthal und das Theater: Die Vorträge des Hofmannsthal Symposiums Wien 1979.* Vienna: Karl M. Halosar, 1981.
Mayer-Pasinski, Karin. *Max Klingers Brahmsphantasie.* Frankfurt: Rita G. Fischer, 1982.
McGrath, William J. *Dionysian Art and Populist Politics in Austria.* New Haven: Yale University Press, 1974.
Mennicke, Karl. *Über Max Schillings Mona Lisa.* Berlin: Drei Masken-Verlag, 1915.
Merian, Hans. "'Cavalleria rusticana.'" *Die Gesellschaft* 7 (1891): 1448–52.
———. "Leoncavallo's 'Pagliacci' und die modern-realistische Oper." *Die Gesellschaft* 9 (1893): 734–55.
Meyer, Theo, ed. *Theorie des Naturalismus.* Stuttgart: Reclam, 1973.

Mitchell, Donald. *Gustav Mahler: The Wunderhorn Years.* Boulder: Westview Press, 1976.

Morgan, David. "The Idea of Abstraction in German Theories of Ornament from Kant to Kandinsky." *Journal of Aesthetics and Art Criticism* 50 (1992): 231–42.

Morton, Marsha L., and Peter L. Schmunk, eds. *The Arts Entwined: Music and Painting in the Nineteenth Century.* New York: Garland, 2000.

Muecke, D. C. *The Compass of Irony.* London: Methuen, 1969.

Naegele, Philipp Otto. *Gustav Mahler & Johann Sebastian Bach.* Northampton, Mass.: Smith College, 1983.

Nagel, Wilibald. "Johann Sebastian Bach und die Deutsche Musik der Gegenwart." *Die Musik* 1, no. 3 (1901): 204–8.

———. "Praeludium." *Die Musik* 1, no. 1 (1901): 3–4.

Needham, Gerald. "Naturalism." In *groveart.com,* www.groveart.com (May 24, 2002).

Nelson, Thomas K. "Klinger's *Brahmsphantasie* and the Cultural Politics of Absolute Music." *Art History* 19 (1996): 26–43.

Neue Pinakothek: Erläuterung zu den Ausgestellten Werken. Munich: Bayerische Staatsgemäldesammlungen, 1982.

Niefanger, Dirk. "Historische und historistische Verfahren: Skizzenhaftes zu Paul Ernst und Hugo von Hofmannsthal im Kontext einer 'historistischen' Moderne." In *Historismus und Moderne,* edited by Harald Tausch, pp. 181–90. Würzburg: Ergon, 1996.

Niemann, Walter. *Die Musik der Gegenwart.* 5th ed. Berlin: Schuster & Loeffler, 1913.

Nietzsche, Friedrich. *Beyond Good and Evil.* Translated by Marion Faber. Oxford: Oxford University Press, 1998.

———. *The Birth of Tragedy and The Case of Wagner.* Translated by Walter Kaufmann. New York: Vintage, 1967.

———. *Human, All Too Human.* Translated by Marion Faber, with Stephen Lehmann. Lincoln: University of Nebraska Press, 1984.

———. *Human, All Too Human.* Translated by R. J. Hollingdale. Cambridge: Cambridge University Press, 1996.

———. *Kritische Studienausgabe.* 15 vols. Edited by Giorgio Colli and Mazzino Montinari. Munich and Berlin: Deutscher Taschenbuch Verlag and de Gruyter, 1988.

———. *The Portable Nietzsche.* Edited and translated by Walter Kaufmann. New York: Penguin, 1954.

———. *Selected Letters of Friedrich Nietzsche.* Edited and translated by Christopher Middleton. Chicago: University of Chicago Press, 1969.

———. *Unfashionable Observations.* Translated by Richard Gray. Stanford: Stanford University Press, 1995.

———. *Unmodern Observations.* Edited by William Arrowsmith. New Haven: Yale University Press, 1990.

Nodnagel, Ernst Otto. *Jenseits von Wagner und Liszt.* Königsberg: Ostpreussischen Druckerei und Verlagsanstalt, 1902.
Noé, Günther von. "Das Zitat bei Richard Strauss." *Neue Zeitschrift für Musik* 125 (1964): 234–38.
Nordau, Max. *Degeneration.* Lincoln: University of Nebraska Press, 1993.
Notley, Margaret. "Brahms as Liberal: Genre, Style, and Politics in Late Nineteenth-Century Vienna." *19th-Century Music* 17 (1993): 107–23.
———. "Late Nineteenth-Century Chamber Music and the Cult of the Classical Adagio." *19th-Century Music* 23 (1999): 33–61.
Nottebohm, Gustav. *Beethoveniana.* Leipzig: Breitkopf & Härtel, 1872.
———. *Ein Skizzenbuch von Beethoven.* Leipzig: Breitkopf & Härtel, 1865.
Ostwald, Peter. *Schumann: The Inner Voices of a Musical Genius.* Boston: Northeastern University Press, 1985.
Painter, Karen, ed. *Mahler and His World.* Princeton: Princeton University Press, 2002.
Paret, Peter. *The Berlin Secession: Modernism and Its Enemies in Imperial Germany.* Cambridge, Mass.: Harvard University Press, 1980.
———. *German Encounters with Modernism, 1840–1945.* Cambridge: Cambridge University Press, 2001.
Partsch, Erich Wolfgang, ed. *Gustav Mahler: Werk und Wirken.* Vienna: Vom Pasqualatihaus, 1996.
Pascal, Roy. *From Naturalism to Expressionism.* New York: Basic Books, 1973.
Peukert, Detlev. *Weimar Republic: The Crisis of Classical Modernity.* Translated by Richard Deveson. New York: Hill and Wang, 1992.
Pfitzner, Hans. *Briefe.* Edited by Bernhard Adamy. Tutzing: Hans Schneider, 1991.
Popp, Susanne. "Preface." In Max Reger, *Concerto for Piano and Orchestra, F minor, Op. 114,* pp. III–X. London: Eulenberg, 1990.
Popp, Susanne, and Susanne Shigihara, eds. *Reger-Studien 3: Analysen und Quellenstudien.* Wiesbaden: Breitkopf & Härtel, 1988.
Puffett, Derrick. *Richard Strauss: Salome.* Cambridge: Cambridge University Press, 1989.
Rarisch, Klaus M. "Über die typographische Mittelachse des 'Phantasus' von Arno Holz." *fulgura frango,* www.fulgura.de/autor/holz/ueber/achse.htm (May 28, 2003).
Reger, Max. *Briefe an Karl Straube.* Edited by Susanne Popp. Bonn: Dümmler, 1986.
———. *Briefe eines deutschen Meisters: ein Lebensbild.* Edited by Else von Hase-Koehler. Leipzig: Koehler & Amelang, 1928.
———. "Degeneration und Regeneration in der Musik." *Neue Musik-Zeitung* 29 (1907): 49–51. Reprinted in *"Die Konfusion in der Musik": Felix Draeseke's Kampfschrift von 1906 und ihre Folgen,* edited by Susanne Shigihara, pp. 250–58. Bonn: Gudrun Schröder Verlag, 1990.

———. *Der junge Reger: Briefe und Dokumente vor 1900.* Edited by Susanne Popp. Wiesbaden: Breitkopf & Härtel, 2000.

Repp, Kevin. *Reformers, Critics, and the Paths of German Modernity: Anti-politics and the Search for Alternatives, 1890–1914.* Cambridge, Mass.: Harvard University Press, 2000.

Riegl, Alois. *Late Roman Art Industry.* Translated by Rolf Winkes. Rome: Giorgio Bretschneider, 1985.

Riemann, Hugo. "Degeneration und Regeneration in der Musik." In *Max Hesses Deutscher Musikerkalender für das Jahr 1908.* Reprinted in *"Die Konfusion in der Musik": Felix Draeseke's Kampfschrift von 1906 und ihre Folgen,* edited by Susanne Shigihara, pp. 245–49. Bonn: Gudrun Schröder Verlag, 1990.

Riethmüller, Albrecht. *Ferruccio Busonis Poetik.* Mainz: Schott, 1988.

Ringbom, Sixten. *The Sounding Cosmos: A Study of the Spiritualism of Kandinsky and the Genesis of Abstract Painting.* Åbo: Åbo Akademi, 1970.

Rinsum, Annemarie van, and Wolfgang van Rinsum. *Deutsche Literaturgeschichte.* Vol. 7, *Realismus und Naturalismus.* Munich: Deutscher Taschenbuchverlag, 1999.

Roethel, Hans K., and Jean K. Benjamin, *Kandinsky: A Catalogue Raisonné of the Oil-Paintings.* 2 vols. Ithaca: Cornell University Press, 1982–.

Röhring, Klaus, ed. *Max Reger 1873–1973: Ein Symposion.* Wiesbaden: Breitkopf & Härtel, 1974.

Rose, Margaret A. *Parody: Ancient, Modern, and Post-modern.* Cambridge: Cambridge University Press, 1993.

Rose, Paul Lawrence. *Wagner: Race and Revolution.* New Haven: Yale University Press, 1992.

Rothfarb, Lee A. *Ernst Kurth as Theorist and Analyst.* Philadelphia: University of Pennsylvania Press, 1988.

Ruhmer, Eberhard, ed. *Neue Pinakothek: Erläuterung zu den Ausgestellten Werken.* Munich: Bayerische Staatsgemäldesammlungen, 1982.

Ruprecht, Erich, ed. *Literarische Manifeste des Naturalismus, 1880–1892.* Stuttgart: Metzler, 1962.

Ruprecht, Erich, and Dieter Bänsch, eds. *Literarische Manifeste der Jahrhundertwende, 1890–1910.* Stuttgart: Metzler, 1970.

Safranski, Rüdiger. *Nietzsche: A Philosophical Biography.* Translated by Shelley Frisch. New York: W. W. Norton, 2002.

Salmi, Hannu. *Imagined Germany: Richard Wagner's National Utopia.* New York: Peter Lang, 1999.

Sanders-Brahms, Helma. *Das Dunkle zwischen den Bildern.* Edited by Norbert Grob. Frankfurt: Verlag der Autoren, 1992.

Scheltinga Koopman, E. Th. "Die Funktion der Musik in Thomas Manns 'Tristan' und 'Zauberberg.'" *Duitse Kroniek* 17 (1965): 83–100, 130–42.

Scher, Steven P. *Verbal Music in German Literature.* New Haven: Yale University Press, 1968.
Schering, Arnold. *Die neue Bachgesellschaft, 1900–1910.* Leipzig: Breitkopf & Härtel, 1911.
———, ed. "Mitgliedversammlung der Neuen Bach-Gesellschaft." *Bach-Jahrbuch* 5 (1908): 144–56.
Scherzinger, Martin. "The Finale of Mahler's Seventh Symphony: A Deconstructive Reading," *Music Analysis* 14 (1995): 69–88.
Schlawe, Fritz. *Literarische Zeitschriften 1885–1910.* Stuttgart: Metzler, 1961.
Schlötterer, Roswitha, ed. *Richard Strauss–Max von Schillings: Ein Briefwechsel.* Pfaffenhofen: W. Ludwig Verlag, 1987.
Schmierer, Elisabeth, Susanne Fontaine, Werner Grünzweig, and Matthias Brzoska, eds. *Töne–Farben–Formen: Über Musik und die bildenden Künste.* Laaber: Laaber Verlag, 1995.
Schmutzler, Robert. *Art Nouveau.* New York: Abrams, 1962.
Schnebel, Dieter, ed. *Bach und die Moderne.* Wiesbaden: Harrassowitz, 1995.
Schneider, Max. *Arnold Böcklin: Ein Maler aus dem Geiste der Musik.* Basel: Holbein-Verlag, 1943.
Schnitman, Sophia. "Musical Motives in Thomas Mann's *Tristan.*" *Modern Language Notes* 86 (1971): 399–414.
Schoenberg, Arnold. *Harmonielehre.* Leipzig: Universal, 1911.
———. *Style and Idea: Selected Writings of Arnold Schoenberg.* Edited by Leonard Stein. New York: St. Martin's Press, 1975.
———. *Theory of Harmony.* Translated by Roy E. Carter. Berkeley: University of California Press, 1978.
———. "Über Oktaven- und Quinten-Parallelen: aus meiner Harmonielehre." *Die Musik* 10, no. 1 (1910): 96–105.
Scholz, Gottfried. "The Image of Giovanni Pierluigi da Palestrina in Pfitzner's *Palestrina.*" *Musical Quarterly* 85 (2001): 76–83.
Schönberg, Kandinsky, Blaue Reiter und die Russische Avantgarde. Journal of the Arnold Schönberg Center 1 (2000).
Schorske, Carl. *Fin-de-Siècle Vienna: Politics and Culture.* New York: Alfred Knopf, 1980.
Schreker, Franz. *Der ferne Klang: Oper in drei Aufzugen. Studienpartitur.* Schliengen: Argus, 1998.
Schuh, Willi. *Der Rosenkavalier: Vier Studien.* Olten: Vereinigung von Freunden der Oltner Liebhaberdrucke, 1968.
———. "Zu Hofmannsthals 'Ariadne'-Szenarium und -Notizen." *Die neue Rundschau* 71 (1960): 84–90.
Schutte, Jürgen, and Peter Sprengel, eds. *Die Berliner Moderne.* Stuttgart: Reclam, 1987.

Schweitzer, Albert. *J. S. Bach.* Translated by Ernest Newman. 2 vols. Boston: Humphries, 1911.

Shaw-Miller, Simon. *Visible Deeds of Music: Art and Music from Wagner to Cage.* New Haven: Yale University Press, 2002.

Sheehan, James. *Imperial Germany.* New York: New Viewpoints, 1976.

Shigihara, Susanne, ed. *"Die Konfusion in der Musik": Felix Draeseke's Kampfschrift von 1906 und ihre Folgen.* Bonn: Gudrun Schröder Verlag, 1990.

———. *Reger-Studien 5.* Wiesbaden: Breitkopf & Härtel, 1993.

Siebigke, Christian Albrecht. "J. S. Bach." In *Museum berühmter Tonkünstler,* vol. 2, part 1, pp. 1–30. Breslau: A. Schall, 1801.

Simms, Bryan. *Music of the Twentieth Century: Style and Structure.* New York: Schirmer Books, 1996.

Singer, Hans Wolfgang. *Max Klinger: Radierungen, Stiche, und Steindrucke 1873–1903.* Berlin: Amsler und Ruthardt, 1909. Reprint and English translation, *Etchings, Engravings and Lithographs, 1878–1903.* San Francisco: Alan Wofsy, 1991.

Sitsky, Larry. *Busoni and the Piano.* New York: Greenwood Press, 1986.

Solie, Ruth, ed. *Musicology and Difference: Gender and Sexuality in Musical Scholarship.* Berkeley: University of California Press, 1993.

Sponheuer, Bernd. *Logik des Zerfalls: Untersuchungen zum Finaleproblem in den Symphonien Gustav Mahlers.* Tutzing: Hans Schneider, 1978.

Stahl, Erich. "Hanswurst in der Operette." *Die Gesellschaft* 1 (1885): 917–18.

———. "Die Operette: eine unzeitgemäße Betrachtung." *Die Gesellschaft* 1 (1885): 448–50.

———. "Viktor E. Neßler und die Wagnerianer." *Die Gesellschaft* 1 (1885): 117–19.

Steinberg, Michael P. "Opera and Cultural Analysis: The Case of Hans Pfitzner's *Palestrina.*" *Musical Quarterly* 85 (2001): 53–62.

Stephan, Rudolf. *Musiker der Moderne: Porträts und Skizzen.* Edited by Albrecht Riethmüller. Laaber: Laaber Verlag, 1996.

———. *Vom musikalischen Denken: Gesammelte Vorträge.* Edited by Rainer Damm and Andreas Traub. Mainz: Schott, 1985.

Stern, Fritz. *The Politics of Cultural Despair.* Berkeley: University of California Press, 1961.

Stinson, Russell. *Bach: The Orgelbüchlein.* New York: Schirmer, 1996.

Strauss, Franz, and Alice Strauss, with Willi Schuh, eds. *Richard Strauss–Hugo von Hofmannsthal Briefwechsel: Gesamtausgabe.* Zurich: Atlantis, 1955. English edition, *A Working Friendship: The Correspondence between Richard Strauss and Hugo von Hofmannsthal.* Translated by Hanns Hammelmann and Ewald Osers. New York: Vienna House, 1974.

Strauss, Richard. *Betrachtungen und Erinnerungen.* Edited by Willi Schuh. Munich and Mainz: Piper and Schott, 1989.

———. *"Wir beide wollen springen": Ein Meisterlied aus der Zeit des Jugendstils.* Edited with an introduction by Alfons Ott. Tutzing: Hans Schneider, 1968.

Szeemann, Harald, ed. *Der Hang zum Gesamtkunstwerk: Europäische Utopien seit 1800.* Aarau: Sauerländer, 1983.

Thatcher, David S. "Nietzsche and Brahms: A Forgotten Relationship." *Music & Letters* 54 (1973): 261–80.

Thomé, Horst, ed. *Paul Ernst: Außenseiter und Zeitgenosse.* Würzburg: Königshausen & Neumann, 2001.

Toller, Owen. *Pfitzner's Palestrina: The "Musical Legend" and Its Background.* London: Toccata Press, 1997.

Tönnies, Ferdinand. *Community and Society.* Edited and translated by Charles P. Loomis. East Lansing: Michigan State University, 1957.

Treitler, Leo. *Music and the Historical Imagination.* Cambridge, Mass.: Harvard University Press, 1989.

Tresidder, Jack. *Dictionary of Symbols.* San Francisco: Chronicle Books, 1997.

Tuchman, Maurice, et al., eds. *The Spiritual in Art: Abstract Painting, 1890–1950.* New York: Abbeville Press, 1986.

Varnedoe, J. Kirk T., and Elizabeth Streicher. *Graphic Works of Max Klinger.* New York: Dover, 1977.

Vazsonyi, Nicholas, ed. *Searching for Common Ground: Diskurse zur deutschen Identität 1750–1871.* Cologne: Böhlau, 2000.

Velten, Klaus. *Schönbergs Instrumentationen Bachscher und Brahmsscher Werke als Dokumente seines Traditionsverständnisses.* Regensburg: Bosse, 1976.

Vriessen, Gustav. *August Macke.* Stuttgart: Kohlhammer, 1953.

Wagner, Cosima. *Cosima Wagner's Diaries.* Volume II. Edited by Martin Gregor-Dellin and Dietrich Mack. Translated by Geoffrey Skelton. New York: Harcourt Brace Jovanovich, 1980.

Wagner, Günther, ed. *Jahrbuch des Staatlichen Instituts für Musikforschung Preußischer Kulturbesitz 1995.* Stuttgart: Metzler, 1995.

Wagner, Richard. *Art and Politics.* Translated by W. Ashton Ellis. Lincoln: University of Nebraska Press, 1995.

———. *The Art-Work of the Future and Other Works.* Translated by W. Ashton Ellis. Lincoln: University of Nebraska Press, 1993.

———. *Prelude and Transfiguration from Tristan und Isolde.* Edited and translated by Robert Bailey. New York: W. W. Norton, 1985.

———. *Religion and Art.* Translated by W. Ashton Ellis. Lincoln: University of Nebraska Press, 1994.

———. *Sämtliche Schriften und Dichtungen.* 5th ed. 12 vols. Edited by Richard Sternfeld and Hans von Wolzogen. Leipzig: Breitkopf & Härtel, 1911.

———. *Tristan und Isolde: Texte, Materialen, Kommentare.* Edited by Attila Csampai and Dietmar Holland. Reinbek: Rowohlt, 1983.

Walker, Alan. *A Study in Musical Analysis.* London: Barrie and Rockliff, 1962.

"Was ist mir Johann Sebastian Bach und was bedeutet er für unsere Zeit?" *Die Musik* 5, no. 1 (1905): 3–78.

Weiner, Marc A. *Richard Wagner and the Anti-Semitic Imagination.* Lincoln: University of Nebraska Press, 1995

———. *Undertones of Insurrection: Music, Politics, and the Social Sphere.* Lincoln: University of Nebraska Press, 1993.

Weiß, Günther, ed. *Neue Mahleriana.* Berne: Peter Lang, 1997.

Weiss, Peg. *Kandinsky in Munich: The Formative Jugendstil Years.* Princeton: Princeton University Press, 1979.

Weyer, Martin. *Die Orgelwerke Max Regers.* Wilhelmshaven: Florian Noetzel, 1989.

Wheeler, Kathleen, ed. *German Aesthetic and Literary Criticism: The Romantic Ironists and Goethe.* Cambridge: Cambridge University Press, 1984.

Williamson, John. "Eugen d'Albert: Wagner and Verismo." *Music Review* 45 (1984): 26–46.

———. *The Music of Hans Pfitzner.* Oxford: Clarendon Press, 1992.

Wilske, Hermann. *Max Reger–Zur Rezeption in seiner Zeit.* Wiesbaden: Breitkopf & Härtel, 1995.

Wiora, Walter, ed. *Die Ausbreitung des Historismus über die Musik.* Regensburg: Bosse, 1969.

Witte, Karsten. "'Das ist echt! Eine Burleske!' Zur *Tristan*-Novelle von Thomas Mann." *German Quarterly* 41 (1968): 660–72.

Worbs, Michael. *Nervenkunst: Literatur und Psychoanalyse in Wien der Jahrhundertwende.* Frankfurt: Europäische Verlagsanstalt, 1983.

Worringer, Wilhelm. *Abstraction and Empathy.* Translated by Michael Bullock. Chicago: Ivan R. Dee, 1997.

Youmans, Charles. "Richard Strauss's *Guntram* and the Dismantling of Wagnerian Musical Metaphysics." Ph.D. dissertation, Duke University, 1996.

Young, Frank W. *Montage and Motif in Thomas Mann's "Tristan."* Bonn: Bouvier, 1975.

Young, Julian. *Nietzsche's Philosophy of Art.* Cambridge: Cambridge University Press, 1992.

Zaunschirm, Thomas, ed. *Arnold Schoenberg: Paintings and Drawings.* Klagenfurt: Ritter Verlag, 1991.

Zierau, Ulla. *Die veristische Oper in Deutschland.* Frankfurt: Peter Lang, 1994.

Zola, Émile. "Aussprüche über die bildende Kunst." *Die Gesellschaft* 1 (1885). Reprinted in *Theorie des Naturalismus,* edited by Theo Meyer, pp. 109–12. Stuttgart: Reclam, 1973.

Zychowicz, James L., ed. *The Seventh Symphony of Gustav Mahler: A Symposium.* Cincinnati: College-Conservatory of Music, 1990.

INDEX

Titles of artworks, musical compositions, and literary works may be found under the name of the artist, composer, or author, unless otherwise indicated. Page numbers in italic refer to illustrations or their captions.

Compositor:	Integrated Composition Systems
Music Engraver:	Don Giller
Indexer:	Kevin Millham
Text:	11.25/13.5 Adobe Garamond
Display:	Adobe Garamond